THE CONSTITUTION OF THE UNITED KINGDOM

The Constitution of United Kingdom, Fifth Edition
The Cover Pictorial Narrative

This image of the UK Constitution comprises a series of visual signifiers. Essential elements of the UK constitution are broken down into a technicolour assortment of contrasting geometric forms and then re-assembled in a contemporary constitutional context. The viewer's eye is drawn to Number 10 at the heart of the composition, signifying 10 Downing Street, and so representing the PM and the executive branch of the state. The equestrian statue of King Richard I at the summit of the composition is a visual evocation of Plantagenet absolute monarchy, and it is juxtaposed below with a brightly coloured ballot box in the lower foreground which stands for the importance of representative democracy. To the left, embodying Parliament as legislator, soars the Elizabeth Tower of the Palace of Westminster with Big Ben striking 12.15. This registers the landmark date of Magna Carta and the early recognition of citizen rights limiting Royal authority. Further to the left, the cascading red robes flowing over the emblem of the House of Lords alerts us to the abolition of the remaining hereditary peers. Above the zero to the right, we find the judicial branch represented by the tower of the Middlesex Town Hall building, home to the UK Supreme Court. The triangle framing the right hand side of the composition contains references to the Irish Republic and to Northern Irish, Scottish and Welsh devolution. The Irish Harp (Irish Republic) within the European Union arranged above the levels of multi-layered government. For Northern Ireland, there is a dark blue and purple polygon depicting the famous jagged edged Giant's Causeway, with the Windsor Framework agreement stretching below it. In the right corner the Scottish cross of St. Andrew with a superimposed Scottish heraldic lion are mirrored by the Welsh white and green flag with heraldic dragon. In the left hand corner, at the foundation of the composition stands a still youthful looking King Charles III clad in gold rimmed coronation robes and bearing the St Edwards Crown and Sceptre as overriding symbol of the continuity of constitutional monarchy but also presiding over the Commonwealth which is depicted behind him.

Putachad
Artist

Constitutional Systems of the World
General Editors: Peter Leyland, Andrew Harding,
Rosalind Dixon, Heinz Klug, and Maartje de Visser

In the era of globalisation issues of constitutional law and good governance are being seen increasingly as vital issues in all types of society. Since the end of the cold war there have been dramatic developments in democratic and legal reform, and post-conflict societies are also in the throes of reconstructing their governance systems. Even societies already firmly based on constitutional governance and the rule of law have undergone constitutional change and experimentation with new forms of governance and their constitutional systems are increasingly subjected to comparative analysis and transplantation. Constitutional texts for practically every country in the world are now easily available on the internet. However, texts which enable one to understand the true context, purposes, interpretation, and incidents of a constitutional system are much harder to locate, and are often extremely detailed and descriptive. This series seeks to provide scholars and students with accessible introductions to the constitutional systems of the world, supplying both a road map for the novice and, at the same time, a deeper understanding of the key historical, political, and legal events which have shaped the constitutional landscape of each country. Each book in the series deals with a single country or a group of countries with a common constitutional history, and each author is an expert in their field.

The Constitutional Systems of the following nations have so far been covered by the series:

Australia	Hong Kong SAR	Pakistan
Republic of Austria	Italy	Romania
Belgium	Independent Central	Russian Federation
Brazil	Asian States	Singapore
Canada	India	South Africa
China	Indonesia	Spain
Commonwealth	Ireland	Taiwan
Caribbean	Israel	Thailand
Czechia	Japan	United Kingdom
European Union	Malaysia	United States
Finland	Mexico	Vietnam
France	Myanmar	
Germany	New Zealand	

Link to series website
www.bloomsbury.com/uk/series/constitutional-systems-of-the-world/

The Constitution of the United Kingdom

Fifth Edition

Peter Leyland

·HART·
OXFORD · LONDON · NEW YORK · NEW DELHI · SYDNEY

HART PUBLISHING

Bloomsbury Publishing Plc

Kemp House, Chawley Park, Cumnor Hill, Oxford, OX2 9PH, UK

1385 Broadway, New York, NY 10018, USA

Bloomsbury Publishing Ireland Limited, 29 Earlsfort Terrace, Dublin 2, D02 AY28, Ireland

HART PUBLISHING, the Hart/Stag logo, BLOOMSBURY and the Diana logo are trademarks of Bloomsbury Publishing Plc

First Edition, 2007
Second Edition, 2012
Third Edition, 2016
Fourth Edition, 2021

Copyright © Peter Leyland, 2026

Peter Leyland has asserted his right under the Copyright, Designs and Patents Act 1988 to be identified as Author of this work.

All rights reserved. No part of this publication may be: i) reproduced or transmitted in any form, electronic or mechanical, including photocopying, recording or by means of any information storage or retrieval system without prior permission in writing from the publishers; or ii) used or reproduced in any way for the training, development or operation of artificial intelligence (AI) technologies, including generative AI technologies. The rights holders expressly reserve this publication from the text and data mining exception as per Article 4(3) of the Digital Single Market Directive (EU) 2019/790.

While every care has been taken to ensure the accuracy of this work, no responsibility for loss or damage occasioned to any person acting or refraining from action as a result of any statement in it can be accepted by the authors, editors or publishers.

All UK Government legislation and other public sector information used in the work is Crown Copyright ©. All House of Lords and House of Commons information used in the work is Parliamentary Copyright ©. This information is reused under the terms of the Open Government Licence v3.0 (http://www.nationalarchives.gov.uk/doc/open-government-licence/version/3) except where otherwise stated.

All Eur-lex material used in the work is © European Union, http://eur-lex.europa.eu/, 1998-2020.

A catalogue record for this book is available from the British Library.

A catalogue record for this book is available from the Library of Congress.

ISBN: PB: 978-1-50999-686-5
HB: 978-1-50999-690-2
ePDF: 978-1-50999-688-9
ePub: 978-1-50999-687-2

Typeset by Amnet
Printed and bound in Great Britain

To find out more about our authors and books visit www.hartpublishing.co.uk. Here you will find extracts, author information, details of forthcoming events and the option to sign up for our newsletters.

Contents

Table of Cases xi
Table of Legislation xv

1. **UK Constitution: Context and History** 1
   Introduction 1
   Constitutional Contexts 2
   Constitutional History 10
   Conclusion 26
   Further Reading 26

2. **Sources of the Constitution** 27
   Introduction 27
   Statute Law 28
   The Common Law 29
   European Union Law 30
   European Convention on Human Rights 31
   Legal Treatises 31
   The Law and Customs of Parliament 32
   The Royal Prerogative 33
   Conventions as a Constitutional Source 33
   Defining Conventions 34
   The Practical Importance of Constitutional Conventions ... 38
   Conclusion 42
   Further Reading 43

3. **Constitutional Principles** 45
   Introduction 45
   Parliamentary Sovereignty 47
   The Rule of Law and Separation of Powers 63
   Conclusion 77
   Further Reading 77

4. **Constitutional Monarchy** 79
   Introduction 79
   What Is the Royal Prerogative? 81

    The Constitutional Role of the Monarchy 84
    Does the Monarch Retain Real Power 89
    What Is the 'Crown'? 90
    Liability of the Crown in Tort and Contract 91
    Evaluation: Preservation, Reform, or Abolition? 92
    Conclusion 94
    Further Reading 96

5. **Parliament** 97
    Introduction 97
    General Elections 100
    Parliament: Composition and Procedure 104
    The House of Lords 112
    Parliament as Legislator 119
    Parliament as Watchdog 126
    Conclusion 137
    Further Reading 138

6. **Government and Executive** 141
    Introduction 141
    The Prime Minister and the Government 142
    Ministers and Civil Service 157
    Conclusion 171
    Further Reading 172

7. **The Constitutional Role of the Courts** 173
    Introduction 173
    The Role of the Courts 176
    Administrative Law and Judicial Review 184
    The Constitutional Protection of Rights and the Human
    Rights Act 1998 201
    Conclusion 214
    Further Reading 215

8. **Devolution** 217
    Introduction 217
    Historical Backdrop 218
    Institutional Features: Scotland and Wales 219
    A New Form of Devolution for Northern Ireland 223
    Intergovernmental Relations: A Revised Approach 226

Devolution and the Courts 230
The Scottish Referendum 2014 and Scottish Devolution
Mark II 234
Finance and Tax-Raising 236
Brexit and the State of the Union 238
Conclusion 244
Further Reading 244

9. **Local Government** 247
   Introduction 247
   Types of Local Government: Counties, Cities, Towns 253
   Local Government Finance and Service Delivery 255
   The Accountability of Local Government 256
   Conclusion 258
   Further Reading 258

10. **The UK Constitution: The Way Ahead?** 261
    Introduction 261
    Parliament and Civil Service: Challenges to Core Institutions 262
    The Protection of Citizen Rights 265
    The Configuration of the UK as Nation State Post Brexit 266
    Is There a Case for the Introduction of a Codified
    Constitution? 267
    Conclusion 271
    Further Reading 272

Index 273

Table of Cases

Court of Justice of the European Union
Amministrazione della Finanze dello Stato v Simmenthal SpA
  (Case 106/77) EU:C:1978:49, [1978] ECR 629 54
R v Secretary of State for Transport, ex parte Factortame Ltd
  (Case C-213/89) EU:C:1990:257, [1990] ECR I-2433 54
Van Gend en Loos (Case 26/62) EU:C:1963:1, [1963] ECR 1,
  [1963] CMLR 105 .... 30, 53

European Court of Human Rights
Hirst v United Kingdom (No 2), App no 74025/01, (2006)
  42 EHRR 41, 6 October 2005 211

United Kingdom
A v Secretary of State for the Home Department [2004]
  UKHL 56, [2005] 2 AC 68 .... 203, 207-8, 210
Anderson, Reid and Doherty v Scottish Ministers [2001] UKPC D5,
  [2002] HRLR 6 231-2
Anisminic v Foreign Compensation Commission [1969] 2
  AC 147, HL 192
Associated Provincial Picture Houses Ltd v Wednesbury
  Corporation [1948] 1 KB 223 .... 186, 196, 198, 205
Attorney-General v De Keyser's Royal Hotel Ltd [1920] AC 508 82-3
Attorney-General v Guardian Newspapers Ltd (No 2) [1990]
  1 AC 109 167
Attorney-General v Jonathan Cape Ltd [1976] QB 752 35
AXA General Insurance, Petitioners [2011] CSIH 31, 2011 SC 662 234
Axa General Insurance Ltd v Lord Advocate [2011] UKSC 46,
  [2012] 1 AC 868 234
Begum case. *See* R (on the application of SB) v Head Teacher
  and Governors of Denbigh High School
Belmarsh case. *See* A v Secretary of State for the Home Department
Bradlaugh v Gossett (1884) 12 QBD 271 109
British Railways Board v Pickin [1974] AC 765 49
Bromley v Greater London Council [1983] 1 AC 768, HL 199
Buick's (Colin) Application for Judicial Review [2018] NICA 26,
  [2018] 7 WLUK 129 233
Bulmer v Bollinger [1974] 2 All ER 1226 30
Burmah Oil Co Ltd v Lord Advocate [1965] AC 75 .... 29, 65

Table of Cases

Campbell v Mirror Group Newspapers Ltd [2004] UKHL 22, [2004]
2 WLR 1232 205
Case of Proclamations (1611) 12 Co Rep 74 .... 37, 80, 83
Conway v Rimmer [1968] AC 910 91
Council of Civil Service Unions v Minister for the
  Civil Service (GCHQ case) [1985] AC 374 .... 83, 84, 173, 196
Darnel's Case (1627) 3 State Trials 36 13
Douglas v Hello! Ltd [2001] 2 WLR 992, CA 205
Duncan v Cammell Laird and Co Ltd [1942] AC 624 91
Ellen Street Estates v Minister of Health [1934] 1 KB 590 50
Entick v Carrington (1765) 19 State Tr 1029 .... 29, 64
Five Knights' Case. *See* Darnel's Case
v British Rail Engineering Ltd [1983] 2 AC 751 179
GCHQ case. *See* Council of Civil Service Unions v Minister
  for the Civil Service
Ghaidan v Godin-Mendoza [2004] UKHL 30, [2004] 3 All ER 411 203
H v Lord Advocate [2012] UKSC 24, [2013] 1 AC 413 28
Inland Revenue Commissioners v National Federation of
  Self-Employed and Small Businesses Ltd [1982] AC 617 195
Jackson v Attorney-General [2005] UKHL 56,
  [2006] 1 AC 262 .... 48, 49, 56, 58, 113, 123, 214
Liversidge v Anderson [1942] AC 206 65
Lord Chancellor's Practice Direction: Judicial Precedent
  [1966] 1 WLR 1234 178
M v Home Office [1994] 1 AC 377 .... 29, 73-4
Manchester City Council v Pinnock [2010] UKSC 45, [2011]
  2 AC 104 .... 204, 213
Martin v HM Advocate [2010] UKSC 10, 2010 SC (UKSC) 40 232
Nottingham City Council v Secretary of State for the Environment
  [1986] AC 240 198-9
O'Reilly v Mackman [1983] 2 AC 237, HL 193
Padfield v Minister for Agriculture, Fisheries and Food [1968] AC 997 192
Pepper v Hart [1993] AC 593, [1993] 1 All ER 42 178
Porter v Magill [2001] UKHL 67, [2002] 1 All ER 465 257
Prohibitions del Roy (1607) 77 ER 1342, 12 Co Rep 63 .... 39, 70
R v British Broadcasting Corporation, ex parte Prolife
  Alliance [2003] UKHL 23, [2003] 2 WLR 1403 .... 205, 208-9, 210
R v Chaytor [2010] UKSC 52, [2011] 1 AC 684 .... 111, 112
R v Chief Constable of West Midlands Police, ex parte Wiley
  [1995] 1 AC 274 91
R v Disciplinary Committee of the Jockey Club, ex parte Aga Khan
  [1993] 2 All ER 853 194
R v North and East Devon Heath Authority, ex parte Coughlan
  [2001] QB 213, [2000] 2 WLR 622, CA 197

R v Panel on Takeovers and Mergers, ex parte Datafin [1987]
  1 All ER 564, CA.. 194
R v Secretary of State for Foreign Affairs, ex parte World Development
  Movement Ltd [1995] 1 WLR 386 197
R v Secretary of State for the Home Department, ex parte Brind
  [1991] 1 AC 696... 65
R v Secretary of State for the Home Department, ex parte Daly
  [2001] 1 AC 532, [2001] 3 All ER 433, HL 206
R v Secretary of State for the Home Department, ex parte Fire Brigades Union
  [1995] UKHL 3, [1995] 2 AC 513, [1995] 2 All ER 244 ....83, 195
R v Secretary of State for the Home Department, ex parte
  Northumbria Police Authority [1989] QB 96 83
R v Secretary of State for Transport, ex parte Factortame (No 2)
  [1991] 1 AC 603, [1991] 3 CMLR 769...............................53, 54, 178, 179,
R v Shaylor [2002] UKHL 11, [2003] 1 AC 247 209
R (On the application of AAA (Syria) and others) v SS for the Home
  Department [2023] UKSC 42, [2023] 1 WLR 4433 192-3
R (on the application of Bradley) v Secretary of State for Work
  and Pensions [2008] EWCA Civ 36, [2009] QB 114 137
R (on the application of Cart) v Upper Tribunal [2011] UKSC 28,
  [2012] 1 AC 663... 190
R (on the application of Chester) v Secretary of State for Justice and McGeoch
  v Lord President of the Council [2013] UKSC 63, [2014] 1 AC 271 211
R (on the application of Equitable Members Action Group) v
  HM Treasury [2009] EWHC 2495 (Admin), [2009] All ER
  (D) 63 (Oct) 137
R (on the application of Evans) v Attorney-General [2015]
  UKSC 21, [2015] 1 AC 1787 ....88, 168
R (On the application of HS2) v Secretary of State for Transport
  [2014] UKSC 3, [2014] 1 WLR 324... 53
R (On the application of Miller) v Secretary of State for Exiting
  the European Union [2016] EWHC 2768 (Admin),
  [2018] AC 61 74
R (On the application of Miller) v Secretary of State for Exiting
  the European Union [2017] UKSC 5, [2018] AC 61
  (Miller 1) 22, 23, 37, 50, 52, 55, 75, 80,
                                  83, 146, 173, 174, 176, 181, 195, 226, 267
R (on the application of Miller) v The Prime Minister [2019] UKSC 41,
  [2020] AC 373 (Miller 2) 37, 39, 84, 87, 89, 98, 173, 174, 175, 176
R (On the application of Privacy Internation) v Investigatory
  Powers Tribunal [2019] UKSC 22, [2020] AC 491 192
R (on the application of Rogers) v Swindon NHS Primary Care
  Trust and Secretary of State for Health [2006] EWCA Civ 392,
  [2006] 1 WLR 2649... 210

xiv *Table of Cases*

R (on the application of SB) v Head Teacher and Governors of
 Denbigh High School [2005] EWCA Civ 199, [2005] 2 All
 ER 396, CA; [2006] UKHL 15, [2007] 1 AC 100, HL 209, 210
R (on the application of South Wales Sea Fisheries) v National
 Assembly for Wales [2001] EWHC Admin 1162, [2002]
 RVR 134 232
R (On the application of Tortoise Media Ltd) v Conservative and
 Unionist Party [2025] EWCA Civ 673, [2025] 1 WLR 4186 194
Recovery of Medical Costs for Asbestos Diseases (Wales) Bill:
 Reference by the Counsel General for Wales [2015] UKSC 3,
 [2015] AC 1016 232
Roberts v Hopwood [1925] AC 578, HL 198
Robinson v Secretary of State for Northern Ireland [2002]
 UKHL 32, [2002] NI 390 232-3
Roy v Kensington and Chelsea and Westminster Family Practitioner
 Committee [1992] 1 AC 624 194
Starrs and Chalmers v Procurator Fiscal, Linlithgow [2000]
 HRLR 191, HCJ Appeal 231
Stockdale v Hansard (1839) 9 Ad & El 1 108
Thoburn v Sunderland City Council [2002] EWHC 195 (Admin),
 [2003] QB 151, [2002] 3 WLR 247 .... 28, 51, 54
UK Withdrawal from the European Union (Legal Continuity) (Scotland)
 Bill – A Reference by the AG and Advocate General for Scotland [2018]
 UKSC 64, [2019] AC 1022 233
Wednesbury case, *See* Associated Provincial Picture Houses Ltd v Wednesbury
 Corporation
X (Minors) v Bedfordshire County Council [1995] 2 AC 633 92
YL v Birmingham City Council [2007] UKHL 27, [2008] 1 AC 95 204

United States
Brown v Board of Education of Topeka 347 US 483 (1954) 179
Bush v Gore 531 US 98 (2000) 179, 182
Dobbs v Jackson Women's Health 597 US 215 (2022) 179
Marbury v Madison (1803) 1 Cranch 137, 5 US 137 (1803) 49, 179

Table of Legislation

European
European Charter of Fundamental Rights 25, 211, 240
    European Convention on Human Rights 3, 8, 10, 25, 27, 29,
        31, 45, 50, 55, 56, 64, 98, 176, 180, 202, 203, 204, 205, 206, 207,
        208, 210, 211, 212, 213, 214, 231, 232, 268
    Art 2 .... 206, 210
    Art 3 206
    Art 4(1)-(3) 206
    Art 5 .... 206, 207, 232
    Art 6 .... 71, 180, 189, 231
    Art 7 206
    Art 8 .... 204, 206
    Arts 8 – 11 206
    Art 9 209
    Art 10 208
    Arts 14, 15 207
    Art 46 211
    Protocol 1 206
Schengen Agreement 21, 24
Treaty of Amsterdam 1999 .... 20, 30
Treaty of Lisbon 2009 (TEU) 20, 21, 30
    Art 4.3 54
    Art 50 22
Treaty of Maastricht 1992 (Treaty on European Union) (TEU) 20, 21, 30, 106,
    Art 5.3 217
Treaty of Nice 2003 .... 20, 30
Treaty of Rome 1957 (EEC Treaty) 19, 29, 30, 52, 53
    Art 5 54

France
Constitution 11
    Art 2 209
Loi no 2004-228 of 15 March 2004 209

India
    Constitution 18

Ireland
Constitution 1937 18

Italy
Constitution 1948
    Art 104 181
    Art 138 62
Law 59/97 150

Pakistan
Constitution 18

South Africa
Constitution 1996 2

Soviet Union
Constitutions 2

United Kingdom

Primary Legislation
Acquisition of Land Act 1919 51
    s 7(1) 51
Act of Settlement 1701 .... 14, 28, 41, 46, 70, 72, 89, 183
Act of Union 1536 'for laws and justice to be ministered in Wales' 16, 218
Act of Union 1545 16
Act of Union 1707 .... 17, 28, 51, 218
Act of Union 1800 .... 17, 18, 28
Anti-Terrorism, Crime and Security Act 2001 .... 207, 208
Appellate Jurisdiction Act 1876 115
Audit Commission Act 1998 257
Bill of Rights 1689 .... 13, 14, 16, 28, 40, 41, 45, 51, 69, 70, 83, 88, 89, 100, 174
    Art I 14
    Art IV 14
    Art VI 14
    Art IX 49, 53, 100, 108, 111
British Railways Act 1968 49
Cities and Local Government Devolution Act 2016 251
Civil Contingencies Act 2004 8
Communications Act 2003 171
Constitutional Reform Act 2005 .... 41, 46, 72, 74, 115, 180, 181, 183, 184
    Pts 1, 2 72
    Pt 3 176
    s 2 181

```
         s 3 ................................................................................. 74, 181
         ss 26, 27 .................................................................................. 177
         s 40 ......................................................................................... 231
         Sch 9 ....................................................................................... 231
Constitutional Reform and Governance Act 2010 ................ 40, 84, 162, 163, 166
         Pts 1, 2 ..................................................................................... 84
         s 3  166
         ss 5, 6 ..................................................................................... 166
         s 7(4) ...................................................................................... 166
         s 8  166
Coronavirus Act 2020 ........................................................................... 7
Corporation Tax (Northern Ireland) Act 2015 .............................................. 224
Criminal Justice Act 1988
s 171 ............................................................................................... 83
Criminal Justice and Public Order Act 1994 ................................................... 64
Crown Proceedings Act 1947
         ss 1, 2 ...................................................................................... 91
         s 28 ......................................................................................... 91
Damages (Asbestos-related Conditions) (Scotland) Act 2009 ....................... 234
Data Protection Act 1998 ..................................................................... 171
Data Protection Act 2018 ................................................................ 76, 171
         Pt 5 ......................................................................................... 169
         Sch 12 ..................................................................................... 169
Defence Act 1842 ................................................................................. 82
Deregulation and Contracting Out Act 1994 ........................................ 75, 135
Dissolution and Calling of Parliament Act 2022 ................................ 39, 86, 157
Education Act 1944 ............................................................................. 249
Employment Protection (Consolidation) Act 1978 ........................................ 163
Environmental Protection Act 1990
         s 159 ......................................................................................... 91
Equal Pay Act 1970 ............................................................................. 163
European Communities Act 1972 ........................... 23, 29, 30, 45, 53, 54, 55, 76
         ss 2, 3 .................................................................................... 179
European Parliamentary Elections Act 1999 ................................................... 57
European Referendum Act 2015 ............................................................... 22
European Union Act 2011 ..................................................................... 30
         ss 2, 3 ....................................................................................... 30
         s 6 ............................................................................................ 22
European Union (Notification of Withdrawal) Act 2017 ................................. 55
European Union (Withdrawal) Act 2018 ..................... 23, 29, 30, 50, 55, 75, 135
         ss 2-4 ........................................................................................ 23
         s 2(1) ........................................................................................ 55
         s 5 ........................................................................................... 179
         s 5(2) ....................................................................................... 179
         s 5(4) ........................................................................................ 25
```

xviii *Table of Legislation*

s 6(5A)-(5D)	180
s 8	31
European Union (Withdrawal) Act 2019	124
European Union (Withdrawal Agreement) Act 2020	23, 171, 179, 180, 239
s 26	180
Sch 4	135
Federation of Malaya Independence Act 1947	19
Fixed-term Parliaments Act 2011	39, 41, 60, 86, 156
Freedom of Information Act 2000	76, 110, 163, 167, 168, 169, 267
Pt II	154, 168
s 1	168
ss 23, 24	168
ss 26-29	169
s 53	169
Government of Ireland Act 1914	57
Government of Ireland Act 1920	17, 223
Government of Wales Act 1998	29, 52, 176, 231, 232
Government of Wales Act 2006	220, 223, 232
s 95	232
s 108(4)	232
Greater London Authority Act 1999	249, 250
ss 154, 155	250
Health and Social Care Act 2008	
s 145	204
House of Lords Act 1999	56, 115
House of Lords (Hereditary Peers) Act 2025	115
Housing Act 1925	51
Housing Act 1985	249
Pt III	249
Human Rights Act 1998	3, 8, 10, 25, 27, 29, 31, 45, 50, 52, 55, 56, 64, 71, 76, 77, 98, 150, 176, 180, 185, 189, 191, 193, 195, 198, 199, 201, 202, 203, 204, 205, 206, 207, 209, 210, 211, 212, 213, 214, 216, 231, 265, 266, 267, 268, 270, 271
s 2	203, 212, 213
s 3	202, 203, 204, 212
s 4	203, 208
s 6	204, 208, 210
s 6(2)	203
s 6(3)(b)	204
s 7	195
s 19	203
Hunting Act 2004	49, 56, 123
Indian Independence Act 1947	18
Instruments of Government (under the Lord Protector)	13

Intelligence Services Act 1994	153
Interpretation Act 1978	178
Irish Free State (Agreement) Act 1922	18
Judicial Review and Courts Act 2022	190
s 2	190
Legal Aid, Sentencing and Punishment of Offenders Act 2012	66, 190, 202
Legislative and Regulatory Reform Act 2006	135
Life Peerage Act 1958	56, 115
Local Government Act 1888	248
Local Government Act 1894	248
Local Government Act 1933	248
Local Government Act 1972	248, 253, 254
s 101	255
s 151	257
Local Government Act 1974	
Pt III	257
Local Government Act 1985	249, 254
Local Government Act 1988	256
Local Government Act 1992	
s 13(1)	254
Local Government Act 1999	256
Local Government Act 2000	62, 247, 255
Pt III	256
s 21	248
Local Government Finance Act 1982	257
Local Government Finance Act 1992	255
Local Government (Scotland) Act 1994	254
Local Government (Wales) Act 1994	254
Localism Act 2011	62, 248, 254, 257
s 53(3)	62
Sch 5	257
Magna Carta 1215	11, 12, 51, 69, 79, 80, 201, 268
Art 39	12, 201
Mental Health (Public Safety and Appeals) (Scotland) Act 1999	
s 1	232
Merchant Shipping Act 1988	53
Pt II	54
s 14	53
Metropolis Management Act 1855	198
Ministers of the Crown Act 1975	150
Municipal Corporation Act 1835	248
National Audit Act 1983	133
National Health Service and Community Care Act 1990	
s 60	91

Nigeria Independence Act 1960 50
Northern Ireland Act 1998 .... 25, 29, 52, 176, 223, 224, 231, 233, 239, 266
    Pt II 224
    s 5(2) 224
    s 5(6) 224
    ss 10, 11 223
    s 16 225
    ss 16A-16C 225
    s 68 225
    s 73 225
Northern Ireland (Elections) Act 1998
    s 1 224
Northern Ireland (Executive Formation and Exercise
    of Functions) Act 2018 233
Northern Ireland (St Andrews Agreement) Act 2006
    ss 17, 18 225
Official Secrets Act 1911 .... 163, 167
    s 2 167
Official Secrets Act 1989 .... 163, 167, 201
Online Safety Act 2023 9
Overseas Development and Co-operation Act 1980
    s 1 197
Parliament Act 1911 .... 16, 28, 36, 41, 42, 56, 57, 58, 59, 86,
    105, 113, 114, 116, 123, 156
    s 2 57
    s 2(1) 56, 57
Parliament Act 1949 .... 16, 41, 56, 57, 58, 113, 123
Parliament Recognition Act 1689 .... 13, 14
Parliamentary and Health Services Commissioners Act 1987 136
Parliamentary Commissioner Act 1967 136
    Schs 1, 2 136
Parliamentary Standards Act 2009 111
Parliamentary Voting System and Constituencies Act 2011 61
    s 8 61
Peerages Act 1963 142
Petition of Right 1628 .... 12, 13, 28
Police and Criminal Evidence Act 1984 27
Police, Crime, Sentencing and Courts Act 2022 266
Political Parties, Elections and Referendums Act 2000 101
Prevention of Terrorism Act 2005 .... 208, 211
Prison Act 1952 206
Public Order Act 1986 201
Public Order Act 2023 266
Race Relations Act 1976 163

Table of Legislation xxi

Recall of MPs Act 2015
    s 1 111
Reform Act 1832 15
Reform Act 1867 15
Reform Act 1883 15
Reform Act 1884 15
Rent Act 1977
    Sch 1 203
Representation of the People Act 1867, 30 & 31 Vict. c. 102
    (Second Reform Act 1867) 32
Representation of the People Act 1918 29
Representation of the People Act 1969 29
Republic of Ireland Act 1948 18
Retained EU Law (Revocation and Reform) Act 2023 135
Safety of Rwanda (Asylum and Immigration) Act 2024 193
    ss 2-4 193
Scotland Act 1998 .... 29, 52, 176, 222, 230, 231, 235, 237
    Pt IV 237
    ss 5 – 8 221
    s 28 50
    s 28(7) 226, 234
    s 29 234
    s 29(2)(b) 230
    s 29(2)(d) 213
    ss 31, 32 222
    s 33 223
    s 33(2) 233
    s 44 231
    ss 45, 46 222
    Sch 5 .... 221, 235
Scotland Act 2012 237
Scotland Act 2016 .... 37, 236, 237
    s 1 222
    s 2 226
Security Services Act 1989
    s 3 63
Senior Courts Act 1981
    s 31 193
    s 31(3) 194
Sex Discrimination Act 1975 163
Sexual Offences Act 1967 124
Sexual Offences (Amendment) Act 2000 57
Statute of Westminster 1931 18
Succession to the Crown Act 2013

ss 2, 3 89
Supreme Court Act 1981. *See* Senior Courts Act 1981
Transport (London) Act 1969 199
Treaty of Union 1707 17
Tribunals and Courts Act 2007
   s 11A 190
Tribunals Courts and Enforcement Act 2007 189
United Kingdom Internal Market Act 2020 .... 228, 263
Wales Act 2014 237
Wales Act 2017 .... 37, 222
   s 2 226
   s 3 .... 221, 223
   ss 17, 18 237
   ss 23-44 237
   Sch 1 221
War Crimes Act 1991 57
War Damage Act 1965 .... 29, 65
Welsh Church Act 1914 57
Zimbabwe Act 1979 19

Secondary Legislation

Civil Procedure Rules (SI 1998/3132)
   Pt 54 193
Defence of the Realm Regulations 1914 82
Rules of the Supreme Court (SI 1965/1776)
   Ord 53 193
South Wales Sea Fisheries (Variation) Order 2001 (SI 2001/1338) 232

United States
Bill of Rights 1791 11
Constitution 2, 11, 68, 69, 117, 124, 128, 179, 182, 211
   Art II, s 2 182
   Amendments 1-10 (Bill of Rights 1791) 11
Patriot Act 2001 211

Other Materials

Anglo-Irish Treaty 1921 218
Balfour Declaration 1926 18
Belfast Peace Agreement (Good Friday Agreement) 1998 .... 25, 213, 224, 239
BBC Charter 236
Cabinet Manual (2011) 37, 156, 271

Civil Servive Code (Cabinet Office) updated August 2019	162, 167
Code of Conduct - Panel on Takeovers and Mergers	194
Codes under the Constitutional Reform and Governance Act	
civil servants	166
diplomats	166
special advisers	166
Covid-19 Public Enquiry	
Module I (2024)	6
EU Withdrawal Agreement	24, 25, 240, 263
s 10	25
Art 153	31
Art 158	31
Arts 160, 161	31
Good Friday Agreement (Belfast Agreement) 1998	25, 213, 224, 233
House of Commons Standing Order 14(1)	124
Judge Over Your Shoulder: A guide to good decision making (6th edn, Government Legal Department, 2022)	73, 200
Ministerial Code 2010	160
4.1	149
Ministerial Code 2019	
4.6	165
Ministerial Code, November 2024	143, 148, 149, 160, 161, 264
5.3	148
10	146
Northern Ireland Protocol	239, 240, 241, 263, 266
Prison Rules under Prison Act 1952	206
Producers' Guidelines of the BBC	208
Programme Code of the Independent Television Commission	208
'Salisbury Convention'	41, 114, 123
Sewel (Legislative Consent) Convention	24, 37, 175, 226, 227, 228, 267
'Stormont Brake' 2023	25
UK- EU Trade and Cooperation Agreement, 19 May 2025	266
Windsor Framework 2023	25, 225, 240, 241, 244, 266

1

UK Constitution
Context and History

Democracy – Freedom of Expression – Mass Media – Constitutionalism, Good Governance – History – Monarchy – Parliament – United Kingdom – Empire – Commonwealth – Europe

INTRODUCTION

OUR DISCUSSION BEGINS by explaining why the unwritten UK constitution is unusual. In general the constitution is *the* text that sets out the fundamental and superior law of the nation. It not only describes the main institutions of the state, but also provides a framework of basic rules that determine the relationship between these institutions. In addition, it will usually provide in outline the legal and non-legal rules and procedures that define the system of central and local government. At the same time, the constitution normally places limits on the exercise of power and sets out the rights and duties of individual citizens. Tom Paine explained that it is the property of a nation, and not of those who exercise the government: 'A constitution is a thing antecedent to the government, and always distinct there from.'[1] In nearly every other state the term *constitution* refers to this document (or series of documents) that contains this *fundamental* and *superior* law of the nation. The constitution of the UK is unwritten/uncodified in the sense that it is not contained in any single document. Furthermore, a codified constitution, as a form of *higher order* law, will generally be entrenched. A specified procedural device (eg a referendum or a higher majority plus federal ratification) must be followed to introduce changes, which makes

---

[1] T Paine, *Rights of Man* [1791] (London, Penguin, 1969) 213.

a codified constitution relatively difficult to amend. In contrast to most others, the UK constitution is not entrenched. In consequence, it is relatively flexible, in the sense that any aspect can be changed by way of ordinary legislation and certain aspects can be modified by convention (discussed in Chapter 2).

The next point to stress is that constitutions will often be designed to deliver a particular system of government, and, at the same time, respond to prevailing local conditions. The founding fathers who drafted the constitution of the United States were keen to include strong institutional inhibitions on the exercise of anything approximating to kingly powers, while also creating a federation with a territorial division of authority between central government and state governments. On the other hand, the Soviet constitutions in Russia under Lenin and Stalin following the revolution in 1917 were conceived to deliver an ideological commitment to a socialist state of workers and peasants. The capitalist system of economics and individual property is expressly rejected in the text of these constitutions. We might compare these to the South African constitution, which was drafted following a protracted struggle to overturn a previous regime based on apartheid. The 1996 constitution seeks to achieve reconciliation between ethnic groups, and it is intended to create a democratic state committed to non-racialism and non-sexism and to the advancement of human rights and freedoms and the achievement of equality. The UK lacks a written constitution which has been custom-built to achieve particular goals,[2] but rather the nation has acquired in piecemeal fashion over the span of several centuries a constitution which supports a liberal democratic system of government.

CONSTITUTIONAL CONTEXTS

What is Liberal Democracy?

Now, we need to be clear about what is meant by *liberal democracy*.[3] In setting out a model of democracy Professor Sunstein explains that 'the central goal of a constitution is to create the preconditions for a well functioning democratic order, one in which citizens are genuinely able

---

[2] See eg H Klug, *The Constitution of South Africa: A Contextual Analysis* (Oxford, Hart Publishing, 2010).
[3] For further discussion see J Morison, 'Models of Democracy: From Representation to Participation' in J Jowell and D Oliver (eds), *The Changing Constitution*, 5th edn (Oxford, Oxford University Press, 2005).

to govern themselves',[4] and he advocates a form of deliberative democracy which is marked out by political accountability and a high degree of reflectiveness and a general commitment to reason giving. More commonly, the term *liberal democracy* refers to the fact that power and legitimacy are reached through the indirect consent of the population as a whole. The consent to be governed is achieved after an electoral process delivers representatives to a Parliament. The majority in Parliament vote for laws which, to some extent at least, reflect the will of the majority. However, when looking at constitutional systems, it would be a mistake to believe that a system of majority rule, in itself, satisfies the credentials of liberal democracy. This is because, while it may be accepted that in some matters the will of the majority should prevail, in regard to others, a crucial feature of 'liberal democracy' is that there are limitations on majority rule. For example, the interests of minorities must always be protected to some degree. In practical terms, this means that political parties may offer policy choices to the electorate regarding say, higher or lower levels of taxation, the role of the public sector, and particular policies to pursue in education, health, social services, and law and order. However, the constitutional arrangements in a liberal democratic system must prevent the tyranny of the majority from prevailing by establishing strong constitutional guarantees. This is normally achieved in the field of civil liberties by means of a charter or bill of rights, which will set out the extent of rights which will be protected (eg freedom of speech and religion, freedom to demonstrate, freedom from arbitrary arrest, and so on). However, the UK with its uncodified constitution relied on ordinary laws and a tradition of restraint demonstrated by the executive organs of the state, until the Human Rights Act 1998 (HRA 1998) incorporated the European Convention on Human Rights (ECHR) into domestic law.

The UK Constitution, Constitutionalism, and Good Governance

The UK constitution has evolved in the sense that the rules which have come into being have been accumulated as a response to circumstances, and they can be regarded as the residue of a historical process with particular laws and conventions incorporated following significant events. Apart from describing institutions and procedures, the starting point in

[4] C Sunstein, *Designing Democracy: What Constitutions Do* (Oxford, Oxford University Press, 2001) 6.

drafting a codified constitution or modifying an existing constitution is to come as close as possible to reaching a consensus on any limits imposed on the majority. As we observed above, each constitution reconciles these issues in its own individual fashion. Unlike most other constitutions, the UK constitution has not been designed according to an ideology or theory to deliver a particular system of government. Despite lacking any guiding principle, the UK system could also be said to display the characteristics of what might be described as *constitutionalism*.[5]

The vast majority of constitutions set out a framework of rules which, if applied and interpreted in the spirit intended, would produce if not a version of liberal democracy, at least conditions of good governance. The point to stress is that the constitution needs to be supported by mechanisms which allow the commitments in the text to be implemented. In many constitutions there is a significant gulf between the statement in the constitution and actual compliance. In the majority of cases it is achieving substantial conformity with the rules that becomes the crucial issue. Indeed, as one well-known commentator puts it: 'The fundamental notion of the *Rechtsstaat* or the rule of law was . . . not conceived out of the blue and introduced without resistance. It was, in fact, the fruit of political conflict and scholarly disputes stretching over many centuries.'[6] Rather than compliance with strict constitutional rules, in the UK the interpretation of some of the important constitutional conventions may arise as a matter of debate and controversy (see discussion of conventions in Chapter 2 and of individual ministerial responsibility in Chapter 6).

The first point is to note that any exercise of political power will be bounded by a system of higher order rules which will usually be set out clearly in the constitution. The second point is to recognise what these rules are likely to concern. For example, in virtually every case these rules will specify the institutional framework for passing valid legislation, and a distinction will often be drawn between what can be the permissible content of ordinary legislation as opposed to law relating to the constitution itself. Further, the higher order rules contained in the constitution will outline the method for the formation of the government, and the rules may place limits on the action taken by the executive organs of the state, including the civil service and the police, in the implementation

---

[5] A Harding and P Leyland, 'Comparative Law in Constitutional Contexts' in E Örücü and D Nelken (eds), *Comparative Law Handbook* (Oxford, Hart Publishing, 2007) 322ff.
[6] R Van Caenegem, *An Historical Introduction to Western Constitutional Law* (Cambridge, Cambridge University Press, 1995) 17.

of law. Finally, the constitution may provide that a court (often a constitutional court) has the capacity to invalidate legislation or executive action which fails to comply with the law of the constitution. Constitutionalism is defined in terms of adherence to the rules and to the spirit of the rules. As Professor De Smith has observed: '[this] becomes a living reality to the extent that these rules curb arbitrariness of discretion and are in fact observed by the wielders of political power.'[7]

A genuine constitution for reformers in the eighteenth century, such as Tom Paine, restrained and regulated the exercise of absolute power. Apart from its positive aspects, namely dealing with the generation and organisation of power, a constitution may be taken to comprise a series of devices designed to curb discretionary or unlimited power. It seeks to establish different forms of accountability[8] not simply through a system of freely elected government, but by placing restrictions on the power of the majority. This accountability is reliant on transparency, and it is acted out in a number of familiar ways:[9] an obligation for the government to be responsible to the elected Parliament; legal limits established by the courts (often including a constitutional court) on the exercise of public power; formal financial accountability in public affairs; accountability through contractual agreement where public services are provided by private organisations; and, additionally, accountability through the intervention of constitutional oversight bodies such as parliamentary select committees, ombudsmen, and courts (discussed in later chapters).

Moreover, the constitution also results in further ground rules in the form of laws, codes of practice, and conventions being adopted to ensure fair play at every level.[10] Finally, an equally significant characteristic of constitutionalism is a degree of self-imposed restraint which operates beyond the text of the constitution and its attendant rules, especially on the part of political actors and state officials. The point to stress here is that all nations have a constitution of some kind, but constitutionalism is only established in a true sense where political behaviour is actually contained within certain boundaries. In the first place, the rules need to

---

[7] S De Smith, 'Constitutionalism in the Commonwealth Today' (1962) 4 *Malayan Law Review* 205.

[8] See C Harlow, *Accountability in the European Union* (Oxford, Oxford University Press, 2002) ch 1, 'Thinking about Accountability'.

[9] For a discussion of the development of such mechanism in the UK, see D Oliver, *Constitutional Reform in the UK* (Oxford, Oxford University Press, 2003) chs 1–3.

[10] Loughlin points out: 'Like all representational frameworks, a constitution is a way of organising, and hence also of generating, political power . . . and orchestrating the public power of the state': see M Loughlin, *The Idea of Public Law* (Oxford, Oxford University Press, 2003) 113.

embody a defensible constitutional morality which accords with principles of good governance[11] but the constitution also represents a sufficiently widely accepted political settlement. In the second place, there must be a general adherence at all levels to the constitutional rules and the wider body of law and conventions associated with them. In the UK, as we will soon discover, there is a debate about the adequacy of constitutional safeguards, especially in relation to the exercise of executive power, but although the rules are often embodied in informal conventions, there is generally a high degree of compliance by the main political actors.

Democracy, Accountability, and the Digital World

At the outset, before proceeding to map the sources of the uncodified UK constitution in Chapter 2, it is useful to identify how the core themes of fitness for purpose and constitutional accountability can be identified as of central importance to this study. The crisis precipitated by Covid-19 highlighted the multi-dimensional challenges to the foundations of the democratic constitution as the effect was discernible at many different levels relating to politics, law, and governance. From a citizen perspective the pandemic exercised a pervasive grip on ordinary lives. It resulted in an almost instantaneous transformation in the relationship between the citizen and the administrative state in the delivery of services. The expectation of direct personal contact was replaced by an entirely different, often 'virtual' experience. In the NHS, consultations with GPs or specialists were frequently undertaken by telephone or online. The experience of virtual delivery was replicated in many other fields. Universities delivered courses online at undergraduate and graduate level; courts and tribunals administered justice without any physical meeting, and so on.

The government response to Covid-19 deeply affected the functioning of core political institutions at the heart of UK democracy.[12] The crisis meant that following the 2020 Easter recess both Houses of Parliament agreed to meet remotely. The absence of MPs from across the nation impacted on the capacity of the House of Commons to function as a

---

[11] For a discussion of 'good governance' from a global perspective, see F N Botchway, 'Good Governance: The Old, The New, The Principle and The Elements' (2001) 13 *Florida Journal of International Law* 159.

[12] The preparations and response to Covid-19 has since been subject to a major independent public inquiry set up in June 2022 chaired by Baroness Heather Hallett. https://covid19.public-inquiry.uk/. The inquiry is in distinct stages. The Module I report was published in July 2024.

mirror of the nation by acting in its familiar role as a revising body and a government oversight body. Parliament was first required to approve the direct legal response to Covid-19 in the form of the Coronavirus Act 2020. In so doing, with only three days allocated for consideration of a complex piece of legislation, it provided some cursory legitimation of the government response. The bill not only included the imposition of unprecedented lockdown measures but was also replete with broad delegated powers.[13]

At the same time, in order to handle the crisis, decisions were taken by government with far-reaching consequences for individual citizens, businesses, and for the national economy. For several months daily televised press conferences were staged by the Prime Minister (PM), Cabinet ministers, and senior medical advisers and broadcast live on national TV. These regular appearances were intended to keep the public informed on the management of the crisis, and official statements setting out policy initiatives were followed by questions from journalists and selected members of the public. In Chapter 5, the role of debates, parliamentary questions, and departmental select committees in holding the government to account is evaluated, but at a moment when Parliament was unable to gather physically, this daily spectacle diverted attention away from the parliamentary task of holding government ministers to account for government policy. Much of the routine work of parliamentary committees continued in virtual form. However, the subsequent failure to reach consensus with all political parties on the safe resumption of parliamentary activities, including a requirement to resume physical voting in place of proxy voting, had serious implications by breaching the principle of equality. In consequence, a significant minority of MPs who felt unable to attend the building on health grounds were excluded from full participation in the democratic process. In sum, notwithstanding the controversial nature of some temporary rule changes, the precautions relating to Covid-19 have transformed many of the procedures followed within Parliament and has had a residual impact on the way Parliament works.

Viewed from a territorial perspective, the response to Covid-19 provides at intermediate level a particular snapshot of the impact of devolution on the multi-layered UK system of governance (discussed in more detail in Chapter 8). Although health is a devolved competence there was an obvious need for inter-governmental consultation and co-operation with Scotland, Wales, and Northern Ireland in the rapid formulation of policy. Legislative consent (Sewel) motions were duly obtained from the devolved legislatures in respect to the Coronavirus bill, but conflicting

[13] S Tierney and J King, 'The Coronavirus Bill', UK Const L Blog (24 March 2020).

policy changes were later introduced without adequate consultation. Initially, as government reacted to pressing events the leaders and ministers of the devolved administrations were invited to COBRA meetings. COBRA is an emergency committee, usually chaired by the PM or other senior minister, which includes relevant ministers, officials, police, military, and experts convened to deal with matters of national emergency.[14] Joint meetings of medical and scientific advisers across the UK were also held. However, once the (emergency) inter-governmental COBRA meetings were discontinued there was no resort to the Joint Ministerial Committee, the only other official channel for consultation, nor was any replacement protocol agreed to review lockdown policy.[15] As a result, there was an obvious failure to co-ordinate the relaxation and the tightening of the respective measures in place in Scotland, Wales, and Northern Ireland during the course of the Covid-19 crisis 2020–21.[16] Devolution was intended to allow significant policy divergence. Given the obvious political differences, particularly between nationalist parties and the then Conservative government, tensions and differences of emphasis were perhaps inevitable. Nevertheless, such problems in coordinating policy relating to public health and safety might not have arisen if recommendations to revise the Joint Ministerial Committee as a formal structure for inter-governmental relations had been implemented as a sector-specific mechanism to co-ordinate policy and reconcile differences between the devolved governments and the UK government at Westminster. In other words, confused signals relating to the guidance given to the public might have been avoided by addressing this particular 'black hole at the heart of the constitutional architecture'.[17]

Next, the constitutional impact of the Covid-19 crisis can be considered with reference to questions of legal regulation and human rights. Codified constitutions invariably include a constitutional charter of positive rights which are enforceable under the constitution. By way of contrast, citizens in the UK have 'negative rights'. They are traditionally able to do anything which does not conflict with a specific law. Of course, the HRA 1998 incorporated the ECHR into domestic law (see Chapter 7) and some important rights have been legally protected under

---

[14] See Civil Contingencies Committee and Civil Contingencies Act 2004.

[15] See 'Inter-governmental relations in the United Kingdom' House of Lords Select Committee on the Constitution, 11th Report of Session 2014–15, 27 March 2015, 57.

[16] G Evans, 'Devolution and COVID-19: Towards a "New Normal" in the Territorial Constitution?' [2021] *PL* 19.

[17] R Rawlings, *Brexit and the Territorial Constitution* (The Constitution Society, 2017) 15.

specific statutes, but only on a piecemeal basis when Parliament has chosen to intervene. From March 2020 the British public were exposed to the circulation of misinformation relating to the virus, available from social media and the internet in the form of Facebook, Twitter, YouTube etc. The threat has included the promotion of potentially lethal advice concerning preventative measures to minimise infection and the use of scientifically untested cures. While state-regulated public service broadcasting such as the BBC were increasingly recognised as a reliable source (related to a Trusted News Initiative), the proliferation of misinformation from the internet went unchecked. This is because, in a classic case of regulation failing to keep up with technology, the platforms circulating the information have not been placed under a duty of care and thereby made subject to adequate legal control. As recognised by parliamentary committees with an interest in the field conducting pre-legislative hearings, the prospect of legislative intervention raises important questions because any new law has to steer a course between conflicting considerations. On the one hand, there is a need to establish an effective regulatory regime but, on the other, such regulation must minimise the inhibition of free expression. Evidence from specialist parliamentary committees point to a range of factors which might determine the efficacy of 'online harms' regulation. For example, the definition of a statutory duty of care making internet companies responsible for the safety of their users; the introduction of comprehensive list of harms in order to set standards against which harms can be measured by a regulatory authority; and the appointment of a competent and adequately funded independent regulatory authority (OFCOM) equipped with sufficient powers of enforcement.[18] Democratic legitimacy calls for robust parliamentary oversight which reinforces the independence of a regulatory regime responsible for policing a controversial policy domain. However, any new law in this field which will also apply to the use of social media at elections[19] and the spread of hate speech. The legislation must therefore have regard to the protection of free speech in conformity with international human rights law.[20] As we will see in Chapters 6 and 7, statutory regulatory bodies reporting to ministers are made accountable to Parliament

---

[18] See the Online Safety Act 2023.

[19] Defending Our Democracy in the Digital Age, All Party Parliamentary Group on Electoral Transparency, January 2020. See also Online Harms White Paper – Initial consultation response, February 2020, www.gov.uk/government/consultations/online-harms-white-paper/public-feedback/online-harms-white-paper-initial-consultation-response.

[20] 'Misinformation in the COVID-19 Infodemic', House of Commons, Digital, Media and Sport Committee, Second Report of Session 2019–21, HC 234, 21 July 2020, 38.

and the situation relating to rights protection changed significantly under the HRA 1998 which, in effect, incorporated the rights contained in the ECHR into UK domestic law, including the right to free expression.

The accelerated streamlining of the practice of public administration by Covid-19 and the need for remote engagement with the citizen brings to mind a spectre of modernity reminiscent of George Orwell's *1984* or Fritz Lang's *Metropolis*. The trend has been a resort to automated decision-making by government.[21] This reminds us that in regard to the executive branch government[22] accountability mechanisms need to keep pace with changes in practice. Typically, automation is used by reducing a decision, often made under a delegated statutory power, to an algorithm, thus virtually eliminating the need for human involvement. From the citizen's perspective the process comes to involve only a form-filling exercise with the applicant typically responding to a series of questions. The outcome then depends on whether the criteria have been met when assessed by a computer (or an official); nonetheless, as will be apparent in Chapters 5 and 6, the Secretary of State remains notionally responsible to Parliament for the decision.[23] In principle, assuming the data supplied is accurate, this method provides speedy, consistent decision-making and minimises the time needed to process applications. If unchecked, however, remote systems are obviously open to fraudulent abuse. The lack of transparency over the extent of deployment of automation is a further concern. Another issue, taking into account the complexity of many types of decision-making, is whether an appropriate balance has been struck between rule and discretion to allow for proper input to avoid injustice. It has been pointed out that pre-existing parliamentary oversight has not been geared up to contain this increasingly 'dehumanised dystopia' which has the potential to become a pernicious form of executive authority.[24]

CONSTITUTIONAL HISTORY

In general, constitutions are formally adopted as a specific text of special importance introduced at a decisive moment in a nation's history to

---

[21] A Le Sueur, 'Automated Decision-Making' in A Horne and A Le Sueur (eds), *Parliament, Legislation and Accountability* (Oxford, Hart Publishing, 2016) 183ff.
[22] The Government Digital Service is a unit within the Cabinet Office.
[23] A parallel trend towards automation is discernible at the level of devolved government and local government.
[24] Le Sueur (n 21) 196.

achieve obvious goals. For example, the constitution of the United States was approved after the success over the British in the American War of Independence. The 'Bill of Rights' was adopted as the first 10 amendments in 1791, but apart from a further 17 amendments the constitution has remained in its original succinct form.[25] The First Republic in France was introduced shortly after the revolution of 1789, and the most recent Fifth Republic was introduced in 1958 to redress the instability of previous constitutions by bolstering the presidential role.[26] In modern times there has been no single domestic event that has required a comprehensive revision of the UK constitution and so the UK has no constitutional text with this special status. Rather, the constitution is comprised of a variety of sources including statute law, common law, and constitutional conventions (the sources of the constitution are discussed in Chapter 2). The constitutional arrangements for the UK have evolved in phases reflecting the political, social, and economic experiences of many centuries. The events selected for coverage are dealt with thematically rather than in chronological sequence, and they are intended to set the scene for the discussion that follows in subsequent chapters.

Qualifying Absolute Monarchy

The first recurring theme worth mentioning involves certain qualifications which have been placed in the exercise of the absolute authority of the monarchy. An obvious starting point looks back to medieval times, and relates to the dispute between King John and his barons which culminated in the drawing up of the Magna Carta of 1215.[27] The feudal system originally operated on the basis that the King's barons or nobles held their lands from the King in exchange for an oath to him of loyalty and obedience, but with the obligation to provide a fixed number of knights whenever these were required for military service. By the reign of King John this feudal obligation for service was expressed through the imposition of arbitrary financial payments determined by the King and his entourage of royal officials, which were often used to maintain an army. The barons were dissatisfied with what they regarded as a form

---

[25] M Tushnet, *The Constitution of the United States of America: A Contextual Analysis*, 2nd edn (Oxford, Hart Publishing, 2015).
[26] S Boyron, *The Constitution of France: A Contextual Analysis* (Oxford, Hart Publishing, 2013).
[27] www.bl.uk/treasures/magnacarta/translation.html; C Breay, *Magna Carta: Manuscripts and Myths* (London, British Library, 2002).

of unjust taxation, and they were sufficiently united to insist on the King recognising a disparate catalogue of demands. The shopping list of grievances was very much a top-down settlement favouring the barons and covering not only the celebrated right to justice in Article 39 but also the freedom of the Church, recognition that London and other cities should enjoy their own liberties and customs, navigation of rivers, inheritance, guardianship of land, seizure of property, and feudal dues. As one commentator has observed: '[A] common core was an undertaking by the crown to observe a precisely formulated code of behaviour towards their subjects or, in other words, to respect their rights and liberties as specified in the charters.'[28] The charter has become famous as a constitutional document. This is partly because it refers to some fundamental rights, for instance by providing that no one should be denied justice or punished except by judgment of their peers or by the law of the land. But also because, at the beginning of the seventeenth century as resistance to absolute royal authority was increasingly evident, it was re-launched and elaborated under Chief Justice Sir Edward Coke as the Petition of Right of 1628. The impact of the original charter, however, was marginal as within weeks King John, encouraged by the Pope, reneged on his promise to uphold the undertakings contained therein. Although only selected provisions of the Magna Carta were later confirmed by future Kings and the English Parliament, certain rights and liberties, in particular the right to fair trial, may be traced back to the original document, which crucially included limitations on royal power.[29]

The limitation on royal authority by constitutional means was achieved in stages. The Tudor monarchs, notably Henry VIII and Elizabeth I, were very powerful and personally active in the affairs of government, but by this period Parliament also became increasingly important. While these Tudor monarchs were able to dominate Parliament, they also ruled through Parliament in order to legalise their actions: 'the sixteenth century had a concept of the supremacy of law, embodied in the rule of the common law and sovereignty controlled by statute, which limited the free power of monarchy and was so recognised, in theory and practice by the Crown.'[30]

The seventeenth century was of great constitutional significance. The Stuart Kings, particularly Charles I (1625–49), sought to claw back the initiative from Parliament by re-asserting the divine right of kings to

---

[28] Van Caenegem (n 6) 17.
[29] A Arlidge and I Judge, *Magna Carta Uncovered* (Oxford, Hart Publishing, 2014).
[30] G Elton, *England Under the Tudors*, 2nd edn (London, Methuen, 1974) 483.

govern. An obvious problem for the King was that Parliament had to be summoned when he wished to raise taxes, for example, to pursue foreign policy, to fight wars, or to crush insurrection. The Petition of Right in 1628, which arose after a person had been imprisoned for refusing to pay a loan imposed by the King (see *Darnel's Case* 1627, also known as 'the *Five Knights' Case*[31]) had already signalled dissatisfaction, because Parliament in 1628 rejected the idea of taxation without its consent, and, at the same time, some MPs began to question the Crown's authority to impose arbitrary imprisonment and martial law.[32] The struggle between the Crown and Parliament came to a head with the Civil War (1642–49). As well as contesting the right to impose taxes without Parliament's consent, mentioned above, the King's authority to summon and dismiss Parliament at will was also called into question. The resistance of MPs to the King's demands when Parliament was recalled culminated in an event of symbolic importance. The King entered Parliament in person with soldiers at his side in order to arrest five dissenting MPs. The Speaker of the House of Commons refused to co-operate with the King's demands in an act of open defiance. At this point factions within Parliament were prepared to resort to armed insurrection to resist the King's demands. In the struggle that followed, parliamentary forces prevailed over those of Charles I, and the King was tried and executed in 1649. Oliver Cromwell's Commonwealth under the Instruments of Government lasted only a few years, however, before the restoration of the monarchy with the accession of Charles II in 1660.

Charles II's reign was relatively uneventful in regard to constitutional matters. However, he was succeeded by his brother James II, who was not only a Roman Catholic, but, like his father Charles I, was prepared to disregard the will of Parliament. The use of his royal authority to promote Catholics to prominent positions in what had become a strongly Protestant nation sparked a strong backlash with far-reaching constitutional implications. With the prospect of revolt on the horizon, James dissolved Parliament in 1688 before fleeing the country. In the meantime, the opponents of James II invited William of Orange (a Dutch Protestant), who was married to James's daughter Mary, to take up the throne on certain conditions. The position of the King in relation to Parliament was set out in the Bill of Rights of 1689, later enacted as the Parliament Recognition Act of 1689.

---

[31] 3 *State Trials* 36–37.
[32] S Willms, 'The Five Knights' Case and Debates in Parliament of 1628: Division and Suspicion under King Charles I' (2006) 7(1) *Constructing the Past*, Article 11.

This landmark document was not a charter of citizens' rights in the modern sense, because it was not concerned to define comprehensively the rights of citizens. Nonetheless, it is extremely important for setting in place certain fundamentals of the contemporary constitution. In particular, it confirmed that it was illegal for the Crown to execute laws, raise taxes, or keep an army in peacetime without the consent of Parliament (Articles I, IV, and VI). It provided not only that a freely elected Parliament should meet on a regular basis, but also it gave formal recognition to the privileges of Parliament, which included a right to free speech and debate for MPs, and it gave them the right to regulate their own proceedings without limitation or interference either from the Crown or from the courts. Shortly afterwards, the Act of Settlement 1701 regulated the succession to the throne and also established the security of tenure of judges. In sum, as Hill observes: 'The men of property [were] secure and unfettered in their control of local government; as taxpayers they determine government policy . . . [they] won freedom – freedom from arbitrary taxation and arbitrary arrest, freedom from religious persecution, freedom to control the destinies of their country through their elected representatives . . .'[33] (The constitutional role of the Crown is considered further in Chapter 4.)

The Emergence of Parliament and the Path to Democracy

As has just been stressed, the UK Bill of Rights of 1689 established that ultimate sovereignty was vested in the King in Parliament, not in the King alone. The power of the Crown and the prerogatives of the Crown were thereafter restricted. In theory at least, unlimited authority had been granted to Parliament as the body with unrestricted law-making capacity. However, this change was only a limited step towards parliamentary democracy in a modern sense. The problem was that Parliament represented elite groups and it mainly protected property rights. The idea of a representative Parliament had been in evidence at least from Edward I's Model Parliament of 1295, whose membership was based on the principle of two knights from each county, two burgesses from each borough, and two citizens from each city. Further, by 1341 the House of Commons was meeting separately.[34] In fact, the composition and powers of Parliament

---

[33] C Hill, *The Century of Revolution* (London, Abacus, 1978) 263 and 265.
[34] www.parliament.uk/about/living-heritage/evolutionofparliament/originsofparliament/birthofparliament/overview/edward.

re-emerged as an issue of great constitutional importance during the course of the late eighteenth and early nineteenth centuries. As well as the development of political ideas associated with popular 'revolutions' in America and France which recognised citizen rights, the nation itself was experiencing rapid transformation. There were new pressures associated with industrialisation, the growth of population, and the rapid expansion of towns and cities. While the complexion of the nation and the distribution of its population was in the course of changing, well into the nineteenth century only a small minority of men had the right to vote as the franchise was based on the value of the property owned or rented. Equally, the geographical division into constituencies sending members to the House of Commons no longer corresponded to the new locations of the centres of population in the industrial cities and towns of the Midlands and the North. Reform Acts in 1832, 1867, 1883, and 1884 went some way towards extending the right to vote and to redistributing seats more evenly but it was not until 1918 that universal suffrage for men and votes for women over 30 were secured, with women securing equal voting rights in 1928.[35]

The extension of the franchise had far-reaching constitutional consequences. It prompted the emergence of more representative political parties. The Labour Party associated with the trade union movement was formed and based its support on the industrial working class while the Tory Party and Whig Party of the eighteenth and nineteenth centuries had by the twentieth century morphed into the Conservative Party and the Liberal Party. MPs were given a direct mandate from this broader electorate to introduce programmes of social reform, and, having obtained a majority in the elected House of Commons, the government in power claimed authority to achieve its political goals. On the other hand, the House of Lords (sometimes referred to as 'the Upper House') comprised the titled nobility (titles were originally granted directly by the King, but by the nineteenth century candidates were nominated by the PM) who originally derived their wealth and influence from the ownership of land. Peers were able to pass on their titles to the next generation by heredity, and as members of the House of Lords they had a traditional right to sit and vote in Parliament. During the nineteenth and early twentieth centuries the landed aristocracy began to use this voting power in the House of Lords first to delay the process of parliamentary reform, and later to oppose the manifesto commitments and budget proposals of the elected

---

[35] J Vernon, *Modern Britain: 1750 to the Present* (Cambridge, Cambridge University Press, 2017) 191ff.

Liberal Government. This opposition precipitated a constitutional crisis. The House of Lords as the unelected legislative chamber was expected to defer to the House of Commons in financial matters. However, when it not only blocked legislative proposals but also refused to pass a budget in 1909 it was forced to agree to its powers being significantly qualified by way of the Parliament Acts of 1911 and 1949. The composition of the House of Lords remains unresolved, but a category of peers appointed for their lifetime only (life peers) which included women was introduced in 1958, and hereditary peers have since been excluded from participating in the business of the House. (The role of Parliament is discussed in Chapter 5.)

Defining the Nation: What is the United Kingdom?

Another dimension to domestic constitutional evolution has concerned the formation of the UK, comprising England, Wales, Scotland, and Northern Ireland. In Chapter 8 we will consider the constitutional implications of recent devolution provisions, but at the outset, it is useful to be familiar with the territorial reach of the sovereign nation. In the case of Wales, conquest of the principality by England was completed under Edward I between 1272 and 1307.[36] Royal authority over Wales was later set out in Henry VIII's reign, first by an Act of Union of 1536 'for laws and justice to be ministered in Wales' which also allowed Wales to return MPs to Westminster, and second, by a further Act of Union of 1545 which contained the details of the political and legal assimilation of the union between England and Wales.[37]

Edward I and other English kings ultimately failed in their attempts to overwhelm Scotland by force, but the thrones of Scotland and England were eventually united, when in 1603 James VI of Scotland succeeded Elizabeth I as James I of England.[38] James had been unsuccessful in his attempt to effect a union of the two kingdoms in an administrative sense. Under the restored constitutional monarchy of William III and Mary, which was set in place by the Bill of Rights of 1689, it was not long before the Scots were faced with a choice. In essence, either the Parliaments of England and Scotland would have to unite, or there would have to be a

---

[36] A Harding, *England in the Thirteenth Century* (Cambridge, Cambridge University Press, 1993) 305ff.
[37] Elton (n 30) 178.
[38] Ibid 474.

separation of the monarchies. Taking account of the economic advantages of fusing the two nations, the Scottish Parliament opted for union. The Treaty of Union and the Act of Union with Scotland 1707 were of enormous significance. This agreement was recognition that England and Scotland were to come under a single Parliament of Great Britain and that the rule of succession for the two thrones would be the same. However, as part of the deal Scotland retained many of its national institutions (church, legal system, and educational system).[39]

The relationship between England and Ireland has been both turbulent and complex. In brief, England had assumed direct rule over Ireland in 1534, and Henry VIII declared himself King of Ireland in 1541. The Catholic majority (later to generally support the Nationalist cause) were hostile to British rule, which tended to favour Protestant settlers (termed 'Unionists' as they remained loyal to the Crown and favoured maintaining close association with Westminster) introduced into Ireland mainly from Scotland by the English. There were many periods of rebellion, which were sometimes brutally suppressed. Following resolutions by the Parliaments in Westminster and Dublin, Ireland was eventually united with England at the beginning of the nineteenth century. This union was achieved by the Act of Union of 1800, which also confirmed the place of Irish MPs at Westminster.[40] However, the prevailing arrangements were not acceptable to Irish Nationalists (who formed a substantial majority, particularly in the South of Ireland), some of whom resorted to intermittent violent struggle. Apart from repressive measures to confront the unrest, the political response of the Liberal Party (pioneered by WE Gladstone) was to attempt to introduce a considerable degree of Irish self-government in domestic affairs, but each of the Home Rule Bills of 1886, 1893, and 1912 was unsuccessful.[41] This was largely because they failed to satisfy the competing claims of Nationalists and Unionists. To accommodate deep-seated differences, the Government of Ireland Act of 1920 was based on partition between the six counties in the North, comprising Northern Ireland with a Parliament in Belfast, and the remainder of Ireland with a Parliament in Dublin. However, the 1920 Act was only implemented in the North. A form of devolved government based at Stormont was set up in 1921 and Unionists secured a promise to allow the North to give its consent before any future assimilation with the South. The situation

---

[39] J Miller, *Early Modern Britain, 1450–1750* (Cambridge, Cambridge University Press, 2018) 359ff.
[40] A Briggs, *The Age of Improvement* (Harlow, Longman, 1975) 196ff.
[41] R Tombs, *The English and Their History* (London, Allen Lane, 2014) 507ff.

concerning devolved government in Northern Ireland will be discussed further (in Chapter 8). Almost at the same time, the British Government reached an agreement with representatives of a provisional government of Ireland to allow an Irish Free State to be established. The Irish Free State (Agreement) Act of 1922 excluded the 26 counties of the South from jurisdiction of the UK Parliament under the Act of Union of 1800. The current Irish constitution dates from 1937, and the Republic left the Commonwealth under the Republic of Ireland Act 1948, which paved the way for the formation of an independent Republic of Ireland in 1949.[42]

In sum, the term *United Kingdom* now refers to a sovereign state which includes England, Wales, Scotland, and Northern Ireland. The implications of the devolved systems of government introduced in Scotland, Wales, and Northern Ireland are discussed in Chapter 8.

Empire to Commonwealth

At the beginning of the twentieth century the UK was a powerful imperial nation. A quarter of the world's population was ruled directly or indirectly from Westminster. Despite victory in World War I (1914–18) and World War II (1939–45), the diminution of Britain's military, economic, and political influence was reflected in the transition from this vast empire to a Commonwealth of self-governing states. Viewed from a constitutional perspective this transition occurred in phases. First, there were self-governing colonies, referred to as dominions, which included Canada, Australia, South Africa, and New Zealand. The Balfour Declaration of 1926 later enacted through the Statute of Westminster 1931 established that the Westminster Parliament would not legislate for the dominions without their consent. In the words of one commentator: 'Its main effect was to end the Empire-wide writ of the United Kingdom Parliament.'[43]

After World War II, the British withdrew from India, and the Indian Independence Act of 1947 resulted in partition and the eventual formation of the independent nations of India and of Pakistan.[44] Malaya was

---

[42] See O Doyle, *The Constitution of Ireland: A Contextual Analysis* (Oxford, Hart Publishing, 2018) 6ff; B Hadfield, 'The United Kingdom as Territorial State' in V Bogdanor (ed), *The British Constitution in the Twentieth Century* (Oxford, Oxford University Press, 2003) 598ff.

[43] R Holland, 'Britain, Commonwealth and the End of Empire' in V Bogdanor (ed), *The British Constitution in the Twentieth Century* (Oxford, Oxford University Press, 2003) 638.

[44] See S Aziz, *The Constitution of Pakistan: A Contextual Analysis* (Oxford, Hart Publishing, 2018) 22ff; A Thiruvengadam, *The Constitution of India: A Contextual Analysis* (Oxford, Hart Publishing, 2017) 29ff.

granted independence under the Federation of Malaya Independence Act 1957. The rapid decolonisation of Africa began with Ghana gaining independence in 1957. In the West Indies, Jamaica and Trinidad were granted independence in 1962. Withdrawal from Africa was completed when, after a protracted dispute and civil war, the Zimbabwe Act of 1979 formally granted independence to Zimbabwe (formerly Southern Rhodesia). In each of these nations the Westminster Parliament gave up its local jurisdiction and a new constitution was adopted, usually featuring prominent elements of the Westminster model, together with a system of law based on the common law. The British Commonwealth has continued as a club of nations of ex-British colonial status with the Crown symbolically at its head. The nations co-operate in the common interests of their peoples and in the promotion of human rights, international understanding, and world peace.[45]

The European Union and Brexit

As the influence of empire and Commonwealth waned, and UK economic involvement with the United States diminished after World War II, so the importance of Europe increased. The Treaty of Rome 1957, which set up the Common Market (European Economic Community (EEC)) without UK inclusion, was a first step towards Churchill's vision of a 'United States of Europe'[46] which would be able to avoid the recurrence of war by featuring a close partnership between France and Germany together with other nations. The UK eventually joined the EEC (subsequently the European Community (EC) and now the European Union (EU)) on 1 January 1973 after protracted negotiations. Although the UK signed up to a mainly economic treaty, from a constitutional perspective, membership of this supra-national organisation resulted in a sacrifice of sovereign power in a number of areas.[47] A new hierarchy of law was recognised which meant that a set of European institutions were capable of making laws which could override the authority of the UK national Parliament and UK domestic courts (this issue is discussed in Chapters 3 and 7). Despite being highly controversial within the main political parties (Conservative, Labour, and

---

[45] For a statement of the reaffirmation of the principles agreed in the Harare government meeting 1991, see for example: https://library.commonwealth.int/Portal/DownloadImage File.ashx?objectId=2619.
[46] Winston Churchill set out these ideas in a speech delivered in Zurich in 1946.
[47] J Murkens, 'The UK's Reluctant Relationship with the EU' in R Schütze and S Tierney (eds), *The United Kingdom and the Federal Idea* (Oxford, Hart Publishing, 2018) 162ff.

Liberal Democrat), EU membership was entered into without consulting the electorate. However, the *post hoc* 1975 referendum appeared to have settled the issue of association with Europe decisively in favour of continued EU membership after a passionate campaign during which otherwise strict rules of party loyalty (including collective Cabinet responsibility, discussed in Chapter 6) were suspended. A latent Euro-scepticism was encouraged by Mrs Thatcher as PM in the 1980s but its expression was then mainly confined to a relatively small faction within the Conservative Party.

During the latter part of the twentieth century and the beginning of the twenty-first successive EU treaties granted membership to many more nations (from 9 in 1973 up to a total of 28 states including the UK) and extended the range of policy areas subject to EU law.[48] The negotiation of the treaties (Maastricht (1992), Amsterdam (1999), Nice (2003), and Lisbon (2009)) and the drafting of the European constitution were mainly undertaken as a top-down exercise, carried out by senior politicians and officials representing Member States. Moreover, formidable obstacles had to be cleared in order to reach agreement. In formulating a constitution and thereby setting an agenda for Europe the most influential nations were committed to very different objectives. For example, political leaders in France, Germany, Italy, Belgium, and Holland were keen to strengthen the EU as a political entity (a 'European Super State') committed to public services and social support.[49] On the other hand, the UK supported a mainly economic union comprising a large market place. This goal was in line with the domestic trend towards a limited state sector and increased economic liberalisation.

Since its expansion in May 2004 economic uncertainty has, on occasion, shaken the EU and the Euro currency to its foundations. Before the Covid-19 emergency of 2020, EU crisis management was needed during the European debt crisis of a decade earlier. The economic impact of this crisis potentially reached beyond Greece to include Portugal, Spain, Ireland, Italy, and even France. This has influenced the political environment. The general apathy and indifference that pervaded the European political space has been increasingly occupied by far right political parties, with little apparent commitment to the liberal democratic ideals of the EU.[50] Outside the UK, the phenomenon of Euro-scepticism was

[48] See I Ward, *A Critical Introduction to European Law*, 3rd edn (Cambridge, Cambridge University Press, 2009), ch 1.
[49] U Haltern, *The Constitution of the European Union: A Contextual Analysis* (Oxford, Hart Publishing, 2025), ch 2.
[50] C Pinelli, 'The Populist Challenge to Constitutional Democracy' (2011) 7 *European Constitutional Law Review* 5.

also apparent well before the Brexit referendum, in referendums on the draft European constitution held in France and Holland in 2005 in which the wider electorate voted decisively against, despite strong endorsement from the ruling political elite.[51]

The hand of opponents to the EU was undoubtedly strengthened by a relative lack of democratic accountability relating to the EU and its institutions.[52] The European Parliament (EP) consists of members elected in Member States. Its authority was enhanced under the Treaty of Lisbon, but it has limited powers and often only operates on the fringes of the law-making process.[53] In contrast, the Commission, exercising executive power at EU level, is unelected. There is no transnational party system capable of rising above national politics, and none of the EU treaties fully addresses the issue of the role and input of national Parliaments and other accountability mechanisms. The absence of political accountability coupled with bureaucracy at EU level which is often portrayed in the media as wasteful, helps to explain the hostility to the EU from Eurosceptic opponents. The perception of an accountability gap has contributed to a gulf opening up between national governments, European institutions, and prevailing public opinion within many of the Member States.[54]

In the UK, the support for the UK Independence Party (UKIP) was not sufficiently concentrated to break the mould of a two- or three-party system at general elections but its popularity exerted pressure on the Conservative Party which already had a vigorous Eurosceptic faction.[55] Ironically, UKIP, as a vociferous anti-EU party, polled sufficient votes at Euro elections to win an increasing number of seats in the Strasbourg Parliament.[56] In many respects the UK remained on the fringes of the wider Euro project. In the aftermath of the Maastricht Treaty it declined to join the Euro currency, it negotiated opt-outs from closer Eurozone integration (eg the Schengen agreement and abolition of border controls, home affairs, and justice policy)[57] and the UK government (2010–15)

---

[51] R Bellamy and S Kröger, 'Domesticating the Democratic Deficit? The Role of National Parliaments and Parties in the EU's System of Governance' *Parliamentary Affairs* (2014) 67, 437–57.
[52] Harlow (n 8) 24.
[53] 'The Role of National Parliaments in the EU', *House of Lords, European Union Committee*, 9th Report of Session 2013–14, HL Paper 151.
[54] Ibid paras 161–63.
[55] See T Shipman, *All out War: The Full Story of Brexit* (London, William Collins, 2017).
[56] In the European Parliament elections UKIP secured 13 seats in 2010 and 24 seats in 2014.
[57] Murkens (n 47) 164ff.

introduced legislation to prevent the creeping encroachment of EU law by requiring national referendums to be held to gain prior approval for the extension of certain laws emanating from Brussels.[58]

In order to settle the issue of UK membership against a background of growing opposition to Europe, primarily within the Conservative Party and anti-European fringe groups (UKIP), PM David Cameron negotiated revised terms of membership with the EU before holding a national 'in/out' referendum[59] on 23 June 2016.[60] The 'leave' result, with 51.9 per cent voting in favour of leaving the EU (which had become known as Brexit), was not widely anticipated.[61] Cameron, whose political authority had been fatally undermined, resigned. The government under his successor PM Theresa May entered Brexit negotiations with the EU immediately without any consensus on an exit strategy or any alternative trade agreement on the table. Rather, it faced a catalogue of intractable and interrelated questions with profound consequences for the economy but also impacting upon constitutional principles in many different ways.

Constitutional Consequences

In observing a shift away from Parliament and towards popular sovereignty, it is important to remember this referendum was not legally binding and that the result was only marginally in favour of Brexit.[62] Nevertheless, on assuming office, Mrs May's government unsuccessfully attempted to trigger the Article 50 Brexit process using the prerogative power. By doing so, the decision to leave could have been finalised entirely without direct reference to Parliament. The government were, in effect, claiming that the executive was empowered directly by the people on whose behalf it could act, without further reference to representative institutions.[63] In the first *Miller* case the majority in the UK Supreme Court (UKSC) found *inter alia* that the effect of the referendum would depend on the terms of the statute that had authorised it and held that

---

[58] See European Union Act 2011, s 6 (now repealed).

[59] See 'The referendum on UK membership of the EU: assessing the reform process', *House of Lords, European Union Committee*, 3rd Report of Session 2015–16, HL Paper 30.

[60] The question will be: 'Should the United Kingdom remain a member of the European Union or leave the European Union?' See the European Referendum Act 2015.

[61] The turnout was 72 per cent.

[62] A Young, 'Populism and Parliamentary Sovereignty' in L Burton Crawford, P Emerton, and D Smith (eds), *Law under a Democratic Constitution* (Oxford, Hart Publishing, 2019) 176.

[63] A Blick, *Stretching the Constitution: The Brexit Shock in Historic Perspective* (Oxford, Hart Publishing, 2019) 55.

legislation would be required to trigger Brexit.[64] By determining the legality of the exercise of the prerogative power the UKSC was required to determine the distribution of power between the executive branch and Parliament. In the words of Sir John Laws: '... the issue that was at the heart of the case: should our constitutional law allow the executive to initiate our departure without legislative authority to that effect? Behind this question there is the larger one: how far should our constitutional law allow the executive to make or unmake domestic law?'[65]

For many opponents of EU membership, a prime objective was the restoration of sovereignty. In Chapter 3 it will be observed that since the European Communities Act 1972 community law prevailed over domestic law. Sovereignty became conflated with the idea of 'taking back control' over law-making from EU institutions and removing the jurisdiction of the European Court of Justice. The cumulative effect of transposing EU directives over nearly 50 years into domestic law was to regulate activities stretching across many fields (eg trading standards, food, pharmaceuticals, agriculture). From a technical legal standpoint the task of eliminating this vast body of law in order to deliver a clean Brexit was not possible in a limited time frame.[66] In order to maintain order and stability as from the date of withdrawal (end of January 2020), the starting point of the withdrawal legislation was to ensure existing EU law remained valid and enforceable in the UK.[67] In other words, the UK remains subject to a substantial body of EU law. Moreover, there is an external paradox identified by Professor Craig:

> ... even if the UK takes the hardest of hard Brexit strategies, there will, nonetheless, be very significant constraints on the sovereign choices available to the UK Parliament. This flows, in part, from the fact that many trading standards are set at the global level, largely as a result of negotiations between the EU and the USA, and these will continue to apply in a post-Brexit world.[68]

However, the legislation also allows for the selective repatriation of EU laws by conferring wide delegated powers on the government, thus

---

[64] R (On the application of Miller) v Secretary of State for Exiting the European Union [2017] UKSC 5.

[65] J Laws, 'The Miller Case and Constitutional Statutes' in M Elliott, J Williams, and AL Young (eds), The UK Constitution After Miller: Brexit and Beyond (Oxford, Hart Publishing, 2018) 210.

[66] See eg European Union (Withdrawal) Act 2018 and the European Union (Withdrawal Agreement) Act 2020.

[67] European Union (Withdrawal) Act 2018, ss 2–4 convert EU law to domestic law.

[68] P Craig, 'Brexit and the UK Constitution' in J Jowell and C O'Cinneide (eds), The Changing Constitution (Oxford, Oxford University Press, 2019) 118.

increasing the power of the executive rather than of Parliament. In turn, this raises further issues of constitutional accountability, as there is only limited opportunity for parliamentary scrutiny by relevant committees of both Houses of Parliament (see further Chapters 5 and 6).[69]

Many other problems related to Brexit matters involve a series of interrelated questions which continue to have a cumulative impact on the constitution and the law. If we turn briefly to devolution, the electorate in Scotland and Northern Ireland had supported the 'remain' position. Leaving to one side how the disappearance of EU funding has impacted on the devolved parts of the UK, it is highly significant that many EU laws concern functions devolved as part of a quasi-federal system of territorial governance.[70] The UK government, however, not only had responsibility for negotiating the Withdrawal Agreement, but also the power to enact in the Westminster Parliament the legislation needed to implement it. The underlying political friction over the approach to Brexit between the positions of the then Conservative government at Westminster and the devolved governments exposed the fragility of the mechanisms for inter-governmental relations (see Chapter 8) and, in particular, the constitutional convention designed to deal with legislative overlap. In an attempt to mitigate the homogenising effect of parliamentary sovereignty the Sewel Convention normally requires the Westminster Parliament to obtain the consent of the devolved legislatures before it proceeds with any bill applying to Scotland, Wales, or Northern Ireland. The EU Withdrawal Bill was passed although a legislative consent motion had been withheld by the Scottish Parliament. Mrs May's government simply chose to ignore a key convention which, as we shall see later, was not legally enforceable (see Chapters 3 and 8).

It was noted above that the UK chose not to enter the Schengen agreement which has the effect of regulating EU immigration and removing border controls between some EU states. However, UK withdrawal impacts on the reciprocal control of borders. In relation to this constitutional study, the post-Brexit prospect of a customs border between Northern Ireland, which remains part of the UK, and the Republic has an incalculable impact on the trading position between the two nations. In addition, common EU membership of the UK and the Irish Republic was implicit as a pre-condition of the 1998 Northern Ireland peace settlement. As will become apparent in Chapter 8, the UK and

---

[69] See 'European Union (Withdrawal) Bill: interim report', HL Select Committee on the Constitution, 3rd Report of Session 2017–19, 7 September 2017, HL Paper 19, para 44.

[70] S Tierney, 'Drifting Towards Federalism?' in R Schütze and S Tierney (eds), *The United Kingdom and the Federal Idea* (Hart Publishing, 2018) 121.

Irish governments are jointly required to act as impartial co-guarantors of the Good Friday Agreement set in place by the Northern Ireland Act 1998. The Agreement itself relies on cross-border institutions such as the North-South Ministerial Council and it is based on the common denominator of EU citizenship allowing freedom of movement and of trade.[71] While the Brexit NI Backstop deal and resulting legislation specifies the continuation of North-South Cooperation and the prevention of any new land border arrangements, this objective has been difficult to reconcile with the precise terms of UK withdrawal and the range of political opinion within NI.[72] In particular, under this (NI Backstop) agreement as the UK is no longer part of the EU single market goods from the remainder of the UK entering NI ports and airports were made subject to rigorous customs controls. This special status is controversial and has faced resistance by the main NI unionist parties as it means that NI, in effect, remains within the single market. In 2023 the so-called 'Windsor Framework' was negotiated with the EU by the government of PM Rishi Sunak to overcome many of the problems encountered in implementing the original Northern Ireland 'backstop' deal, and it included as a concession to Unionists the so-called *Stormont Brake* granting the NI Assembly a veto on any extension of European regulations.[73]

In the absence of a codified constitution, another important dimension to Brexit concerns the impact of withdrawal on the protection of citizens' rights. UK departure brings to an end the European status of citizenship encompassing a range of civil, political, and social rights contained in the European Charter of Fundamental Right.[74] The ECHR, incorporated into domestic UK law by the HRA 1998, remains in place but EU primary and secondary legislation also plays an important role in securing certain categories of human rights (for example, employment rights, equality and non-discrimination rights, privacy rights, and the family rights of migrants). Without any special constitutional entrenchment the repatriation of EU laws in crucial areas such as employment rights will remove a layer of rights protection from UK law.[75]

---

[71] B Dickson, 'Devolution in Northern Ireland' in J Jowell and C O'Cinneide (eds), *The Changing Constitution*, 9th edn (Oxford, Oxford University Press, 2019) 262.
[72] EU Withdrawal Agreement, s 10.
[73] The Windsor Framework: A New Way Forward, CP 806, February 2023.
[74] See European Union (Withdrawal) Act 2018, s 5(4). S Kadelbach, 'Brexit and What it Means' in S Kadelbach, R Hofmann, and R Klump (eds) *Brexit and What it Means* (Baden Baden, Nomos, 2019) 16.
[75] C O'Cinneide, 'Human Rights and the UK Constitution' in J Jowell and C O'Cinneide (eds), *The Changing Constitution*, 9th edn (Oxford, Oxford University Press, 2019) 92.

CONCLUSION

This chapter has sought to convey the spirit of the elusive and traditional UK constitution by introducing a series of core themes that frame the study that follows. At the same time, it provides a preliminary glimpse into how a unique combination of law, custom, and practice, understood to comprise the constitution, is having to encounter a storm of contemporary challenges headed by Brexit, Covid-19, and populism (to name but a few issues). Indeed, the extent of current uncertainty is posing what has been a recurring, but no less crucial problem that needs to be kept in mind throughout our journey: is the established political culture and tradition sufficiently robust to safeguard the status and the spirit of the traditional constitution? Finally, perhaps the most distinctive characteristic of the UK constitution to emerge so far, certainly in comparison with other constitutions, is the fact that it has never been subject to a process of formal codification resulting in any single constitutional document or related series of documents. In the next chapter we will consider in more depth the respective contribution of the diverse sources of the UK constitution.

FURTHER READING

Arlidge A and Judge I, *Magna Carta Uncovered* (Oxford, Hart Publishing, 2014).
Bagehot W, *The English Constitution* (London, Fontana, 1963).
Blick A, *Stretching the Constitution: The Brexit Shock in Historic Perspective* (Oxford, Hart Publishing, 2019).
Bogdanor V, *Beyond Brexit: Towards a British Constitution* (Oxford, IB Tauris, 2019).
Elliott M, Williams J, and Young AL, *The Constitution after Miller: Brexit and Beyond* (Oxford, Hart Publishing, 2018).
Haltern U, *The Constitution of the European Union: A Contextual Analysis* (Oxford, Hart Publishing, 2025).
Holland R, 'Britain, Commonwealth and the End of Empire' in V Bogdanor (ed), *The British Constitution in the Twentieth Century* (Oxford, Oxford University Press, 2003).
Maitland F, *The Constitutional History of England*, 10th edn (Cambridge, Cambridge University Press, 1946).
Mount F, *The British Constitution Now* (London, Heinemann, 1993).
Sunstein C, *Designing Democracy: What Constitutions Do* (Oxford, Oxford University Press, 2001).
Van Caenegem R, *An Historical Introduction to Western Constitutional Law* (Cambridge, Cambridge University Press, 1995).

2
Sources of the Constitution

Statute Law – Common Law – European Union – European Convention on Human Rights – Legal Treatises – Law and Customs of Parliament – Royal Prerogative – Conventions

INTRODUCTION

THE UNITED KINGDOM has a constitution but it is not a codified constitution. In other words there is no single document (or series of documents) that is known as the constitution. The lack of a codified constitution also means that there is no body of rules which is antecedent to the institutions of state and government and which could therefore be said to form an act of foundation. Despite the fact that there is no fundamental law relating to the constitution, it is possible to approach a description of the constitution by reference to a number of key constitutional sources. To take an obvious example, the Human Rights Act 1998 makes the individual rights defined under the European Convention on Human Rights (ECHR) of central constitutional importance, but, at the same time, many other statutes may be of relevance to constitutional practice in the field of human rights: for instance, the Police and Criminal Evidence Act 1984 deals more specifically with police powers and the rights of the individual.

In many nations today the constitution is linked to a system of representative government, but in the UK in particular, there is much less reliance on legal rules and safeguards, and much more reliance on constitutional conventions which are underpinned by a commitment to a democratic system of government. The evolution of the constitution has been possible because conventions are capable of being easily modified to accommodate changing circumstances. All constitutions are to some extent uncodified, with their own conventions, but a distinguishing feature of the UK constitution is that so much of its constitutional practice is governed by conventions. In consequence, particular attention in this chapter is devoted to discussing conventions as a source of the constitution and their significance in relation to constitutional practice. First, however, we will consider the other sources of the constitution.

STATUTE LAW

In the UK, the basic principle of the constitution is the doctrine of parliamentary sovereignty. Since the Bill of Rights of 1689 the courts have recognised Acts of Parliament as the highest source of law. In one sense it might be true to say that all statutes passed by Parliament that have not been repealed are part of the constitution. This is because each one has been passed to set out or refine particular areas of law and there is a coincidence between ordinary law and the constitution. However, in practical terms, it is obvious that certain statutes are of special *constitutional* importance. The Petition of Right 1628 concerned the principle of no taxation without representation. The Bill of Rights 1689, although not a modern Bill of Rights, as discussed in Chapter 1 secured a Protestant succession to the monarchy (a position that was confirmed by the Act of Settlement 1701). The Bill of Rights also formally confirmed that the seat of power had swung towards Parliament as part of a constitutional monarchy.

The nature of constitutional statutes was considered in *Thorburn v Sunderland City Council*[1] and has been recognised subsequently by Lord Hope giving judgment in the UK Supreme Court (UKSC).[2] While Laws LJ in *Thoburn* did not set out any special test to determine the question of what would qualify, it was explained that constitutional statutes are pieces of legislation which condition the legal relationship between citizen and state in some general, overarching manner, or which enlarge or diminish the scope of what might be regarded as fundamental constitutional rights. A number of important constitutional statutes that will be the subject of discussion in later chapters were recognised by Laws LJ as falling into this category (constitutional statutes are discussed at greater length in Chapter 3). The Acts of Union with Scotland in 1707 and with Ireland in 1800 dealt with arrangements for combining the English Parliament first with the Scottish Parliament and then the Irish Parliament. The Parliament Act 1911 imposes limits on the legislative powers of the House

---

[1] [2003] 3 WLR 247.
[2] See *H v Lord Advocate* [2012] UKSC 24 at para [30].

of Lords. The Representation of the People Act 1918 extended the vote to all men over 21 and women over 30, and the Representation of People Act 1969 reduced the voting age so that all adults over 18 could vote. The European Communities Act 1972 incorporated the Treaty of Rome and in so doing placed important limitations on the sovereignty of the Westminster Parliament.[3] The Scotland Act 1998, the Government of Wales Act 1998, and the Northern Ireland Act 1998 set out the principles for devolution. The Human Rights Act 1998 had the effect of incorporating the ECHR directly into English law and in so doing provides the UK with what is, in effect, a bill of rights.

THE COMMON LAW

In a system where judicial precedent applies, judicial decisions are binding and are used to develop the law on a case-by-case basis. The common law has always been an important source of the UK constitution. Certain aspects of private law, particularly concerning contract and tort, are comprised of rules originating from judicial decisions. There are particular landmark cases that have expanded the common law in a constitutional context.[4] These decisions remain of constitutional significance. For example, the case of *Entick v Carrington*[5] concerned trespass and placed limits on the powers of the Crown and Secretary of State to interfere with the person or property of the citizen without lawful authority.[6] More recently, the UK Home Secretary was found to be in contempt of court for ignoring an order of the High Court in *M v Home Office*[7] (discussed in Chapter 3). However, it is important to note that decisions of the courts (including the UKSC, formerly the House of Lords) may be amended and overridden by later statutes, eg the decision in *Burmah Oil v Lord Advocate*[8] prompted the UK Parliament to pass the War Damage Act 1965, which had retrospective effect. The courts accept the validity of Acts of Parliament and thus validate the concept of parliamentary sovereignty. Although they do not directly challenge legislation,

---

[3] The European Union (Withdrawal) Act 2018 repeals the European Communities Act 1972.
[4] See M Elliott and K Hughes (eds), *Common Law and Constitutional Rights* (Oxford, Hart Publishing, 2020).
[5] (1765) 19 State Tr 1029.
[6] A Tomkins and P Scott (eds), *Entick and Carrington: 250 Years of the Rule of Law* (Oxford, Hart Publishing, 2015).
[7] [1994] 1 AC 377.
[8] [1965] AC 75.

part of their role is to interpret statutes under established rules of statutory interpretation (see Chapter 7).

EUROPEAN UNION LAW

As we noted in Chapter 1, despite the implementation of the decision to leave the EU from January 2020, EU law, more than five years after withdrawal, remains a significant source of UK law. Although now repealed, the European Communities Act 1972, which came into force on 1 January 1973, made the law of the European Community (now the EU) an important constitutional source.[9] In *Van Gend en Loos* the European Court of Justice explained the implications for Member States of becoming a member:

> The Community [now EU] constitutes a new legal order of international law for the benefit of which the States have limited their Sovereign rights ... Independently of the legislation of member states, Community law therefore not only imposes obligations on individuals but is also intended to confer upon them rights which become part of their legal heritage.[10]

Some categories of EU law have direct effect in Member States, which meant that any rights or obligations enjoyed by or imposed on any individual under the treaties could be enforced in the English courts. This body of law was always confined to those areas covered by the Treaty of Rome 1957 and subsequent treaties. Each treaty (Maastricht, Amsterdam, Nice, and Lisbon) was incorporated into UK domestic law by statute. But any extension of powers was made subject to any UK opt outs. Also, the European Union Act 2011 was passed in an attempt to prevent the incremental ceding of power to the EU.[11] In particular, the Act introduced a complicated series of 'locks'. For example, it provided for parliamentary approval and a referendum to be held throughout the UK on new EU treaties and proposed EU treaty changes.[12] In summary, the effect of the European Union (Withdrawal) Act 2018 was that on Brexit day the existing body of EU law was converted into UK law.[13] While a significant

---

[9] Lord Denning famously described the treaties as an 'incoming tide' in *Bulmer v Bollinger* [1974] 2 All ER 1226.
[10] Case 26/62 [1963] ECR 1 at 12.
[11] The Act enabled the UK to ratify a Protocol to allow additional European Parliament seats for the UK and 11 other Member States during a current European Parliament term.
[12] European Union Act 2011, ss 2 and 3.
[13] M Elliott and S Tierney, 'Political Pragmatism and constitutional principle: the European Union (Withdrawal) Act 2018' [2019] *PL* 37.

body of law emanating from Europe continues to apply in the UK there is ambiguity under the Brexit legislation over whether some directives will have vertical or horizontal effect.[14] The Act also gives broad delegated powers for ministers to make regulations to deal with deficiencies arising from UK withdrawal.[15] Prior to Brexit, EU membership also meant that rulings from the Court of Justice of the European Union (CJEU or ECJ) would be binding on domestic courts within the UK. The jurisdiction of the CJEU continued to apply in many areas over a transitional period and beyond, but the CJEU no longer has general jurisdiction over the UK in relation to any acts taking place after 1 January 2021.[16]

EUROPEAN CONVENTION ON HUMAN RIGHTS

Since the Human Rights Act 1998 came into force in October 2000 the ECHR, an international treaty, is incorporated as part of UK domestic law. The ECHR can be regarded as amounting to a constitutional charter of rights. As we shall see in later chapters, the ECHR is an international treaty setting out basic individual rights including: right to life; liberty and security; prohibition of torture and slavery; right to fair trial; no punishment without law; right to respect for privacy and family life; freedom of thought, conscience, and religion; freedom of expression; freedom of assembly and association; and prohibition of discrimination. All public bodies, including the courts, are legally required to act in a way which is compatible with the above rights, and a remedy may be sought if these rights are breached (see Chapter 7).

LEGAL TREATISES

The lack of a codified constitution has meant that academic and legal treatises that describe and analyse the nature of the constitution as it has evolved assume special status. For example, there are classic works that may be cited with authority when seeking to establish how the constitution operates. Walter Bagehot's *The English Constitution* provided an influential account of parliamentary democracy during the

---

[14] Vertical effect of EU law is the principle which has allowed individuals to enforce EU law against the state, while horizontal effect concerns whether EU law applies in proceedings between individuals and non-state bodies, including private companies.
[15] European Union (Withdrawal) Act 2018, s 8.
[16] See eg Withdrawal Agreement, Arts 153, 158, 160, 161.

mid-Victorian period. It was famous for making a distinction between the 'efficient' and the 'dignified' parts of the constitution. The book was published at about the same time as the Second Reform Act of 1867 extended the right to vote to 1.5 million male householders and distributed more parliamentary seats to the main industrial towns. Probably the most influential contribution has been made by *Introduction to the Study of the Law of the Constitution* by AV Dicey, which was first published in 1885. Although this study was and still is controversial, for instance in the sense that it might be characterised as hostile to modern forms of democracy, Dicey nevertheless provides arguably the most persuasive explanation of the core concepts of parliamentary sovereignty and the rule of law. Parliamentary practice and procedure, which is obviously an important part of the contemporary constitution, is frequently determined by reference to *A Practical Treatise on the Law, Privileges, Proceedings and Usage of Parliament*, now in its 23rd edition. This work is referred to simply as '*Erskine May*' after the constitutional theorist who produced the original volume. Contemporary studies by constitutional experts are also relevant where there is a lack of clarity over aspects of constitutional practice. However, relying on academic sources is apt to present problems, since experts may differ in their interpretation of how constitutional doctrine applies. For example, the studies by Professor Christopher Forsyth and Sir William Wade and by Professor Paul Craig on the subject of administrative law adopt markedly different approaches.[17] Constitutional treatises should be regarded as *subordinate* sources, which are only resorted to by the courts and other constitutional players when there is no other established authority.

THE LAW AND CUSTOMS OF PARLIAMENT

The law and customs of Parliament refers to the resolutions of the two Houses of Parliament that establish parliamentary practice (standing orders of the House). This body of rules is of great political importance, ranging from the regulation of debates to the functions of the leaders of the government and opposition. MPs and Peers can change these rules. For example, the recommendations of the Select Committee on Procedure (1978) were adopted following the 1979 general election

---

[17] See C Forsyth and I Gosh, *W Wade and C Forsyth's* Administrative Law, 12th edn (Oxford, Oxford University Press, 2022); P Craig, *Administrative Law*, 10th edn (London, Sweet & Maxwell, 2025).

resulting in the introduction of the House of Commons Departmental Select Committees to scrutinise the work of government departments. In 2015 the 'English votes for English laws' procedure was introduced by this route (discussed in Chapters 5, 8, and 9). It is important to note that as parliamentary rules and procedures are established by standing orders, they fall outside the scope of both legislation and common law.

THE ROYAL PREROGATIVE

Many powers are exercised by ministers and officials under primary or secondary legislation, but the *royal prerogative* refers to those powers which have been left over from the period when the monarch was directly involved in the process of government. These remaining powers, now mainly exercised by ministers, include: making treaties; declaring war; deploying the armed forces; regulating the civil service; and granting royal pardons. The prerogative powers continue to be important for the operation of government in these areas, and they have been recognised by judges in developing case law.[18] (The nature and extent of prerogative powers are discussed in more detail in Chapter 4.)

CONVENTIONS AS A CONSTITUTIONAL SOURCE

Conventions are a particularly important source of the UK constitution and they are also crucial to understanding how the constitution functions. In the remainder of this chapter conventions will be discussed in more detail. An observer of the UK constitution would build up a very incomplete account of its workings if attention was given only to legal rules, since conventions, in the words of one commentator, 'provide the flesh which clothes the dry bones of the law'. It is evident that: 'The legal structure of the constitution is everywhere penetrated, transformed and given efficacy by conventions.'[19]

Conventions are the source of the non-legal rules of the constitution. They may be characterised as being associated with laws but at the same time they are distinct from them. They lubricate the formal

---

[18] R Hazell and T Foot, *Executive Power: The Prerogative, Past, Present and Future* (Oxford, Hart Publishing, 2022).
[19] Sir Ivor Jennings, *The Law and the Constitution*, 5th edn (London, University of London Press, 1959) 81 and 113.

machinery of government and assist in making government work. In this sense they have an important *practical* dimension. It is very difficult to settle constitutional disputes without understanding them. Moreover, conventions allow what would otherwise be a rigid legal framework to be kept up to date with the changing needs of government because they are capable of evolving. In subsequent chapters we will be looking in detail at a number of conventions, but first we need to understand why conventions have been difficult to define and note the different areas in which they apply.

DEFINING CONVENTIONS

The difficulty in defining conventions is mainly because they encompass a wide range of practices, some of which are a lot more certain than others.[20] The important thing to remember is that they determine many of the practices of government and aspects of conduct of state institutions. They are not the result of a legislative or a judicial process but rather often arise from what might be considered the hardening of usage over a period of time. A failure to adhere to an important convention might lead Parliament to cast a disputed practice into legislative form.

Perhaps the most influential definition derives from AV Dicey, who explained that[21]

> the 'conventions of the constitution' consist of maxims or practices which, though they regulate the ordinary conduct of the Crown, of ministers, and of other persons under the constitution, are not in strictness laws at all.

In recognising that conventions were mainly the customary rules which determined how the discretionary powers of the state were exercised, Dicey drew a special distinction between laws, which he explained were enforceable in the courts, and conventions. He maintained that conventions were 'rules intended to regulate the exercise of the whole of the remaining discretionary powers of the Crown'. It is important to recognise that for Dicey the key characteristic is that conventions, unlike laws, are not enforceable in the courts. Conventions consist of the understandings, habits, practices, maxims, and precepts that are necessary to

---

[20] See R Brett Taylor, 'Foundational and regulatory conventions: exploring the constitutional significance of Britain's dependency on conventions' [2015] *PL* 614.

[21] AV Dicey, *Introduction to the Study of the Law of the Constitution*, 10th edn (Basingstoke, Macmillan, 1959) 24.

regulate the conduct of the sovereign, the Prime Minister (PM), ministers, and officials, and also that of other constitutional players. It is true to say that conventions are not directly enforced in quite the same way as laws, but that the existence of conventions has been recognised by the courts as part of judicial reasoning. For example, in *Attorney-General v Jonathan Cape Ltd*[22] the Attorney-General on behalf of the government was unsuccessful in getting the court to enforce in the public interest the confidentiality requirement which forms part of the convention of collective Cabinet responsibility, by getting the court to issue an injunction to prevent a former Cabinet minister from serialising his memoirs. However, as one commentator notes:

> The Attorney-General may be said to have been victorious in this case in gaining judicial acceptance of the principle that a legal obligation of confidentiality attaches to Cabinet proceedings, even though the court decided that the Crossman diaries no longer ... retained their confidential character, and so fell outside the protection of the law.[23]

Sir Ivor Jennings, approaching the task of definition from a different perspective, suggested that three questions should be posed in order to identify a valid convention.[24] The first task is to determine whether there is a precedent for the practice. Finding this out involves ascertaining how often and how consistently a practice has been observed previously. The second question asks whether those operating the constitution have accepted the convention as binding. Could it be said that an obligation is created by the practice under consideration? While the first question merely requires a descriptive response, this second question is much more problematic. Some conventions are both relatively easy to identify and also to follow, and they are accordingly regarded as binding, for example, the requirement that the PM must be a member of the elected House of Commons. However, this is not always the case. For example, the convention of individual ministerial responsibility is of enormous constitutional importance. It concerns the accountability of the executive to Parliament, but there is considerable uncertainty over the exact way in which it applies. As we shall see in Chapters 5 and 6, there is debate among experts concerning how ministers are accountable to Parliament for shortcomings in their department, and, in particular, the circumstances when resignation by a minister is required. The

---

[22] [1976] QB 752.
[23] C Turpin and A Tomkins, *British Government and the Constitution*, 7th edn (London, Butterworths, 2011) 181.
[24] Jennings (n 19) 131ff.

final question posed by Jennings acknowledges the strong pragmatic dimension to the constitution. It asks whether there is a good *political* reason for the existence of a convention. By taking another example we can see what Jennings had in mind. The deference of the House of Lords to the House of Commons is very important. The legitimacy of the Commons has increased because it is the democratically elected House of Parliament. This approach also illustrates that many conventions have arisen because of usage over a period of time. During the constitutional crisis that followed the rejection of the budget in 1909 (explained further below) PM Asquith reminded King George V that it had been established that the sovereign acts upon the advice of his or her ministers. He asserted respectfully that there was no longer any doubt that the final decision-making power rests with the elected government enjoying the confidence of Parliament.

In some situations it may be difficult to know whether a practice has actually been recognised as a convention. Determining the validity of a convention may come down to establishing whether the actors regard the conduct as binding upon them. Dicey believed that conventions formed part of a constitutional morality that is positive. Conventions are followed because a failure to obey them would lead to *legal* difficulties. For example, Parliament must assemble each year to pass financial resolutions and make a budget to raise taxes and pay for the government, armed forces, local government, etc. Dicey's account does not explain why parliamentary sessions continue beyond setting a budget. In contrast, Jennings believed that disregarding conventions would result in *political* rather than legal problems. The refusal of the House of Lords to pass the budget in 1909 serves as an excellent illustration. This action by the Lords was in clear breach of a convention, and this failure to pass a Finance Bill prompted a political crisis for the obvious reason that a government without a budget to pay officials and the armed forces, and so on, could not govern. From the moment of the budget's rejection a stalemate existed between the elected House of Commons and the mainly Conservative hereditary peers in the House of Lords. After protracted negotiations, King George V agreed to create sufficient peers to secure the passage of a Parliament Bill, curbing the powers of the Upper House, but only if there was a mandate from the electorate for the reform. After the general election in December 1910 returned a Liberal-dominated coalition committed to reform, the Conservative peers in the House of Lords backed down and passed the Bill. Apart from removing the general veto over legislation exercisable by the House of Lords, the Parliament Act of 1911 placed in statutory form what had been regarded as a convention, namely, that the House of Lords could not veto or delay money Bills.

In the first *Miller* case the UKSC was called upon to consider the legal status of the Sewel convention.[25] It applies to legislation emanating from the Westminster Parliament but affecting devolved matters falling under the remit of the devolved legislatures.[26] The convention normally requires devolved legislatures to grant legislative consent motions but what is the legal position if consent is refused? The court adopted a definition of constitutional conventions consistent with Professor Dicey who regarded conventions as constitutional rules which needed to be followed, often for legal reasons but, unlike laws, these rules are not justiciable in the courts.[27] The UKSC stated: 'Judges are neither the parents nor guardians of political conventions; they are merely observers. As such, they can recognise the operation of a political convention … but they cannot give legal rulings on its operation or scope because those matters are determined within the political world'.[28] Despite the fact that this convention is set out in the Scotland Act 2016 and the Wales Act 2017 the court refused to recognise these obligations as being legally enforceable. An unconvincing distinction was drawn in the second *Miller* case[29] between unenforceable conventions and enforceable principles of parliamentary accountability based on the democratic mandate recognised from the Case of the Proclamations.[30]

We can conclude this brief overview by recognising that there is no way of knowing with certainty what an established convention is, except from the behaviour of the sovereign, politicians, or other officials responsible for operating it as part of the constitution. At least, it might be said of some conventions that they are rules of political practice that are regarded as binding by those to whom they apply. The Cabinet Manual published in 2011 (now in need of revision) seeks to perform this function in relation to the application of some key conventions relating to PM, ministers, and civil servants. In this sense it could be

---

[25] G Anthony, 'Sovereignty, Consent and Constitutions' in M Elliott, J Williams, and AL Young (eds), *The UK Constitution After Miller: Brexit and Beyond* (Oxford, Hart Publishing, 2018) 192ff.

[26] A McHarg, 'Constitutional Change and Territorial Consent: The Miller Case and the Sewel Convention' in M Elliott, J Williams, and AL Young (eds), *The UK Constitution After Miller: Brexit and Beyond* (Oxford, Hart Publishing, 2018) 155.

[27] Dicey (n 21) 448.

[28] *R (on the application of Miller) v SS for Exiting the European Union* [2017] UKSC 5, para [146].

[29] *R (on the application of Miller) v The Prime Minister* [2019] UKSC 41 (*Miller 2*).

[30] (1611) 12 Co Rep 74.

claimed that conventions therefore provide a *prescriptive* view of what should happen in a range of given situations. However, Professor Griffith rejected an approach to the constitution which is over-dominated by backward-looking conventions and he takes a much more pragmatic view – 'the constitution is what happens' and goes on to suggest 'if it works, it's constitutional'.[31] Since it is difficult to reach a satisfactory definition beyond this discussion, it will be informative to introduce some of the main conventions applying to the respective state institutions. Their constitutional importance will become more fully apparent as we proceed in subsequent chapters.

THE PRACTICAL IMPORTANCE OF CONSTITUTIONAL CONVENTIONS

Before discussing the various elements of the constitution in more detail, it will be helpful to be familiar with some of the main constitutional conventions. It will be apparent from the examples discussed already that many of these conventions are imprecise and may change over time. Most of the important conventions applying to the monarchy bear witness to the passage of authority away from the Crown. In the majority of cases there is very little discretion left with the monarch. For example, it has long been established that the Royal Assent to Bills that have completed their passage through the House of Commons and the House of Lords is never refused by the reigning monarch. To do so would undermine the capacity of a representative Parliament to pass legislation. By way of contrast, there are conventions where some discretion may have to be exercised. It is a well-established convention that the sovereign appoints the leader of the majority party in the House of Commons to form a government and become PM. Assuming one party enjoys such a majority, the leader of that party will always be chosen to form a government but, as we will see in Chapter 4, if no party emerges from a general election as a clear winner the monarch might be required to seek advice on whom to call upon first to form a government while maintaining strict political neutrality.[32] The lack of clarity on such important questions has led to calls for statutory procedures to be set in place which would determine the outcome should such circumstances recur.[33]

---

[31] J Griffith, 'The Political Constitution' (1979) *MLR* 1 at 19.
[32] V Bogdanor, *The Coalition and the Constitution* (Oxford, Hart Publishing, 2011) 19.
[33] Fabian Commission Report, *The Future of the Monarchy* (14 July 2003). See Fabian Society website, publications archive.

The pivotal constitutional convention which was considered in *Miller 2*[34] (see Chapters 4 and 7) requires the sovereign to act upon the advice of the PM and his or her ministers. In practice, although the business of government is conducted in the name of the Crown the key decisions are taken at ministerial level. Also, the King's speech given from the throne in the House of Lords at the opening of each session of Parliament setting out government policy is always written by the PM. Another long-established convention recognises that the sovereign in person cannot sit as a judge in his or her own courts.[35]

Turning next to the executive branch, the roles of the PM and Cabinet have developed and continue to develop by convention. Sir Robert Walpole, usually regarded as the first PM, depended heavily on the King's patronage and mainly operated as the King's spokesman in Parliament. Walpole, who was officially appointed First Lord of the Treasury, disliked the use of the term 'Prime Minister', which carried with it the connotation that he was the King's favourite.[36]

Modern PMs continue to consult the monarch by having regular meetings, but by the nineteenth century the appointment of PMs came to depend on the results of the election process. The person sent for had to be capable of forming a government commanding a majority in Parliament. It has also been established by convention that the PM and the Chancellor of the Exchequer must be members of the House of Commons and, as a result, directly accountable to the electorate.

We shall see later that the PM's powers have grown enormously. Until relatively recently there had been negligible statutory intervention setting out the formal limits on any of the prime ministerial powers. However, the provisions establishing the date of elections on a regular five-year interval contained in the Fixed Term Parliaments Act 2011 (FTPA 2011) and the Dissolution and Calling of Parliament Act 2022 restoring the convention allowing the PM to choose the election date stand out as an important exception (see Chapter 6). In a different sense the precise relationship between the PM and the Cabinet has never been defined with any precision. For example, it has been suggested that during the course of the twentieth century, the Cabinet system changed from the Cabinet acting as the sole decision-making body to the situation that prevailed up to the late 1970s where decision-making took place within Cabinet committees. Under PMs Thatcher and Blair, the Cabinet, rather than

---

[34] Above n 29.
[35] See the famous case of *Prohibitions del Roy* (1607) 12 Co Rep 63.
[36] H Wilson, *A Prime Minister on Prime Ministers* (New York, Summit Books, 1977) 8.

acting as decision-making body or a principal forum for debate, met for regular collegiate team-building and informal exchanges of views on policy matters at senior ministerial level.[37]

The Constitutional Reform and Governance Act 2010 provides a good example of legislation seeking to clarify an area that previously depended largely on convention. As we shall see in Chapter 6, the Act puts the running of the civil service on a statutory footing with formal recognition of the PM's power to manage the service. At the same time it sets out procedures for the appointment of special advisers to the PM's personal office and in other government departments. The role of 10 Downing Street (ie the PM's office) and the Cabinet Office in co-ordinating government had expanded according to the requirements of the office of PM from the period of World War I until the development of the contemporary machinery of government, but this occurred without any formal regulation by statute.

Further conventions of central constitutional importance relating to the PM and Cabinet are discussed in later chapters. In particular, collective Cabinet responsibility requires the Cabinet to unite around a policy position or for dissenters to resign. The convention arose from the need to provide the sovereign with advice that was not conflicting (see Chapter 6). Individual ministerial responsibility concerns the accountability of ministers and the executive to Parliament and requires ministers to be directly answerable to Parliament for their actions (see Chapters 5 and 6).

In relation to parliamentary conventions, looking back historically it has already been observed that the attempt of monarchs in the seventeenth century to govern without Parliament led to conflict between Parliament and the King. Since the Bill of Rights 1689 it has been established that Parliament is summoned at least once a year. Furthermore, it is a convention of fundamental constitutional importance in the Westminster type of parliamentary system that the government should command a majority in the House of Commons, and that if it is unable to do so the government should fall. The rationale behind the convention is obvious. The government requires a majority in the elected chamber to pass the legislation it needs to govern effectively. Therefore, if the ruling party or parliamentary grouping lost a vote on a major bill followed by losing an unambiguous vote of confidence, the PM would offer his or her resignation.[38] The strong impetus towards party organisation and discipline

---

[37] A Seldon, 'The Cabinet System' in V Bogdanor (ed), *The British Constitution in the Twentieth Century* (Oxford, Oxford University Press, 2003) 129.
[38] A King, *The British Constitution* (Oxford, Oxford University Press, 2007) 336ff.

within Parliament (particularly the House of Commons) resulted from the application of this convention, which has been recognised since 1832.[39] However, in Chapter 5 it will be suggested that the convention was called into question in the 2017–19 parliamentary session. The government of PM May suffered a succession of defeats on the pivotal question of gaining approval for the withdrawal agreements negotiated from the EU without seeking a vote of confidence as required under the FTPA 2011 or offering her personal resignation.

Also, the so-called 'Salisbury convention' recognises that the House of Lords should not use its delaying power under the Parliament Acts 1911 and 1949 in respect of legislation which forms part of the electoral programme of a governing party, once again showing deference to the elected House of Commons. Many procedural questions relating to Parliament are determined by convention and these include: the time allocated in the House of Commons to the official opposition; the fact that political parties are represented on committees according to the percentage of MPs supporting them; and the 'pairing' arrangements for MPs, through which government and opposition whips allow for the non-attendance of MPs for votes in the House of Commons. Finally, the Speaker is elected by members of the House of Commons to preside over the House. Although the MP selected as Speaker will have been a member of the government or opposition party, it is a convention of the highest importance that as Speaker, she or he will act with strict impartiality.

In relation to judges and the courts, the Bill of Rights 1689 and the Act of Settlement 1701 formally recognised the importance of judicial independence by securing the tenure of judges and there are a number of other conventions relating to the judicial role. It is generally acknowledged that the professional conduct of judges should not to be questioned in Parliament, except where there is a substantive motion for dismissal. (Senior judges can only be dismissed by Parliament using this procedure, and no senior judges have been dismissed in modern times.) Until very recently there was no clear separation of powers in the UK, as we will see when discussing the role of the Lord Chancellor in Chapter 7. The Constitutional Reform Act 2005 has established a Supreme Court outside of Parliament and reformed a system of judicial appointments that previously depended upon informal soundings to determine the suitability of possible judicial candidates (see Chapter 7). Nevertheless, it was already an accepted convention that judicial appointments were

---

[39] R Brazier, *Constitutional Practice: The Foundations of British Government*, 3rd edn (Oxford, Oxford University Press, 1999) 217.

made on merit (and not on the basis of political affiliation) and that serving judges should not have any active involvement with party politics. (In Chapter 7 we will assess how the courts deal with questions of legality under the rule of law and judicial review procedure.) The other side of this coin is the convention that ministers, as members of the executive branch, should avoid direct comment on specific cases under consideration by the courts (particularly if the case involves the government). For example, Lady Chief Justice Baroness Carr expressed concern after both the PM and Leader of the Opposition had made disparaging comments at Prime Minister's Questions (PMQs) about a judicial decision in a controversial immigration case.[40]

CONCLUSION

In this chapter we have observed that the uncodified UK constitution is comprised of a number of different sources, but statute law might be regarded as the predominant source of the constitution, as is evidenced by the recent battery of legislation reforming aspects of the constitution (devolution, human rights, and freedom of information Acts have been introduced since 1997, to name but a few examples). The doctrine of sovereignty proposes that Parliament is all-powerful and, in theory at least, has the capacity to determine the nature of the constitution. The limits of this doctrine will be critically examined in the next chapter. However, a substantial part of the discussion has concentrated on conventions as a constitutional source. Conventions vary, ranging from well-established practices that will be applied with predictable outcomes to rather vague guidelines that are open to interpretation in the way that they are applied. Failure to adhere to conventions can have far-reaching consequences. The constitutional crisis following the budget in 1909, discussed in Chapter 5, was caused because the House of Lords chose to ignore the convention that recognised the predominance of the House of Commons over the House of Lords on financial matters. Legislation in the form of the Parliament Act 1911 was necessary to prevent a similar situation occurring. In essence, conventions provide built-in flexibility which may be a distinct advantage. The application of a convention might fill a gap between constitutional tradition and practice, in the sense of defining what the actors should do to make the constitution work, and

---

[40] 'Top judge "deeply troubled" by PMQs exchange of Gaza family's right to live in the UK', *The Guardian*, 18 February 2025.

political reality, in the sense of helping to determine by reference to the past how any conduct might be modified to take account of changing circumstances. However, it can also be argued that a systematic process of codification is necessary to clear up the many ambiguities surrounding the way many conventions apply.

FURTHER READING

Allison J, *The English Historical Constitution* (Cambridge, Cambridge University Press, 2007).

Bagehot W, *The English Constitution* (London, Fontana, 1963).

Dicey AV, *Introduction to the Study of the Law and the Constitution*, 10th edn (Basingstoke, Macmillan, 1959).

Harding A, 'Conventions and Practical Interpretation in Westminster-type Constitutional Systems' [2022] *I-Con* 1–23.

Loughlin M, *The Foundations of Public Law* (Oxford, Oxford University Press, 2010).

Marshall G, *Constitutional Conventions: The Rules and Forms of Political Accountability* (Oxford: Oxford University Press, 1987).

Ward I, *The English Constitution: Myths and Realities* (Oxford, Hart Publishing, 2004).

3
Constitutional Principles

Parliamentary Sovereignty – Express Repeal – Implied Repeal – Enrolled Act Rule – Legislative Supremacy – Primary Legislation – Constitutional Statutes – European Convention on Human Rights – Political Sovereignty – Referendum – Rule of Law – Predominance of Law – Arbitrary Powers – Equality before the Law – Judicial Independence – Separation of Powers – Fusion of Powers

INTRODUCTION

ANY DISCUSSION OF THE BRITISH CONSTITUTION depends upon a knowledge of the sources of the uncodified constitution, allied to familiarity with the main principles which underpin the current workings of the constitution. These concepts can be linked to landmarks in constitutional history mentioned earlier, but, at the same time, they are of central importance to current practice, and they are open to interpretation in different ways. For example, it was noted in the opening chapter that the Bill of Rights of 1689 makes the Crown subject to the will of Parliament and that it also recognises that Parliament (Crown, Lords, and Commons) has unlimited legislative authority. In short: 'The principle inherent in the Bill of Rights is the supremacy of Parliament in law.'[1] It will be necessary when discussing the sovereignty of Parliament to assess what this apparently absolute doctrine now means, given that the European Communities Act 1972, prior to its repeal, was interpreted as allotting special status to EU law, and the Human Rights Act 1998 (HRA 1998) requires judges to interpret statutes according to the European Convention on Human Rights (ECHR).

Another point worth making at the outset is that these doctrines are related to each other. Laws gain their legitimacy from a democratically elected sovereign Parliament. At the same time, when implementing any

---
[1] C Munro, *Studies in Constitutional Law*, 2nd edn (London, Butterworths, 1999) 128.

such laws, there needs to be a way of protecting citizens from arbitrary treatment and this means discretionary powers given to officials and the police must have legal bounds. Dicey was at pains to stress that: 'In England the idea of legal equality, or of the universal subjection of all classes to one law administered by the ordinary courts, has been pushed to the utmost limit.'[2] The rule of law was regarded by Dicey as *the* idea that has the potential under the common law to qualify the supremacy of Parliament, but we will soon discover that the rule of law is difficult to define and it is not a neutral concept. Rather, it needs a strong moral dimension in order to guide all forms both of law making and law enforcement.[3]

The final concept discussed in this chapter is separation of powers. Constitutions necessarily describe different kinds of powers and functions and delineating the distinction between such powers and functions is frequently a central issue in drafting a constitution. The objective is almost invariably to prevent the concentration of too much unchecked power in one set of hands. Obviously, the UK lacks a custom-designed constitution embodying a strict separation of powers. Nevertheless, the concept and language of separation of powers is still relevant. Two aspects are mentioned as a prelude to the discussion that follows later in this chapter. First, the judicial review procedure that has developed under the rule of law results in the judicial branch overseeing the activities of the executive branch to prevent abuses of power. In this regard, the issue of judicial independence has been addressed at important moments in constitutional history to allow the courts to perform such a role. For example, the Act of Settlement of 1701 (see Chapter 1) protected judges from summary dismissal, and the Constitutional Reform Act 2005 (see Chapter 7) sets in place a system for judicial appointments that seeks to minimise executive interference. Second, in the UK there is no separation between the legislative and executive branches since ministers must be Members of Parliament. Such a fusion between legislative and executive functions at the heart of the system (as exemplified in the former position of the Lord Chancellor: see Chapter 7) has led commentators to consider whether formal and informal 'checks and balances' which exist as part of constitutional practice are sufficient to achieve adequate constitutional accountability by ensuring the containment of a powerful executive branch.

---

[2] AV Dicey, *Introduction to the Study of the Law of the Constitution*, 10th edn (Basingstoke, Macmillan, 1959) 193.

[3] See L Fuller, *The Morality of Law* (Yale University Press, New Haven, 1969); J Jowell, 'The Rule of Law' in J Jowell and C O'Cinneide (eds), *The Changing Constitution*, 9th edn (Oxford, Oxford University Press, 2019) 17.

PARLIAMENTARY SOVEREIGNTY

Defining Legal Sovereignty

The legal sovereignty of Parliament was regarded by Dicey as *the* founding principle of the constitution. In his words, it meant that 'Parliament... has under the English constitution the right to make or unmake any law whatever; and, further, that no person or body is recognised by the law of England as having a right to override or set aside the legislation of Parliament', and it is 'the very keystone of the law of the constitution',[4] in the sense that the sovereignty of Parliament is a fundamental rule upon which no legal limits could be placed. This emphasis on the absolute power of Parliament is because in the absence of a codified constitution the all-powerful position of Parliament in its capacity to act as law-maker assumes special importance. In the first place, parliamentary sovereignty holds that, in theory at least, Parliament comprising the House of Commons, the House of Lords, and the sovereign has the capacity without any legal limits to pass or repeal any law. As Blackstone remarked, it confirms that 'Parliament can do everything that is not naturally impossible'.[5]

Second, a corollary of the sovereignty of Parliament is that provisions in a more recent statute will prevail over those in an older statute. This is the essence of the doctrine of implied repeal, and it would appear to follow from this proposition that Parliament cannot bind its successors. This limitation is because any pre-existing law can be superseded by an Act passed by a later Parliament. And it is a rule that has special importance in a constitutional context, because, on one view, if this applies strictly, it means that the entrenchment of constitutional principles/a bill of rights is not possible.

The capacity of Parliament to reconstitute itself and entrench basic principles has been the subject of much theoretical debate in academic circles.[6] For example, a critique by Sir Ivor Jennings of the orthodox theory argues that the rule of recognition as explained by Dicey is a common law concept.[7] It has been accepted by the courts that statute

---

[4] Dicey (n 2) 40 and 70.
[5] W Blackstone, *Commentaries on the Laws of England*, Book 1 (Oxford, Oxford University Press, 2016) 161.
[6] See J Goldsworthy, *The Sovereignty of Parliament: History and Philosophy* (Oxford, Oxford University Press, 1999) ch 2, 'Defining Parliamentary Sovereignty'.
[7] I Jennings, *The Law and the Constitution*, 5th edn (London, University of London Press, 1959) 152ff.

law is superior to the common law. In consequence, it follows that Parliament can enact legislation changing this rule by drafting a statute that requires the courts to accept that some Acts of Parliament are protected from repeal by simple majority vote. In other words, if judges are subordinate to Parliament then Parliament can tell the judges what rules to follow in determining whether or not a statute is unconstitutional. At a practical level, following the far-reaching changes of recent years, it will be important for us to consider below whether the conference of power on other bodies has had a significant impact on sovereignty. To put it simply, has sovereignty really shrunk, as some commentators have contended?[8]

There is an influential view developed by Wade[9] and Allan which maintains that Parliament's sovereignty is itself established through judicial acceptance under the common law: 'Legislation obtains its force from the doctrine of Parliamentary sovereignty, which is itself a creature of the common law and whose detailed content and limits are therefore of judicial making. Parliament is sovereign because the judges acknowledge its legal and political supremacy.'[10] The next step in this argument is to maintain that a statute which flies in the face of common law values, for example because the measure is outrageously undemocratic, might be declared invalid by the courts. (As noted when discussing the *Jackson* case below, some House of Lords judges have repeated the highly controversial suggestion that primary legislation *in extremis* might by challenged in the courts.[11]) One obvious objection to the common law view takes things back a stage further and questions the legal source of judicial authority to make the common law: 'The only alternative consistent with the argument is to think judges conferred authority on themselves.'[12]

Third, the sovereignty of Parliament means that there is no other body that has authority to challenge the validity of laws made by Parliament in the proper manner. This aspect of the doctrine contradicts a view held earlier that 'an Act of Parliament could be disregarded in so far as it was contrary to the law of God or the law of nature or natural justice ... [when] the supremacy of Parliament was finally demonstrated

---

[8] Munro (n 1) 149.

[9] W Wade, 'The Basis of Legal Sovereignty' (1955) *Cambridge Law Journal* 172.

[10] T Allan, *Law, Liberty and Justice* (Oxford, Oxford University Press, 1993) 10. The point has been made that it could hardly, without circularity, be a doctrine based on statutory authority.

[11] See Lord Steyn, Lord Hope, and Baroness Hale in *Jackson v Attorney-General* [2005] UKHL 56, [2006] 1 AC 262.

[12] J Goldsworthy, *The Sovereignty of Parliament: History and Philosophy* (Oxford, Oxford University Press, 1999) 240.

by the Revolution of 1688 any such idea has become obsolete'.[13] Article 9 of the Bill of Rights of 1689 provided that 'proceedings in Parliament ought not to be impeached or questioned in any court or place out of Parliament'. This assertion has been taken to mean under the 'enrolled act rule' that statutes passed by Parliament cannot be challenged by the courts in regard to their validity. For example, in *British Railways Board v Pickin*[14] the plaintiff was adversely affected by a private Act of Parliament, namely the British Railways Act 1968. He attempted to argue that it was invalid on the grounds that Parliament had been misled as to relevant facts during the Bill's passage through Parliament and also that certain procedural rules (standing orders) of the House of Commons had been ignored. The challenge was rejected on final appeal to the House of Lords. Lord Morris confirmed: 'When an enactment is passed there is finality unless and until it is amended or repealed by Parliament.' On the issue of the courts not being able to question the way legislation is passed, *Pickin* remains good authority. However, in *Jackson v Attorney-General*[15] (discussed in more detail below) it was unanimously held that the courts had jurisdiction to determine whether the disputed statute (the Hunting Act 2004) was a valid Act of Parliament. Had the court decided that this was not a valid statute, it would not have been able to set aside the legislation (the legislation would remain in force), but the court had the power 'to ascertain the validity of a purported Act of Parliament'.[16]

A further crucially important point about legal sovereignty that will be relevant in relation to many issues under discussion in this book is that this principle determines the relationship between Parliament and the courts. It means that, although the courts have an interpretative function in regard to the application of legislation, it is Parliament, and not the courts, which has the final word in determining the law. This is markedly different from most codified constitutions. For example, in the United States, the US Supreme Court held in *Marbury v Madison*[17] that it could determine whether laws passed by Congress and the President were in conformity with the constitution, permitting judicial review of constitutional powers. The situation in the United States is that ultimately there is judicial rather than legislative supremacy (see further Chapter 7).

---

[13] Munro (n 1) 130.
[14] [1974] AC 765.
[15] Above n 11.
[16] AL Young, 'Hunting Sovereignty: Jackson v Her Majesty's Attorney General' [2006] PL 192.
[17] (1803) 1 Cranch 137.

Before we further examine the current limits of sovereignty it is worth pointing out that, with each of the measures of constitutional reform introduced post-1997, great care was taken to preserve the sovereignty of the Westminster Parliament (eg in regard to devolution, see section 28 of the Scotland Act 1998). Also, the HRA 1998 is specifically designed not to undermine the doctrine of sovereignty. The courts cannot invalidate primary legislation which conflicts with rights under the ECHR; they are empowered only to make what is called a 'declaration of incompatibility' (see Chapter 7 for a more detailed discussion).

Express Repeal, Implied Repeal, and Constitutional Statutes

In explaining the limits of parliamentary supremacy, it is important to understand the difference between express and implied repeal. Express repeal is relatively easy to explain. This is when a later statute declares that the whole or part of an earlier statute is being amended or repealed by the provisions that are being currently introduced. In *legal* terms there is general agreement among judges and legal commentators that the power of the Westminster Parliament expressly to repeal legislation remains in place as demonstrated by the Brexit legislation (see reference to the *Miller 1* case below).[18] However, it would be more accurate to say that any limitations to this power are likely to be political rather than legal. For example, if Parliament decided to remove the right to vote at elections the resulting law would be legally valid, but the attempt to take away such a basic right might, at the same time, precipitate demonstrations and civil unrest. Similarly, there would be no legal impediment to Parliament repealing, for example, the Nigeria Independence Act of 1960 with provisions that purported to re-impose colonial status. Such an Act would, however, be unenforceable, and would no doubt also result in strong condemnation from Nigeria itself.

If we turn to implied repeal, the situation in regard to the scope of Parliament's power is less clear when there is a lack of consistency between an earlier and a later statute, without any guidance as to which will apply. There was, at one time, clear judicial authority to support the idea that a later statute will always prevail over an earlier one. A seminal case on this point is *Ellen Street Estates v Minister of Health*.[19] A court had to determine what should happen where a provision (or provisions)

---

[18] See eg European Union (Withdrawal) Act 2018.
[19] [1934] 1 KB 590.

in an earlier statute clashed with those in a later statute, and whether an attempt to bind a future Parliament was valid. This conflict concerned the construction of the Acquisition of Land Act 1919 and the Housing Act 1925. Section 7(1) of the Acquisition of Land Act 1919 was phrased so that it might appear to apply notwithstanding the provisions in later statutes. The compensation scheme in this Act was more generous than that in the Housing Act 1925. A litigant was seeking to take advantage of the earlier scheme. However, the Court of Appeal held that, even if it had been the intention of the earlier Parliament to bind future Parliaments, the provisions of the later statute would take precedence. Maughan LJ stated: 'The legislature cannot, according to our constitution, bind itself as to the form of subsequent legislation and, it is impossible for Parliament to enact that in a subsequent statute dealing with the same subject-matter there can be no implied repeal.'[20]

The doctrine stated by Maughan LJ has been significantly qualified by more recent constitutional developments. Dicey was able to argue in the late nineteenth century that parliamentary legislation was supreme in the hierarchy of law, and that all statutes emanating from Parliament had equal authority, with the most recent prevailing. It is clear that this is no longer the case since certain Acts of Parliament have come to have special significance.

In *Thoburn v Sunderland City Council*[21] it was stated:

> In the present state of its maturity the common law has come to recognise that there exist rights which should properly be classified as constitutional or fundamental ... And from this a further insight follows. We should recognise a hierarchy of Acts of Parliament: as it were 'ordinary' statutes and 'constitutional' statutes.

Laws LJ proceeded to reason that the two categories must be distinguished on a principled basis. In essence, he suggests that constitutional statutes are pieces of legislation which condition the legal relationship between citizen and state in some general, overarching manner, or which enlarge or diminish the scope of what might be regarded as fundamental constitutional rights. Such legislation might do both these things. The special status of constitutional statutes follows the special status of constitutional rights. Many examples can be cited from the well-known landmarks of constitutional history. Any such list would include: the Magna Carta 1215; the Bill of Rights 1689; the Act of Union 1707;

---

[20] Ibid, at 597.
[21] [2003] QB 151.

the Reform Acts which distributed and enlarged the franchise; the HRA 1998; the Scotland Act 1998; the Government of Wales Act 1998; the Northern Ireland Act 1998, and so on. After making this distinction Laws LJ controversially suggests that ordinary statutes may be impliedly repealed while constitutional statutes may not be repealed in this way. There would be a requirement for express or specific words in the later statute to achieve the result.[22] In brief, it would appear that this amounts to recognition of a higher order of laws operating at a constitutional level. An area where the constitutional status of statutes will be put to the test is in situations where the government uses its power to dominate Parliament to produce legislation that has a fundamental impact on constitutional rights as in *Miller 1*.[23]

Sovereignty, EU Law, and Brexit

By now it will be obvious that EU law emanating from the Treaty of Rome and developed by the European Court of Justice (ECJ) fundamentally qualified the concept of parliamentary sovereignty for as long as the UK remained a member. The EU at supra-national level operated as an additional institutional layer of government. For example, it consists of the European Commission, which is formed from Commissioners appointed by the governments of Member States. This body is expected to represent the interests and objectives of the EU and is mainly concerned with initiating proposals, decision-making, and the implementation of rules throughout the EU. The Council of the EU, which comprises ministers from Member States, exercises legislative and executive powers and functions. Further, there is a European Parliament, which consists of members elected in each Member State. Although the European Parliament was not originally designed as a law-making body, it has to be consulted in the legislative process under the co-decision procedure. The important point to stress is that the EU legislative process gives rise to particular forms of law which have applied in the UK. Most prominently, it recognises regulations, which have general application in all Member States, and directives, which are sometimes capable of having direct effect in the event that they are not implemented by individual Member States. EU

---

[22] AL Young, 'The Future of Constitutional Adjudication' in M Elliott, J Williams, and AL Young (eds), *The Constitution after Miller: Brexit and Beyond* (Oxford, Hart Publishing, 2018) 295.
[23] R *(On the application of Miller) v SS for Exiting the European Union* [2017] UKSC 5.

membership meant that for as long as the European Communities Act 1972 and successive legislation incorporating later treaties remained in force, the UK Parliament had, in practical terms, surrendered its powers to legislate in regard to those areas covered by EU law. The effect of EU law was to confer rights directly on individuals and national courts had to protect those rights. This body of law has direct effect within Member States and it has to be applied by the courts. However, in the *HS2* case the UK Supreme Court (UKSC) stated: 'If there is a conflict between a constitutional principle, such as that embodied in article 9 of the Bill of Rights, and EU law, that conflict has to be resolved by our courts as an issue arising under the constitutional law of the United Kingdom.'[24]

When considering the limits of sovereignty we need to be clear about the status of EU law within individual Member States. The decision in *Van Gend en Loos*[25] paved the way for the establishment of the supremacy of this body of law by developing the doctrine of primacy. It was in this ruling that the ECJ held that 'the [EU] constitutes a new legal order of international law for the benefit of which the states have limited their sovereign rights, albeit within limited fields, and the subjects of which comprise not only Member States but also their nationals.' For our purposes, the radical impact of EU law can be demonstrated by reference to the landmark decision in *R v Secretary of State for Transport, ex parte Factortame (No 2)*.[26] The facts concerned the granting of fishing rights. The Merchant Shipping Act 1988 (section 14) established a new register of UK vessels that was only open to those that satisfied certain conditions. One of these conditions specified only vessels that were 75 per cent UK-owned were eligible for registration. It was argued by the applicants, who were directors of Spanish companies, that this requirement infringed the anti-discrimination provisions of the Treaty of Rome on grounds of nationality. The matter was referred by the House of Lords to the ECJ in Luxembourg.

The ECJ ruled that domestic courts were required to ensure effective protection of EU law rights. The Merchant Shipping Act 1988 obviously contravened rights recognised under EU law, and it followed that the UK domestic courts should not be precluded from granting interim relief to protect these rights. In line with its earlier decision in the *Simmenthal Case*[27] the ECJ had focused on the effectiveness principle and on

---

[24] *R (On the application of HS2) v Secretary of State for Transport* [2014] UKSC 3, para [79].
[25] [1963] CMLR 105.
[26] [1991] AC 603, [1991] 3 CMLR 769.
[27] Case 106/77, *Amministrazione della Finanze dello Stato v Simmenthal SpA* [1978] ECR 629.

the obligation of national courts under Article 5 (now Article 4.3 of the (Lisbon) Treaty on European Union (TEU)) to ensure observance by setting aside obstructive national rules which precluded or limited the grant of an appropriate remedy. The ECJ did not actually specify the conditions under which a national remedy, such as interim relief, should be granted in a given case. The House of Lords was left to decide this point in accordance with national principles. However, the ECJ made clear that a rule that absolutely prohibited the grant of interim relief would contradict the principle of effectiveness.[28]

In *Factortame (No 2)* the House of Lords recognised that domestic legal systems were required under the Treaties to enforce directly effective rights under EU law. Following the ruling by the ECJ,[29] an injunction was issued by the highest UK court preventing the minister from enforcing the nationality requirements under Part II of the Merchant Shipping Act 1988 which were in conflict with EU law. Lord Bridge stated: 'to insist that, in the protection of rights under [EU] law, national courts must not be inhibited by rules of national law from granting interim relief in appropriate cases is no more than a logical recognition of [the] supremacy [of EU law].'[30] This decision confirmed that, in those areas covered by the Treaties, Parliament no longer reigned supreme; it was European and not domestic law which predominated.

UK membership of the EU represented a significant qualification to the principle of parliamentary sovereignty. Some influential commentators argued that it also created a new rule of recognition by diluting the fundamental principle recognised by Dicey,[31] while others viewed the change as a leap from an 'historical' constitution to 'legal' constitution.[32] In any event, the doctrine of primacy required that EU law prevail over domestic law in all areas covered by the Treaties. Although the European Communities Act 1972 and the legislation incorporating subsequent Treaties passed through Parliament in the same way as other statutes, these measures can be regarded, as recognised by Sir John Laws in *Thorburn*, as a special kind of 'constitutional' legislation having prospective effect. The UKSC has since confirmed that 'The primacy of EU law means that, unlike other rules of domestic law, EU law cannot be implicitly displaced by the mere enactment of legislation which is

---

[28] See P Craig, 'Brexit and the UK Constitution' in J Jowell and C O'Cinneide (eds), *The Changing Constitution*, 9th edn (Oxford, Oxford University Press, 2019) 104ff.
[29] Case-213/89.
[30] [1991] AC 603 at 658.
[31] W Wade, 'Sovereignty: Revolution or Evolution?' [1996] 112 LQR 568.
[32] V Bogdanor, *Beyond Brexit: Towards a British Constitution* (London, Tauris, 2019) 86.

inconsistent with it.'[33] After it was established in the courts that the will of Parliament had been to make domestic law subject to EU law, a major exception to the principle of implied repeal had been established.

This brief analysis of sovereignty is directly related to EU membership and the Brexit situation. In *Miller 1* the majority in the UKSC held that the 1972 Act operated as a partial transfer of law-making powers by Parliament to the EU but, at the same time, Parliament remained sovereign during EU membership. In other words, during the period of EU membership Parliament retained the capacity to expressly repeal EU law. Further, the UKSC reasoned that a change affecting the 1972 Act, as the conduit through which EU law flowed, was of such fundamental constitutional importance that it could not be introduced using the prerogative power alone, but would require primary legislation enacted by Parliament. Following the decision in *Miller 1* the legislation to trigger Brexit was duly passed.[34] Of course, later in the process the European Union (Withdrawal) Act 2018 repealed the 1972 Act and, in so doing, removed the conduit through which EU law flowed. It did not, however, invalidate the pre-existing body of EU law. In fact the Withdrawal Act provides that 'EU-derived domestic legislation ... continues to have effect in domestic law on and after exit day'.[35]

The Human Rights Act 1998 and Sovereignty

A limit to the doctrine of implied repeal is equally relevant to any discussion on human rights.[36] In effect, the HRA 1998 incorporates the rights contained in the ECHR. The Act allows the courts to provide effective legal remedies for the breach of Convention rights while formally adhering to the doctrine of parliamentary sovereignty. As we shall see later (Chapter 7), the effect of the Act is to put all public authorities (government and civil service, local and devolved government, the police, and the courts) under a legal duty to uphold this charter of rights. To inhibit non-compliance, ministers, when introducing parliamentary Bills, are required to issue a statement to the effect that the proposed legislation will be compatible with Convention rights, and this state-

---

[33] R *(On the application of Miller) v Secretary of State for Exiting the European Union* [2017] UKSC 5, paras [66], [78], [81].
[34] See European Union (Notification of Withdrawal) Act 2017.
[35] European Union (Withdrawal) Act 2018, s 2(1).
[36] AL Young, *Parliamentary Sovereignty under the UK Human Rights Act* (Oxford, Hart Publishing, 2009) ch 2.

ment is published on the face of the Bill. The Act appears at one level specifically to preserve parliamentary sovereignty if a court makes a declaration of incompatibility. This does not invalidate primary legislation. However, in an important sense here, too, there is no implied repeal, since the courts have been required from 2 October 2000 to interpret all subsequent legislation in a way that is compatible with Convention rights, if it is possible for them to do so. The purposive construction of subsequent statutes (the rule of construction which requires the courts to give priority to Convention rights when interpreting any statute) results in this provision under the HRA 1998 prevailing over a subsequently enacted statute. This exception to sovereignty is confined to situations where the courts are called upon to interpret the will of Parliament in respect to Convention rights.[37] Unlike the New Zealand model, there is no provision in the HRA 1998 to apply the doctrine of implied repeal when interpreting the Act, which means that Convention rights will be presumed by the courts to be protected, unless it is expressly stated to the contrary in a subsequent statute. (See Chapter 7 for further discussion of the effects of the HRA 1998.)

The *Jackson* Case: A Revised Interpretation of Sovereignty?

The decision *Jackson v Attorney General*[38] by the House of Lords must be viewed in light of the wider debate over the respective roles of Parliament and the judiciary.[39] It has already been noted above that the issue of parliamentary sovereignty took centre stage when the courts were called upon to consider the validity of the Hunting Act 2004, which banned the hunting of foxes with dogs in the face of strong opposition from the hunting lobby. Also, we have seen how the Parliament Acts 1911 and 1949 radically modified the powers of the House of Lords.[40] The Hunting Act 2004 was relatively unusual in that it had been repeatedly rejected by the House of Lords, and the House of Commons eventually invoked the override procedures set out under section 2(1) of the Parliament Act 1911 and the Parliament Act 1949 which allowed legislation to be passed

---

[37] Ibid 152ff.
[38] Above n 11.
[39] See J Jowell, 'Parliamentary Sovereignty under the New Constitutional Hypothesis' [2006] *PL* 562.
[40] The Life Peerage Act 1958 and the House of Lords Act 1999 modified the composition of the second chamber.

into law without the approval of the House of Lords.[41] It is important to remember that by passing the Parliament Acts of 1911 and 1949 Parliament had, in effect, reconstituted itself after the settlement of 1689 by changing the method for approving legislation in circumstances specified in these Acts. The claimants attempted to argue that the 1949 Act, which had reduced the delaying power of the Upper House to one year, was made by a form of subordinate legislature,[42] and that it had not been validly enacted. In consequence, they sought a declaration that it should have no legal effect. It was possible to present such a case because the Parliament Act 1949 also depended upon section 2(1) of the Parliament Act 1911 and, therefore, it too only received the approval of the House of Commons and the Crown (and not the House of Lords). The effect of the 1949 Act was to increase the powers granted to the House of Commons, and the claimant's case further rested on the proposition that this extension by the House of Commons of its own authority ran counter to the principle that delegates are prevented from increasing their own powers.

The House of Lords (Judicial Committee) rejected this argument. Their Lordships held that the Parliament Act 1911 clearly provided that 'any' legislation passed in accordance with section 2 would be an Act of Parliament, and that such legislation should not be classified as a species of subordinate legislation. Taking full account of the historical background leading up to its passage, their Lordships preferred to view the effect of the Parliament Acts 1911 as a restriction of the powers of the House of Lords rather than an extension of the powers of the House of Commons. It was also held that there was nothing in the 1911 Act which prevented the use of the procedure laid down in its provisions to amend the Act. In other words, the 1949 Act, which had the effect of doing precisely this, by restricting the delaying power to one year, was deemed to be valid. According to Dicey, the basic rule of the constitution is that Parliament has unlimited sovereignty. Parliament is omnipotent and therefore any valid law passed by Parliament would be recognised by the courts and it would trump any previous Act, including a law modifying the role of Parliament.[43]

On the other hand, critics of Dicey, notably Jennings, believed that legal sovereignty merely refers to the fact that the legislature has for the time being powers to make laws of any kind in the manner and

---

[41] The Parliament Acts have been invoked on rare occasions: the Government of Ireland Act 1914, the Welsh Church Act 1914, the War Crimes Act 1991, the European Parliamentary Elections Act 1999, the Sexual Offences (Amendment) Act 2000.

[42] According to a view expressed by W Wade, *Constitutional Fundamentals* (London, Stevens, 1980) 27–28.

[43] See quote from Dicey (n 2) and ibid, ch 1.

form required by law,[44] implying that effective qualifications to sovereignty might be effectively included. This judgment has not resolved the academic dispute, but some *obiter* statements depart from a Diceyan position by envisaging possible limits to parliamentary sovereignty. Lord Steyn and Baroness Hale stated that new laws could be passed to change *manner and form* in respect to the passage of legislation, by for example introducing a two thirds majority rule applying under particular conditions. Certain limits to sovereignty were linked to the exceptions contained in the Parliament Act 1911. Seven judges (out of nine) opined that any statute not receiving the consent of the House of Lords, which extended the life of a Parliament beyond the five years stipulated in the Parliament Act of 1911, would not be recognised by the courts as valid.[45] On this view, it can be claimed that Parliament has bound its successors in regard to any Bill containing such a provision.

The panel of judges in the House of Lords have been criticised at a technical level, perhaps unfairly, for failing clearly to resolve the conflicting legal issues raised in *Jackson*.[46] However, it should be stressed that it is the political context which is of central importance here. In the first place, under the rules of the constitutional game as it is currently played, opening up the possibility of a successful direct challenge to legislation because of its failure to gain the approval of the unelected House of Lords would undermine the democratic process, and therefore probably precipitate a response from Parliament anyway. In the second place, as Lord Bingham recognised in his judgment, the modification to the principle in the Parliament Acts which has allowed the elected House of Commons to prevail over the House of Lords has been accepted by political players from all parties since the passage of the 1911 and 1949 Parliament Acts. Reference to the importance of practice appears to confirm the famous observation that 'the constitution is no more and no less than what happens'.[47] Finally, an emerging judicial view is also implied in some of the judgments which questions the unqualified supremacy of Parliament and foresees the possibility of judicial intervention to invalidate legislation where it involves flagrant abuse of power (threats to human rights, removal of judicial review, etc).[48] It should be apparent that a significant

---

[44] Jennings (n 7) 152ff.
[45] Young (n 16) 193.
[46] E Wicks, 'R (Jackson) v Attorney-General [2005]: Reviewing Legislation' in S Juss and M Sunkin (eds), *Landmark Cases in Public Law* (Oxford, Hart Publishing, 2017) 231ff.
[47] J Griffith, 'The Political Constitution' [1979] *MLR* 1, 19.
[48] M Elliott, 'The Sovereignty of Parliament, the hunting ban and the Parliament Acts' [2006] *Cambridge Law Journal*, March 3.

Political Sovereignty: Elections, Referendums, and Brexit

Dicey argued that *political sovereignty* (as opposed to legal sovereignty, which rests with Parliament) lay with the electorate and it is therefore associated with representative and responsible government. Political sovereignty is based on the doctrine of the mandate. It means that manifesto policies are carried out by legislation passed by Parliament (we will be noting that the extension of franchise actually strengthened the power of government, not that of Parliament). However, the formidable powers to legislate without constitutional qualification allow a government with a popular mandate to make wide-ranging changes, including constitutional reforms. Thus, according to the *Whitehall Model* of executive dominance expounded by Birch, the government controls Parliament and not Parliament the government.[49] Indeed, the term 'elective dictatorship' was used in a similar way by Lord Hailsham to explain how parliamentary sovereignty had turned into the sovereignty of the House of Commons, which in turn is dominated by the party machine in the hands of the Prime Minister (PM) and the civil service.[50] However, it has already been observed in the introduction that a revised notion of popular sovereignty has been emerging as part of the contemporary constitution which relies on consulting the electorate through referendums (see Chapter 1).

According to the traditional model of the constitution which largely applied until the mid-1970s, MPs were elected as representatives of their constituents and were sent to Parliament to decide matters on their behalf. Where there was a matter of major constitutional importance (eg the Parliament Act 1911 restricting the powers of the House of Lords) which arose and needed to be settled urgently by reference to the wider citizenry, a general election was used to determine the issue. Two elections were held in 1910 to ensure the government had a mandate for House of Lords reform. In February 1974, at a time when the nation was in the throes of a miner's strike which was causing fuel shortages and power cuts, an early election was called on 'who governs Britain?'. Similarly, PM May, although no longer able to request a dissolution herself, sought

---

[49] Birch originally expounded this view in 1967; now see A Birch, *The British System of Government*, 10th edn (London, Routledge, 1998) 163ff.
[50] Lord Hailsham, 'Elective Dictatorship' (Richard Dimbleby Lecture, 1976).

in 2017 (unsuccessfully) to use a general election called under the FTPA 2011 to obtain a strong mandate for a Brexit deal.

In 1975 PM Harold Wilson turned to a national referendum to allow the expression of sincerely felt pro- and anti-Common Market (now EU) views which were causing deep political divisions in his own party on the understanding that collective responsibility would be resumed subsequently (see Chapters 1 and 6). In this instance, the decisive vote in favour had the desired effect of removing for a generation the question of EU membership from the forefront of UK politics. In contrast, far from resolving the issue, the narrow outcome of the 2016 Brexit referendum was the prelude to a prolonged acrimonious debate over UK withdrawal. Professor Bogdanor explains the result under what he views as the transformed post-Brexit British Constitution as the emerging sovereignty of the people trumping the sovereignty of Parliament (in the sense that that a majority of the electorate had voted to leave while there was still a majority in favour of remain in Parliament).[51] This view is difficult to reconcile with recent developments. Although, there were persuasive political reasons for both actions, PM Cameron was not required to resign following the referendum, nor was the government or Parliament legally obliged to act on the result by triggering Brexit. Further, this referendum was held at the behest of the PM. The entire electorate as the 'sovereign people' have only exceptionally been able to express their will directly. There is no established constitutional mechanism to allow them to do so. This avenue has been chosen only when it suited the PM and the government.

Moreover, against a background of the rise of 'populism', the projection of such a 'sovereignty of the people' interpretation of events is in danger of neglecting an overarching normative question facing liberal democracy, namely, the extent to which there should be deference to the will of the people.[52] As Professor Goldsworthy observes:

> It may be true that the will of the people should usually prevail, but it must always be subject to moral limits ... One of the advantages of representative democracy is that public affairs can be given more careful and well informed scrutiny than the vast majority of individual members of the general public can undertake.[53]

While the Brexit referendum provided an important snapshot of public opinion as a response to a single question, the outcome did not reconcile

---

[51] Bogdanor (n 32) 109.

[52] AL Young, 'Populism and Parliamentary Sovereignty' in L Burton Crawford, P Emerton, and D Smith (eds), *Law under a Democratic Constitution* (Oxford, Hart Publishing, 2019) 195ff.

[53] J Goldsworthy, 'Response to Contributors' in L Burton Crawford, P Emerton, and D Smith (eds), *Law under a Democratic Constitution* (Oxford, Hart Publishing, 2019) 293.

deep-seated differences which split the nation almost down the middle. Not only were questions raised, especially about the probity of the campaign advocating withdrawal, but the public who voted could not have been aware of the consequences, since no viable alternative package of measures had been put to them. It would appear to follow, accepting the deference to the sovereignty of the people argument, that a second referendum was essential to determine the terms of withdrawal. Notwithstanding a vigorous popular campaign for a second referendum, none was forthcoming from the resulting political maelstrom. The denial of democratic choice was mainly because such a referendum might have undermined the objectives of the government while negotiating Brexit and caused a reversal of the original referendum's outcome.

The Brexit scenario underlines the fact that without a codified constitution specifying conditions for the holding of referendums, an antidote is needed to the 'Ad hoc manner in which referendums have been used as a tactical device by the government of the day . . .'.[54] Parliamentary committees of both Houses have recommended that Parliament should judge [through legislation] what issues should be subject to referendums, with the litmus test being whether a fundamental constitutional issue is at stake. At the same time there is recognition of the need to formulate ground rules in terms of form and procedure requirements.[55] In sum, while the Brexit referendum was undoubtedly a highly significant constitutional event, the claim to have moved to a constitution based on the sovereignty of the people is difficult to substantiate. Apart from the EU referendums in 1975 and 2016, the plebiscite held on whether to change the electoral system to the alternative vote method, arising from the 2010 coalition agreement between the Conservatives and Liberal Democrats, has been the only other nationwide referendum held in the UK.[56]

Although national referendums have been very rare, since 1975 regional referendums have become an increasing part of the contemporary UK constitution.[57] They were employed in Scotland, Wales, and Northern Ireland in relation to the introduction of devolution, and the Westminster

---

[54] 'Referendums in the United Kingdom' Report with Evidence, House of Lords, Select Committee on the Constitution, 12th Report of Session 2009–10, HL Paper 99, 49.

[55] 'Lessons learned from the EU referendum' Public Administration and Constitutional Affairs Committee of the House of Commons, Twelfth Report of Session 2016–17, HC 496. Op cit HL Paper 99, 49.

[56] Parliamentary Voting System and Constituencies Act 2011. This was a legally prescriptive referendum which would have required a change to the voting system had the electorate voted for it (see s 8).

[57] P Leyland, 'Referendums, Popular Sovereignty and the Territorial Constitution' in R Rawlings, P Leyland, and AL Young (eds), *Sovereignty and the Law* (Oxford, Oxford University Press, 2013).

government conceded a binding referendum on Scottish independence which was held in September 2014 (see Chapter 8). Equally, the introduction of an elected Mayor and Assembly for London depended on first gaining approval in a London-wide referendum. In effect, referendums have been used in each of these cases to consolidate major constitutional change. Popular endorsement arguably lends more permanence to the reform. Margaret Thatcher's government was able simply to abolish the Greater London Council as a level of local government. However, it would be much more difficult in terms of practical politics for the central government to sweep away devolution and/or the London Mayor and Assembly without first seeking approval by way of a referendum. In addition, since 2000 there have been statutes to introduce regional government and local government reform employing referendums which go beyond testing the water in advance of reform but rather these referendums were under the Local Government Act 2000 and the Localism Act 2011 and were intended as a mechanism to promote deeper participation in the political process. It is also worth noting that the implementation of proposals for elected regional assemblies (which were never introduced) also depended on a referendum being held in each region.[58]

In terms of the overall national picture this discussion reveals that there are no clear ground rules on the conduct of referendums. In comparison, codified constitutions are likely to specify in some detail the circumstances when referendums must be held. For example, in Italy the adoption of constitutional amendments is made conditional on popular approval.[59] As we have seen, referendums have been included in recent statutes for many different reasons. This trend promises to have an impact in ways that may not have been anticipated. It is very expensive to organise referendums, which might act as a disincentive to holding them with any frequency. For reasons of cost, these changes will almost certainly mean that referendum questions will be combined routinely with other elections.[60] In consequence, voting in the UK may increasingly involve selecting candidates to serve at various levels of government and deciding other local policy questions at the same time. In turn, the more frequent reliance on referendums to determine such issues may have the effect of eroding the position of elected politicians otherwise expected to act as decision-makers on behalf of the wider electorate under the traditional model of the constitution.

---

[58] *Your Region, Your Choice: Revitalising the English Regions*, Cm 5511(2002).
[59] Italian Constitution 1948, Art 138.
[60] Localism Act 2011, s 53(3).

THE RULE OF LAW AND SEPARATION OF POWERS

Defining Rule of Law

The conception of the rule of law expounded by Dicey needs to be understood together with the doctrine of parliamentary sovereignty. This is because the related concept of the rule of law, in effect, imposes qualifications to what appears to be the unlimited nature of parliamentary sovereignty. The rule of law is formally defined by Dicey as having three rather different connotations.[61]

First, it recognises the predominance of regular law over arbitrary power. There is an assertion that no one should be punished except for a clear breach of the law established in the *ordinary* courts. In a more general sense, the rule of law means that there should be an absence of arbitrary power and it suggests that government and other public bodies require lawful authority in order to act. The role of the courts in policing the exercise of state power is the central concern of the modern law of judicial review. In terms of the functioning of government in a contemporary context, this requirement limits wide discretion placed in the hands of the executive which is not subject to strict legal qualification. In practice however, it is not uncommon for modern legislation to grant discretionary powers. For example, section 3 of the Security Services Act 1989 empowered the Home Secretary to issue a warrant authorising the taking of action for the purpose of assisting the security service to discharge any of its functions in connection with the obtaining of information. This could be done without the need to actually specify any suspected offence.

Second, the Diceyan approach to the rule of law requires strict equality before the law in the sense that no one is above the law and all persons are equally subject to the jurisdiction of the ordinary courts. This is a principle which, in theory, applies from the highest government ministers and top officials to the most humble citizens. It means that the government and the executive should be amenable to control by the courts. This control element was important for Dicey as it forms the basis of his criticism of the *droit administratif* (see discussion of the red light and green light theories of administrative law in Chapter 7). While the French system is characterised as affording special protection to officials, in contrast, the rule of law principle of equality was demonstrated

---

[61] AV Dicey, *An Introduction to the Law of the Constitution*, 10th edn (Basingstoke, Macmillan, 1959) 188ff.

by the famous decision in *Entick v Carrington*.[62] This was the occasion when Lord Camden CJ made an affirmation of the normal process of law. It was held that, in the absence of a statute or common law granting authority, the actions by the representatives of the King were unlawful.

On closer examination, the idea of equality can be seen to be qualified in a number of respects. In the first place, certain groups enjoy legal immunity. To take some obvious examples, MPs are granted special (parliamentary) privileges, the King has immunity from legal proceedings, and diplomats also enjoy immunity. In the second place, inequality is present because discretionary powers are given to officials. They are granted powers that members of the public do not have (eg to raise taxes or to make compulsory purchases of land). Also, legislation frequently distinguishes one category of persons from another. To cite some examples, as part of housing law landlords are granted rights not granted to tenants, and likewise under employment law employers enjoy distinct rights to their employees.

Third, in the absence of a codified constitution, Dicey pointed out that the rights of individuals have been defined and enforced by the courts. He argued that the British constitution is a result of the ordinary law of the land, in the sense that remedies protecting the liberties of the citizen have been developed under the common law. The concept of negative liberty works on the basis that, rather than setting out rights in positive form, conduct is lawful unless it contravenes specific law. From a Diceyan standpoint, the common law principles of natural justice (see the discussion of judicial review in Chapter 7) that are applied by the courts might be regarded as an expression of the rule of law. However, the view that rights in general can be protected in this way is difficult to sustain in the constitution as it functions today. In practice, there has been increasing reliance on statute law to set out rights and qualify rights. The most important recent example of this trend was the enactment of the HRA 1998. The HRA 1998 has the effect of incorporating the ECHR into domestic law, and so from 2 October 2000 the Convention became a surrogate 'Bill of Rights' for the UK. (See Chapter 9 for wider discussion of the debate surrounding constitutional codification.)

The numerous statutory provisions, including the deliberate use of ouster clauses (see Chapter 7) to constrain judicial intervention may reduce or qualify rights casting doubt on the extent of Dicey's faith in the common law as the primary legal means for protecting the citizen's liberties against the state. For example, the Criminal Justice and Public Order

---

[62] (1765) 19 St Tr 1030.

Act 1994 placed further restrictions on the right of citizens to demonstrate and introduced important qualifications to the right to silence in criminal trials. Faced with such assaults on individual liberty, judicial eloquence has often not been backed up by effective action. In *Liversidge v Anderson*[63] Lord Atkin stated:

> In this country, amid the clash of arms, the laws are not silent. They may be changed but they speak the same language in war as in peace. It has always been one of the principles of liberty for which on recent authority we are now fighting, that the judges are no respecters of persons and stand between the subject and any attempted encroachment on his liberty by the executive.

Lord Atkin's worthy defence of freedom is found in a dissenting judgment. The minister's decision to detain persons of external origin without cause was upheld by the House of Lords. It has been suggested that the outcome might have been different in today's climate of increased judicial activism, but the point is that the courts cannot be depended upon to uphold rights, especially when there is a climate of great public fear and concern. Further, in *R v Secretary of State for the Home Department, ex parte Brind*,[64] the House of Lords was not prepared to intervene to prevent a government broadcasting ban aimed at political parties sympathetic to paramilitary organisations in Northern Ireland who were not prepared to denounce the use of violence to secure their political aims. In general, the rule of law prevents governments from legislating retrospectively because of the injustice that such measures would be likely to cause. There have been exceptions, for example where the implications of a court ruling threaten to have far-reaching consequences for the government.[65]

The Response to Dicey

Does the rule of law enable us to distinguish democratic government from dictatorship and does it provide a sound basis for setting out constitutional rights? According to Dicey's view, a society is governed under the rule of law *only* if it meets his criteria, and it ultimately amounts to a *political* judgment whether a nation achieves such standards. In Dicey's formulation an emphasis is placed on individual rights rather than social

---

[63] [1942] AC 206.
[64] [1991] 1 AC 696.
[65] For example, the decision in *Burmah Oil Co v Lord Advocate* [1965] AC 75 prompted the War Damages Act 1965.

rights. The concept has the effect of excluding all but his definition of what comprises a liberal democracy from having the rule of law. Jennings launched a substantial critique of Dicey's conception of rule of law[66] because he argued that the rule of law must amount to more than: 'law and order is better than anarchy'. It is a doctrine which must be seen to exist within a context of democratic government. The problem is that without a moral dimension the rule of law could as easily be applied to a tyranny as to a liberal democratic society. It could describe any society where law and order exists. Ferdinand Mount has attacked Dicey's doctrine of the rule of law as being inescapably narrow, addressing rudimentary personal rights such as free speech and assembly but overlooking 'the complex and diverse local and national bureaucracies both inside and outside the governmental system which had already become a feature of British life'.[67]

It is not surprising then that the Diceyan view has faced sustained criticism from left-of-centre advocates of progressive social reform, like Jennings, Robson, and Laski, because the rule of law overlooks the problem of addressing collective rather than individual social and economic rights.[68] Formal equality under the law means very little if a large proportion of the population suffers from economic and social marginalisation. From a left-of-centre standpoint constitutional rights need to be defined beyond the liberal agenda of freedom of speech, religion, and assembly, to include basic rights to housing, health, and education. Furthermore, in the current environment particularly in light of introduction of court fees and cuts to the availability of legal aid contained in the Legal Aid, Sentencing and Punishment of Offenders Act 2012, viewed from the standpoint of potential claimants the question of equality in terms of access to the law itself is controversial. A reduction in the availability of legal assistance means that for many people the prospect of obtaining redress in the courts is not a realistic option. As a result there has been the emergence of alternative forms of redress, such as ombudsmen, law centres, and mediation.

On the positive side, the rule of law has left the UK with a political and legal culture with an emphasis on due process. Put in simple terms, there is an expectation that government and the apparatus of state power will be exercised by ministers and officials operating within the law. In turn,

---

[66] *The Law of the Constitution*, 5th edn (London, University of London Press, 1959) 54ff.
[67] F Mount, *The British Constitution Now: Recovery or Decline?* (London, Mandarin, 1993) 58.
[68] Jowell (n 3) 5ff.

this power is arbitrated by an independent judiciary. It is generally the case that rule of law principles operate as a set of institutional restraints to the exercise of executive power. The rule of law addresses certainty in decision-making and it determines how a satisfactory balance between rule and discretion can be reached when putting the law into effect. The problems might arise if the courts become too intrusive, as many would argue that the judges should have a subordinate role to a democratically elected Parliament and any government formed from it.[69] Nevertheless, the judicial oversight function is very important and is closely related to the role of judicial review in its supervisory role under the ultra vires principle which will be discussed later (see Chapter 7). As Sir Stephen Sedley observes in his defence of the development of judicial review, the position was concisely summarised by Lord Nolan: 'The proper constitutional relationship of the executive with the courts is that the courts will respect all acts of the executive within its lawful province, and the executive will respect all decisions of the courts as to what its lawful province is'.[70]

Dicey developed these ideas in a different era. The rule of law was presented as an ideal. Now it should be the basis for criticising, not admiring, the legal culture of the UK. In response to the profound changes that have taken place since Dicey, public lawyers and political theorists have been required to adapt these principles. We need to consider in the light of current constitutional practice the reality of questions about the ability of government to predominate over Parliament, often referred to in this book by Lord Hailsham's term 'elective dictatorship'. Indeed, it has been suggested that the UK has witnessed the triumph of a 'Model of Governance' over a 'Model of Law' in which regulation has become the basic technique of administration, and administrative programmes are reduced to numbers and evaluated according to measures of value for money.[71] If this is the case, how can the situation be redressed? In subsequent chapters (see Chapter 7 in particular) we will see the need to identify the shortcomings of the mechanisms for control at the level of the administrative state and in regard to the conferment of rights.

---

[69] See M Loughlin, *Public Law and Political Theory* (Oxford, Oxford University Press, 1992) 197ff; for the more recent debate see N Barber, R Ekins, and P Yowell (eds), *Lord Sumption and the Limits of the Law* (Oxford, Hart Publishing, 2016).
[70] S Sedley, *Law and the Whirligig of Time* (Oxford, Hart Publishing, 2018) 250. See also Barber, Ekins, and Yowell (n 69) at 247ff.
[71] See eg C Harlow and R Rawlings, *Law and Administration*, 4th edn (Cambridge, Cambridge University Press, 2022) 50ff, and C Harlow, *Accountability in the European Union* (Oxford, Oxford University Press, 2002) 189.

In a somewhat different sense, the rule of law might imply that law and order is always better than anarchy. However, the rule of law is not achieved simply by the semblance of order (eg citizens generally conforming to arbitrary and unjust law in Nazi Germany 1933–45 or in Soviet Russia, particularly under Stalin 1922–53) but it depends on restraints that apply to governments and that governments apply to themselves. The terms of reference of the Hutton Inquiry established by Tony Blair as PM provided scope to investigate the inner workings of government following disquiet over the justification for UK involvement in the Iraq war.[72] PM Major set up the Scott Inquiry (discussed in Chapter 6) following the collapse of the Matrix Churchill trial. Both investigations were sanctioned not withstanding the potentially far-reaching implications for the government. The rule of law suggests that law and order and political liberty are mutually dependent, and it demands respect for what we termed *constitutionalism* (see Chapter 1). In the UK this will usually be associated with adherence to procedural rules and adherence to important constitutional conventions (discussed in Chapter 2).

Separation of Powers

The rationale behind the prescriptive doctrine of separation of powers is to avoid the concentration of power in the hands of a single person or body. The diffusion of authority among different centres of decision-making has long been regarded as a safeguard against totalitarianism and a means of preventing the abuse of power. Contemporary views of the separation of powers originate from eighteenth-century thought. In *The Spirit of Laws*[73] Montesquieu stated, referring to England, that all would be lost: 'if the same man or the same ruling body, whether of nobles or of the people, were to exercise these three powers, that of law making, that of executing public resolutions, and that of judging crimes and civil causes'. Tom Paine had written in 1792:[74] 'From the want of a constitution in England to restrain and regulate the wild impulse of power, many of the laws are irrational and tyrannical, and the administration of them vague and problematical.' The constitution of the United States is heavily influenced by the idea of limiting and checking power. A clear distinction is

---

[72] *Report of the Inquiry into the Circumstances Surrounding the Death of David Kelly CMG by Lord Hutton* [2004] HC 247.

[73] Baron de Montesquieu, *De L'Esprit des Lois* [1748] Book XI, ch 6.

[74] T Paine, *Rights of Man* [1791] (London, Penguin, 1969) 217.

made between legislative, executive, and judicial functions. For example, the legislative body is an elected Congress comprising the Senate and the House of Representatives. Congress is able to initiate legislation but this requires presidential approval. Equally, the President can initiate legislation, which requires approval from Congress. Another feature is that the government is formed from outside Congress, although Congress has assumed a crucial role in keeping check on the government by a network of committees. The President has executive power and is responsible for appointing the government. However, the most important nominees for government and also for the Supreme Court require the approval of the Senate. An element of tension between the three branches is deliberately built into the system. The Watergate Affair involved the investigation by Congress of serious malpractice and a subsequent cover-up by the President, and it demonstrated that even the President could be forced to resign for a gross abuse of power.[75]

The UK constitution, by way of contrast, had no clear separation of powers. Rather, there is a limited separation of functions and a considerable number of overlapping powers. This does not mean, of course, that legal process is not employed as means of subjecting governmental power to legal control. But it might be more accurate to characterise the constitution as having a number of checks and balances. These will be considered at greater length in Chapters 5 and 6. Although the concept of *separation of powers* has not been deliberately incorporated into the UK constitution there is a long history of placing limits on the exercise of power. The Magna Carta, which was drawn up in 1215 as an agreement between the King and his barons, was an early attempt to place formal limits on the exercise of royal power. In the seventeenth century the attempt by James I, and more especially Charles I, to revive the doctrine of absolute kingship based on divine right led to the civil war between King and Parliament between 1642 and 1649. The conflict arose from the attempt to rule and raise taxes without the assent of Parliament. It resulted in a victory for Parliament and a short spell of republican rule under Oliver Cromwell.[76] Clearly, the supremacy of Parliament over the absolute supremacy of kings was demonstrated again by the passage of the Bill of Rights of 1689, which engineered the change to the royal succession. However, apart from securing a Protestant succession, the Bill of Rights was primarily intended to make far-reaching limitations

---

[75] M Tushnet, *The Constitution of the United States*, 2nd edn (Oxford, Hart Publishing, 2015) 34.
[76] C Hill, *The Century of Revolution* (London, Routledge, 2001) 117ff.

on the absolute power of the monarch.[77] In the first place, it provides that Parliament cannot be suspended by the monarch except with its own consent. Second, it confirmed that the levying of taxes must be approved by Parliament, and third, it states that a standing army cannot be formed in peacetime without the consent of Parliament. The courts accepted this political settlement as law by recognising that statutes passed by Parliament, not, as previously, 'enacted by the monarch in Parliament', had to be enforced and that its enactments take precedence over the common law. In sum, Parliament had imposed conditions on the power of the King.[78]

Fusion of Powers

It has already been pointed out several times that the UK constitution evolved gradually. It was not designed according to a blueprint which took on board the concept of separation of powers. In consequence, until very recently there has been no clear demarcation between legislative, executive, and judicial functions in the contemporary state. In fact there are institutions which combine more than one of these functions. The sovereign is technically part of all three branches. From the throne in the House of Lords, the King opens each session of Parliament. The government governs in her name. Justice is dispensed through the royal courts. In practice however, there is a strong element of constitutional limitation on the exercise of royal power. This is to the extent that there is no active contribution to the routine workings of government. In addition to legislation such as the Act of Settlement of 1701, this has often been achieved by the recognition of important conventions in relation to the exercise of prerogative power. Also, it was confirmed in Lord Coke's landmark judgment in *Prohibitions del Roy*[79] that the King, in person, was not able to judge disputes.

The most obvious overlapping of powers is in Parliament. Rather than having a clear separation between legislature and executive as exemplified in the US constitution, the UK government is formed from within Parliament. It survives only if it is able to maintain its majority in the House of Commons. Indeed, this is what Walter Bagehot writing in the

---

[77] Munro (n 1) 6.
[78] M Loughlin, *The Foundations of Public Law* (Oxford, Oxford University Press, 2010) 259ff.
[79] (1607) 12 Co Rep 63.

nineteenth century was keen to emphasise when he stated that 'the efficient secret of the English Constitution may be described as the close union, the nearly complete fusion of executive and legislative powers'.[80] After the majority party in the House of Commons is recognised as the government, its continuation in office depends upon being able to maintain a majority whenever there is a vote on government legislation or on major issues of confidence. The whips (party managers) have emerged to deliver this majority. As a result, there is no real impediment to the legislative competence of Parliament. This is because the government is able to count on its majority in the House of Commons to secure the passage of its legislative programme. What we described earlier as the supremacy of Parliament is, in fact, normally the supremacy of the executive. It was noted earlier that this feature of the constitution has been termed 'elective dictatorship'. (In Chapters 1 and 5 it is pointed out that exceptionally under the minority government (2017–19) Parliament was able to assert its role at the expense of the executive). A central concern is to prevent the abuse of power by establishing legal means of controlling power, and a key question for any student of the constitution is whether ministers as Members of Parliament are made sufficiently accountable to Parliament for their actions (see Chapters 5 and 6).

Parliament, the Lord Chancellor, and the UK Supreme Court

As part of the traditional constitution there has been an overlap between legislative, executive, and judicial powers in several different ways. The ancient office of Lord Chancellor (LC) demonstrated this overlapping of powers and functions most graphically. First, the LC as a member of the House of Lords was head of the judiciary and President of the Chancery Division of the High Court. This position allowed the incumbent to sit personally as a judge in the House of Lords and the Judicial Committee of the Privy Council and to determine which other Law Lords sat on appeals. Second, this was because the incumbent held executive office as ministerial head of a government department and, by virtue of this position, was given a seat at the Cabinet table. Third, the LC not only had the right to participate in the legislative proceedings of the House of Lords but also presided over the House as its Speaker.[81] As we will see in Chapter 7, after the HRA 1998 was passed incorporating Article 6 ECHR,

---

[80] W Bagehot, *The English Constitution* [1867] (London, Fontana, 1963) 65.
[81] D Woodhouse, *The Office of Lord Chancellor* (Oxford, Hart Publishing, 2001).

doubts were raised over the propriety of Law Lords being members of the legislature and of the LC acting as a Cabinet minister while sitting as a judge in such a court. The Constitutional Reform Act 2005 had the effect of removing the LC's right to sit as a judge on the UK's highest court[82] and recognised the constitutional importance of separation of powers while it also provided for the introduction in 2009 of a Supreme Court to replace the judicial committee of the House of Lords as the UK's high appellate court.[83]

In common with other ministers, the LC introduced legislation and participated in debates. This position produced a direct conflict of interest. For instance, the LC's Department (now renamed the Ministry of Justice) had a central role in the appointment of senior judges. Parliament is primarily a legislative and scrutinising body, but it contained the Judicial Committee of House of Lords, which was until October 2009 the highest domestic appellate court. Nevertheless, the House of Commons and the House of Lords can sit as courts that have the power to discipline their own members. Further, the Attorney-General is the law officer of the Crown. In this capacity the Attorney-General acts as the government's principal legal adviser, but the Attorney-General is also a minister who is able to initiate criminal and civil proceedings in the courts when this is seen as in the public interest. There is an expectation that ministerial duties will be performed independently of the government but there may be a clear conflict of interest. (For example, the Scott Inquiry was critical of the advice given by the Attorney-General over the use of public interest immunity certificates to prevent evidence going before the courts.)

Separation of Powers and Judicial Independence

In the light of the overlapping of powers characteristic of the constitution, to what extent does the UK have an independent and impartial judiciary? Senior judges are not appointed on grounds of their political affiliations and they have been granted protection against summary dismissal since the Act of Settlement of 1701. The rule of law doctrine, as explained above, requires the government/executive to operate according to the law. An independent judicial branch is required to ensure that

---

[82] See Constitutional Reform Act 2005, Parts 1 and 2.
[83] A Le Sueur, 'The Conception of the UKs New Supreme Court' in A Le Sueur (ed), *Building the UK's New Supreme Court* (Oxford, Oxford University Press, 2004).

this occurs. In recent times the judicial review procedure has become the principal method of challenging the legality of the actions of public bodies, whether they are operating under statutory powers or under prerogative powers.[84] Procedural reforms and the development of the grounds of judicial review have contributed to a heightened profile for the courts and greater judicial activism. There has been an enormous increase in the number of cases coming before the courts. During the late 1980s civil servants were alerted by a general circular called 'The Judge over your Shoulder' to be aware of judicial review.[85] In the estimation of some commentators, the courts were assuming the guise of a surrogate opposition at a time when the official party political opposition in Parliament was particularly weak. However, there is a danger that the authority of Parliament could be undermined by excessive judicial activism.[86]

Indeed, ministers have claimed that instances of judicial activism undermine the authority of Parliament and their ability to implement policy. On the other hand, securing executive accountability to the law must equally be regarded as central to the rule of law and to judicial review.[87] The friction between the executive and the courts is often most obvious in areas of government competence falling under the Home Office. The examples which follow will serve to illustrate this in different ways. In *M v Home Office*[88] an asylum seeker from Zaire was seeking judicial review of a decision by the Immigration Service (an executive agency which is part of the Home Office) to deport him, but the hearing coincided with the date set for his repatriation. The prospect of deportation before the judicial proceedings were complete led M's lawyers to make an emergency application to the court to put matters on hold. The application was successful and an undertaking to the judge was given from the Home Office not to act while the case was pending. This instruction was not adequately communicated by the Home Office to the Immigration Service. In the meantime, M was flown out of the country. Contempt proceedings were brought by M's lawyers against the Home Secretary for ignoring a court order. This boiled down to a question of whether the courts were in a position to issue coercive orders against

---

[84] Harlow and Rawlings (n 71) 711ff.
[85] *Judge Over Your Shoulder: A guide to good decision making* (6th edn, Government Legal Department, 2022).
[86] See eg M Loughlin, 'Sumption's Assumptions' in N Barber, R Ekins, and P Yowell (eds), *Lord Sumption and the Limits of the Law* (Oxford, Hart Publishing, 2016).
[87] P Craig, *UK, EU and Global Administrative Law: Foundations and Challenges* (Cambridge, Cambridge University Press, 2015) 156ff.
[88] [1994] 1 AC 377.

ministers. The sovereign's courts were taking punitive action against the Crown in the guise of her ministers.[89]

The House of Lords held that the judge in the original case had jurisdiction to issue injunctions, including interim injunctions, against ministers and other officers of the Crown. At the same time, an injunction would be binding against the Home Secretary personally, notwithstanding the fact that he was operating in an official capacity and according to advice given to him. Reaching this conclusion involved drawing a distinction between the immunity from judicial process enjoyed by the King or Queen in person, and making a finding against a minister in his or her official capacity (or that minister's department) or against a minister personally. It was reasoned that a finding of contempt against a government department would, in circumstances such as those applying in the instant case, 'vindicate the requirements of justice' and ensure that orders of the court are obeyed. This is a highly significant outcome, since it illustrates that the courts will intervene if a government department seeks to interfere with the administration of justice.

The relevance of judicial independence was highlighted vividly in 2016 after some extreme supporters of Brexit, aided by elements of the media,[90] projected the original Divisional Court decision in *Miller 1*[91] as judicial interference with a legitimate political process which had been set in train by the referendum. The response in headlines and articles included unwarranted personalised attacks on the credibility of the individual judges who decided the case, and threats to mount protests outside the UKSC, as well as calls to reform the system of judicial appointments. The PM and Lord Chancellor/Secretary of State for Justice responded by emphasising the importance of judicial independence, in line with their statutory duty now set out under the Constitutional Reform Act 2005, but this fell short of expressing unequivocal condemnation.[92] In view of the inflammatory language and inaccurate reporting, they were criticised for choosing to temper their remarks by voicing support for freedom of the press. The point being that the institutional integrity of the courts

---

[89] C Forsyth, 'M v Home Office [1992] Ministers and Injunctions' in S Juss and M Sunkin (eds), *Landmark Cases in Public Law* (Oxford, Hart Publishing, 2017).

[90] The headline on the front page of Daily Mail on 4 November 2016 featured photographs of the judges in their wigs and robes: In giant letters 'Enemies of the People' followed by 'Fury over "out of touch judges who defied . . . Brexit voters". . . and . . . could trigger constitutional crisis'.

[91] [2016] EWHC 2768.

[92] Under section 3 ministers '. . . must uphold the continued independence of the judiciary'.

depends upon responsible reporting by the press and broadcast media.[93] In the prelude to the final appeal judgment in *Miller 1*, the UKSC was careful to stress that the Court was not deciding political issues resolvable by ministers and Parliament but that it is the 'duty of judges to decide issues of law brought before them by individuals and entities exercising their rights of access to the courts in a democratic society'.[94] This discussion demonstrates the ongoing constitutional importance of upholding judicial independence.

A Redefinition of Power?

It has been explained that concepts of the separation of powers have often attempted to distinguish legislative, executive, and judicial functions and propose that one organ of government should not exercise the functions of another. However, if we examine the role of the executive in the UK, we find there is an overlapping of both executive and legislative powers and executive and judicial powers. The executive functions of ministers and their departments are frequently combined with powers to formulate delegated legislation. It is common for legislation to provide scope for sub-rules and regulations to be drawn up by officials. The term 'Henry VIII clause' is applied when there is wide discretion in the making of delegated legislation.[95] At the same time, the growth of the administrative state has resulted in officials now sometimes deploying algorithms having judicial functions in many policy areas ranging from the allocation of means-tested benefits to the calculation of personal taxation.

At this point, it is worth asking how useful this eighteenth-century conception of separation of powers is, given the present shape of the state and taking account of the way power is currently exercised. The position has changed radically over recent years. For example, since 1979, the UK has experienced privatisation of public utilities; complex layers of state regulation; deregulation; new public management; the creation of 'next steps' agencies; contracting in the public sector; compulsory competitive tendering in local government; public-private partnerships; the citizen's charter; and health service reorganisation (to name but a

---

[93] See K Ewing, 'A Review of the Miller Decision', UK Const L Blog (10 November 2016); N Barber and J King, 'Responding to Miller', UK Const L Blog (7 November 2016).
[94] *R (on the application of Miller) v Secretary of State for Exiting the European Union* [2017] UKSC 5, para 3.
[95] See eg the Deregulation and Contracting Out Act 1994 and the European Union (Withdrawal) Act 2018.

few of the most prominent initiatives). State institutions, particularly central and local government, are increasingly tied into relationships with business, with the voluntary sector, and with consumer groups in many different ways. These modified approaches clearly have important implications in the shaping and management of our public institutions. Frequently services are publicly funded, but the service is delivered under contract by the private sector (such services ranging from prisoner escort, street cleaning, and refuse disposal to school meals). It will be apparent that the term 'governance' has been used to describe the divergent patterns and tangled interweaving of public and private bodies.[96] In addition, the HRA 1998, Freedom of Information Act 2000, and Data Protection Act 2018 have imposed additional obligations on public authorities in their dealings with the citizen. Another dimension was the prevalence of EU law as part of the domestic scene, which meant that the UK had a 'multi-layered' constitution[97] comprising policy networks at sub-national (ie devolved), national, and supra-national level. UK withdrawal from the EU has resulted in a legal divorce; the repeal of the European Communities Act 1972, and the removal of the nations' formal institutional involvement but the major part of this body of law remains valid. Nonetheless, there are increasingly dense networks through which power is exercised. Channels of accountability and perception between the political masters and end users are often blurred (take, for instance, the hostile public reaction to many aspects of EU policy prior to Brexit). Such complexity may even call into question the predominant role of the state, and, in particular, the capacity of any government to intervene effectively by legislative means to address contemporary problems. For example, levels of immigration have remained high despite legislative initiatives in this field by successive administrations. As the UK constitution lacks any sense of overall design, the extent to which the separation of powers should have a central future role can be questioned. The most important consideration may be avoiding potential conflicts of interest between constitutional players rather than reshaping the institutions according to a particular model. In sum, these developments suggest that it is no longer realistic to analyse our constitution in terms of a unitary, self-correcting constitution.[98]

---

[96] See eg R Rhodes, *Understanding Governance: Policy Networks, Governance, Reflexivity and Accountability* (Buckingham, Open University Press, 1997).

[97] See N Bamforth and P Leyland, 'Introduction' in N Bamforth and P Leyland (eds), *Public Law in a Multi-Layered Constitution* (Oxford, Hart Publishing, 2003).

[98] P Craig, 'Dicey: Unitary, Self-Correcting Democracy and Public Law' (1990) 106 *Law Quarterly Review* 205.

CONCLUSION

The idea which has been central to this discussion is that under a constitutional framework, whether formal or informal, power must have limits, and in order to achieve such limits there needs to be a division of power. In the UK constitution the separation of powers is an untidy concept. The idea certainly does not apply in the strict sense, as it does to a much more obvious extent in the United States. It is more accurate to conclude by emphasising that there are conventions that are observed which safeguard some *division* of power and functions between the various branches of government. The idea of checks and balances rather than separation of powers conveys the importance of creating a tension between institutions with different constitutional functions. But reaching a satisfactory balance between these considerations remains problematic and the far-reaching changes that have been introduced in recent years threaten to present further challenges (see particularly Chapters 1, 7, and 10).

FURTHER READING

Allan T, *Law, Liberty and Justice: The Legal Foundations of the British Constitution* (Oxford, Oxford University Press, 1993).

Bingham T, *The Rule of Law* (London, Allen Lane, 2010).

Dicey AV, *Introduction to the Study of the Law of the Constitution*, 10th edn (Basingstoke, Macmillan, 1959).

Elliott M, 'Parliamentary Sovereignty in a Changing Constitutional Landscape' in J Jowell and C O'Cinneide (eds), *The Changing Constitution*, 9th edn (Oxford, Oxford University Press, 2019).

Goldsworthy J, *Parliamentary Sovereignty: Contemporary Debates* (Cambridge, Cambridge University Press, 2010).

Gordon M, *Parliamentary Sovereignty in the UK Constitution* (Oxford, Hart Publishing, 2015).

Jowell J, 'The Rule of Law' in J Jowell and C O'Cinneide (eds), *The Changing Constitution*, 9th edn (Oxford, Oxford University Press, 2019).

Loughlin M and Tierney S, 'The Shibboleth of Sovereignty' (2018) 81(6) *Modern Law Review* 989–1016.

MacCormick N, *Questioning Sovereignty: Law, State and Practical Reason* (Oxford, Oxford University Press, 1999).

Rawlings R, Leyland P, and Young AL (eds), *Sovereignty and the Law* (Oxford, Oxford University Press, 2014).

Young A, *Parliamentary Sovereignty and the Human Rights Act* (Oxford, Hart Publishing, 2009).

4

Constitutional Monarchy

Magna Carta – Royal Prerogative – Glorious Revolution – Abdication Crisis – Constitutional Monarchy – Head of State – The Crown – Defender of the Faith – Conferment of Honours – Liability in Contract and Tort – Preservation – Abolition

INTRODUCTION

THE UNITED KINGDOM has a hereditary monarch as head of state. The King performs an important role as the personification of the nation. He appears on the national and international stage, and in this capacity he is often associated with occasions of pomp and ceremony that evoke memories of imperial glory. It is particularly this feature that distinguishes the British monarchy from its counterparts in the Netherlands, Belgium, and Scandinavia. However, as we shall see in the discussion that follows, although only limited power is exercised by the King on his own initiative, many constitutional functions still require his direct involvement. The path to constitutional monarchy has involved both the deliberate curtailment of royal power and its gradual erosion. The terminology is somewhat misleading. The government is still described as 'His Majesty's government', central government acts in the name of the Crown, and the courts are presided over by His Majesty's judges, but in modern times the monarch, although head of state, has a greatly subordinate constitutional role to Parliament, the government, and the courts. This is now accepted by reigning monarchs without question. In this chapter we will discuss the institution of the monarchy, the royal prerogative, and the nature of the Crown as part of the current constitutional framework.

During the Middle Ages and Tudor times kings and queens ruled through the exercise of the royal prerogative, but the idea that the powers of the monarch should be limited by law can be traced back at least as far as the Magna Carta of 1215. It was later established that general laws could not be made by way of proclamation – only Parliament could enact laws. It was also recognised that the King himself could not act as a judge, but must act through the judges in the courts. Since the *Case of Proclamations*[1] it has been recognised that the scope of the prerogative can be determined by the courts.[2] As we noted in Chapter 1, the events of the seventeenth century, and in particular the Civil War 1642–49 and the 'Glorious Revolution' of 1688, are significant in English constitutional history because they signalled the decisive end of any pretensions to absolute monarchy, with most powers over legislation and delegated legislation eventually passing to Parliament. This coincided with the emergence of the doctrine of the supremacy of Parliament described by Dicey. This trend was reinforced in the eighteenth century with the Hanoverian succession of George I in 1714 to the throne, by which time ministers were directly responsible for the day-to-day running of government. The scope of government activity was then much more limited, with only a few Whitehall departments (such as the Treasury, the Foreign Office, and the Board of Trade), but as the foundations of the modern administrative state were laid in the late nineteenth and twentieth century, with the role of government being greatly expanded, so the monarch became increasingly peripheral to the central activities of the executive. In this sense, by the time of Queen Victoria it could be said of the monarch that: 'she reigns but does not rule'.[3]

The abdication crisis which erupted in 1936, once again, confirmed the pre-eminence of Parliament and prime ministerial government over the monarch.[4] Edward VIII shortly after succeeding to the throne decided he would like to marry his mistress, the American divorcee, Mrs Simpson. The Prime Minister (PM), Stanley Baldwin, with the support of his Cabinet and the leader of the opposition, made it clear that, given the King's position as head of the Church of England and the marriage vows that would be entailed, this match was constitutionally unacceptable. Edward therefore had to choose between the hand of Mrs Simpson and continuing on the throne. Confronted with what amounted to an ultimatum from the PM and his government, Edward gave up the throne in favour of his brother, who became King George VI.

It will already be apparent from these examples that the evolution from a ruling monarchy to a constitutional monarchy took many hundreds of

---

[1] (1611) 12 Co Rep 74.
[2] *R (on the application of Miller) v Secretary of State for Exiting the European Union* [2017] UKSC 5.
[3] C Munro, *Studies in Constitutional Law*, 2nd edn (London, Butterworths, 1997) 256.
[4] A Taylor, *English History 1914–45* (London, Pelican, 1975) 490ff.

years. Moreover, the link with the past has special significance because, for a nation which has not experienced a recent political revolution, the monarchy represents tradition and continuity. The King, as a symbol of national identity, can be said to personify the state. He performs an important constitutional role but is, in fact, left with very little real political power. It is a convention of the highest constitutional importance that the monarch always follows the advice of his or her ministers. Many of the most far-reaching powers which formerly were exercised by the monarch, mainly prerogative powers, are now in the hands of the PM and the government. Although these powers are exercised by the government, they are still performed in the name of the monarch.

WHAT IS THE ROYAL PREROGATIVE?

The majority of issues involving the use of the prerogative are concerned with governing the country. The prerogative includes crucial areas such as the conduct of foreign affairs, defence, and national security, and when outlining the King's constitutional role it will be apparent that he has a major presence in many areas but exercises only limited power because the prerogative is now in the hands of the PM, ministers, or officials. The royal prerogative comprises residual powers and functions which were originally associated with the monarch. In considering the royal prerogative and its exercise it is useful to draw out a contrast between what appears to be the site of legal power as opposed to the constitutional reality of where power actually resides. In practical terms, the powers encompassed by the term 'prerogative' are of great importance for the effective working of government. They range from the conduct of foreign affairs, the making and ratification of treaties, the preservation of national security, the maintenance of the defence of the realm, and the exercise of the enormous powers of patronage available to the PM. Certain prerogatives are now regulated by constitutional conventions to enable government to function. The way these powers are exercised has been considered by parliamentary committees, and there have been recommendations to introduce statutory regulation in order to achieve greater clarity in respect to the scope and application of the prerogative and to achieve increased parliamentary approval and scrutiny.[5]

---

[5] See eg '"Taming the Prerogative": Strengthening Ministerial Accountability to Parliament', *Public Administration Select Committee*, HC 422, March, 2004; 'Review of the Executive Royal Prerogative Powers: Final Report', *Ministry of Justice*, CM 7170, October 2009.

The prerogative involves distinguishing between of two elements: (a) the *personal* prerogatives of the monarch; and (b) the *political* prerogatives, that is, those used by the government/executive/Crown in foreign affairs and domestic policy. Generally speaking, government operates within the parameters conferred by Parliament under statutory provisions. There are certain areas where the prerogative provides the legitimation for the use of a common law power and confers certain immunities on those using it. Considerable controversy has arisen over the definition and extent of the prerogative, particularly between the accounts of Sir William Blackstone in the eighteenth century, who stresses the 'special pre-eminence' of the King's powers, and Dicey in the nineteenth century, who was of the view that:

> The prerogative appears to be both historically and as a matter of actual fact nothing else than the residue of discretionary or arbitrary authority, which is at any given time legally left in the hands of the Crown . . . Every Act which the executive government can lawfully do without the authority of the Act of Parliament is done in virtue of this prerogative.[6]

This is a broad definition embracing all the non-statutory powers of the Crown of a residual (ie leftover) nature. Judicial decisions have tended to reflect the Diceyan position.

The centrality of the concept of parliamentary sovereignty to the constitution means that, as a general rule, statutory powers prevail over the prerogative. Parliament has the capacity to curtail prerogative powers. In situations where there is a conflict between statute and the prerogative, the statute will always prevail. The leading case illustrating this principle is *Attorney-General v De Keyser's Royal Hotel Ltd*.[7] In 1916 during the course of World War I the government, acting in the name of the Crown, took control of a hotel to accommodate the headquarters of the Royal Flying Corps under the Defence of the Realm Regulations. It then denied the legal owners any right to compensation. Compensation appeared to be available to them under statute, namely, the Defence Act 1842. It was argued by the Crown that since it had been acting under prerogative power in wartime any compensation for the requisition of this hotel was a matter within its discretion. However, the court held that this was now governed by statute. The statutory power in effect superseded the prerogative. Lord Atkinson stated that

---

[6] A Dicey, *Introduction to the Study of the Law of the Constitution*, 10th edn (London, Macmillan, 1959) 424.
[7] [1920] AC 508.

after the statute has been passed, and while it is in force, the thing it empowers the Crown to do can thenceforth only be done by and under the statute, and subject to all the limitations, restrictions and conditions by it imposed, howsoever unrestricted the Royal prerogative may theretofore have been.'

But the *De Keyser* principle also suggests that where a statutory provision covers the same grounds as the prerogative, the latter falls into abeyance and might be re-activated should the statute be repealed.

There may be areas where statutory powers and prerogative powers can exist in parallel without inconsistency.[8] However, the House of Lords held in 1995 that it was unlawful to act using the prerogative power where Parliament has given a minister a specific statutory power. In *R v Secretary of State for the Home Department, ex parte Fire Brigades Union*[9] there was a successful challenge by the Fire Brigades Union when the minister sought to introduce a method for compensating victims under his prerogative powers. In doing so, in effect, he was bypassing the scheme which had not yet been activated but had already been approved by Parliament under section 171 of the Criminal Justice Act 1988. In *Miller 1*:[10]

> all 11 Justices . . . agreed that the relevant legal principles governing the existence and effect of a relevant prerogative stem from the *Case of Proclamations*, the Bill of Rights 1689, the frustration principle and *De Keyser's Royal Hotel* . . . [and that] general prerogative powers, and particularly the foreign affairs treaty prerogative, did not extend to include an ability to modify domestic law . . .[11]

In a somewhat different context, the decision of the House of Lords in the *GCHQ* case[12] is of great importance. The challenge concerned a decision (under her prerogative powers) by the PM, as Minister for the Civil Service, to ban the union membership of civil servants at the government communication headquarters in Cheltenham without any prior consultation. In a famous judgment in which Lord Diplock explained the principles of judicial review (see Chapter 7), it was established beyond any doubt that, in principle, the exercise of prerogative powers by ministers could be subject to judicial review. While in general prerogative

---

[8] *R v Secretary of State for the Home Department, ex parte Northumbria Police Authority* [1989] QB 96.
[9] [1995] 2 All ER 244.
[10] *R (on the application of Miller) v Secretary of State for Exiting the European Union* [2017] UKSC 5.
[11] M Elliott, J Williams, and AL Young, 'The Miller Tale: An Introduction' in *The UK Constitution after Miller: Brexit and Beyond* (Oxford, Hart Publishing, 2018) 21.
[12] *Council of Civil Service Unions v Minister for the Civil Service* [1985] AC 374.

powers can be challenged, certain types of exercise of the prerogative are non-justiciable.[13] For example, these areas would include decisions relating to: the making of treaties, the defence of the realm, the prerogative of mercy, the grant of honours, and the appointment of ministers. The application for judicial review was ultimately unsuccessful in the *GCHQ* case because the PM was able to bring forward sufficient evidence to show that the failure to consult in the proper way had been made because of legitimate concerns over the risk to national security.

There has been an important trend towards qualifying prerogative powers. The running of the civil service is no longer one of the personal prerogatives of the PM. Although the management of the service remains with the PM, it has been placed on a statutory footing for the first time under Part 1 of the Constitutional Reform and Governance Act 2010. The Act does not apply to the management of the diplomatic and security services which still remains under the prerogative (see Chapter 6). Under Part 2 of the same Act, treaties which are negotiated under ministerial prerogative powers must now be laid before Parliament for ratification.

THE CONSTITUTIONAL ROLE OF THE MONARCHY

Bagehot observed that without entering into 'the combat of politics ... the Crown does more than it seems'[14] and the extent of this contribution is borne out as we survey the range of conventions and residual powers associated with the monarch. The pivotal convention which applies to the monarch is that he or she is bound to act on the advice of his or her ministers. The fact that the UK constitution can be described as a constitutional monarchy rests upon this and other conventions. In other words, many things are done in the name of the monarch, and are performed under prerogative powers, but the monarch's action is frequently governed by constitutional practice or by other *political* actors. However, there are also important technical questions over whether the residue of important, but sometimes ill-defined prerogative powers left in the hands of a reigning monarch can be justified in a contemporary constitutional context. For example, given the difficulties that have arisen with the formation of a government (discussed below) it has been suggested that

---

[13] The issue of justiciability of the prerogative was considered by the UK Supreme Court in *Miller 2* (see n 29 below).

[14] W Bagehot, *The English Constitution* (London, Fontana, 1963) 100.

legislation should be passed to determine who would become PM in the event of a future hung Parliament.[15]

The constitutional role of the monarch might be summarised under the following headings:

(1) *The formation of a government* – The basic rule is that following a general election the monarch will always call upon the leader of the majority party in the House of Commons to form a government. A majority in the House of Commons is, of course, necessary to ensure that legislation can be passed. Given that the ability of voters to elect a government is the principle at the heart of parliamentary democracy, it is extremely important that the monarch accepts the verdict of the electorate in performing this role. The electoral system usually provides a clear winner, but this is not always the case. For example, after the February 1974 election neither the Conservatives nor Labour secured an overall majority. Labour emerged from the election with 301 seats, five more than the Conservatives, but the Conservatives polled a higher aggregate total of votes. To form a government either the Labour Party or the Conservative Party required the support of a combination of Liberals, Scottish Nationalists, Welsh Nationalists, and Northern Ireland MPs. The constitutional role of the monarch in this situation is to ensure that a viable government is formed. This means the monarch should ask the leader of the party most likely to be able to sustain a government to become PM. After the February 1974 election, Edward Heath, the incumbent PM, did not resign but was unable to reach agreement with the Liberals. In consequence, Queen Elizabeth II had no real alternative to sending for Harold Wilson, whose Labour Party had the largest number of seats. Mr Wilson managed to govern for six months with a minority government before calling another election. After the 2010 general election which also delivered a hung Parliament, the incumbent Labour PM, Gordon Brown, remained in 10 Downing Street until it was clear after negotiations between politicians that the Conservative and Liberal Democrats had reached an agreement to form a government (rather than a Labour-led rainbow agreement of Liberal Democrats and other minor parties). At this point Gordon Brown was in a position to recommend to the Queen that she should invite David Cameron to form a government.[16] Crucially, the political actors were required to follow the protocol recognised by the Cabinet Office manual setting out the relevant rules and conventions. In consequence,

---

[15] See eg D Bean, *The Future of the Monarchy* (London, The Fabian Society, 2003).
[16] R Blackburn, 'The 2010 General Election Outcome and Formation of the Conservative-Liberal Democratic Coalition Government' [2011] *PL* 30.

the Queen's neutrality was not compromised, as it might have been had she been drawn into the government formation process.

All the main political parties (Conservative, Labour, and Liberal Democrat) now elect their leader by processes involving the balloting of MPs and party members, but until 1965 the Conservative Party did not have a formal method for electing its leader. As a result, when a serving Conservative PM had to leave office prematurely, the monarch performed the task of deciding who should be the successor. This occurred with the resignations of PM Eden in 1956 and PM Macmillan in 1963.

(2) *The calling of elections* – The Fixed Term Parliaments Act 2011 removed the power to determine the timing of an election from the PM by setting general elections at five-year intervals, but the Dissolution and Calling of Parliament Act 2022 has restored the convention under which an election is called by virtue of His Majesty's prerogative. In practice, the PM choose the date of election and requests a dissolution within the five-year window set by the Parliament Act 1911. Once the decision is taken by the PM to call an election, the monarch is obliged, according to convention, to dissolve Parliament. There have been exceptional situations. One such arose in February 1974 when no party emerged from the election with a majority in the House of Commons. It has been suggested that, had Harold Wilson been unable to win a vote in the House of Commons after being invited to form a government, the Queen might have been in a position to refuse a request for a dissolution of Parliament for another election, at least until other party leaders had been given the opportunity to attempt to form a government that was acceptable to Parliament.[17]

(3) *Ministerial appointments* – In regard to ministerial appointments at all levels the monarch follows the advice of the PM in approving the selections that the PM makes. There is no requirement that the monarch is consulted by the PM over the suitability of these choices, and there is no longer power to refuse any of these choices. In the eighteenth and nineteenth centuries there were some instances when the monarch was reluctant to take advice. There is nothing that formally prevents the monarch expressing his or her opinion about the suitability of the choices proposed by the PM. George VI was reported to have expressed clear reservations when Winston Churchill selected Lord Beaverbrook as Minister for Aircraft Production and member of the War Cabinet in 1940, but nevertheless the PM's choice prevailed.[18]

---

[17] See further R Brazier, *Constitutional Practice: The Foundations of British Government*, 3rd edn (Oxford, Oxford University Press, 1999) see ch 3, 40ff.

[18] M Hastings, *Finest Years: Churchill as Warlord 1940–45* (London, Harper Collins, 2009) 82.

(4) *Appointments and honours* – There are many other official appointments which are conferred by the monarch, but these choices are nearly always made on the advice of the PM. These include the creation of peers, the appointment of archbishops and bishops, the appointment of all senior judges, and the conferment of most honours, such as knighthoods. However, the King is personally able to select members of the royal household, including his Private Secretary. In addition, there are a few honours that remain in the personal gift of the King.

(5) *Assent to legislation* – In respect to passing of legislation, it should be remembered that, following its passage through Parliament, the royal assent is required for a Bill to become law. It is an established convention (certainly since Queen Anne's refusal in 1708 to sign the Scottish Militia Bill – and on that occasion she was acting on ministerial advice) that the monarch never refuses to give the royal assent to legislation, and that to do so would be unconstitutional. However, it might be argued that there could be extreme circumstances when refusal of the royal assent would be justified, for example, if Parliament approved legislation that sought to postpone indefinitely a general election in peacetime. The royal assent is also required for legislation passed by the Scottish Parliament, Northern Ireland Assembly, and Welsh Parliament (formerly Assembly).

(6) *Following ministerial advice and collective responsibility* – It is a crucially important convention of the constitution that the King always acts on the advice of his ministers.[19] This doctrine is demonstrated at the opening of each session of Parliament. The King's speech setting out his government's policy is, in practice, always written by the government. Another equally important convention, collective Cabinet responsibility, is derived from the idea that any advice to the monarch should be unambiguous. This convention requires that members of the Cabinet are bound to defend the policy agreed around the Cabinet table, or alternatively, should resign from the government (this convention is discussed in greater detail in Chapter 6). It should be stressed that there is no active involvement by the monarch in the routine business of government. He has access to classified information and has confidential weekly meetings with the PM during which he is briefed on government policy. On these occasions the King can express his views and provide advice. However, the PM is not under any obligation to take account of these views. It is of crucial importance that the monarch is perceived as being above politics and impartial when it comes to performing his main constitutional functions. Queen Elizabeth II resisted any such association during her

---

[19] See *Miller 2* (n 29 below) in relation to the prorogation of Parliament.

long reign, but although Charles as heir to the throne was, on occasion, criticised for his involvement with sensitive, mainly environmental, issues which might have a political dimension, since ascending to the throne as King Charles III he has avoided any direct involvement in controversial political questions.[20]

(7) *Commander-in-chief of the armed forces* – The King performs an important symbolic function as the nominal head of each of the armed forces, but under the Bill of Rights 1689 the keeping of an army by the Crown is made subject to the consent of Parliament. While the forces are now largely regulated under statute, ministers act under the prerogative to direct the armed forces in their strategic operations.

(8) *Head of state* – As head of state, the King represents the nation on the international stage. In this capacity he hosts events at home and makes visits abroad. However, the PM, the Foreign Secretary, or other senior ministers will be entirely responsible for determining any matters of government policy or negotiating treaties that involve meetings with other heads of state or heads of government, and in this capacity ministers will be acting under their prerogative powers.

(9) *Head of the Commonwealth* – At the turn of the twentieth century the British monarch was the figurehead for the British Empire. Independence has been conferred on virtually all former colonial possessions and many have joined the British Commonwealth,[21] which seeks to promote co-operation between member nations.[22] The Queen has a mainly symbolic role at its head and she remains titular head of state of a number of commonwealth nations, including Canada, Australia, New Zealand, and much of the Commonwealth Caribbean.[23] During her reign Queen Elizabeth II attended Commonwealth summits and made frequent visits to Commonwealth countries to help keep this loose association of nations together and King Charles shows every sign of continuing to perform this role.

(10) *Head of the Church of England* – The historic role of the monarch as Head of the Church of England and defender of the (Anglican) faith harks back to the bitter conflicts of the reformation in the sixteenth century. Of course, the contemporary approach of monarchs has

---

[20] This question was brought to public attention after a contested information request by a *Guardian* journalist in 2005 for the release of correspondence concerning environmental issues between the Prince and various ministers and finally resolved by the courts in 2015. See *R (Evans) v Attorney General* [2015] UKSC 21.
[21] Currently the organisation comprises 54 independent countries and 2.4 billion people: https://thecommonwealth.org/about-us.
[22] I Jennings, *The Queen's Government* (Middlesex, Penguin, 1969) 36ff.
[23] D O'Brien, *The Constitutional Systems of the Commonwealth Caribbean* (Oxford, Hart Publishing, 2014) 39ff.

changed to acknowledge an open multi-faith society in the twenty-first century. A person is no longer disqualified from succeeding to the throne by marrying a Roman Catholic.[24] However, the legal requirement for an Anglican succession remains in place,[25] although it is widely regarded as an anachronism.[26]

DOES THE MONARCH RETAIN REAL POWER?

A famous summary of the constitutional role was provided by Bagehot in the nineteenth century when he stated: 'she has the right to be consulted, the right to encourage and the right to warn', meaning by this that the monarch had become a 'dignified' rather than an 'efficient' (ie working) element of the constitution.[27] We have already observed that in nearly every case the monarch's powers and discretions are constrained by established conventions. Recent experience supports this view.[28] With the outcome of Brexit at a crucial stage a request was made by PM Johnson for an extended prorogation of Parliament in September 2019. This was a matter of great political controversy because a prolonged suspension of Parliament (for five weeks) would arguably limit democratic debate and scrutiny of the ongoing Brexit process at a crucial time. The power to order prorogation of Parliament is a prerogative power. It can only be exercised by the Crown but any prorogation is triggered by the advice of the PM. It was acknowledged in *Miller 2*[29] that following such a request Her Majesty was obliged by constitutional convention to accept the PM's advice (as she had in fact done). In other words, she was not regarded as an active player; rather, the question for the Supreme Court to decide was whether she had been given lawful advice by the PM. As mentioned in Chapter 7, prorogation was unanimously found by the Court not to be justified and therefore it was declared invalid. By contrast, the hung Parliament after the February 1974 election (almost a dead heat between the parties) required some active intervention in deciding which political leader should be given the first chance to form a government. This

---

[24] Succession to the Crown Act 2013, ss 2 and 3.
[25] Bill of Rights 1689 and Act of Settlement 1701.
[26] R Blackburn, 'Queen Elizabeth II and the Evolution of the Monarchy' in M Qvortrup (ed), *The British Constitution: Continuity and Change* (Oxford, Hart Publishing, 2013) 173.
[27] W Bagehot, *The English Constitution* (London, Fontana, 1963) 111.
[28] H Kumarasingham, 'Viceregalism at Westminster: The Role and Powers of the Queen in the 2019 Brexit Constitutional Crises' in H Kumarasingham (ed), *Viceregalism* (London, Palgrave Macmillan, 2020).
[29] *R (On the application of Miller) v The Prime Minister* [2019] UKSC 41, para [30].

illustrates that there may be occasions when a convention is not clearly defined, and where considerable discretion is left in the monarch's hands.

In terms of a capacity to 'advise' Queen Elizabeth II accumulated experience of having worked with 14 different PMs since she acceded to the throne in 1952. The monarch is kept very closely in touch with the exercise of governmental power by means of a weekly audience with the PM during which he or she is fully briefed about the affairs of government, and has access to all Cabinet papers. The meetings with the PM are strictly confidential, which allows the opportunity to express views about matters of government policy. For example, it was widely reported that there were misgivings expressed by Queen Elizabeth over certain aspects of PM Thatcher's domestic policy during the late 1980s. Also, in times of crisis, the King or Queen is kept fully informed of the latest developments. It should be emphasised that the PM is not under any obligation to take account of any royal opinions. Indeed, if a declared position on controversial political matters were to leak out, this would undermine the reputation for impartiality which is so important to the monarch's constitutional role. Bagehot could almost be describing the present position when he summed up the powers of Queen Victoria more than 100 years ago as the rights to be consulted, to encourage, and to warn ministers, but it has been suggested in light of the monarch's current role that the right to be informed and to advise could now be added to the list.[30]

WHAT IS THE 'CROWN'?

The Crown refers to the King in his official or his personal capacity. It is also the generic term used to refer to persons or bodies exercising powers which historically were the monarch's personal powers. Thus the 'Crown' is applied to the executive branch of government. Ministers are of course technically servants of the Crown and in general statutory powers are conferred by Parliament on ministers in person.[31] The blanket concept of the Crown conflicts with reality because it suggests that the various diverse elements of the executive are a unified whole, with the concept of the Crown masking the fact that there are often conflicts and tensions between central government departments. We have already noted that the political

---

[30] R Brazier, 'The Monarchy' in V Bogdanor (ed), *The British Constitution in the Twentieth Century* (Oxford, Oxford University Press, 2003) 78.

[31] H Wade and C Forsyth, *Administrative Law*, 11th edn (Oxford University Press, 2014) 35ff.

prerogative is exercised by, or on the advice of, the Crown. In consequence, the term 'Crown' as it is employed in the UK is a product of constitutional history, and it might be described as anachronistic. Comparable powers in Europe or the United States would be constitutionally exercised by, or on the advice of, what is called the state, executive, or government.

The Crown has enjoyed certain legal immunities. For example, Public Interest Immunity (PII) may apply in a judicial context relating to withholding the disclosure of evidence by public bodies in the public interest[32] and the Crown may be able to avoid liability under a statute that is not expressed as being applicable to it. Such immunity has allowed public bodies to remain outside the scope of statutory provisions which otherwise provide for social welfare, employment rights, and public safety. However, most contemporary legislation has tended to restrict or entirely dispense with this immunity.[33] The intention has been to ensure that government departments are not shielded from obligations that are placed upon them.

LIABILITY OF THE CROWN IN TORT AND CONTRACT

The UK lacks a well-developed theory of the state and of a state administration,[34] which means that contracts are entered into by Crown servants as agents acting on behalf of the Crown itself. It has been established that officials responsible for negotiating contracts on behalf of a government department are not personally liable under contract because it is the principal (the department) and not the agent (the official) who is responsible. A general right to sue the Crown under contract is provided by section 1 of the Crown Proceedings Act 1947, which removes the need to obtain the leave of the Attorney-General to bring an action against the Crown. Until 1947, prior to this enactment, a petition of right was required to recover damages from the Crown.[35]

Similarly, under section 2 of the Crown Proceedings Act 1947, the Crown (as opposed to the state) is liable in tort (which covers the other civil

---

[32] See Crown Proceedings Act 1947, s 28, *Duncan v Cammell Laird and Co Ltd* [1942] AC 64, *Conway v Rimmer* [1968] AC 910, *R v Chief Constable of West Midlands Police, ex p Wiley* [1995] 1 AC 274. For further discussion of PII particularly in relation to Matrix Churchill etc see A Tomkins, *The Constitution after Scott* (Oxford, Oxford University Press, 1998) 167ff.

[33] See eg National Health Service and Community Care Act 1990, s 60, and Environmental Protection Act 1990, s 159.

[34] See further J Allison, *A Continental Distinction in the Common Law* (Oxford, Oxford University Press, 2000) 32.

[35] Wade and Forsyth (n 31) ch 20.

wrongs under the common law). For example, it can sue or be sued in the courts where there is a claim for negligence. In addition, as an employer, the Crown is liable for torts committed by its employees while in the course of their employment. It is also worth pointing out that other public bodies such as local authorities are in a similar position to the Crown with regard to their general exposure to liability in tort. In most respects, the Crown is treated in the same way as any other defendant, that is, to initiate an action against the Crown a litigant sues the department concerned or the Attorney-General. There are, however, fundamental limitations to the award of damages against the Crown and other public bodies.[36] If policy matters were routinely amenable to challenge by means of a claim for damages, this would be an indirect method of influencing the formulation and application of policy by democratically elected and publicly accountable bodies.[37]

EVALUATION: PRESERVATION, REFORM, OR ABOLITION?

The monarchy is a costly institution to preserve and it has been the subject of considerable controversy in recent years. In fact, there has been a torrent of media criticism which has ebbed and flowed. This adverse exposure has drawn attention to: the failure of royal marriages; Queen Elizabeth's initially detached reaction to the death of Princess Diana (the former wife of Prince Charles and mother of his children, William and Harry); and the much publicised tensions between Harry and Meghan (Duke and Duchess of Sussex) and other members of the royal family. However, Prince Andrew's conduct has certainly caused the most obvious damage to the image of the royal family. First over a reputation for profligacy at the expense of the taxpayer as a national trade ambassador (2001–11). Subsequently, in regard to serious allegations relating to alleged sexual encounters with under-aged girls facilitated by the convicted sex offender Jeffrey Epstein. In 2025 his credibility suffered a further blow as the release of email correspondence from Epstein established that a BBC televised interview in 2019 purporting to refute accusations against him had contained manifest inaccuracies. This has attracted prolonged adverse media coverage for the royal family as an institution. In response, Andrew was required to step down from his activities as a working royal in 2019 and then in 2025, the King removed all his remaining titles together with a previous entitlement to enjoy the benefit of residing in

---

[36] See eg *X (Minors) v Bedfordshire County Council* [1995] 2 AC 633.
[37] C Harlow, *Understanding Tort Law*, 3rd edn (London, Sweet & Maxwell, 2005) 150.

a property owned by the Crown estates (subsidised by the taxpayer).[38] Notwithstanding this catalogue of controversy associated with the royal family, the approval ratings for the monarchy have remained positive.[39]

Walter Bagehot's account of the Victorian constitution recognises a special dichotomy characterising the constitution as involving an interaction between 'dignified' and 'efficient' elements, with the monarchy in all its ceremony and splendour not only epitomising the dignified aspects but having real importance as a powerful symbol of constitutional continuity.[40] Certainly, the British monarchy is an institution which retains many arcane procedures, and its members have been accommodated at taxpayers' expense in palatial finery. On the one hand, the associated pomp and ceremony of the formal splendour of the State Coronation in 2023 to mark the accession to the throne of King Charles III,[41] the trooping of the colour to celebrate the King's birthday, and the state opening of Parliament are attractions for some citizens and many visitors from abroad. On the other, such spectacles on a grand scale can be objected to as expensive and anachronistic luxuries. For example, the cost of staging the Coronation in 2023 was £72.8 million. There have been calls to review the extent to which state funding through the 'civil list' should go beyond supporting the monarch and his immediate heirs, and to assess whether the public purse should extend to a total of seven royal palaces and to pay for transport in royal yachts, trains, and planes.[42] In fact, it has long been suggested that the British monarchy should be trimmed in size, assume a lower profile, and become more informal like its Scandinavian counterparts.[43] Perhaps this slimming down process has already begun. The decision by Prince Andrew to withdraw from public duties in 2019 was perhaps inevitable given the serious allegations made against him. At the beginning of 2020 Harry and Meghan decided to step back from their royal duties and, as a result, they are no longer in receipt of public funds.[44]

---

[38] 'King Charles officially strips Andrew of HRH style and prince title, *The Guardian* 6 November 2025.

[39] https://yougov.co.uk/politics/articles/52165-royal-favourability-trackers-may-2025.

[40] P Leyland 'The Westminster Model Constitution Home and Abroad: Texts and Contexts' in N Son Bui and M Pongsapan (eds), *Comparative Law in Asia: Essays in Honour of Andrew Harding* (Oxford, Hart Publishing, 2025) 82.

[41] D Torrance, 'The Coronation of King Charles III and Queen Camilla', *House of Commons Library*, Research Briefing, 28 July 2025, CBP 9789.

[42] R Blackburn and R Plant, 'Monarchy and the Royal Prerogative' in *Constitutional Reform: The Labour Government's Constitutional Reform Agenda* (London, Longman, 1999) 145.

[43] T Bull, 'Institutions and Divisions of Powers' in H Krunke and B Thorarensen (eds), *Nordic Constitutions: A Comparative and Contextual Study* (Oxford, Hart Publishing, 2018) 43ff.

[44] www.royal.uk/statement-her-majesty-queen-0 (18 January 2020).

An equally trenchant objection is that: 'The monarchy remains symbolic of privilege over people, of chance over endeavour, of being something, rather than doing something. We elevate to the apex of our society someone selected not on the basis of talent or achievement, but because of genes.'[45] Given this type of criticism, namely of a class-based system founded on privilege by birth right, it is not surprising that republican alternatives have gained a more prominent place on the political agenda.[46] For instance, there have been proposals to replace the monarchy with a republican constitution.[47] However, in devising an alternative it would be difficult to match the range of significant constitutional functions which are exercised by a reigning monarch to a new office without including significant changes to the role of PM, the Cabinet, and the civil service. The design of the office of President as Head of State viewed from an international perspective can have many forms. The United States (or French) variant of an elected President with formidable executive powers and the ability to veto legislation[48] would be much too radical a departure for the UK constitution to take on board. On the other hand, a directly elected President with a mainly ceremonial role similar to that granted to the President of the Irish Republic could serve as a possible model. Even if the type of role for a future President is defined, a further question which arises concerns reaching agreement on the type of candidates who might be suitably qualified to stand for election and hold such a high profile public office. Indeed, the difficulty in reaching sufficient consensus upon an acceptable alternative was demonstrated when a referendum for the removal of Queen Elizabeth II as head of state was held in Australia in 1999. Despite misgivings over the status quo expressed in opinion surveys, the Australian electorate rejected the republican alternative presented to them.

CONCLUSION

Many nations throughout the world have not accepted the republican case and continue to have constitutional monarchies. Spain can be cited

---

[45] 'Time for the Monarchy to Step Aside' (2000) *The Observer*, 30 June.
[46] A Gray and A Tomkins, *How We Should Rule Ourselves* (Edinburgh, Canongate, 2005); I Mclean, *What's Wrong with the British Constitution* (Oxford, Oxford University Press, 2010) ch 12.
[47] Commonwealth of Britain Bill 1995–96; A Tomkins, *Our Republican Constitution* (Oxford, Hart Publishing, 2005).
[48] M Vile, *Politics in the USA* (London, Hutchison, 1976) 183ff.

as an example of a European nation which has welcomed the introduction of a constitutional monarchy in recent times. After the catastrophic Spanish Civil War (1936–39), which was followed by a generation of fascist dictatorship, Juan Carlos was named by Franco as his successor. His accession to the throne in 1975 reinstated a recognised dynasty and provided a means of reconnecting with a legitimate tradition associated with the nation's history. However, Juan Carlos was intent on democratic reform and after elections were held a hereditary monarchy became the central feature of a new liberal democratic constitution adopted in 1978. Under the constitution the King has limited powers but he acts as a symbol of the 'unity and permanence' of the state and also stands in a position of neutrality, safeguarding the regular functions of the institutions of the state.[49] The robustness of the new constitution was tested in 1981 when decisive action by the King, at the very pinnacle of the constitution, thwarted a military coup. At the same time, this intervention arguably demonstrated the value of a constitutional monarchy which is backed by strong public support.

Turning back to the UK, there is wide acknowledgement (even by detractors) that Queen Elizabeth II during her long reign (1952–2022) performed her constitutional functions with an unflinching dedication to duty. Despite the political turmoil associated with the brief premiership of Liz Truss (see Chapters 6 and 10), which happened to coincide with the passing of Queen Elizabeth, King Charles III who took over has performed his constitutional duties from the outset with meticulous regard to established convention (subject only to illness). William, Prince of Wales, shows every indication of being equally sure-footed as an eventual successor. The prospect in the future that an unsuitable individual might be in line inevitably raises doubts about the viability of the institution.[50] However, the abolition of the monarchy is not on the immediate horizon. As has been noted above, it would require a written constitution embodying the comprehensive codification of the current conventions relating to the monarch, many of which have been discussed in this chapter. Indeed, notwithstanding the criticisms set out above, it can still be argued that the institution of the monarchy in the UK is very important in constitutional terms, because the reigning King or Queen personifies the nation as head of state and confirms a link with the nation's past

---

[49] V Comella, *The Constitution of Spain: A Contextual Analysis*, (Oxford, Hart Publishing, 2013) 8, 71ff.
[50] R Blackburn, 'The Prince of Wales at 70 and the Survival of the Monarchy' [2019] *PL* 447, 449.

constitutional history. Moreover, as Bagehot stressed, the presence of an experienced and respected monarch acts as a stabilising influence, particularly during times of war or of political crisis.

FURTHER READING

Bagehot W, *The English Constitution* (London, Fontana, 1963).

Bogdanor V, *The Monarchy and the Constitution* (Oxford, Oxford University Press, 1995).

Blackburn R, 'Monarchy and Crown Prerogative, 20 Years Later: An Answer to Professor Brazier' [2024] *PL* 5989.

Blackburn R, 'Queen Elizabeth II and the Evolution of the Monarchy' in M Qvortrup (ed), *The British Constitution: Continuity and Change* (Oxford, Hart Publishing, 2013).

Blackburn R, 'The Prerogative Power of Dissolution of Parliament: Law, Practice and Reform' [2009] *PL* 766.

Brazier R, 'The Monarchy' in V Bogdanor (ed), *The British Constitution in the Twentieth Century* (Oxford, Oxford University Press, 2003).

Craig P, 'Prerogative, Precedent and Power' in C Forsyth and I Hare (eds), *The Golden Metwand and the Crooked Cord* (Oxford, Clarendon Press, 1998).

Freedland M, 'The Crown and the Changing Nature of Government' in M Sunkin and S Payne (eds), *The Nature of the Crown: A Legal and Political Analysis* (Oxford, Oxford University Press, 1999).

Hazell R and Morris B (eds), *The Role of Monarchy in Modern Democracy: European Monarchies Compared* (Oxford, Hart Publishing, 2020).

Twomey A, 'Miller and the Prerogative' in M Elliott, J Williams, and AL Young (eds), *The UK Constitution after Miller: Brexit and Beyond* (Oxford, Hart Publishing, 2018).

5

Parliament

General Election – First Past the Post – Additional Member System – House of Commons – Backbencher – The Speaker – House of Lords – Hereditary Peer – Life Peer – Government and Opposition – Legislation – Parliamentary Select Committees – Parliamentary Privilege – Watchdog Functions – Henry VIII Clause – Ombudsman – National Audit Office – Public Accounts Committee

INTRODUCTION

IN THE UNITED KINGDOM, Parliament is the body in which the legislative power is vested. It consists of an elected House of Commons and a House of Lords that is largely comprised of life peers (appointed for their lifetime) but with a residual membership of hereditary peers (whose titles are inherited), bishops, and Law Lords (see later discussion on the composition of the House of Lords). In addition, in order for legislation approved by Parliament to become law, the royal assent is required. Apart from acting as the legislature for the UK, Parliament authorises the levying of taxation and controls national expenditure and it keeps a check on the executive. In this capacity it provides the main forum for providing political accountability. It also acts as a sounding board for the nation by debating issues of public concern and by giving the public and other vested interests the chance to lobby their MPs.

Before reviewing the institutional structure in more detail, several preliminary contextual observations are called for relating to the high degree of recent political volatility and the uncertainty regarding Parliament's role. First, for most of the period when the proposals for exiting the EU were being considered by Parliament (2017–19), far from being an endorsement of the Brexit referendum result sought by the Prime Minister (PM) in the 2017 election, no single party enjoyed a majority in the House of Commons, and this had a significant impact in the way it functioned.[1] The trend towards what is termed in this book 'elective dictatorship' (see Chapters 3, 6, and 7) recognising that the executive has the upper hand in controlling Parliament was reversed.[2] An assertive House of Commons, working across party lines, inflicted numerous defeats on the government and passed legislation in opposition to the government to prevent a 'no deal' Brexit.[3] Furthermore, the attempt by the government to circumvent Parliament by prorogation (ie suspension) was unanimously found to be unlawful by the UK Supreme Court (see Chapter 7).[4] A Conservative government was elected with a substantial overall majority in December 2019 and in 2024 a Labour government was elected with an even larger majority. In regard to the independence of backbenchers in conducting the business of the House, there is some evidence that MPs have been on occasion prepared to stand up to the party whips than was the case in most post World War II parliaments but as manifesto commitments have been turned into government legislation there has also been a resumption of executive dominance.

As already noted, since Brexit the supremacy of EU law is no longer recognised.[5] In theory, Parliament resumes its place as a sovereign legislature as recognised by Dicey in the late nineteenth century, with apparently unlimited capacity to pass or repeal any law. But, in practice, apart from the ultimate sanction of elections, parliamentary power is subject to arguably increasing constraints. First, in dealing with questions of legality the interpretative role of the courts introduces a degree of uncertainty relating to the validity of legislation and, of course, Convention rights contained in the European Convention on Human Rights are binding under the treaty and enforceable domestically under the Human Rights Act 1998.[6] Next, there is the territorial dimension – devolution grants law-making powers within defined limits to devolved legislatures confining the range of its routine legislative authority. It is also noteworthy that for law-making purposes the introduction of the English Votes for

---

[1] A Blick, *Stretching the Constitution: The Brexit Shock in Historical Perspective* (Oxford, Hart Publishing, 2019) 44.

[2] A King, *The British Constitution* (Oxford, Oxford University Press, 2007) 82ff.

[3] M Russell, 'Parliament, politics and anti politics' in *Parliament and Brexit* (The UK in a Changing Europe, March 2020) 4–6; T Hickman, 'Contempt of Parliament, Political Satire and the Case of Rt Hon Rees-Mogg MP', UK Const L Blog (12 September 2019).

[4] *Miller 2*, discussed in Chapter 7.

[5] P Craig, 'Brexit and the Constitution' in J Jowell and C O'Cinneide (eds) *The Changing Constitution*, 9th edn (Oxford, Oxford University Press, 2019).

[6] M Elliott, 'Parliamentary Sovereignty' in J Jowell and C O'Cinneide (eds), *The Changing Constitution*, 9th edn (Oxford, Oxford University Press, 2019).

English Laws (EVEL) procedure (discussed below) has turned Westminster into a predominantly 'English Parliament'.[7]

In a number of other ways Parliament has faced challenges as the central forum for democracy. For instance, although not legally binding, the Brexit referendum was essentially used as a populist device which had the effect of favouring the wishes of the people over those of Parliament as the core institution of deliberative democracy (see discussion of popular sovereignty in Chapter 3). As Young observes, the effect is to 'undermine democratic debate by challenging representative institutions which aim to facilitate the formation of consensus'.[8]

In terms of the accountability of the executive to Parliament, the Speaker of the House of Commons, Sir Lindsay Hoyle, criticised the government in 2020 for using presidential-style press conferences by the PM (and other ministers) from 10 Downing Street (initially during the Covid-19 crisis) to publicise policy initiatives, rather than announcing them in Parliament where the government is open to democratic scrutiny.[9] Lastly, as the full impact of Brexit is felt, Parliament is faced with a fresh set of challenges, particularly concerning the repatriation of law and the oversight of the resulting legislation and delegated legislation which will be generated by this process.[10]

This chapter will consider Parliament's role as part of the contemporary constitution. However, it should be remembered that a power struggle between Parliament and the monarch was an important feature of constitutional history. Parliament first emerged as merely an advisory body to the King. It was made up of the land-owning aristocracy and the established church, who were represented in the House of Lords. The House of Commons consisted of elected representatives of the gentry on a roughly geographical basis. Parliament functioned as a kind of representative body of local interests available for consultation, but by the fifteenth century it also assumed a more prominent role in passing legislation. Under the Tudor monarchs (Henry VIII, Mary I, and Elizabeth I) it reverted to a more passive role. However, although it could be summoned and dismissed at will, Parliament was required by the King

---

[7] P Silk, 'Devolution and the UK Parliament' in A Horne and G Drewry (eds), *Parliament and the Law*, 2nd edn (Oxford, Hart Publishing, 2018), 196ff.

[8] A Young, 'Populism and Parliamentary Sovereignty' in L Burton Crawford, P Emerton, and D Smith (eds), *Law under a Democratic Constitution* (Oxford, Hart Publishing, 2019) 193.

[9] www.bbc.co.uk/news/uk-politics-53533809.

[10] Over a transition period legislation was required to ensure that measures, mainly in the field of the environment, trade, agriculture, and fisheries, were available to replace EU laws with the end of the transition period at the end of 2020.

to approve requests for the raising of revenue. The constitutional clashes of the seventeenth century were a direct result of attempts by the King to rule without recourse to Parliament. This overlooked the established practice that the King could not enact statutes without the consent of the two Houses of Parliament. 'Parliamentarian theories maintained that God originally conferred the highest powers of government on the community as a whole, rather than a single person.'[11] During the seventeenth century such responses to absolute monarchy led to Parliament asserting its role. The Civil War was waged by Parliament against King Charles I, and constitutional constraints were finally placed on the monarchy towards the end of the seventeenth century by the Bill of Rights of 1689. This established that Parliament must meet on a regular basis. It also conferred special privileges on Parliament. For example, Article 9 of the Bill of Rights provides that the freedom of speech and debates and proceedings in Parliament shall not be called into question by any court.[12]

GENERAL ELECTIONS

Before we look at the way both Houses of Parliament operate, it is important to investigate the relationship between the House of Commons and representative government. In order to do this, there will be a brief discussion of the electoral system.[13]

First Past the Post

The first-past-the-post method of election in the UK has contributed to the political dominance of large parties. During the eighteenth and nineteenth centuries, the Tories and Whigs were the names of the parties in the ascendancy, but both tended to represent narrow factional interests, in particular, the landed gentry and the industrial entrepreneurs. By the end of the nineteenth century the Conservatives (originating from the Tories) and Liberals (originating from the Whigs) were the main parties

---

[11] J Goldsworthy, *The Sovereignty of Parliament: History and Philosophy* (Oxford, Oxford University Press, 1999) 96.

[12] P Evans, 'Privilege, Exclusive Cognisance and the Law' in A Horne and G Drewry (eds), *Parliament and the Law*, 2nd edn (Oxford, Hart Publishing, 2018) 17.

[13] For an overview, see J Curtice, 'The Electoral System' in V Bogdanor (ed), *The British Constitution in the Twentieth Century* (Oxford, Oxford University Press, 2003).

who alternated in power. The Labour Party as the political voice of the trade union movement was founded in the late nineteenth century. After World War I, Labour began to replace the Liberals as the main left-of-centre party, briefly forming the government in 1924, and again between 1929–31. Since the end of World War II, apart from the minority Labour government in 1974, the Conservative/Liberal Democratic coalition government (2010–15), and the minority Conservative government (2017–19), the Conservative and Labour Parties have alternated between government and opposition.

The first-past-the-post (simple plurality) system operates by dividing the nation into 650 approximately equal constituencies in terms of population, each of which sends a single member to Parliament. It produces MPs who represent clearly defined geographical areas and, as we shall see, an MP might be regarded as an 'ombudsman' for his or her own constituents. Candidates selected by the political parties, and independent persons who pay the required deposit of £500 and are able to get sufficient nominations, can stand at general elections or at by-elections. The Political Parties, Elections and Referendums Act 2000 regulates the conduct of political parties and establishes an election commission to oversee the electoral process. The Act also requires political parties to be registered and it imposes restrictions on the source of donations to prevent foreign and anonymous support for political parties. The Act further requires that any donation of over £5000 to a political party is declared. Both the Labour and Conservative Parties faced criticism following the 2005 election for accepting loans from donors in order to circumvent the provisions of this Act.

The electoral system is extremely straightforward to understand. A voter is presented with a list of candidates and the parties they represent, and simply puts a cross next to the name of his or her preferred candidate. The candidate receiving the most votes wins the seat. This is whether or not the candidate receives a majority of the votes cast in that constituency. Although it is not in any sense proportionate, 'first past the post' registers the relative support between the parties with the widest following in the country. The major parties nearly always win the seats in their heartlands, but the outcome of elections is decided in more marginal constituencies, where a shift in support between the main parties may lead to a change in the member elected. The system favours parties polling nationally over 30 per cent of the popular vote. For example, Labour were returned to government with a huge overall majority of 180 seats in the 1997 General Election but with just under 44 per cent of the popular vote.

After the 2010 General Election for the first time since February 1974 no party emerged with an overall majority of seats in Parliament.[14] Although the Conservatives improved their percentage vote by 4 per cent they failed to achieve sufficient seats for an overall majority. The Labour Party share of the vote fell by 6 per cent, which was its poorest showing since 1918. The Liberal Democrats marginally increased their share of the popular vote but won five seats fewer than in 2005. Nevertheless, on this occasion as the third largest national political party holding the balance of power between the other two major parties they were in a position to negotiate a coalition deal with the Conservative Party which lasted for the full parliamentary term. As already mentioned, after the 2017 election from which the Conservatives emerged as the largest party a minority Conservative government was formed under PM May. The government was able to remain in office because of a confidence and supply voting agreement in the House of Commons reached with the 10 Democratic Unionist Party (DUP) MPs (elected from Northern Irish constituencies).

A serious drawback of the First Past the Post System (FPP) is the manifest distortion in representation it causes in the absence of any proportional element. The 2024 general election provides an excellent illustration as the Labour Party achieved 411 seats with an overall majority of 164 seats but polled less than 34 per cent of the popular vote. In this election voters appear to have voted tactically and switched their support in most constituencies to the party most likely to defeat the Conservatives. On the other hand, Reform UK with 14.3 per cent and the Green Party with 6.7 per cent of the popular vote were only able to get five MPs and four MPs respectively elected to the Westminster Parliament. Recent results also shows that the system tends to favour a party enjoying a high level of popular support in particular areas or parts of the nation. In the 2019 election the Scottish National Party won 48 seats with only 3.9 per cent of the popular vote the seats were confined entirely to Scottish constituencies. To tackle this issue, some correction on a proportional basis would address this clear discrepancy. For example, the Independent Commission under Roy Jenkins which reported in 1998 recommended a mixed system with 80–85 per cent elected by alternative vote in individual constituencies and the remaining 15–20 per cent of the Commons elected from a party list. The list would have provided a proportional

---

[14] National parties = Conservative 36.1 per cent popular vote, 307 seats (47.5 of seats); Labour 36.1 per cent popular vote (40 per cent of seats); Liberal Democrats 24 per cent popular vote, 57 seats (8.8 per cent seats).

'top up' element.[15] A mixed system with a party list top up is used for the elections to the Scottish Parliament. By contrast the Welsh Senedd has recently opted for a proportional closed party list system of election (see Chapter 8).

Social Media and Electronic Voting

The manner in which elections are fought is rapidly evolving. As the Democracy and Digital Technologies committee stated in a report on the need to regulate the use of social media at election times published in 2020: 'Democracy faces a daunting new challenge. The age where electoral activity was conducted through traditional print media, canvassing, and door knocking, is rapidly vanishing. Instead it is dominated by digital and social media. They are now the source from which voters get most of their information and political messaging.'[16] The Cambridge Analytica scandal exposed the exploitation of the illegal use of databases for the targeting of voters, and social media has been deployed to circumvent strict spending limits applicable at election times.[17]

However, while there has been an increase in postal voting, electronic voting at general elections by computer is not on the immediate horizon. This would cut down the expense of elections and allow results to be declared as soon as the polls close (assuming a secure system is devised).

Quite apart from the normal electoral process, more frequent consultation online from the citizen's home is in prospect. Such an innovation would amount to an entirely new form of participatory democracy by allowing dialogue between the government and the wider citizenry. The prospect of broadening consultation to inform decision-making by central and local government might be welcomed. It could help deliberations on many routine matters. On the other hand, the holding of online plebiscites as indicators of the public mood would have to be rigorously controlled, as testing the water in this way could easily be abused by government. For example, in order to justify the introduction of repressive legislation following a violent crime or terrorist attack the Home

---

[15] The Report of the Independent Commission on the Voting System (The Jenkins Commission), (1998) Cm 4090.
[16] 'Digital Technology and the Resurrection of Trust', House of Lords, Select Committee on Democracy and Digital Technologies, Report of Session 2019–21, 29 June 2020.
[17] P Birkinshaw and M Varney, *Government and Information Rights*, 5th edn (Haywards Heath, Bloomsbury, 2019) 167.

Secretary might calculate on getting instant approval for such measures in an electronic vote.

PARLIAMENT: COMPOSITION AND PROCEDURE

Government and Opposition

The adversarial style in the House of Commons resting on a tension between the government benches facing His Majesty's opposition is fundamental to the Westminster style of Parliament. The official opposition has a vital part to play in the parliamentary system.[18] It will be obvious that the role of the opposition is to oppose the government of the day, both by raising reasoned objections to its legislative proposals, and by criticising its performance as a government. The opposition also has to present itself as a government-in-waiting. As well as having a distinct set of policies, it has an alternative leader and government team in what is termed a 'Shadow Cabinet'. On top of any earnings as MPs, the Leader of His Majesty's Opposition and the opposition Chief Whip are paid salaries, which is further acknowledgement of their formal status. In order to perform its function, the official opposition and other opposition parties are granted parliamentary time, and they are represented on all parliamentary committees. The opposition has a particularly important role in relation to public expenditure. Not only is a senior member of the opposition appointed as chair of the influential Public Accounts Committee but also a certain amount of time, called supply days (now opposition days), is set aside to debate in detail the estimates for public expenditure.

The opposition will often choose a sensitive topic which is likely to cause embarrassment to the government for debate, in anticipation that the debate will attract adverse publicity and a modification of policy. But the outcome of debates and votes in the House of Commons is often a foregone conclusion when a government has an overall majority. This is because the government whips are nearly always able to ensure a majority for the ruling party (see references to 'elective dictatorship'[19]). However, an effective opposition may be able to cause long-term political

---

[18] A Birch, *The British System of Government*, 10th edn (London, Routledge, 1998) 134ff.

[19] From Lord Hailsham's phrase: *Elective Dictatorship* (London, British Broadcasting Corporation, 1976).

damage to the government. For example, although the administration of PM Major survived for several years afterwards, the government's credibility was seriously damaged by criticisms of economic mismanagement levelled at it by the opposition following the UK's forced withdrawal from the European Exchange Rate mechanism on 16 September 1992. A degree of co-operation between government and opposition is required to allow many parliamentary procedures to operate and to facilitate the passage of legislation. For example, there will usually be agreement over the amount of time to be devoted to clauses of a government bill. Finally, as a potential leader, the PM may confide in the Leader of the Opposition on matters of national importance or crisis, for example, where there was a national emergency during the Covid pandemic or when UK armed forces are engaged in action overseas.

The Speaker and the Role of Backbench MPs

As already noted, the House of Commons consists of 650 elected MPs, each of whom represents an individual constituency which is based on geographical area. MPs who are not members of the government or shadow government are referred to as 'backbenchers'. Apart from representing their constituents, MPs participate in debates, vote on legislation, and serve on parliamentary committees. The House of Commons is presided over by the Speaker (and three deputies), elected by MPs. The Speaker detaches him/herself from previous party associations and has enormous authority over the House of Commons. Looking back historically, the Speaker was the elected official who spoke for his or her fellow members by communicating requests to the King or Queen. In the present set-up, apart from presiding over debates and determining the order in which members speak, the Speaker performs an important quasi-judicial function in giving rulings on procedural points of order that arise, as well as performing a quasi-judicial function when dealing with internal disciplinary issues concerning the conduct of MPs. The procedural tasks performed by the Speaker includes determining whether a bill is considered to be a money bill (under the 1911 Parliament Act the House of Lords cannot delay money bills from becoming law). It is important to note that the Speaker is disqualified from direct participation in debates. In addition, the Speaker retains a historic role in formally representing the views of the House of Commons to the monarch.

MPs are sent to Parliament to represent their constituents, but they are not delegates. They may win their seat on the basis of manifesto pledges made by a political party to the electorate. However, once elected, there is no formal mechanism available to individual electors to compel their MP to follow manifesto policies. On the other hand, the political party to which MPs belong (exceptionally there may be MPs who do not belong to a major political party) is in a position to exert pressure to encourage them to toe the party line. MPs are free to dissent from this position and vote with the opposition or abstain from voting. For instance, the divisions in the Conservative Party over the EU led to numerous rebellions by Eurosceptic MPs. This made it difficult for the government of PM Major (1990–97) to introduce legislation incorporating the Treaty of Maastricht (which extended the role of Europe with the formation of the EU). The matter was subject to a vote of confidence, but the government narrowly prevailed. In 1995 the same divisions in the Conservative Party in the House of Commons prompted Major to trigger a leadership election that he was able to win against his Eurosceptic opponent. PM Blair, who enjoyed a much larger majority, lost the support of a significant minority of backbench MPs over some issues (eg the introduction of foundation hospitals and the war against Iraq). Behind the scenes, the party machine in the form of the party 'whips' exert strong pressure on individual members. In consequence, MPs who persistently vote with the opposition may lose the endorsement of their party ('have the whip withdrawn'). This punishment can be imposed on a temporary or on a permanent basis.

Also, there is a geographical and local dimension to the role of MPs which has been reinforced with the electoral success of the Scottish National Party (SNP) in Scotland. MPs seek to represent the interests of their constituents and promote what they regard as their constituency interests. There are many examples of MPs articulating local views on contentious matters. For example, one such issue has concerned opposition voiced in Parliament to proposals to build a third runway at London's Heathrow Airport. Local opposition is spearheaded in Parliament by local members. MPs will take up grievances on behalf of their constituents. But there may be limits to such support. MPs may be reluctant to back a local cause when this conflicts with the official party line.

The adversarial character of parliamentary politics has exerted an enormous influence on the procedures that have developed. Originally, a two-party system derived from having rival factions outbidding each other to act as advisers to the monarch (one in government; the other in opposition). In order to succeed in an adversarial system political parties have tended to be made up of broad coalitions of individuals with diverse shades of opinion. The factions need to keep together for a government to maintain its majority in Parliament. Nevertheless, if the policies of a party change too much, or if the leadership loses touch with the grass roots, the tension caused may result in rebellions inside the party and defections to other parties. One of the most dominant PMs of recent times, Margaret Thatcher, faced a leadership contest and was forced to step down because of divisions in her own parliamentary party.[20]

As well as providing executive oversight (see section below) parliamentary questions provide an important opportunity for individual members to raise matters on behalf of constituents and of general concern. MPs are expected to represent the interests of constituents whether or not those individuals are political supporters. 'Question Time' is the highlight of the parliamentary day, and it brings matters to the attention of the wider public. It will be pointed out below that 'Question Time' is also a procedure that permits MPs to call the executive to account for its actions. Early-day motions are another method for drawing attention to a matter of concern. There are limited opportunities for backbench MPs to initiate debates on subjects that they feel are important. Adjournment debates are available for raising issues and are held at the end of parliamentary business. These may be matters that cause embarrassment to the government, but emergency debates are granted only occasionally by the Speaker.

The question of representation in Parliament, and particularly in the House of Commons, should also be considered in terms of the extent to which a gender and ethnic balance has been achieved.[21] Nancy Astor, the first female MP, was elected in 1918, but since then until quite recently, women have been grossly under-represented. The situation has improved significantly since 1997. Following the 2024 general election, female representation reached a record high of 35 per cent, with the election of 190 Labour, 29 Conservatives, 32 Liberal Democrats, and 11 Scottish Nationalist female MPs.[22] Turning to ethnic representation, up until 1987 there were no non-white MPs but by 2024, there were 90 MPs from ethnic backgrounds, making up 13 per cent of the total.[23] Improved representation of women and ethnic minority MPs is, at least partly, attributable to changes in the selection procedures for prospective candidates adopted by the main political parties.

---

[20] P Hennessy, *The Prime Minister: The Office and Its Holders since 1945* (London, Penguin, 2001) 433.
[21] See eg R Campbell and J Lovenduski, 'Winning Women's Votes? The Incremental Track to Equality' [2005] *Parliamentary Affairs* 837.
[22] R Kelly, Women elected to the House of Commons, 24 June 2025. https://commons library.parliament.uk/research-briefings/sn06652/.
[23] E Uberoi, House of Commons Library, Briefing Paper, CBF 1156, 16 March 2020.

Parliamentary Privilege

Parliament has been given a number of important legal privileges which allows it to conduct its constitutional role without interference from the Crown or from the courts, and these amount to a source of constitutional law in their own right.[24] The grant of these special privileges by the sovereign must be related to the struggle between the King and Parliament which came to a head in the seventeenth century with the English Civil War of 1642–49 and the 'Glorious Revolution' of 1688. As has already been mentioned, the English Bill of Rights of 1689 provided under Article 9 that the freedom of speech and debates or proceedings in Parliament ought not to be impeached or questioned in any court or place outside Parliament. In the absence of a codified constitution as a form of guarantee, these privileges have been demanded from the monarch by the Speaker of the House of Commons and confirmed (as a symbolic gesture) at the beginning of each parliamentary session.[25] In effect, this acknowledges the independence of Parliament, and Parliament is granted special rights to do certain things without having its legitimacy or its authority challenged by the sovereign, the government, or the courts. This means that, for example, in theory, MPs have an unqualified freedom of speech. In practice, this means that what is said in Parliament cannot be the subject of defamation actions or prosecution in the courts. However, if this privilege is abused MPs may be disciplined by Parliament itself. The absolute freedom of speech can be regarded as the most significant of the privileges enjoyed today. This immunity has the potential to enable MPs to voice concern about matters of public concern in Parliament in circumstances where they would otherwise be forced to remain silent. It permits accusations in Parliament which, if repeated outside, would result in legal proceedings. For example, in 1955 at the height of the so-called 'Cold War' Kim Philby was exposed in Parliament as a spy. This revelation was the prelude to uncovering of the biggest security scandal in British history.

In *Stockdale v Hansard*,[26] which concerned whether a report published under the authority of the Commons was susceptible to civil action, the courts conceded jurisdiction to the House of Commons and refused to provide a remedy. This was after being presented with a Speaker's warrant asserting that it was not for the court to inquire into the business

---

[24] C Munro, *Studies in Constitutional Law*, 2nd edn (London, Butterworths, 1999) ch 7.
[25] Evans (n 12) 17ff.
[26] (1839) 9 Ad & El 1.

of Parliament. Lord Denman stated: 'Whatever is done within the walls of either assembly must pass without question in any other place.' Further, the case of *Bradlaugh v Gossett*[27] confirmed that the courts have no power to intervene in relation to the internal management and procedures of the House of Commons. It also recognised that Parliament is able to determine the nature and limits of parliamentary privilege. The recognition of parliamentary privilege has meant that Parliament has the right to control its own internal proceedings without question. Moreover, Parliament is a court which can discipline and, if necessary, imprison its own members for misbehaviour. As we will see, in recent years further steps have been taken to oversee the activities and behaviour of MPs.

Parliamentary Standards and the Conduct of MPs

The conduct of some MPs became a particular cause of concern during the 1990s and again in 2009 following the disclosure of apparently excessive claims for expenses. In 1994 Lord Nolan, a senior judge from the judicial panel in the House of Lords, was given the task of reformulating guidelines in respect to regulating the conduct of MPs and setting up the Committee on Standards in Public Life. Public duty, selflessness, integrity, objectivity, accountability and openness, honesty, and leadership were identified as forming the principles that should underpin the codes of practice. These principles obviously apply to MPs. Furthermore, Members of Parliament are required not to bring the office of Member of Parliament into disrepute. Failure fully to disclose such interests is regarded as a serious matter, which will lead to disciplinary action.[28] The reputation of the House has been tainted by scandals in relation to MPs receiving cash to ask parliamentary questions and, as mentioned above, in relation to their claims for expenses.[29]

The Parliamentary Commissioner for Standards has an investigatory role and MPs are required to co-operate with any investigation that is undertaken. The Standards Commissioner performs the functions previously carried out by separate Select Committees on Members' Interests and on Privileges. These committees were combined in 1995, with the formation of a new House of Commons Select Committee on Standards

---

[27] (1884) 12 QBD 271.
[28] See *First Report of the Committee on Standards in Public Life*, Cm 2850 (1995).
[29] R Kelly, M Hamlyn, and O Gay, 'The Law and the Conduct of Members of Parliament' in A Horne and G Drewry (eds), *Parliament and the Law*, 2nd edn (London, Bloomsbury, 2018) 48ff.

and Privileges. It is chaired by a respected member of the opposition, has 11 members, and a quorum of five, with the power to appoint sub-committees. This Committee oversees the work of the officer of the House of Commons. The Parliamentary Commissioner for Standards is responsible for the maintenance of the Register of Members' Interests and advises MPs on the registration requirements, but the Commissioner also has the task of investigating specific complaints about the conduct of MPs. The Committee on Standards considers matters relating to privileges referred to it by the House, and matters relating to the conduct of MPs, including specific complaints about MPs' conduct which have been made to the Commissioner and referred by the Commissioner to the committee. In particular, the committee has power to order the attendance of any MP before the committee, and to require that specific documents or records in the possession of an MP relating to its inquiries, or to the inquiries of the Commissioner, be laid before the committee. Reports by the Commissioner demonstrate that these procedures are strictly enforced, but also reveals the complexity and ambiguity of some of the rules governing what MPs and ministers are expected to enter on the register.[30]

A major public scandal erupted in 2009 in regard to inflated and in some cases fraudulent expenses claims from MPs. The matter came to light after Freedom of Information requests from three journalists investigating such claims were successful.[31] There had been attempts to prevent detailed disclosure from taking place in the courts made by the Speaker of the House of Commons[32] and some MPs had been keen to pass a private member's bill that would have made them exempt, or partially exempt, from the provisions of the Freedom of Information Act.[33] The argument by the press that the publication of details of MPs' expenses claims was in the public interest was upheld by the Information Commissioner and later confirmed by the High Court. To understand this affair in context it should be recognised that MPs in the UK received a salary of £74,000 (£93,904 April 2025), which is about average in comparison with their European counterparts,[34] but were allowed to claim up £100,000 for office expenses. The House of Commons had published a Green Book which was intended to provide detailed guidelines about the rules

---

[30] Select Committee on Standards and Privileges, *Thirteenth Report*, 20 July 2006.
[31] See P Leyland, 'Freedom of Information and the 2009 Parliamentary Expenses Scandal' [2009] *PL* 675.
[32] See 'Speaker "Leaned On" over Expenses' BBC News, 28 May 2009.
[33] The Freedom of Information (Amendment) Bill was introduced in 2006 but failed to complete its parliamentary stages in 2007.
[34] http://news.bbc.co.uk/1/hi/uk_politics/7961849.stm#France.

concerning the financial allowances available to MPs. Some MPs, including one Cabinet minister, sold their secondary properties at a profit after having received repayments and mortgage relief, but avoided payment of capital gains tax on the sale. The payment of family members as staff was another practice which was called into question. The publication of details also revealed what might be termed 'creative abuse of the rules' with inappropriate claims, some of which appear almost comical in the light of the principles set out in the Green Book for Members referred to above. The catalogue of abuse which was placed in the public domain caused considerable damage to the credibility of the entire political class in the eyes of the general public. Parliament responded by passing the Parliamentary Standards Act 2009 which established an Independent Parliamentary Standards Authority with responsibility for overseeing the pay and expenses of MPs. Subsequent reform allows voters to petition for the removal of miscreant MPs from office. Under this legislation the possibility of unseating an MP arises when an MP is either: imprisoned; suspended from the House for 10 days or more; or found guilty of submitting false claims of expenses. If such a petition receives the support of at least 10 per cent of voters in a constituency the sitting MP loses his or her seat.[35] Nevertheless, the question of the conduct of MPs and their effectiveness has remained a major ongoing concern. Following a manifesto commitment in the 2024 election manifesto by Labour the Modernisation Committee of the House of Commons has launched an important investigation with a view to reform which will have three main aims: driving up standards; improving culture and working practices; and reforming procedures to make the Commons more effective.[36]

Another interesting aspect relating to parliamentary privilege arose when in *R v Chaytor and others*,[37] a group of three MPs and a peer facing criminal charges of false accounting relating to their expense claims,[38] argued on final appeal before a nine-judge panel of the Supreme Court that the Crown Court had no jurisdiction to try them on the grounds that this would infringe parliamentary privilege. Article 9 of the Bill of Rights of 1689 was used to suggest that freedom of speech and debates or proceedings in Parliament ought not to be impeached or questioned in any court. After examining the relevant law, Lord Rodgers pointed

---

[35] Recall of MPs Act 2015, s 1.
[36] A Blick and D Govan (eds), 'The Constitution in Review: A Report from the United Kingdom Constitution Monitoring Group', Issue 1, 1 July 2024–31 December 2024, *The Constitution Society*.
[37] [2010] UKSC 52.
[38] Kelly, Hamlyn, and Gay (n 29) 38ff.

out that the very fact that the House authorities co-operated with the police in the investigations suggested that they did not regard the allegations as falling into the category over which a privileged claim would be made. Lord Phillips concluded that 'precedent, the views of Parliament and policy all point in the same direction. Submitting claims for allowances and expenses does not form part of, nor is incidental to, the core essential business of Parliament, which consists of collective deliberation and decision making'.[39] Moreover, it was further held that the House does not assert any exclusive jurisdiction to deal with criminal conduct, even where this relates to or interferes with proceedings in committee or in the House.

THE HOUSE OF LORDS

We turn next to consider the role of the House of Lords. While it is generally acknowledged that the House performs an important revising function, its role and composition have been a matter of constitutional debate for more than a century. Although members of the House of Lords are not elected, the so-called Upper House has broadly similar functions to the House of Commons. It scrutinises legislation as it passes through Parliament, and it requires the government to account for its policies. The House of Lords operates as a revising chamber with more time available and, in many cases, more expertise to perform this task. The House of Lords, which serves as the second chamber in the UK, is a very unusual body. In common with the Canadian Senate, it is entirely unelected and, as well as having a legislative role, it used to perform the crucial judicial function of being the highest domestic appellate court, although a UK Supreme Court was established in 2009 to perform this judicial appellate function. The House of Lords has been the subject of reform on several occasions; the most recent and far reaching, certainly in terms of composition, was in 1999, when the hereditary element was heavily pruned. This was to be the prelude to further reform, but, to date, there has been a lack of consensus as to what should happen next. While most commentators and politicians recognise that a second chamber should continue to have a role as a body which revises legislation and helps to scrutinise the executive, there has been much disagreement over the composition of the House of Lords or any such body that might replace it.

---

[39] *R v Chaytor and others* [2010] UKSC 52, para [62].

The democratic legitimacy of the Lords has been called into question since the extension of voting rights during the course of the nineteenth century. As a hereditary body the House of Lords largely represented the landed aristocracy, but the social and economic changes resulting from the Industrial Revolution, including the growth of towns and cities, the emergence of powerful industrial interests, and the activities of protest movements and organised labour had an important bearing on politics. The response of the House of Lords to electoral reform is particularly relevant to this discussion. When the first Reform Bill of 1832 proposed a limited extension of voting rights and a fairer distribution of seats, the landed aristocracy in the House of Lords attempted to prevent the Bill's passage through Parliament. It resisted again at the beginning of the twentieth century when a Liberal government was elected on a radical social programme which included the state provision of an old age pension and a social security scheme. These policies were partly bankrolled by increased taxes and inheritance duties for rich landowners.[40] The tactics of the Conservative opposition in the House of Lords, which thwarted the government's attempts to introduce many of its policies by voting them down, triggered a constitutional crisis. The clash between the two Houses culminated in the rejection by the House of Lords of the Finance Bill (Budget) of 1909. This intervention departed from what was believed to be a convention that prevented the Lords from blocking money Bills. To overcome the stalemate, the Liberal government was required to contest two elections in 1910. The first was on the budget, and the second on the government's proposals to curtail the powers of the Lords permanently. The prospect that the King would create enough Liberal peers to vote in favour of the Parliament Bill and thereby overwhelm the opposition prompted sufficient Conservatives in the House of Lords to back down and vote in favour of reform.

The Parliament Act, which became law in 1911, clipped the wings of the House of Lords by replacing its capacity to veto legislation with a delaying power of two years (this was later reduced to one year by the Parliament Act 1949). The delaying power has been used on only a handful of occasions since 1949. The reluctance to invoke this power confirms the subordinate role of the House of Lords.[41] It is mainly a revising chamber. In addition, the Parliament Act 1911 entirely removed any rights to veto or delay financial Bills. Nevertheless, in order to

---

[40] R Tombs, *The English and Their History* (London, Penguin Books, 2014) 528.
[41] As was pointed out in Chapter 3, the constitutional status of the Parliament Acts was considered by the House of Lords in *Jackson v Attorney-General* [2005] UKHL 56.

provide some balance between the two Houses the 1911 Act left the House of Lords with an absolute power to reject any legislation which sought to prolong the lifetime of a Parliament and, at the same time, it reduced the maximum period between parliamentary elections from seven to five years. The present House of Lords is left with the power to delay legislation for up to a year. It can also amend legislation emanating from the Commons, but any such amendments may not be accepted by the Commons. Furthermore, in order minimise gridlock between the two Houses the so-called 'Salisbury convention' acknowledges that the government's manifesto commitments, in the form of government Bills, are not voted down by the (unelected) House of Lords at second reading stage.[42]

Composition of the House of Lords

As an institution which first became prominent in medieval times, the House of Lords contained a number of different categories of hereditary peers. Viewed from a historical standpoint the Upper House of peers represented the families who had been elevated to the nobility by the King (dukes, marquises, earls, viscounts, and barons). Many were able to trace their ancestry back hundreds of years and this category included the King and Royal Dukes.

The power to appoint peers, which originally lay with the sovereign, has since the eighteenth century been in the hands of the PM, whose nominees are confirmed routinely by the sovereign. An independent advisory appointment body, called the House of Lords Appointments Commission (HOLAC), was set up in the year 2000 to select potential members of the Lords, but it has an uncertain role in the appointment process because its recommendations are not currently binding on the PM and other candidates can be nominated by the PM without the approval of HOLAC.

By the time the Parliament Act 1911 reformed the House of Lords, it was already evident to many that birth right was not a legitimate qualification for service in a modern legislature. Moreover, the predominance of hereditaries was iniquitous because the Conservatives were able to muster a majority by summoning their supporters amongst the hereditaries to vote. This built-in Conservative majority presented a particular problem for Liberal and later for Labour governments. Nevertheless, until

[42] T (Lord) Bingham, 'The House of Lords: its future?' [2010] *PL* 261, 265.

1999 hereditary peers, then numbering over 758 out of 1,325, remained the largest single group. The House of Lords Act 1999 removed the voting rights of all but 92. Between 1999 and 2025 upon the death of a hereditary peer a ballot was held among the former hereditary peers to establish which of their number would make up the 92 working hereditary peers. However, the right of any remaining hereditary peers to participate in the business of the House will be removed by the House of Lords (Hereditary Peers) Act 2025.

The Lords Spiritual, representing the established Church of England, also assumed a traditional right to sit in the House of Lords. The Archbishops of Canterbury and York and 24 other bishops are entitled to participate in the affairs of Parliament. Although the leaders of other denominations may be given life peerages, there is no guarantee of equivalent representation. A further distinct category of life peers used to be the 12 Law Lords, created under the Appellate Jurisdiction Act 1876, who were appointed to serve on the highest domestic appellate court, the judicial committee of the House of Lords. However, the Constitutional Reform Act 2005 has replaced the judicial committee of the House of Lords with a UK Supreme Court, and this change has ended the anomalous situation which allowed the Lord Chancellor, and the most senior serving judges, to also serve as members of the legislature.

As the replacement of the hereditaries, life peers presently comprise the main category of eligible members. The Life Peerage Act 1958 allowed the appointment of a new category of barons, serving only for their lifetime. In addition, the 1958 Act removed the sex discrimination barrier that had prevented women from sitting in the House of Lords. Currently, 261 female life peers account for nearly a third of the total membership. Although life peerages were available as an alternative to the hereditary principle from 1958, it was not until the election of Labour in 1964 that it became accepted practice to appoint exclusively life peers. Nominees for life peerages have fallen into two main categories. First, a certain number have been created on a regular basis as the political nominees of the main political parties. It has been a convention that, in order to perform the role of opposition effectively, opposition parties should be entitled to make recommendations to the serving PM. A substantial proportion of these political appointments is made up of politicians with experience in the House of Commons or at European, devolved, or local level. The second category of nominees comprises those appointed in recognition of exceptional contributions to the wider community. Included under this head are captains of industry, retired leaders of trade unions, distinguished academics, former senior civil servants, retired generals, admirals, and air marshals, leading figures from the professions, arts, and sciences, and so on. The intellectual distinction and specialist knowledge of many life peers contributes to the high quality of debate in the House of Lords and to the contribution it makes as a body which revises legislation. With the exception of ministers and shadow ministers, peers are not paid, but are entitled to claim back expenses for travel, subsistence, and secretarial costs. At the time of writing in terms of allegiances the declared political affiliation of peers amounted to 281 Conservative, 217 Labour, 177 Cross Bench, 75 Liberal Democrats (with the remaining peers classed as: non-affiliated, bishops, or representing smaller parties). In terms of party politics it will be clear that no political grouping has a majority. The current value of the House of Lords as a revising chamber is commonly attributed to a combination of factors. The party whips are in a weaker position as peers do not face re-election, the membership partly consists of cross benchers and tend to be independently minded. Life peers are appointed for their contribution to public life, industry, the professions or the arts, and as a result, cover an impressive spectrum of relevant expertise.[43]

House of Lords: Further Reform?

As already observed, recent legislation has tackled the anomaly of hereditary peers, but the Parliament Act of 1911 which reduced the powers of the Upper House was enacted as a temporary measure until such time as the composition and the role of a second chamber could be agreed.[44] Quite apart from recalibrating powers and functions, the obvious issues which need to be addressed in proceeding with further reform include: a substantial reduction in the number of sitting members; the method of selection and/or election; and the status of the second chamber as a territorial representative body in comparison to the House of Commons. Many governments have launched proposals for reform[45] but the various options usually featuring a hybrid solution (part elected,

---

[43] See generally P Norton 'Legislative Scrutiny in the House of Lords' in A Horne and A Le Sueur (eds) *Parliament, Legislation Accountability* (Oxford, Bloomsbury, 2016), 117ff.
[44] For an evaluation of reform so far, see G Phillipson, '"The Greatest Quango of Them All", "A Rival Chamber" or "A Hybrid Nonsense"? Solving the Second Chamber Paradox' [2004] *PL* 352.
[45] See R Brazier *Constitutional Reform: Reshaping the British Political System*, 3rd edn (Oxford, Oxford University Press, 2008) 64ff.

part appointed) have controversial implications[46] and have failed to gain sufficient support.[47]

In opposition the Labour Party in 2022 published the Brown Commission report.[48] This reform project addressing many aspects of the constitution places a strong emphasis on the increased devolution of power from London and the South East of England to the regions and nations. For instance, under the US constitution, all US states are granted equal two-member representation in the Senate, irrespective of their size or population. Such an arrangement ensures that bigger states in terms of population do not dominate decision-making. In this sense a reformed second chamber might have the potential to provide a counter balance of territorial representation based on regions throughout the UK. The Brown report elaborates Labour's previous proposals for a Regional Senate by recommending the replacement of the current House of Lords with an elected Senate or Assembly of the Nations and Regions. Limited details are set out in the report and there is very little indication on the wider impact such a radical proposal would have on the House of Commons, electoral system, and the constitution more generally. Although clearly, to avoid direct overlap, the new Senate would be elected on a different election cycle from the House of Commons using a different voting system. The clear intention behind this proposal is to provide increased representation to the regions of the entire nation compensating for the Commons representational bias favouring England which is more heavily populated. As outlined the reformed body would only be able to amend rather than reject legislation. The Senate would be granted a distinct set of new functions, including the scrutiny of a new category of special local legislation, and it would act as guardian of the constitution by exercising a veto power over a list of constitutionally protected statutes.

If the UK followed other nations by introducing an elected Regional Senate, this would provide a transformed institution but also one with an important element of democratic legitimacy. Certainly, the method of election used and gap between elections would need to be on a different basis from the House of Commons; also the terms of office of members would be for a different period. In addition, the constituencies would be drawn so as to provide a significant regional emphasis. However, there

---

[46] The Royal Commission on the Reform of the House of Lords, *A House for the Future*, Cm 4534 (2000).

[47] House of Lords Reform Bill 52, 2012–13.

[48] 'A New Britain: Renewing our Democracy and Rebuilding the Economy' *Report of the Commission on the UK's Future*, 2022.

are reasons for caution in establishing an elected, or mainly elected, body of this kind. If it is accepted that the House of Commons should continue to have a predominant role, the democratic legitimacy of a reformed second chamber arising through election could be problematic. It might lead to the second chamber asserting its authority, and thereby acting as a competitor to the House of Commons. It could, for example, radically amend (even if it lost its present power to delay legislation), disrupting the process of government. Another potential drawback is the danger that an elected second chamber might duplicate the political tribalism of the House of Commons, with members dragooned by the party machine. Politicians mindful of having to face the voters at some future date would be less likely to display the relative independence compared to the Commons demonstrated by many members of the House of Lords in recent years. Moreover, there is evidence to suggest from a comparative study of the situation in Ireland, Spain, and Italy that the contribution of a second chamber as an effective legislative body tends to be undermined where the government enjoys a majority in both Houses.[49] It will be apparent that a radical reform might have unforeseen constitutional consequences and take years to implement. Since the 2024 general election there has been no indication that the Labour government intends to proceed further with any form of the Brown Commission proposals for a Regional Senate.

By second chamber standards world-wide the membership of the House of Lords remains extremely large at around 800 members, and only a limited proportion of peers attend on a regular basis.[50] A less radical and manageable way forward in proceeding with reform, but also one capable of attracting immediate support might concentrate on drastically slimming down the number of sitting members and confirming the position of the HOLAC in selecting life peers while reducing the role of the incumbent PM who currently exercises unchecked discretion in making appointments.[51] Recent proposals by the House of Lords itself have only gone a modest way to answering the compelling case to reduce the size of the House by suggesting a cap of 600 members.[52]

---

[49] M Russell, *Reforming the Lords: Lessons from Overseas* (Oxford, Oxford University Press, 2000) 150–52 and 226–27.

[50] A Smaller House of Lords: The Report of the Lord Speaker's Committee on the Size of the House of Lords (13th Report of Session 2017–19) HC 662.

[51] See L James, P Thomas, A Renwich, M Russell *The Constitutional Landscape: Options for Reform* (The Constitution Unit, March 2025), 20.

[52] Fifth Report of the Lord Speaker's committee on the size of the House, House of Lords, 17 July 2003.

PARLIAMENT AS LEGISLATOR

This section considers the legislative process in more detail. The focus will be on assessing how effective Parliament is as a legislative body and to what extent it is able to deliver high quality legislation.[53]

In the simplest terms, according to the doctrine of the mandate, Parliament has legitimacy because the most important part of it, namely, the House of Commons, is elected. The party with the strongest support in the Commons (usually a majority over other parties) is in a position to form a government. In turn, the government will introduce the policies that have been approved by the electorate. However, this only roughly describes the relationship between Parliament and law-making. To some extent it is possible to see a correspondence between declared political aims at election times, and the legislation that is introduced by government.[54] However, apart from legislation to put into effect manifesto pledges in the main policy areas, governments will also need to introduce laws in response to pressing matters of topical concern which range from management of the economy and regulation of industry to measures in response to the threat of terrorism or disease. Legislation also originates from a variety of other sources, some of which are outside Parliament. Some government Bills arise from the routine work of the Law Commission, which reports on the state of various aspects of civil and criminal law. The introduction of devolution with a separate law-making apparatus has meant that now just over half of all legislation from Westminster applies only to certain parts of the UK.[55]

Public Bills

A process of consultation may precede the introduction of government legislation. In order to facilitate this, a Green Paper or White Paper (government publication setting out intentions) will be issued to elicit responses from individuals and organisations likely to be affected by the proposed legislation. An important innovation in recent years has been the publication of some legislation as draft bills well in advance

---

[53] See A Horne and A Le Sueur (eds), *Parliament Legislation and Accountability* (Oxford, Hart Publishing, 2016).
[54] J Bara, 'A Question of Trust: Implementing Party Manifestos' [2005] *Parliamentary Affairs* 585.
[55] R Hazell, 'Westminster as a "Three-in-One" Legislature' in R Hazell and R Rawlings (eds), *Devolution, Law Making and the Constitution* (Exeter, Imprint, 2005) 228.

of their passage through Parliament in order to give more opportunities for consultation. In line with the practice in the Scottish Parliament, this process of pre-legislative scrutiny has allowed departmental select committees to take evidence, report, and make recommendations on proposals before the legislation goes through its formal parliamentary stages, and there is evidence to suggest that a significant proportion of recommendations have an impact on the final form of the legislation.[56] Parliament is the focus for the activity of pressure groups. The central lobby of the House of Commons is where members of the public can meet their MPs to make representations. The modern trend has been to cultivate contacts with MPs and for MPs to take consultancies with commercial organisations. Labour MPs are frequently sponsored by trade unions, and some MPs, mainly Conservative, are associated with business interests, either as directors or as consultants. An intervention from the MP will be expected when the subject of discussion concerns areas where the pressure or interest group has a direct interest. As mentioned earlier, members are required to declare any such connections on a Register of Members' Interests.

As we review the parliamentary stages of government legislation, it is worth noting that Bills can be introduced in either the House of Commons or the House of Lords. The initial stage for legislation is called the first reading. This simply marks the announcement of the publication of the Bill. The principles contained in the Bill will be debated by the assembled House at the next stage, which is referred to as the second reading. The second reading is the main opportunity for MPs to debate the issues of principle contained in the proposal. If there is disagreement on the principles of the Bill, amendments may be put forward and a vote will take place at the end of the debate. While MPs have a limited opportunity during the debate to criticise the Bill, it should be recognised that it is extremely unusual for a government with an overall majority in the House of Commons to lose a vote on a division following the second reading. However, the minority government of Theresa May (2017–19) not only lost 28 votes but was forced to make concessions on other flagship bills. Defeat on a major platform of the government's legislative programme would usually result in a vote of no confidence (see Chapter 6).[57]

---

[56] J Smookler, 'Making a Difference? The Effectiveness of Pre-Legislative Scrutiny' [2006] *Parliamentary Affairs* 522; *The Briefing Paper Issues in Law Making, Number 5: Pre-Legislative Scrutiny* (Hansard Society, 2004).

[57] M Russell, *The Parliamentary Battle over Brexit* (Oxford, Oxford University Press, 2023).

After a Bill has surmounted the hurdle of being approved by a vote of the whole House, it moves on to the committee stage. This is when the Bill is normally considered by a public bill committee (formerly known as standing committees), although Bills of major constitutional importance (eg European Communities Bill 1972) are considered by a committee of the whole House. There is a different emphasis at this point, as the public bill committee concentrates on examining the provisions in much greater detail, clause by clause. A public bill committee comprises between 16 and 50 members, and the parties are represented on the committee according to their strength in the House of Commons. As a result, the government (assuming it has a majority in the Commons) is guaranteed a majority on the committee. It is also relevant to mention that the whips (who are the party managers) decide on the MPs who will serve on these committees. Members who toe the party line will be favoured, and those who tend to be independently minded will be kept off these committees. This has a significant impact on the approach of standing committees, as the whips are prepared to use their influence to keep the proposals of the government intact in situations where there is opposition to a Bill, and where amendments are likely to be suggested by the committee but resisted by the government. There are occasions when committees may be able to persuade a minister to change or reconsider parts of a Bill, but it is clear that standing committees have limited success in securing modifications from the government. Of course, the opposition may simply use the committee as a platform to present its alternative view and to inconvenience ministers.

The effectiveness of public bill committees has been criticised for reasons other than the tendency towards partisanship just alluded to. Unlike the 'subject' committees that perform this function in the Scottish Parliament, public bill committees are non-specialist, in the sense that MPs assigned to public bill committees are not required to have any special interest or expert knowledge of the subject matter of the legislation. Moreover, public bill committees are not equipped with support staff able to undertake research or to provide the committee with advice. Given that the prime role of such committees is to improve the quality of the measure in question these are serious deficiencies which might result in overlooking potential weaknesses and a failure to introduce carefully considered amendments.[58]

---

[58] J Simpson Caird and D Oliver, 'Parliament's Constitutional Standards' in A Horne and A Le Sueur (eds), *Parliament Legislation and Accountability* (Oxford, Hart Publishing, 2016).

The report stage follows the committee stage and this is when the amended Bill is brought before the whole House. It is still possible for additional amendments to be made by ministers and for the opposition to suggest amendments at this stage. After the completion of the report stage, the Bill receives its third reading. At this point verbal amendments may still be made. There can be short debates at the third reading stage, and the opposition can oppose the Bill by forcing a vote.

After a Bill has successfully negotiated its passage through one House, it is sent to the other where it passes through the same stages. The procedures for the consideration of Bills in the House of Lords are broadly similar to those in the Commons. The committee stage of legislation is different, as in the Lords it will be considered by the whole House. One of the main arguments for retaining a second chamber has been because of the performance of the House of Lords as a revising body for legislation. There are several reasons for this.[59] The life peers, who are, in the main, the working members of the House of Lords, include leading members of the community and politicians. Although many may be past the peak of their careers, these peers will have specialist expertise and, in the case of politicians, useful experience of Parliament and government gained prior to their 'elevation' to the House of Lords. In addition, the House of Lords has more time to devote to detailed consideration of legislation. This element is especially important, as the procedural devices to curtail discussion and debate do not apply in the same way in the Upper House. Perhaps the biggest advantage over the Commons is that the party machine, operating through the whips, is much less effective in the Lords. Peers are more independently minded because failure to support the party line will not affect career prospects. The members are appointed for life, and thus have no election looming over the horizon, and the composition of the Lords is no longer skewed towards one party, as it used to be.[60] The upshot is that since the abolition of most hereditary peers in 1999 the government has suffered defeats in the House of Lords with increasing regularity (for example, a striking 1649 times between 1999 and 2012), and legislation will frequently be amended during its passage through the House of Lords.[61] If this occurs, the amended Bill returns to the Commons, where the Bill may be accepted by

---

[59] The Legislative Process: The Passage of Bills Through Parliament, House of Lords Select Committee on the Constitution, 24th Report of Session 2017–19, 8 July 2019, HL 393, 13.

[60] See M Russell, *The Contemporary House of Lords: Westminster Bicameralism Revived* (Oxford: Oxford University Press, 2013) 131ff.

[61] Ibid 135.

the Commons in its amended form. At this point negotiation is possible between the two Houses over the final form of the Bill. The Commons may simply reject the amendments and return the Bill to the House of Lords for approval.[62] If the House of Lords is unwilling to accept the Bill, it has the option of invoking its powers under the Parliament Acts 1911 and 1949 which will delay the legislation for one year. The power is hardly ever used.[63] The rarity of the application of the Parliament Act is partly because of the Salisbury convention which usually means that the House of Lords will not obstruct legislation introduced as part of an election manifesto commitment. However, there are occasions when government Bills are substantially amended through the intervention of the House of Lords.[64]

It will be apparent that sufficient time needs to be allocated to legislation for Parliament to adequately perform its function as a revising body For instance, public bill committees should be given an opportunity to turn their attention to all the important clauses of a Bill. There is an obvious tension which arises. This is because the government will be keen to expedite its legislative programme in order to ensure that as many of its Bills as possible are fitted into the parliamentary session, while the opposition, which will often be resistant to the character of the changes proposed in a government Bill, could use the revising process as a means of blocking its progress. In addition, there is evidence to suggest that a discernible trend towards fast tracking government legislation has reduced the quality of parliamentary scrutiny.[65]

A number of procedural rules are available to facilitate the passage of legislation and these tend to operate in favour of the government. The *closure* shortens debate by allowing a vote to be taken but this requires the support of 100 members to apply. The *guillotine* involves the allocation of a strict timetable for the debate of each part of the Bill. This agreement may mean that some clauses are not discussed at all. The *kangaroo* at report stage enables only specified clauses to be selected for discussion. The application of these procedures depends on co-operation between government and opposition. A report published by the Constitution

---

[62] R Whitaker, 'Ping-Pong and Policy Influence: Relations between the Lords and Commons, 2005–6' [2006] *Parliamentary Affairs* 536.

[63] The last occasion was in regard to the Hunting Act 2004. See the discussion in Chapter 3 of *Jackson v Attorney-General* [2005] UKHL 56.

[64] See Lord Norton and L Maer, 'Relationship Between the Two Houses' in A Horne and G Drewry (eds), *Parliament and the Law*, 2nd edn (Oxford, Hart Publishing, 2018).

[65] M Russell, 'Should We Be Worried About the Decline of Parliamentary Scrutiny?' [2025] *Public Law* 31–57 at 35ff.

Society has expressed concern that the Modernisation Committee of the House of Commons is not addressing the failure of Parliament to sufficiently scrutinise both legislation and public expenditure.[66]

The requirement of maintaining a majority in Parliament is a feature of the parliamentary system which the UK shares with Italy but, of course, the United States has an altogether different system. A President can and often does have a hostile majority in Congress. The struggle by a President to get legislation through Congress may result in gridlock but, although this might have a bearing on the effectiveness of the Federal government, it does not threaten the continuance of the government in office.[67]

Private Members' Bills and Private Bills

Backbench MPs have limited opportunities to introduce legislation on their own initiative. There is an annual ballot for gaining a place high up in the queue. These Private Members' Bills (PMBs) undergo a similar procedure in both Houses to government legislation but any such proposals depend upon first having 100 sympathetic members to get through the second reading stage and the government allocating sufficient time for the Bill to pass through Parliament. This is the case even when the measure has considerable support. Important reforms, usually cutting across traditional party lines, have been introduced using PMBs, for example, the bill which legalised homosexuality.[68] However, MPs voted recently to circumvent normal procedure under Standing Order 14(1) which gives precedence to government business. This tactic laid the way for the introduction of PMBs designed to delay Brexit, and at the same time, it provides an illustration of the assertiveness of the House of Commons vis-à-vis the government under the minority Conservative government (2017–19).[69]

Unlike Public Bills and PMBs, Private Bills are introduced to grant benefits or impose obligations on a specifically defined class of persons or to a particular private company or public body. Equally, Private Bills may be used to authorise specific works or activities in a particular area. For example, the Channel Tunnel rail link between the Kent coast and

---

[66] Blick and Govan (n 36) 17.
[67] M Tushnet, *The Constitution of the United States of America: A Contextual Analysis*, 2nd edn (Oxford, Hart Publishing, 2015) ch 2.
[68] See the Sexual Offences Act 1967.
[69] See European Union (Withdrawal) Act 2019.

central London was made possible by virtue of a Private Bill. These measures are subject to a somewhat different procedure in Parliament to enable objections to be heard, but they must pass through both Houses and receive the royal assent.

The Demise of English Votes for English Laws (EVEL)

Since devolution, the legislative role of the Westminster Parliament has been affected by the so-called 'West Lothian question'. The problem is that, since the devolved parts of the UK acquired their own Parliament/Assemblies and executives with powers over devolved matters, MPs at Westminster from Scotland, Wales, and Northern Ireland could vote on policy areas affecting England, while English MPs no longer had voting rights over devolved competences. Devolution has modified the role of Westminster MPs representing constituencies in Scotland, Wales, and Northern Ireland because local constituents are more likely to turn to members of the devolved bodies to deal with problems concerning devolved matters coming under the devolved executives – for example, agriculture, education, environment, housing, and health. A Scottish constituent is therefore much more likely to go through a Member of the Scottish Parliament if help is needed with resolving a devolved matter. Thus the workload of Scottish MPs to Westminster has been much reduced.

The government elected in May 2015 sought, at least partly, to address this issue by changing the internal procedure in the Westminster Parliament for the passage of government legislation affecting England. While EVEL applied (2015–21), bills designated by the Speaker as an English Bill went through an extra Grand Committee stage (comprising of only English MPs) in the House of Commons. This Grand Committee could amend or veto the legislation before the bill proceeded to the report stage, taken by the whole House.[70] Such a change which had been introduced without enabling legislation was controversial and proved difficult to implement. For instance, it raised difficult and potentially controversial questions for the Speaker to answer in defining what constituted an England only bill. Further, the Scottish Nationalists and Welsh Nationalists have been and continue to be a significant political force in Scotland and Wales but the involvement of their MPs (and other MPs elected in

---

[70] L Laurence Smyth, 'English Votes for English Laws' in A Horne and G Drewry (eds), *Parliament and the Law*, 2nd edn (Oxford, Hart Publishing, 2018), 207ff.

Scotland and Wales) at Westminster was in danger of being marginalised, turning Westminster increasingly into a Parliament for England. Moreover, the change suited Conservative governments which tended to win a substantial majority of the parliamentary constituencies in England and thereby commanded a routine majority on the English Grand Committee. (The wider impact of devolution is discussed further in Chapter 8.)

PARLIAMENT AS WATCHDOG

In this section of the chapter we will evaluate the oversight function of Parliament. Our focus turns to the mechanisms and procedures that have been formulated to undertake this crucial task and assess their effectiveness. It is worth considering as the discussion proceeds whether Parliament's main function is really as a legislative body or whether it is a body which effectively scrutinises the government. Since 2010 a number of important reforms have been introduced in an attempt to strengthen the authority of Parliament in the face of the government. The ability of Parliament to scrutinise the executive has been often undermined by party interests. For example, government whips on behalf of the party leadership have attempted to keep MPs from their own party with a reputation for independence of mind from serving on parliamentary committees.[71]

Parliamentary Questions

It has already been mentioned that parliamentary questions provide an important opportunity for individual members to raise matters on behalf of constituents. Backbenchers have a chance to interrogate the executive by framing oral questions that are directed at ministers. Questions may be tabled electronically and the answers are prepared by civil servants within the relevant department. Ministers take turns in providing answers on Monday to Thursdays. Such probing can potentially be a source of deep embarrassment to the government. Although routine questions make a significant contribution to executive oversight, media attention tends to be drawn towards PM's Questions on Wednesdays

---

[71] See the failure to secure the selection of the preferred candidate of the government as chair of the joint Intelligence and Security Committee in 2020: https://www.institutefor government.org.uk/blog/battle-chair-intelligence-and-security-committee.

which tends to focus on contentious topical issues and often features a clash between government and opposition. For example, the questioning of PM Thatcher by a Labour MP over the sinking of the Argentinian warship, the *General Belgrano*, during the Falklands conflict, revealed that the vessel was in fact heading away from the British forces, not towards them, as Parliament had previously been led to believe. There are important limitations, however, that reduce the ability of MPs adequately to fulfil their ostensible function of holding the executive to account at question time. First, the balloting procedure which determines whether a question is chosen for oral reply is determined by luck and not according to the gravity or relevance of the matter raised. Second, only limited time is available, with ministers answering questions for around 60 minutes each day except Fridays. Third, questions are limited to a narrow departmental remit. Fourth, compared to MPs who may rely on government sources for information related to questions, ministers are at an advantage as they are supported by civil servants and may be able to choose whether to release sensitive information into the public domain.

Departmental Select Committees

Departmental select committees were established in 1979 to oversee the work of the major government departments. There were originally 14 of these committees but there are now 21. The committees consist of 11 MPs, with the parties represented according to their relative strength in the House of Commons, which means that the governing party will have a majority on the committee. In fact, select committees should be regarded as an important extension of ministerial responsibility, helping to keep track of what ministers do with their responsibility for their departments and other agencies. Unlike the courts, which deal with ultra vires executive action or the abuse of power, the committees are at an advantage in that they can have an informal influence on the formative stage of policy-making, examining at their discretion political, social, and economic issues as they arise.[72]

The departmental select committees have been compared to those within the US system.[73] However, there are substantial differences in their structure and effectiveness. With regard to structure, a central characteristic

---

[72] R Kelly, 'Select Committees: Powers and Functions' in A Horne, G Drewry, and D Oliver (eds), *Parliament and the Law* (Oxford, Hart Publishing, 2013).

[73] F Mount, *The British Constitution Now* (London, Mandarin, 1992) 186.

of the separation of powers under the US constitution is the way the legislature keeps check on the executive by means of Congressional committees. Although their wider reputation has been based on a number of scandals that have been revealed by special investigations (the most notable of all being Watergate in 1973/4), the committees undertake, on a day-to-day basis, the more routine tasks of initiating policy and scrutinising the executive, with their specific terms of reference being administration, policy, and expenditure. In fact, the Congressional committees are powerful bodies which are generously funded and equipped with full-time staff. They have formidable powers to summon before them papers or persons, including Secretaries of State (ministers) and top civil service officials and advisers. The Scottish Parliament and Welsh Assembly (now Parliament) have introduced subject committees which combine the role of standing and select committees. The declared objective is for specialisation to achieve a degree of expertise in a particular area. This also addresses a criticism of the departmental committees working outside the parliamentary legislative process.

In the UK system, Parliament (within the existing framework of the Westminster model) has always assumed the crucial role of acting as a formal check on the executive. It became apparent to many MPs in the 1970s that to perform this task more effectively the place of select committees had to be revised and their inquisitorial powers needed to be strengthened. The new departmental committees were to have a clear function, that being to shadow all the main departments of state, with the aim of examining expenditure, administration, and policy. To assist in their investigative role these committees have limited capacity to employ a staff of expert advisers, mainly on a part-time basis. Serving on these committees provides backbench MPs with an opportunity to be involved in the policy process. These committees also promote a degree of co-operation between MPs of all parties who may identify with the broad objectives of executive accountability. On the other hand, it might be argued that a more adversarial approach would provide greater accountability.

Since 1979, with each new Parliament following a general election, the departmental select committees have been reconstituted. Each is chaired by a member from one of the two largest parties, usually the government party. The committee then decides on appropriate subjects for scrutiny, although it should be noted that this very selectivity can be a source of weakness as well as strength. These subjects will include major matters of policy as well as more detailed administrative questions. It will be immediately apparent that the departmental select committees have a crucial advantage in comparison to public bill committees, in that they have the means to conduct more in-depth inquisitorial investigations which can give them considerable information not available to the mass of individual MPs, rather than being dependent, as these are, on asking particular questions and relying on the co-operation and goodwill of ministers and officials. This information will include not simply evidence before the committee, but also written submissions, departmental (official) briefs, visits (at home and abroad), informal meetings with non-parliamentarians, etc. The published reports of the departmental select committees, and their accompanying volumes of memoranda, provide MPs with a countervailing source of information to that of ministers and the executive departments, and in that sense the committees are of importance in holding ministers to account and in questioning civil servants. One important shortcoming is that the reports of the departmental committees are not debated by the House of Commons as a matter of course.

Ministers and senior civil servants appear regularly before the department select committees. However, ministers (and MPs and peers) can refuse to attend (unless charged with contempt of Parliament and required by a vote of the House of Commons to do so). Nevertheless, it can be problematic requiring attendance when a minister or official refuses to appear before a committee, apparently in defiance of Parliament. One notable instance concerned the director of the Brexit Vote Leave Campaign (Dominic Cummings) in 2016 who declined to give evidence at the Brexit Fake News inquiry in 2018 held by the Digital, Culture, Media and Sport Committee. Although the matter was referred to the House of Commons privileges committee who considered the issue of enforcement, there was no direct power short of a vote of the whole House to compel the individual concerned to provide evidence before the committee.[74]

The Cabinet Office guidance to civil servants who are summoned to appear before these committees was revised following the Scott Report (for further discussion, see Chapter 6). These guidelines encourage officials to be helpful but specifically rule out disclosing advice given to ministers or inter-departmental exchanges on policy issues; disclosing the level at which decisions were taken; and discussing the work of Cabinet committees or their decisions. Furthermore, civil servants are not permitted to express their own views on matters of policy. This supports the view that policy emanates from the politicians and not from civil

---

[74] P Evans, 'Will They Come When You Do Call for Them? Should Select Committees Have Real Power to Compel Evidence?' (London, Hansard Society, 10 June 2021).

servants. To some extent limitations as to time and resources result in a restricted focus of attention and, in consequence, an invariably selective impact on the issues of the day. Dedicated research based on the detailed analysis of the reports of select committees suggests that these committees are increasingly active and that about 40 per cent of their recommendations are accepted by government. Of course, they are less likely to be successful in influencing or challenging flagship policies based on the government's manifesto commitments.[75]

Wright Reforms: Standing Up to the Executive

As scrutinisers of the executive, departmental select committees were intended when introduced in 1979 to be more independent from the government than standing committees. This position was to be achieved by establishing a committee of selection to nominate members thus minimising the influence of the party whips. However, this situation did not long survive the partisanship that dominates the way Parliament operated, and the whips were regularly consulted on the membership of these committees. Indeed, government whips sought to remove the chairs of the Transport Committee and the Foreign Affairs Committee after the 2001 general election. Both of these chairs had earned a reputation for independence and presided over committees that had made reports that were critical of aspects of government policy. However, the failure to re-nominate MPs held in high esteem by colleagues caused a minor rebellion on the backbenches and their re-appointment was eventually confirmed. The situation concerning the election of chairs of select committees changed following the report presided over by Tony Wright MP which had been set up in July 2009 as a response to the MPs' expenses scandal.[76] The report investigated ways in which the House of Commons might be able to resist the dominance of the executive. The election by alternative vote of the chairs of select committees by a secret ballot of the whole House was one of the key recommendations of this report implemented in July 2010. Also, each party now elects its quota of the members of every select committee by secret ballot. The party composition of these committees reflects pro rata party support in the House of Commons. Backbench MPs continue to assert their independence. For example, in

---

[75] M Russell and M Benton, *Selective Influence: The Policy Impact of House of Commons Select Committees* (London, Constitutional Unit, 2011) 7.
[76] House of Commons Reform Committee 'Rebuilding the House', HC 1117 (2008–09).

2020 the preferred nominee of PM Johnson to chair the influential Intelligence and Security Committee which oversees national security was defeated by another backbench Conservative MP. In consequence, the new committee chair, despite being a well-respected MP, was expelled from the Conservative parliamentary party as a punishment. This obvious snub to the authority of the PM suggests that MPs exercise their own initiative when voting and that the party hierarchy would be wise to consult the views of their own backbenchers before endorsing a candidate.[77]

The introduction of a Backbench Business Committee was another significant change that should also strengthen the hand of backbench MPs, as this committee has responsibility for scheduling 35 days of debate. The conferral of these powers on ordinary MPs should mean that in the future the government will have significantly less clout in agenda setting. In 2003 the House of Commons decided that the chairs of the departmental select committees should receive an additional salary, currently £16,500 pa, in recognition of the additional workload the job entails. Serving on and chairing these important committees now provides an alternative career structure for MPs not reaching the front ranks of government or opposition.

The Modernisation Committee of the House of Commons recommended that departmental select committees should have a much extended role and perform all of the following tasks: consider major policy initiatives; consider government responses to major emerging issues; propose changes where evidence persuades the committee that recent policy requires amendment; conduct pre-legislative scrutiny of Bills; examine and report on main estimates, annual expenditure plans, and annual resource accounts; monitor performance against targets in the public service agreements; take evidence from each responsible departmental minister at least annually; take evidence from independent regulators and inspectorates; consider the reports of Executive Agencies; examine treaties within their subject areas; and consider major appointments made by a Secretary of State. In order to enhance the transparency of the process a number of committees have since adopted the practice, with the co-operation of the relevant government department, of holding pre-appointment hearings before certain important public appointments are confirmed.[78] The effectiveness of these committees might be

---

[77] 'Senior Tory kicked out of party after intelligence committee coup', *Financial Times*, 15 July 2020; 'What Chris Grayling rejection as intelligence committee chair reveals', *The Spectator*, 15 July 2020.

[78] See eg Appointments of Michael Cohrs and Alastair Clark to the Interim Financial Policy Committee, Fourteenth Report of Session 2010–12, HC 1125, 7 June, 2011.

further improved. A report by the Liaison Committee of the House of Commons in 2019 emphasises the importance of improved follow up to ensure the implementation of the recommendations of departmental select committees, also stressing the need for higher quality departmental responses which need to be produced within tight deadlines.[79] Given the overlap between policy areas, the importance of the coordination of the scrutiny function of the departmental committees and between the committees of the House of Commons and the House of Lords arises as another relevant issue which needs addressing.[80]

These committees tend to work more effectively at times when there is a narrow government majority, as this encourages a greater degree of inter-party co-operation. For example, in the 2010–11 parliamentary session the departmental select committees for Culture, Media and Sport and for Home Affairs played a prominent part in further uncovering aspects of the *News of the World* hacking scandal. The investigatory role of these committees was well demonstrated in July 2011. Rupert and James Murdoch, Rebekah Brooks, the Metropolitan Police Commissioner, and other senior police officers were questioned by MPs before a live television audience in the style of the 1976 Watergate hearings in the USA. In tandem with the public inquiry chaired by Lord Justice Leveson, the reports from these committees helped shape the official response to the alleged misconduct of the media and the Metropolitan Police.

Public Accounts Committee and National Audit Office

The Public Accounts Committee (PAC) is one of the oldest and most prestigious parliamentary committees. Despite the fact that the scope of government was then much more limited than is now the case, WE Gladstone, as Chancellor of the Exchequer, recognised the need to provide a mechanism of accountability for public expenditure. The PAC was first created in 1861, while the office of Comptroller and Auditor General (described below) followed in 1866. In essence, this framework has survived to the present day.[81]

---

[79] 'The effectiveness and influence of the select committee system' House of Commons Liaison Committee, Fourth Report of Session 2017–19, HC 1860, 9 September 2019, 118ff.
[80] P Leyland, 'The House of Lords Faces up to Brexit' in R Albert, A Baraggia, and C Fasone (eds), *Constitutional Reform of National Legislatures* (Cheltenham, Elgar, 2019) 105.
[81] See J McEldowney, 'The Control of Public Expenditure' in J Jowell and D Oliver (eds), *The Changing Constitution*, 7th edn (Oxford, Oxford University Press, 2011) 355ff.

The House of Commons exercises some degree of control over government finance through the PAC. The PAC, more than most other parliamentary committees, operates in a less-partisan, non party-political way and consists of 15 MPs, the chair being a senior member of the opposition, usually with experience as a Treasury minister. The PAC's remit is limited to the audited accounts of government departments. Ministers and departmental accounting officers (usually the senior civil servant, called a permanent secretary) appear before the PAC to be questioned, even interrogated, on issues arising from the annual audit of departmental accounts. Further, the introduction of television cameras in the House of Commons has brought these proceedings, and the important issues examined, to the wider public. Reports prepared by the PAC each year (30–40 in number) are always debated annually by the House of Commons. The government will be expected to respond to any criticisms made by taking any necessary remedial action.

The PAC is the only parliamentary committee which has comprehensive administrative support in the form of the National Audit Office (NAO), which is headed by the Comptroller and Auditor General (C & AG).[82] The Comptroller used to be appointed by the government of the day, but the National Audit Act 1983 modified the status of the Comptroller and that of the staff (around 750), establishing the post as an officer of the House of Commons. The method of appointment now is by means of a commission, of which the PM and the chair of the PAC are both members. This reinforces the element of independence in the system of accountability. The point to note is that the Comptroller and Auditor General and the NAO are independent of government, and certify the accounts of all government departments and a wide range of other public sector bodies. Most of the PAC's work consists in examining the value for money (VFM) reports undertaken by the NAO, which are intended to measure economy, efficiency, and effectiveness of departments and other bodies in the way they have used their resources. The NAO works closely with the PAC, examining the effectiveness with which governmental bodies implement their assigned policy goals. Reports are based on the annual audit of all government departments. They are passed to the PAC where the evidence contained therein can be used effectively as a tool with which to probe into the details of expenditure, and this gives the reports of the PAC added authority.

---

[82] The National Audit Office reports are available online at www.nao.org.uk/.

A widely publicised example concerned serious delays that occurred in issuing passports in 1999. This problem was caused by the introduction of a new computer system. The backlog led to much anxiety and inconvenience for members of the public who had booked summer holidays abroad. In June 1999 the Passport Agency had around 565,000 applications awaiting processing and applications were taking on average 50 days. The NAO immediately reported to Parliament, and the Committee of Public Accounts compiled evidence largely based on its report. It was acknowledged that the Agency's financial objective had been to recover, via the passport fee, the full cost of passport services but the NAO went on to estimate that the cost of the additional measures taken by the Passport Agency to deal with the manifest failures in implementation amounted to £12.6 million.[83] There have been numerous instances of strongly critical investigations both by the NAO and the PAC. To take a more recent example, in 2005 the PAC investigated the Department for Work and Pensions, concentrating on fraud and error in the benefits system amounting to £3 billion. The PAC recommended simplification of the benefits system, introduction of benchmarking, and measuring performance against other comparable organisations.[84]

Although the PAC and the NAO have a crucial part to play in the process of scrutiny, they are concerned only with past expenditure, that is, on funds that have already been allocated. Essentially, this auditing work, although very important, is Parliament looking over its shoulder at items of expenditure with a paramount concern for the efficient and economical use of public money.[85]

Parliamentary Scrutiny of Delegated Legislation

The pressure on parliamentary time has given rise to an increasing trend towards the delegation of power to the executive. Delegated legislation is published and laid before Parliament before it is introduced, but most of these measures will automatically come into effect after 40 days, unless a challenge is made. The parliamentary Joint Committee on Statutory Instruments can bring to the attention of Parliament measures over which

---

[83] National Audit Office, *United Kingdom Passport Agency: The Passport Delays of Summer 1999*, HC 812, 1998/99.

[84] Public Accounts Committee, *Fourth Report: Fraud and Error in Benefit Expenditure*, HC 411, 2005/06.

[85] C Lee and P Larkin, 'Financial Control and Scrutiny' in A Horne and G Drewry (eds), *Parliament and the Law*, 2nd edn (Oxford, Hart Publishing, 2018) 339ff.

it has concern but it does not have any power to challenge such measures. The ease with which delegated rules can be introduced further illustrates the degree of executive dominance over Parliament.[86] The use of skeleton legislation which allows ministers and their officials to draw up sub-rules has become widespread as a means of dealing with technical detail. The cumulative effect has been to give more broad-based powers to ministers and to officials. The trend towards giving very widely drawn powers in skeleton legislation and so-called 'Henry VIII clauses' was discernible in the Deregulation and Contracting Out Act 1994, which allowed the minister responsible to: 'repeal or amend any Act which authorises or requires the imposition of a burden on any trade, business or profession'. Even more extreme, the Legislative and Regulatory Reform Bill which went before Parliament 2005–06 proposed in its original form to give ministers powers to alter any law passed by Parliament. (This clause was modified following strong objections.) Brexit continued this trend and has created an additional burden for Parliament. The enabling legislation[87] allowed for the selective disapplication of EU law and included Henry VIII clauses granting ministers wide powers to amend existing retained EU law.[88] But also the Brexit bills provided limited scope for parliamentary scrutiny.[89] In short, the volume of delegated legislation, and the powers conferred as a consequence, has contributed to a discernible shift in the balance of power from the legislature to the executive.[90]

E-Petitions and Popular Democracy

E-petitions have been introduced as a way for the public to raise popular concerns before government and Parliament. At least six signatures are required to initiate the process. The government responds to all petitions receiving more than 10,000 signatures and any petition which attracts more than 100,000 signatures will be considered for debate in the House of Commons. For example, a petition to stop allowing immigrants into the UK which had 200,000 signatures was debated by the

---

[86] AL, Young, *Unchecked Power: How Recent Constitutional Reforms are threatening UK Democracy* (Bristol, Bristol University Press, 2024) 65ff.

[87] See eg the EU (Withdrawal) Act 2018 and the Retained EU Law (Revocation and Reform) Act 2023.

[88] European Union (Withdrawal Agreement) Act 2020, Sch 4.

[89] T Poole, 'The Executive in Public Law' in J Jowell and C O'Cinneide (eds), *The Changing Constitution*, 9th edn (Oxford, Oxford University Press, 2019) 196ff.

[90] A Tucker, 'Parliamentary Scrutiny of Delegated Legislation' in A Horne and G Drewry (eds), *Parliament and the Law*, 2nd edn (Oxford, Hart Publishing, 2018) 363ff.

House of Commons in October 2015.[91] An 11-member Petitions Select Committee was established by the House of Commons in 2015 to oversee the running of e-petitions and press for action if there is an inadequate response by government or the public body concerned to a topic that has been raised.[92]

The Parliamentary and Health Service Ombudsman

The office of the Parliamentary and Health Service Ombudsman (PHSO) was introduced by the Parliamentary Commissioner Act of 1967 to plug a manifest gap in dealing with grievances relating to the civil service and governmental agencies exposed by cases such as Crichel Down discussed in Chapter 6.[93] The main function of the PHSO is to investigate cases of maladministration (not actually defined in the Act) referred to the PHSO by MPs, but no actual power to grant a binding legal remedy is given to the PO. Nevertheless, in most cases the recommendations of the PO are followed by the department or public body concerned. The PHSO has formidable investigatory powers and a staff to assist with inquiries. The remit of the PO, first set out in Schedules 1 and 2 to the 1967 Act (later extended by the Parliamentary and Health Services Commissioners Act 1987), applies to most government and quasi-governmental bodies. The filtering of complaints through MPs was insisted upon during the passage of the original bill in order that the role of backbench MPs would not be usurped, and it is certainly true that MPs continue to pursue matters against government departments on behalf of their constituents and often proceed more quickly than the formal approach of the PHSO. Moreover, this lack of direct access has been seen by many critics as a weakness. The filter restriction no longer applies to health service complaints. According to the published figures for 2024–25 the PHSO dealt with 124,000 enquiries and decided 9,085 complaints following primary or detailed investigation.[94] The modest numbers investigated given the huge number of decisions in the public domain show that the trend has been to selectively conduct in-depth investigation. Moreover, there have been high profile investigations by the PHSO which have resulted in awards

---

[91] https://petition.parliament.uk.
[92] www.parliament.uk/business/committees/committees-a-z/commons-select/petitions-committee/.
[93] P Leyland and G Anthony, *Textbook on Administrative Law*, 8th edn (Oxford, Oxford University Press, 2016) ch 6.
[94] The Ombudsman's Annual Report and Accounts 2024–25, HC 998.

of compensation in line with the PHSO's recommendations. For example in regard to losses suffered by householders through the building of the Channel Tunnel rail link. The reports of the PHSO are submitted to the Public Administration Select Committee of the House of Commons and are also laid before the House.[95] In *R (Bradley) v Secretary of State for Work and Pensions*[96] the decision to reject the PHSO's findings of maladministration and to reject her recommendations was successfully challenged by way of judicial review. Many thousands of policyholders had lost out because of misleading advice from the department but offering compensation to the many individuals affected in line with the PHSO's recommendations would have cost several billion. The case is of constitutional importance because the Court of Appeal considered the status of the ombudsman's role in relation to central government. The court found that the Secretary of State must proceed on the basis that the ombudsman's findings of injustice caused by maladministration are correct unless they are quashed in judicial review proceedings. And it was further held that the minister could not simply reject the ombudsman's findings because the minister preferred another view, he or she must have cogent reasons for doing so.

CONCLUSION

The ability of the executive to dominate the Westminster Parliament has been acknowledged by many commentators as a central feature of the legislative process.[97] Indeed, according to Bagehot the almost unbridled capacity to legislate was the 'efficient secret' of the (nineteenth century) constitution as it meant that an elected government could deploy its majority to implement its legislative programme.[98] But by the late twentieth century the government's stranglehold over Parliament was increasingly regarded as a systemic deficiency.[99] Not only can a majority government ensure through the party whips that legislation reaches the statute book, but the intensity of parliamentary scrutiny is often limited, and government legislation frequently

---

[95] 'The Ombudsman in Question: The Ombudsman's Report on Pensions and its Constitutional Implications', HC 1081, 2006.
[96] [2009] QB 114. See also *R (Equitable Members Action Group) v HM Treasury* [2009] EWHC 2495 (Admin).
[97] Lord Hailsham, *The Dilemma of Democracy* (London, Collins, 1978).
[98] W Bagehot, *The English Constitution* (London, Fontana, 1963) 65.
[99] F Mount, *British Constitution Now* (London, Mandarin, 1992) 217.

grants the executive sweeping delegated powers. In recent times, only in the absence of a government majority in the brief interlude between 2017–19 was Parliament able to flex its muscles to thwart the intentions of a weak government. The election of a majority government in 2019 and again in 2024 has led to the return of a powerful executive capable of dominating Parliament.[100] As we will see in the concluding chapter, addressing this issue would require root and branch reform to rebalance the constitution. Such reform would almost certainly include the introduction of a proportional element to the electoral system to reduce the predominance of any single party in the House of Commons, while at the same time reforming the House of Lords to transform it into an, at least partly, elected regional second chamber of some kind. On the positive side, it will be apparent from this discussion that procedural changes and reforms in composition have led to certain improvements in the performance of Parliament. For example, the introduction of departmental select committees shadowing government departments in 1979 undoubtedly re-enforced the effectiveness the House of Commons in overseeing government departments. Also, since the removal of most hereditary peers at the beginning of the millennium the less partisan but more expert House of Lords, despite its lack of democratic legitimacy, has performed a useful role in amending legislation and reporting on pressing questions not covered by the Commons.

FURTHER READING

Abraham A, 'Ombudsman as Part of the UK Constitution: A Contested Role?' (2008) 61 Parliamentary Affairs 206.

Brazier A and Fox R, 'Reviewing Select Committee Tasks and Modes of Operation' (2011) 64 Parliamentary Affairs 354.

Horne A and Drewry G, Parliament and the Law, 2nd edn (Oxford, Hart Publishing, 2018).

Horne A and Le Sueur A (eds), Parliament Legislation and Accountability (Oxford, Hart Publishing, 2016).

Johnson J, 'Select Committees: Powers and Functions' in A Horne and G Drewry (eds), Parliament and the Law, 2nd edn (Oxford, Hart Publishing, 2018).

Kelly, R, Hamlyn, M, and Gay O, 'The Law and the Conduct of Members of Parliament' in A Horne and G Drewry (eds), Parliament and the Law, 2nd edn (Oxford, Hart Publishing, 2018).

---

[100] V Bogdanor, *Beyond Brexit: Towards a British Constitution* (London, Tauris, 2019) 274.

Further reading

Lee C and Larkin P, 'Financial Control and Scrutiny' in A Horne and G Drewry (eds), Parliament and the Law, 2nd edn (Oxford, Hart Publishing, 2018).

Norton, P, 'Parliament' in J Jowell and C O'Cinneide (eds), The Changing Constitution, 9th edn (Oxford, Oxford University Press 2019).

Russell M, The Parliamentary Battle over Brexit (Oxford, Oxford University Press, 2023).

Russell M, Legislation at Westminster: Parliamentary Actors and influence in the Making of British Law (Oxford, Oxford University Press, 2017).

Russell, M, The Contemporary House of Lords: Westminster Bicameralism Revived (Oxford, Oxford University Press, 2013).

Tomkins A, 'What Is Parliament For?' in N Bamforth and P Leyland, Public Law in a Multi-Layered Constitution (Oxford, Hart Publishing, 2003).

6

Government and Executive

Prime Minister – Collective Cabinet Responsibility – Policy Formation – Government 'Spin' – Government Departments – Individual Ministerial Responsibility – Codes of Practice – The Scott Report – Freedom of Information – E-Government Europe

INTRODUCTION

THIS CHAPTER FOCUSES upon the conduct of central government in the UK. First we turn to the pinnacle of government in order to assess the role of the Prime Minister (PM), the Cabinet, and the government more widely. The second part of the chapter proceeds to consider the governmental mechanisms for the implementation of policy by considering the contribution of ministers, the civil service, and the emergence of a contract state. In terms of the exercise of constitutional power, it is helpful to view the UK political system as hierarchical, with the PM, and the Office at 10 Downing Street, at the apex of a triangle. At the next level we find the Cabinet Office, the departments of state, and then below this junior ministers responsible for particular policy domains. In turn, the entire machinery of government relies on a permanent civil service, which is, itself, hierarchical in structure. Once again, a central objective underpinning the discussion is to gauge how effectively the constitution in its current form is able to provide accountable government. The running of the executive branch relies heavily upon imprecise conventions (collective cabinet responsibility and individual ministerial responsibility) and informal rules rather than on enforceable constitutional laws. Between 2010 and 2019 the nation elected weak governments, lacking a decisive parliamentary majority. At the same time, deep-seated political division over Europe exerted enormous pressure on the interpretation, development, and application of pivotal constitutional rules and conventions.

THE PRIME MINISTER AND THE GOVERNMENT

In terms of the broader constitutional context we can see that the composition of Parliament is crucial to the emergence of any government.[1] In most cases the government is formed after a general election by the party or parties capable of commanding a majority in the House of Commons. The predominance of the elected House of Commons over the House of Lords has given rise to the recognition of a strong convention dating back to 1902, that in order to be accountable to the electorate, the PM must be a member of the House of Commons.[2] If one party has an overall majority the leader of that party in the House of Commons will be invited by the monarch to form a government and the leader will become the PM. The procedure for the change of government in the event of a hung Parliament with no party having a majority was put to the test following the 2010 general election. The guiding principle, according to the Cabinet Secretary, was to keep the Queen out of any political controversy. Gordon Brown as incumbent was entitled as PM to remain in 10 Downing Street while the parties negotiated to see what combination of MPs were capable of forming a government. Moreover, it would have been perfectly within the prerogative of the incumbent PM for the new Parliament to have met in order to test the opinion of the House of Commons.[3] After an agreement has been reached or a vote taken, the PM is in a position to continue, assuming the agreement includes the PM's party or the vote supports that party. However, if the incumbent is unsuccessful, then he or she will resign and recommend a successor. After failing informally to muster sufficient support from other parties to stage a vote PM Brown resigned on 11 May 2010, four days after the election, and recommended to the Queen that David Cameron be appointed as his successor.[4] This means that '[p]olitics continue to be organised around the linchpin principle of the Westminster system – the need for governments to secure and

---

[1] R Brazier, *Choosing a Prime Minister: The Transfer of Power in Britain* (Oxford, Oxford University Press, 2020) chapters 1 and 6.
[2] In order to take over as PM in 1963, the Earl of Home (Sir Alec Douglas Home) renounced his title under the Peerages Act 1963, and with it, the right to sit in the House of Lords.
[3] V Bogdanor, *The Coalition and the Constitution* (Oxford, Hart Publishing, 2011) 21.
[4] In the meantime David Cameron had negotiated a coalition deal with Nick Clegg, leader of the Liberal Democrats. See B Young, 'Formation of the Con-Lib Dem Coalition' in R Hazell and B Young (eds), *The Politics of Coalition: How the Conservative-Liberal Democrat Government Works* (Oxford, Hart Publishing, 2012) 30.

retain the confidence of the popularly elected house'.[5] Then, the first job the PM has to perform following his or her appointment is to select a government from the MPs elected to the House of Commons and the peers who are members of the House of Lords.

Prime Minister: Rise and Fall

The PM has no job description and no direct personal mandate from the electorate, rather, the source of the PM's political authority derives from his or her place as leader of the party in office. All major political parties elect a leader with the assumption that, should the party emerge victorious at a general election by obtaining a majority of seats in the House of Commons, the leader will become the next PM. While in office, given the powers at their fingertips mentioned in the sections below, the office holder is in a position of enormous political power but this dominance is also fragile. Indeed, the experience of recent decades confirms that this power may be challenged from within the party. The fall of Margaret Thatcher in 1990 demonstrated that it is possible for even the most powerful of PMs with a strong electoral mandate to lose the support of the parliamentary party and be forced from office. PM Thatcher contributed to her own downfall after more than 11 years in Downing Street. She not only accumulated many political enemies in her own party but also, in spite of the advice of colleagues, stubbornly continued with unpopular policies such as the introduction of the community charge (a form of local poll tax) and her personal hostility to the EU.[6] A Conservative Party leadership election procedure triggered by disaffected MPs generated the momentum to force her eventual resignation.

In 2022 PM Johnson also enjoyed a clear electoral mandate from the 2019 general election but his reputation for integrity and competence was steadily undermined during his premiership and this led to his eventual downfall. Ministers, including the PM, under the ministerial code[7] are meant to uphold good standards of government and they are under an overarching duty to comply with the law. In fact the PM with the support of his most senior civil servant, the Cabinet Secretary, has ultimate responsibility for enforcing the code and thereby protecting the

---

[5] Ibid, 23.
[6] P Hennessey, *The Prime Minister: The Office and Its Holders Since 1945* (London, Penguin, 2001) 433ff.
[7] Ministerial Code, November 2024, https://assets.publishing.service.gov.uk/media/672b46f5f03408fa7966d1d4/November_2024_-_Ministerial_Code.pdf.

constitution.[8] The 'Partygate' affair concerned his participation in, and knowledge of, excessive illegal workplace social gatherings in 10 Downing Street during the Covid lockdowns. After the PM appeared to have misled Parliament over these breaches, a report by a senior civil servant, Sue Gray, pointed to failures of leadership and judgement within No 10 and the Cabinet Office.[9] Johnson himself was served with a fixed penalty notice by the police. This criticism triggered requests from 54 Tory MPs for his resignation. The PM received sufficient votes (211) to temporarily survive a party vote of confidence by Conservative MPs. However, a scandal relating to the appointment of the Deputy Chief Whip, who had been confirmed in post by the PM notwithstanding briefings about the candidate's previous sexual misconduct, prompted a dramatic crumbling of support, with the resignation of a succession of his senior ministers, including the Chancellor of the Exchequer and Health Secretary. His position rapidly became untenable. Johnson's resignation on in July 2022 resulted in a leadership contest not a general election. Truss as the winner assumed the premiership in September 2022.

While Johnson's administration was repeatedly discredited by the personal conduct of the PM and other ministers, the short lived administration that followed (43 days) disregarded fundamental rules of financial prudence. Truss as PM with her Chancellor Kwarteng, despite lacking a direct electoral mandate, attempted to improve the political fortunes of the Conservative government by a policy intended to promote economic growth. This policy called for unfunded tax cuts, mainly favouring business, while capping energy prices. In the absence of plans to drastically reduce public expenditure such an initiative would have caused a substantial unfunded budget deficit. The mini-budget setting out the policy triggered an immediate run on the pound and collapse of the financial markets. In turn, this prompted the replacement of the Chancellor followed by a humiliating policy U turn. Truss herself resigned as PM faced with a dramatic loss of support by Conservative MPs.[10] Another truncated party leadership contest resulted in the selection of PM Rishi Sunak. He assumed office, once again, without seeking an electoral mandate. As there is no official regulation of the leadership procedure the system adopted by the Conservative Party allows a limited

---

[8] 'Executive oversight and responsibility for the UK Constitution', *Select Committee on the Constitution*, 6th Report of Session 2024–25, HL Paper 72, 22ff.

[9] B Maddox, 'Sue Grey's report shows how Boris Johnson has damaged the office of the Prime Minister' *Institute of Government*, 25 May 2022.

[10] A Seldon, *Truss at 10: How Not to Be Prime Ministers* (London, Atlantic Books, 2025) 287ff.

number of signed up party members rather than MPs to decide who ultimately becomes PM when there is a leadership challenge.

Nature of the Office

Once established in office, there is considerable scope to pursue a personal style of leadership. Some PMs, for example John Major, favoured a more collegiate approach (a style referred to as *primus inter pares*) while others such as PMs Thatcher and Blair moulded the office around their own personality, and became known for a more presidential style of leadership (virtually equivalent to an elected absolute monarch). If we look back to trace the constitutional derivation of the post it will be apparent that the office of PM is not defined under the constitution or any Act of Parliament, and, in fact, it originates from the early eighteenth century, when the sovereign as chief executive found it increasingly convenient to rely on a small coterie of ministers. During the reign of George I (1714–27) a leading political figure in the guise of Sir Robert Walpole assumed primacy among the King's ministers with the monopolisation of power and patronage at the head of government in his or her official capacity as First Lord of the Treasury.[11] The incumbent needed to have not only the confidence of the sovereign, but also the ability to command majority support for the King in Parliament.[12] Walpole was only referred to pejoratively as 'Prime Minister', denoting the fact that he was regarded by rivals as the political favourite of a German-speaking King who had limited familiarity with British politics.

As leader of His Majesty's government a current PM assisted by the Cabinet Secretary (top civil servant) is expected to exercise a pivotal role in safeguarding the constitution which of course is not formalised.[13] Many key aspects are set out in the Cabinet Manual or in the codes of practice.[14] For instance, this task will involve ensuring that important constitutional conventions are applied correctly and that the values set out in the codes of practice (discussed below) governing the conduct of

---

[11] H Wilson, *A Prime Minister on Prime Ministers* (Summit Books, New York, 1977) 9ff.
[12] R Crossman, 'Introduction' in W Bagehot, *The English Constitution* (London, Fontana, 1963) 20–22.
[13] 'Executive oversight and responsibility for the UK Constitution', *Select Committee on the Constitution*, 6th Report of Session 2024–25, HL Paper 72, 22ff.
[14] www.instituteforgovernment.org.uk/explainer/cabinet-manual; 'Revision of the Cabinet Manual, House of Lords Select Committee on the Constitution, 6th Report of Session 2021–22, HL Paper 34.

ministers and civil servants are upheld. A notable innovation since the 2024 election has been the appointment of an Independent Adviser on Ministerial Standards to advise the PM and ministers about their adherence to the ministerial code.[15]

Many of the powers that the PM currently exercises are prerogative powers which were previously the personal prerogatives of the Crown. A prerogative of great importance is the right of the head of government to conduct international relations and negotiate treaties with other nations. This power can be limited by statute. In the first *Miller* case[16] the UK Supreme Court confirmed that the prerogative could not be used to trigger Brexit because it would deprive citizens of pre-existing statutory rights without any legislative authority (see Chapter 7). In addition, the prerogative includes extensive powers of patronage. Some appointments, such as appointments to the government, archbishops and bishops, and other honours, are entirely in the gift of the PM, while others are merely confirmed by the PM. These include life peerages,[17] appointments of the most senior civil servants, and senior judicial appointments.

Notwithstanding the different individual styles of leadership, the PM has a predominant role over the conduct of government, and this tended to increase during the course of the twentieth century. The fact that a PM usually has sole charge over appointing and dismissing ministers obviously means that he or she wields enormous power over the Cabinet and other ministers. Perhaps the most famous instance was PM Macmillan's reshuffle in 1962, often referred to as the 'Night of the Long Knives', which resulted in the sacking of a third of the Cabinet. Equally, a minister will be removed from office for obvious misconduct. For example, the Defence Secretary Gavin Williamson was sacked by PM May in 2019 for leaking classified information. However, under the 2010 coalition agreement PM Cameron was not able to dismiss any of the five Liberal Democrat cabinet members without the approval of Deputy PM Clegg. The reshuffle by PM May in 2017 after she failed to achieve a majority in the snap election was heavily constrained by the internal politics over Brexit within her party. In contrast, PM Johnson emerged in a stronger position to fashion a government reflecting his preferences after achieving an overall majority of over 80 seats in the 2019 election. The PM has the capacity not only to change the complexion of the government

---

[15] Ministerial Code, Cabinet Office, November 2024, 10.

[16] *R (On the application of Miller) v Secretary of State for Exiting the European Union* [2017] UKSC 5.

[17] Recommendations for life peerages are now first made by the House of Lords Appointments Commission and approved by the PM.

by means of appointments that are made, but also to remould the institutional structures of government departments to suit the direction of policy (see below).

The PM presides over the government as chair of a Cabinet of up to 22 salaried senior ministers and has unique authority to call Cabinet meetings.[18] The Cabinet and its committees are the focal point of government decision-making. In theory, at least, the Cabinet is bound by the convention of collective cabinet responsibility (explained above). According to Bagehot, it was a combining committee: 'a hyphen which joins, a buckle which fosters, the legislative part of the State to the executive part of the State. In its origins it belongs to the one, in its functions it belongs to the other'.[19] Major policy issues are discussed at Cabinet, and conflicts between departments may be finally resolved over the Cabinet table, but key decisions may be taken in one of the many Cabinet committees which specialise in the various policy areas. The ability of a PM to dominate the Cabinet also arises because the PM is able to determine the composition of, and who chairs, these committees.[20] The PM will preside over the most important committees and is able to set the agenda for Cabinet meetings. This means that decisions of great importance may be reached by Cabinet committee and effectively kept within the PM's inner circle of associates and advisers without providing an opportunity for discussion by the full Cabinet.

Collective Cabinet Responsibility

The convention of collective cabinet responsibility can make an important contribution to the authority of the PM. This constitutional convention at the heart of government originates historically from the need for the head of the government to present the Crown with unified advice on matters of policy.[21] The convention allows for the fact that the decision-making process will be controversial, with ministers frequently expressing divergent views on any issue brought to Cabinet and its sub-committees for final decision. The convention demands confidentiality, as any dissenting opinions are expressed privately. At the end of the discussion, after a free and frank exchange has taken place, the PM, who normally chairs

---

[18] P Hennessey, *Whitehall*, 2nd edn (London, Pimlico, 2001) 306ff.
[19] W Bagehot, *The English Constitution* (London, Fontana, 1963) 68.
[20] www.gov.uk/government/publications/the-cabinet-committees-system-and-list-of-cabinet-committees.
[21] J Sharpe, 'Parliamentary Conventions' (The Constitution Society, 2020) 42ff.

the meeting, is responsible for identifying the feeling of the meeting and noting an agreed position. The ministerial code states that 'Decisions reached by the Cabinet or Ministerial Committees are binding on all members of the government'.[22] This convention means that the government as a whole is thus held accountable to Parliament for decisions made on matters of policy. It follows that if the House of Commons fails to express sufficient support for a major policy the government is likely to fall.[23]

The convention of collective responsibility dictates that a member of the Cabinet who during the discussion voiced opposition to the view that is finally adopted must accept the decision.[24] In theory, this requires the minster to vote and speak actively for the policy, or alternatively that the minister should resign.[25] The resignations of Cabinet ministers Robin Cook and Claire Short from the government of PM Blair over the policy to support the American invasion of Iraq in 2003 were such examples. However, since the 1970s the increasingly acrimonious debate over UK membership of the EU has exposed the limits of the doctrine of collective Cabinet responsibility to the extent that some influential commentators claim that it has been 'irretrievably weakened'.[26] This is largely because both main parties have contained a significant number of pro- and anti-European MPs (and peers) at all levels. As was mentioned in the introductory chapter, the issue of reconciling such divisions with collective responsibility arose in 1975 when PM Wilson decided to organise a referendum on whether the UK should remain a member of the European Economic Community (now EU). During the campaign, in order to minimise the political damage from the deep-rooted party divisions on this issue, an 'agreement to differ' was introduced by the PM, allowing individuals at variance with the official government position to campaign on the other side of the argument. What had been defended by a previous Cabinet Secretary as a key convention was waived (incidentally, not for the first time) on the understanding, first, that the convention still applied with respect to official government and parliamentary business,

---

[22] Ministerial code, Cabinet Office, November 2024, 5.3.
[23] One such example was the collapse in support for PM Chamberlain in 1940 over the conduct of World War II.
[24] Ministerial Code, Cabinet Office, November 2024, 4ff.
[25] Ministers at more junior levels of government will be expected to resign if unwilling to accept government policy.
[26] V Bogdanor, *Beyond Brexit: Towards a British Constitution* (London, IB Tauris, 2019) 134.

and second, that its application in delivering unanimity would resume once the result was announced.

For the 2016 Brexit referendum campaign PM Cameron proceeded on a similar basis by allowing individual ministers to dissent on this exceptional issue from the official pro-remain position, while maintaining their place in the government. This confirmed that the position since PM Wilson seems to be that the PM is able to modify or apply the doctrine at will, but, on this occasion, the deep divisions within the Conservative Party over the terms of Brexit meant that, in effect, collective Cabinet responsibility remained suspended under PM Theresa May. Indeed, the flood of resignations from May's government over disagreement with government policy, despite the intervention of party whips in Parliament in the attempt to secure a Brexit deal, demonstrates the limits of the convention in obtaining unanimity. Between 2017 and 2019 there were 35 ministerial resignations over Brexit, including five at cabinet level, before Mrs May herself finally announced her intention to stand down as PM. Furthermore, as mentioned earlier the downfall of PM Boris Johnson was precipitated by the resignation of senior cabinet ministers followed by other members of the government. The updated version of the ministerial code (2024) issued under PM Keir Starmer recognises the traditional application of the convention of Collective Cabinet Responsibility but prime ministerial toleration of dissent by ministers and its frequent suspension have undermined its effectiveness in promoting unified government.

Shaping Government Departments

The PM is not only able to reshuffle the team of ministers serving in the government, but he or she also has an apparently unlimited capacity to create and to reshape government departments.[27] In another context the accountability issue within departments, between government departments, and between departments, agencies, and other public bodies is determined by the distribution of functions for distinct policy areas. The exercise of this kind of control has the advantage of allowing a PM who has received a mandate from the electorate to fashion the administrative organs of the state to facilitate the policy objectives that are regarded as a priority. A good example, dating from the 1960s, was when PM Wilson created the Department of Economic Affairs to manage economic

---

[27] Ministerial Code, Cabinet Office, May 2010, 4.1.

planning and, then as its contribution to policy diminished, dispensed with the department in 1969.[28]

The Ministers of the Crown Act 1975 allows departmental re-organisation to be made by Order in Council, which is a form of delegated legislation. This provides scope for both transfers of functions and dissolutions of departments. There were many such changes introduced under PM Blair. For example, the Lord Chancellor's Department responsible for courts and judicial appointments was first designated the Department of Constitutional Affairs in 2003 to reflect responsibility for the introduction of devolution and the Human Rights Act, and then re-launched again in 2007 as the Ministry of Justice with additional responsibility for prisons transferred from the Home Office. At the height of the Covid-19 crisis in 2020, without prior consultation or referral to Parliament, the office of PM Johnson announced that the Department of Overseas Development would be combined with the Foreign Office. Despite repeated attempts to redraw departmental boundaries on an ad hoc basis, many inconsistencies remain in the allocation of responsibilities between policy areas.

In many other nations, departmental re-organisation can be undertaken only by a more formal legal process. For example, in Italy a statute was passed in 1997 to allow a re-allocation of functions at the highest level of government between ministries, which has resulted in the compression of 20 ministries into 12.[29]

10 Downing Street and Policy Formation

The growth of the PM's Office at 10 Downing Street, with its own staff and with an expanded profile in co-ordinating the activities of government, means that a structure now exists for policy co-ordination. The capacity of a PM to drive the complex machinery of modern government from the top has increasingly depended on having in place an apparatus of administrative back up.[30] In the first place, the Cabinet Office emerged as the department with overall responsibility for supporting the work of the Cabinet. Its primary function was (and is) to provide secretarial support to the Cabinet, and to the network of Cabinet committees where much of the detailed work of the Cabinet is carried out across

---

[28] S Sked and C Cook, *Post-War Britain: A Political History* (London, Penguin, 1979) 230.
[29] See Italy: Law 59/97.
[30] A Blick and G Jones, *At Power's Elbow: Aides to the Prime Minister from Robert Walpole to David Cameron* (London, Biteback Publishing, 2013).

departments on key issues. In charge of the Cabinet Office, which is at the same time a civil service department, is the Cabinet Secretary. As head of the home civil service, the Cabinet Secretary also has the task of working as a conduit between the government and the civil service more generally. For example, the Cabinet Secretary must guarantee the impartiality of a permanent civil service. In another capacity, the Cabinet Office deals with public sector appointments and promotions within the civil service. The Cabinet Office has overseen many of the public sector reforms that have been introduced in recent years. As noted earlier the Cabinet Secretary, as head of the civil service, presides over the Cabinet Office and from this position is also responsible for in some respects acting as a guardian of constitutionality by upholding the integrity of the civil service. This includes overseeing the conduct of the civil service, and in particular, by ensuring that civil servants do not allow ministers to act unlawfully in breach of the relevant codes of practice for ministers and civil servants.

Since the 1960s the staffing levels have expanded, and there have been repeated attempts to improve the structure and organisation to meet challenges as they have arisen. For example, inside Downing Street itself, the Central Policy Review Staff (CPRS) was introduced by PM Heath in 1971 under the direction of Lord Rothschild to provide advice from outside the civil service. Subsequently, PMs have stamped their mark on the way the Cabinet Office and 10 Downing Street are organised. For example, the CPRS was dispensed with by PM Thatcher, who decided to build up her own Policy Unit into what Hennessey describes as 'what has in effect [become] a proper Downing Street version of a French Prime Ministerial cabinet'.[31] This presented the opportunity for PM Thatcher to introduce her favoured advisers into Whitehall, including, for example, the chief executive of Marks and Spencer, a merchant banker, and two professors of economics. The Policy Unit was formed into a group of experts that took a keen interest in many of the key policy areas of government, and it assumed a position to promote the main principles of Thatcherism throughout the government. This included the introduction of market principles and privatisation. (In a later section of this chapter we will discuss the impact of the 'Next Steps' initiative on the structure of the civil service.) Despite recognising the extensive powers apparently placed in the hands of the office holder, Mount rejects what he calls 'the alternative theory of prime-ministerial government' expounded

---

[31] Hennessey (n 1) 424.

by commentators such as Mackintosh.[32] For example, one barrier to be surmounted by the PM in exercising this power is a fiercely independent civil service that often provides incomplete briefing and advice, and then there are problems of communication and implementation which still have to be overcome before any policy is put into effect.[33]

The PM's Office, based at 10 Downing Street, is relatively small in terms of numbers, certainly when measured against the size of the Cabinet Office and the wider civil service, but it has assumed growing importance in the conduct of government.[34] In the main this has been in respect to giving advice on policy formation, in respect to overseeing the co-ordination and effective delivery of policy, and in respect to the communication of the government message through the PM's press office. The PM is assisted by a Chief of Staff and PMs have tended to surround themselves with a select group of special policy advisers (SPADS) reflecting their own ideological viewpoint. In turn, this trend has confirmed the growing importance of the organisation based at 10 Downing Street. There were 36 SPADS under the Conservative government of John Major, and this figure rose to 78 under the Labour government of Gordon Brown. The number was reduced to 68 under the coalition government led by David Cameron but by December 2019 the figure had escalated to a total of 109.[35] SPADS are not able to directly exercise statutory powers, manage public funds, or issue instructions to civil servants but they play an active role in policy development and can request the supply of data from civil servants (see below).

Moreover, recent PMs have also placed strong emphasis on the effective delivery of policies in the public sector. To this end, the Strategy Unit was set up in 2002, bringing together the Performance and Innovation Unit (PIU), the PM's Forward Strategy Unit (FSU), and parts of the Centre for Management and Policy Studies (CMPS). The Strategy Unit was responsible for carrying out long-term strategic reviews of major areas of policy, and it helped to coordinate the activities of government by undertaking studies of cross-cutting policy issues, and by working with departments to promote strategic thinking and improve policy-making across Whitehall. The Unit conducted investigations and issued regular reports that made practical recommendations. These were designed: to encourage stronger leadership from ministers and senior civil servants;

---

[32] J Mackintosh, *The British Cabinet* (London, Stevens, 1962).
[33] F Mount, *The British Constitution Now* (London, Mandarin, 1992) 136ff.
[34] See A Seldon, 'The Cabinet System' in V Bogdanor (ed), *The British Constitution in the Twentieth Century* (Oxford, Oxford University Press, 2003).
[35] www.instituteforgovernment.org.uk/explainers/special-advisers.

to improve policy formulation and implementation; and to enhance the capacity for co-ordination across government. Although the Strategy Unit itself was disbanded in 2010, under PM Johnson the rebranded No 10 Policy Unit included 44 advisers to the PM.[36]

The use of the internet since the turn of the twenty-first century to promote the government's message represented an important innovation. The citizen is drawn into a new style of participatory democracy based on a transformed relationship between the individual and the information superhighway, which also embraces government and local government. The Strategy Unit seeks to make government more open and accessible through its e-government strategy and UK online campaign, aiming to improve the online information provided by government.[37] 10 Downing Street assumes a leading role on issues that cut across government departments, including promoting information technology. This co-ordinating function may fall outside the remit of other individual government departments.

The PM has a special position in relation to the operation of the intelligence services.[38] As head of the intelligence and security services, with overall responsibility for security matters, the PM chairs the COBRA committee. In this sphere it is the Intelligence and Security Committee, established by the Intelligence Services Act 1994, which provides some parliamentary oversight over the three main organisations responsible for national security, namely MI6, officially the Secret Intelligence Service (SIS); Government Communication Headquarters (GCHQ); and MI5, officially the Security Service.[39] The committee examines expenditure, administration, and policy within what has been termed the 'ring of secrecy'. The committee is appointed by the PM, after consultation with the Leader of the Opposition. It comprises cross-party membership of nine, taken from both the House of Commons and the House of Lords, and is required to report annually to the PM on its work. The introduction of oversight is a useful development, but it is difficult to assess accurately how effectively the committee, tribunal, and Security Services Commissioner perform their respective roles as their most valuable work

---

[36] R Hazell, 'A Profession Comes of Age' in B Yong and R Hazell (eds), *Special Advisers: Who They Are, What They Do and Why They Matter* (Oxford, Hart Publishing, 2014) 203.

[37] J Morison, 'Modernising Government and the E-Government Revolution: Technologies of Government and Technologies of Democracy' in N Bamforth and P Leyland (eds), *Public Law in a Multi-Layered Constitution* (Oxford, Hart Publishing 2003); S Ward and T Vedel, 'Introduction: The Potential of the Internet Revisited' (2006) 59 *Parliamentary Affairs* 210.

[38] www.intelligence.gov.uk/.

[39] www.mi5.gov.uk/output/Page7.html; www.mi6.gov.uk/output/Page79.html.

relates to classified material, which is deliberately placed beyond the public gaze and, as we shall see later in this chapter, such information is designated as an excluded category under Part II of the Freedom of Information Act 2000.

Prime Minister's Press Office, SPADS, and Government Spin

In order to present the government's position effectively the need for a press office has been recognised for many generations, but in recent years the role of the opinion-formers has changed and become much more important.[40] In part, this can be seen as a response to the fact that information is now constantly circulated 24 hours a day, and is available from foreign sources, through the internet, and by satellite. It has become increasingly clear that policy initiatives can be seriously compromised by facing sustained adverse comment on television and radio, and in the press. Ultimately, the public perception of the government through the coverage it receives in the mass media has a major impact on the electoral fortunes of a political party. The role of the media in opinion-forming has transformed the way the business of government is conducted. The PM, as leader of the party, needs to keep in touch with the public mood and has a press office to assist with this task. Press secretaries are appointed to champion the cause of the government, and they have always been political appointments, introduced from outside government and civil service, to work in harmony with the serving PM. However, the pejorative term 'spin doctor' has been applied by critics to suggest that in recent years the function of the press secretary and the press office has gone beyond assisting the PM (and other ministers) with media management and opinion-forming. The task has in fact changed from putting the best possible interpretation on issues that come up, to actually taking the initiative in setting a political agenda for a particular area of government policy. Alistair Campbell, as press secretary and later director of communications at 10 Downing Street (until 2003) was widely criticised in the media for wielding a great deal of power behind the scenes, but without being subject to any direct control. Furthermore, PM Blair decided when he became PM that any policy announcement across the entire government had to be cleared through the Downing Street press office. This practice was introduced to avoid an impression

---

[40] See generally A Blick, *At Power's Elbow: Aides to the Prime Minister from Robert Walpole to David Cameron* (London, Biteback Books, 2013).

of disunity conveyed by the previous government led by PM Major that resulted from inconsistent and contradictory messages being released by individual departments. However, the requirement that policy announcements have to be approved at the centre has meant that Downing Street and the press office have been able to control the political agenda across the entire spectrum of government activity.[41] As a result, enormous power has been placed in the hands of appointed officials who are not directly accountable under the constitution for their activities. In response to some of these criticisms, the independent Phillis report in 2004 attempted to delineate the political and civil service roles more clearly.[42]

In line with the recommendations contained in the report, a new Permanent Secretary, Government Communications was appointed in 2004 whose remit was to focus on a strategic approach to communications across government to better inform and respond to the requirements of citizens and people who use and work in public services. In a complementary role, on the political side of the communications machine, the PM's Director of Communications has responsibility for the day-to-day media activity at 10 Downing Street. The Director of Communications also assists Cabinet ministers and their special advisers with the political context for departmental communications, but does not directly exercise any executive power over the civil service.[43]

In May 2020 the conduct of Dominic Cummings, the PM's chief adviser, drew attention to the limits of the accountability of appointed officials (SPADS), who wield power at the highest level of government but are not directly answerable to Parliament.[44] Eyebrows had already been raised by Cumming's abrasive relationship with civil senior servants and a high-handed role in the appointment, dismissal, and management of other SPADS. At the height of the Covid-19 pandemic he was found to have breached the strict lockdown rules. The failure of Cummings to take responsibility for his unlawful actions by resigning from the post was questionable. The attempt to defend the actions prompted damaging adverse publicity for the government, and its approach to upholding its own lockdown policy, but the case also highlights a systemic problem,

---

[41] See T Daintith, 'Spin: A Constitutional and Legal Analysis' (2001) 7 *European Public Law* 593, at 606.
[42] http://archive.cabinetoffice.gov.uk/gcreview/News/index.htm.
[43] H James, 'What Future for Government Communications?', Speech at the CPPS Seminar, 20 January 2005, available at www.cabinetoffice.gov.uk/about_the_cabinet_office/speeches/james/html.
[44] M Gordon, 'Dominic Cummings and the Accountability of Special Advisers', UK Const L Blog (3 June 2020).

namely, that enforcement of these rules ultimately depends on the PM's judgement as guardian of the constitution. An obvious conflict arose between the application of these ethical rules and personal loyalty towards the PM's most senior adviser.[45] In sharp contrast, after admitting to a similar infringement of the lockdown rules in April 2020, Scotland's Chief Medical officer, Catherine Calderwood resigned following a request to do so by the Scottish First Minster.

General Elections and Confidence Motions

A significant feature of the PM's constitutional role has been the ability to determine the date of a general election within the five-year time frame set out by the Parliament Act 1911. In order to secure a coalition deal with Liberal Democrats in 2010 this convention was qualified. PM Cameron supported the enactment of the Fixed Term Parliaments Act (FTPA) 2011. This stipulated that general elections should take place regularly every five years (subject to some exceptions).[46] Crucially, it removed the PM's discretion to advise the monarch to dissolve the House at a time of the PM's choosing. The crucial question of maintaining the confidence of Parliament was also affected by this change. The Cabinet Manual (CM) drawn up in 2010–11 to identify the basic procedural and ethical rules of government states that the PM holds the position by virtue of his or her ability to command the confidence of the House of Commons.[47] For much of her premiership PM May was unable to muster a clear majority in the House of Commons on the pivotal issue of Brexit. As the votes were not designated 'confidence motions', a series of humiliating defeats, culminating in the rejection of the proposed Brexit withdrawal agreement in 2019 by 432 votes to 202, did not result in the immediate resignation of the government. A formal vote of no confidence was held in January 2019 under the FTPA. For entirely pragmatic reasons the opposition motion was defeated by 325 votes to 306. The upshot was that the government was unable to command an effective majority needed to realise its legislative objectives. Nevertheless, it was able to continue in power contrary to what had long been regarded as a fundamental principle. Inadequate allowance had been made for the implications of passing the FTPA 2011,

---

[45] Ibid.
[46] V Bogdanor *The Coalition and the Constitution* (Oxford, Hart Publishing, 2011) 114ff.
[47] AL Young, *Unchecked Power: How Recent Constitutional Reforms Are Threatening UK Democracy* (Bristol, Bristol University Press, 2024) 152ff.

particularly through the failure to clarify the distinction between confidence and no confidence motions.[48] However, the Dissolution and Calling of Parliament Act 2022 restored the convention. In effect, this allows the PM to choose election day as PM Sunak did in 2024. This power means that the PM in government enjoys an unfair advantage. For example, tax cuts might be introduced as a bribe with an election date in mind.[49]

MINISTERS AND CIVIL SERVICE

Next we turn to the constitutional relationship between ministers and civil servants before proceeding to examine the wider role of the civil service and related issues of accountability which have arisen with the evolution of the machinery of government and related oversight mechanisms.

Individual Ministerial Responsibility

Individual ministerial responsibility is the constitutional convention which is concerned with the accountability between Parliament, the political decision-makers, and the professional civil servants and the administrators responsible for implementing policy in the UK. In essence, a model of the constitution was conceived which sought to accommodate the existence of discretionary public power by the device of ministerial responsibility. The rule of law, as explained by Dicey,[50] works on the basis that the courts police the boundaries of excessive ministerial power under the ultra vires principle, while Parliament oversees the actions of ministers within the limits of these powers. What does this add up to in practice? In a formal and procedural sense, ministers are responsible: this responsibility is in the sense that they are answerable to Parliament for their departments. In this way individual ministerial responsibility describes a 'chain of accountability'. Officials answer to ministers, who answer to Parliament, which, in turn, answers to the electorate. This demonstrates how individual ministerial responsibility emerged as the convention which described constitutional accountability for policy

---

[48] See further M Russell, *The Parliamentary Battle over Brexit* (Oxford, Oxford University Press, 2023).
[49] M Russell and R Hazell, 'In Praise of Fixed Term Parliaments' The Constitution Unit Blog (7 June 2024).
[50] A Dicey, *An Introduction to the Study of the Law of the Constitution*, 10th edn (Basingstoke, Macmillan, 1959) 188ff.

matters, but, as we shall see from the examples cited below, the problem is that accountability is often no more than a requirement to give reasons and explanations for actions or decisions as part of the process of government.

For the convention to operate, the basic requirement is that ministers are members of Parliament. As was recognised in the previous chapter, the answerability of ministers to Parliament is acted out in a number of ways. In particular, the relevant minister in the House of Commons or House of Lords introduces a government Bill concerning his or her department in Parliament; backbench MPs are able to table questions to ministers on a regular basis; ministers are called to account for their policies before departmental select committees; and the Public Accounts Committee in harness with the National Audit Office investigates past government expenditure by undertaking value for money (VFM) audits (see Chapter 5).

Ministers, then, are made accountable or answerable to Parliament by these routine procedures. In terms of general principle, individual ministerial responsibility recognises that the continuation in office of ministers depends upon them enjoying the confidence and support of MPs or peers. In practice, however, attempts to challenge the credibility of a minister are seldom successful when the government in power enjoys a substantial majority in the House of Commons. In 1954 Sir Thomas Dugdale resigned over the famous Crichel Down affair, where blame for departmental incompetence was clearly attributable to officials. Furthermore, the blameworthy action mostly occurred well before this minister took up office. In fact, this sacrifice was prompted for political reasons, and the resignation should be regarded as an exception to general practice. Unless the matter is taken up as a crusade by the press, what Richard Crossman explained, writing half a century earlier, still applies: '[Since] the Government party controls Parliament, both resignations and dismissals for incompetence have become rare. Indeed, the incompetent minister with a departmental muddle to cover up may be kept in office for years . . . more votes will be lost by admitting the incompetence than by concealing it.'[51] The government can nearly always rely upon the support of its backbench MPs to sustain its majority and therefore there will be no need for a minister to fall on his or her sword and resign.

Apart from Crichel Down, there have been few examples of ministers accepting responsibility for policy and resigning. One such was the

---

[51] R Crossman (ed), 'Introduction' in W Bagehot, *The English Constitution* (London, Fontana, 1963) 43 and 45.

resignation of Lord Carrington as Foreign Secretary following the invasion of South Georgia by the Argentinians prior to the Falklands War in 1982. Lord Carrington accepted the blame for not responding to intelligence reports warning about the impending invasion. In October 2002 Estelle Morris, the Secretary of State for Education and Employment, resigned over criticism concerning her handling of a crisis regarding the grading of A-level examinations that prompted a personal loss of confidence over her stewardship of the department.[52] On the other hand, blame can be deflected for political mistakes by a sacrificial resignation, which identifies an individual minister rather than the PM or the government as a whole as being responsible for a policy oversight. For example, Leon Brittan, the Secretary of State for Trade and Industry took full responsibility for a departmental leak relating to the Westland affair, and his resignation in 1986 shielded the PM and the government from intensifying criticism at a time of crisis.[53]

Ministerial responsibility has always been an imprecise convention, which delivers partial accountability. Assuming the minister is the architect of the policy, it would appear to follow that, should the policy design prove to be fundamentally flawed, the minister should be held responsible in front of Parliament and the public, but frequently the responsibility spans a period of time and is distributed between departments and agencies. Ministers will be required at least to supply information, but also in some cases, an explanation, apology, and policy change may follow from the spotlight of public attention in the media. The Windrush scandal[54] which eventually resulted in the resignation of Home Secretary Amber Rudd in April 2018, concerned the outrageous mistreatment over several years, and in some cases the deportation, of older generation Commonwealth citizens of West Indian origin. Several hundred suffered from the policy because they did not have passports and were unable to prove their immigration status. The injustices were caused by a combination of a flawed policy introduced by a previous Home Secretary (Theresa May) in 2012 and maladministration (eg poor decision-making, inadequate policy co-ordination, and destruction of entry records by the Home Office). Although there have been a series of highly critical reports[55] resulting in

---

[52] D Woodhouse, 'UK Ministerial Responsibility in 2002: The Tale of Two Resignations' (2004) 82 *Public Administration* 1.
[53] See G Marshall, 'Cabinet Government and the Westland Affair' [1986] *PL* 184.
[54] C Harlow, 'Windrush: Lessons learned or perhaps not?', UK Const L Blog (6 April 2020).
[55] W Williams, Windrush: Lessons Learned Review, March 2020, HC 93, The Windrush generation, Sixth Report of Session 2017–19, 3 July 2018, HC 990; 'Windrush generation and the Home Office, Eighty-Second Report of Session 2017–19, HC 1518.

changes in Home Office practice, Rudd's resignation as Home Secretary was prompted by the public exposure that she had misled Parliament's Home Affairs Select Committee over the existence of targets for the removal of immigrants and, in so doing, breached the ministerial code. Once again, in 2020 under PM Johnson a series of prominent ministerial failures exposed the limitations of executive accountability at the heart of government. This included the reluctance of the Health Secretary to take direct responsibility for a failure to deliver an effective testing regime at the height of the Covid-19 crisis, and the reaction of the Secretary of State for Education to the fiasco over the publication of school examination results after the cancellation of the exams themselves, based on a defective mathematical formula approved by his department. This outcome had far-reaching consequences for many thousands of school leavers whose university places depended on their examination grades. Not only did the minister refuse to step down but there was an attempt to deflect the blame onto another government agency (Ofqual).[56] Such evidence relating to policy flaws and maladministration demonstrates that notwithstanding the ministerial code accountability is limited, resignations until recently were unusual, and it further supports the view that under the Conservative government political considerations nearly always predominated.

By way of contrast there have been many ministerial resignations prompted by questionable personal behaviour relating to financial probity, personal integrity, abuse of ministerial office, and scandalous sexual behaviour. Perhaps the most famous example was the resignation in 1963 of the Secretary of State for War, John Profumo, for deliberately misleading Parliament. At the height of the 'cold war' he had denied his association with a high-class prostitute who was also having an affair with a Russian military attaché (probable spy) stationed in London.

Many ministers since have resigned for breaches of the ministerial code or for personal misconduct. Peter Mandelson MP left the Blair government in 1998 for failing to declare a loan and again in 2001 after it was alleged he used his position to assist with a passport application. Liam Fox MP stepped down as Secretary of State for Defence in 2011 after being found to have breached the ministerial code by allowing an associate without security clearance to attend meetings at the Ministry of Defence. In 2025 Angela Rayner, Labour's Deputy Prime Minister and Secretary of State for Housing, Communities and Local Government

---

[56] R Brazier, 'Contempt for the Constitution?', UK Const L Blog (6 October 2020). The head of Ofqual resigned.

resigned following a referral to the Independent Adviser on Ministerial Standards (IAMS) which confirmed that she had underpaid stamp duty on a property transaction.[57] Although the amounts involved were relatively trivial this was embarrassing for the government. Prime Minister Starmer had approved a revised Ministerial Code and a widening of the role of the IAMS in the wake of a succession of scandals, particularly under the premiership of Boris Johnson.[58]

The non-resignation of a minister in situations where there is suspicion of personal impropriety in breach of the ministerial code may be particularly damaging to the entire government.[59] Ultimately, the decision rests with the PM. Professor Woodhouse has summed up the position as follows:

> Moving into the twenty-first century, the convention of ministerial responsibility can be defined loosely, as requiring, first, information rather than resignation; secondly, ministerial 'accountability' for everything but 'responsibility' for only some things; thirdly, civil service 'responsibility' for some things but 'accountability' only when this suits ministerial interests.[60]

A reformulation of ministerial responsibility needs to recognises the integral responsibilities of ministers for supervision of their department or agency. In particular, this would require that ministers make sure that adequate resources are available for the effective implementation of policies and that they assume direct control at times when things go wrong as part of explanatory and amendatory responsibility.[61]

Government Accountability and the Scott Report

The reluctance of ministers to resign was further illustrated following publication of the Scott Report.[62] A public inquiry chaired by a senior judge was set up to look into the processes of government after it emerged that arms had been supplied to Iraq with the covert support of

---

[57] www.instituteforgovernment.org.uk/comment/rayner-resignation-starmer-reset.
[58] www.instituteforgovernment.org.uk/explainer/independent-adviser-ministerial-interests.
[59] 'Robert Jenrick under pressure to resign after donor-row documents released' *The Guardian*, 25 June 2020.
[60] D Woodhouse, 'Ministerial Responsibility: Something Old, Something New' [1997] PL 280.
[61] D Woodhouse, 'The Reconstruction of Constitutional Accountability' [2002] PL 262, 86.
[62] *Report of the Inquiry into the Export of Defence Equipment and Dual-Use Goods to Iraq and Related Prosecutions*, 1995–96 HC 115.

government during the Gulf War between Iran and Iraq during the 1980s. This action was clearly in contravention of published government policy at the time. The issue came to public attention following the collapse of a prosecution against two directors of the Matrix Churchill company, which had been contracted to supply a supergun to Iraq. Although government ministers had used public interest immunity to prevent the disclosure of information in court on grounds of national security, the fact that these directors were working in collusion with the secret intelligence services came to light. It appeared that the government had been prepared to suppress this information in order to prevent embarrassment for having misled Parliament over its involvement, even if this meant imprisonment for these directors of Matrix Churchill. Many of criticisms in the report related to the conduct of ministers, including the suggestion that the House of Commons had been misled by one minister, and that guidelines for the signing of public interest immunity certificates had been wrongly interpreted by the Attorney General, but, despite criticism appearing in the report, neither minister resigned.[63] The Scott Report also exposed a lack of candour, which amounted to a failure by ministers to meet the obligations of ministerial accountability by providing adequate information about the activities of their departments, and it was recognised that this failure tended to undermine the democratic process. In response, a revised code of practice was introduced for civil servants and ministers which have made it more difficult to mislead Parliament.[64] In particular, civil servants are committed to core values of integrity, honesty, objectivity, and impartiality which means that they must not deceive or knowingly mislead ministers, Parliament or the wider public when answering parliamentary questions or appearing before departmental select committees, and it requires all government departments and agencies to adopt a whistleblowing procedure to allow concerns over any abuse to be raised. From a legal standpoint, the latest code also confirms the contractual relationship between ministers and civil servants now set out in the Constitutional Reform and Governance Act 2010 and incorporated in the terms and conditions of employment for civil servants.[65]

---

[63] A Tomkins, *The Constitution After Scott: Government Unwrapped* (Oxford, Oxford University Press, 1998) provides a detailed discussion of the report and its implications.
[64] Civil Service Code Cabinet Office, updated August 2019.
[65] See N Bamforth, 'Accountability of and to the Legislature' in N Bamforth and P Leyland (eds), *Accountability in the Contemporary Constitution* (Oxford, Oxford University Press, 2013) 270.

The Role of the Civil Service

In tandem with ministers and SPADS, policy is developed and implemented at central government level by permanent officials employed directly by the Crown. In 2025 around 503,000 individuals were working for the UK Civil Service[66] of whom 315,000 serve in five major departments.[67] In order to consider the issues of accountability in respect to the operation of government itself, we need to explore in more detail the relationship between ministers and civil servants, and the re-organisation of the institutions of central government.[68] In the first place, it is worth noting that until the Constitutional Reform and Governance Act 2010 was enacted there had never been a single statute or a set of delegated rules that regulated the conduct of civil servants or which establishes their constitutional position. For example, civil servants have a special position in law as servants of the Crown, but on matters of employment law, the Equal Pay Act 1970, the Employment Protection (Consolidation) Act 1978, the Sex Discrimination Act 1975, and the Race Relations Act 1976 all apply to the civil service. Civil servants are bound by the Official Secrets Acts 1911 and 1989 and by the Freedom of Information Act 2000 (subject to statutory exceptions discussed below). Civil servants are also regulated by an assortment of codes of conduct and disciplinary codes. As we have already observed in our discussion of ministerial responsibility, some of these codes have an important bearing on the relationship of civil servants with ministers and with Parliament.

For many generations, ministers have been in a position to rely upon a permanent and professional civil service, which, in most cases, has been led by an elite class of Oxford and Cambridge-educated officials, with a reputation for neutrality. The foundations of the modern service were laid following the Northcote-Trevelyan Report of 1854.[69] This groundbreaking report, among other things, established the idea of appointment on merit and led to the division of the civil service into two classes

---

[66] Whitehall Monitor 2025, *Institute for Government*, January 2025. https://assets.publishing.service.gov.uk/government/uploads/system/uploads/attachment_data/file/911987/Statistical_bulletin_-_Civil_Service_Statistics_2020.pdf; https://assets.publishing.service.gov.uk/government/uploads/system/uploads/attachment_data/file/836373/Statistical-bulletin-Civil-Service-Statistics-2019-V2.pdf.

[67] These departments comprise: Works and Pensions, Justice, Revenue and Customs, Defence, Home Office.

[68] See generally G Drewry, 'The Executive: Towards Accountable Government and Effective Governance' in J Jowell and D Oliver (eds), *The Changing Constitution*, 7th edn (Oxford, Oxford University Press, 2011).

[69] Northcote-Trevelyan Report on the Organisation of a Permanent Civil Service 1854.

comprising, on the one hand, policy-makers, and, on the other, more routine workers. The civil service remains a system of centralised hierarchical administration comprised of trained professionals, who operate according to prescribed and objective rules. The structure is designed to enable those at the base of the pyramid of administration to carry out the commands of those at the pinnacle. The role of the civil service is to implement policy, often by putting into effect detailed legislative provisions, and it establishes a system which limits the arbitrary exercise of power by officials. Nevertheless, in the UK, as in other comparable nations (eg France, Italy, and Germany), the legal framework of legislation will inevitably leave scope for the exercise of discretionary power, with the traditional model regarding ministers and civil servants as partners. This means that officials have been allowed some discretion to act, but this discretion is set within strict limits. It will be apparent from our discussion of legal accountability in chapter 7 that the courts can be called upon to intervene to ensure that the exercise of any such discretion remains lawful.

The UK civil service implements policy for whichever government is in power and, unlike in the United States, there is no 'spoils system' allowing politicians to routinely replace the most senior officials with a change of government. The service has a high reputation for intellectual excellence and integrity. It is considered to be neutral, with a capacity to give impartial advice to ministers. However, it has also attracted criticism for lack of managerial competence and efficiency, and for a failure to attract the specialist expertise needed in many areas of government (see eg the Fulton Report 1968,[70] which made more than 100 recommendations).

The situation in regard to the structure and organisation of the civil service has changed significantly in recent years. The Conservative governments between 1979 and 1997 were critical of the traditional approach of many civil servants to questions of policy implementation which, it was argued, resulted in ineffective government. In order to pursue the radical Thatcherite agenda, which departed from the consensual policies of post-war generations, the association between the civil service and established interests in both business and the public and voluntary sector was revised. Since the 1980s there have been radical managerial innovations to help overcome resistance to reform by senior officials. The New Public Management (NPM) initiative and the Next Steps re-organisation in particular were inspired by an ideological commitment to introduce the disciplines of the free market to the processes of government. Indeed, the idea of running a public enterprise on a similar basis to a private

---

[70] *The Report of the Committee on the Civil Service* (Fulton), Cmnd 3638 (1966–68).

business became a prevalent theme in publicly funded bodies throughout Europe and beyond. It depended upon the introduction of a new kind of contracting between the various levels of government and between government and the private sector.

Another manifestation of this change of approach, already alluded to, is that there has been an increase in the appointment by ministers of political advisers and SPADS, who exercise a growing influence on policy-making, and these advisers can also be involved lower down the administrative hierarchy to monitor progress with policy initiatives.

The revised ministerial code recognises that 'The Minister in charge of a department is solely accountable to Parliament for the exercise of the powers on which the administration of the department depends.'[71] It is apparent that in some respects this re-organisation has led to a significant redefinition of the doctrine of ministerial responsibility. Less emphasis is placed upon detailed day-to-day supervision of the entire department. Accountability between the department and the agency tends to be mainly in respect of overall finance and budgeting matters. Particular emphasis is placed on assessing measurable criteria such as financial efficiency. In consequence, greater autonomy brought about by agency status has promoted a divergence of interests between the agency and the department. It has resulted in a division into two distinct accountabilities, but no revised mechanism to address the problem.[72] For example, ministerial responses to parliamentary questions on matters of detailed financial policy might fall under the remit of the agency chief executive, and in some cases the answers to questions provided by the chief executive may be considered inadequate.

Although the precise criteria and terminology are modified to reflect local conditions, aspects of the NPM model have been manifest in much of Europe. This idea is not fundamentally concerned with democratic control and accountability, but rather with control through forms of contractual relationship.

Civil Service Management and the Recognition of Codes of Practice

Concerns have been voiced over the creeping politicisation of the civil service.[73] In a change of practice which has the potential to undermine the independence of what has been regarded as a permanent civil service,

---

[71] Ministerial Code, Cabinet Office, 2019, 4.6.
[72] P Barberis, 'The New Public Management and a New Accountability' (1998) 76 (Autumn) *Public Administration* 45.
[73] A King, *The British Constitution* (Oxford, Oxford University Press, 2007) 233.

a number of Permanent Secretaries have resigned since the 2019 general election following claims that their position was deliberately made untenable by their ministerial bosses.[74] Another example discussed above has been the increased role of special advisers introduced by the PM and other ministers (eg Alistair Campbell, Downing Street Press Secretary and Director of Communications 1997–2003 under PM Blair and more recently Dominic Cummings under PM Johnson 2019–2020). One obvious problem is that these appointees may appear to exercise authority over permanent civil servants but without their respective positions being clearly defined. The Parliamentary Committee on Standards in Public Life had recommended that the role of the civil service and civil servants should be placed on a statutory footing.[75] The Constitutional Reform and Governance Act dispensed with Orders in Council and placed the management of the civil service on a statutory footing. It was now placed under parliamentary scrutiny. The Act also established a Civil Service Commission which is responsible for appointing civil servants.[76] At the same time, it required that a code of conduct be published for the civil service, the diplomatic service, and for special advisers.[77] These codes form part of the terms and conditions of service of civil servants, diplomats, and special advisers and recognise that the core values of integrity, honesty, objectivity, and impartiality set out in the Act must be upheld at all times.[78] Some critics have argued that:

> The quest for defined boundaries and roles at the top of government, where politics and administration intertwine, is misguided. Ambiguity, fuzziness, and grey areas are assets since they enable flexibility, and practical responses to unexpected happenings.[79]

Revised codes have been published but these more explicit rules failed to prevent the intense controversy surrounding the appointment of former *News of the World* editor Andy Coulson as PM Cameron's Director of Communications. He was installed without the routine vetting and

---

[74] Brazier (n 56).

[75] See Parliamentary Committee on Standards in Public Life, *Ninth Report: Defining the Boundaries within the Executive: Ministers, special advisors and the permanent civil service*, 2003; Public Administration select committee, 8th Report, 2001–02, published 19 July 2002; D Oliver, *Constitutional Reform in the UK* (Oxford, Oxford University Press, 2003) ch 3.

[76] See Constitutional Reform and Governance Act 2010, s 3.

[77] Ibid, ss 5, 6, and 8.

[78] Ibid, s 7(4).

[79] G Jones, 'Against a Civil Service Act' [2002] October–December *Public Money and Management* 6.

security clearance experienced by others holding this crucial office. As mentioned above, Dominic Cummings was able to carry on as the PM's chief adviser despite being in apparent breach of the code in March 2020.

Government Openness and the Freedom of Information Act 2000

The Freedom of Information Act 2000 (FOI Act 2000) requires the disclosure of information by the government and other public bodies and, as a result, it has an important impact in delivering accountability in many areas.[80] It will already be apparent that the convention of individual ministerial responsibility, which is central to executive accountability, hinges on an obligation to provide information. Until quite recently, the corridors of Whitehall and public authorities in general were shrouded in a cloak of secrecy. The blanket protection that public bodies had enjoyed under the 'catch-all' section 2 of the Official Secrets Acts 1911 was relaxed to some extent by the Official Secrets Act 1989. The failure of the government in the 1980s to prevent the circulation of the *Spycatcher* book,[81] which had been written by an ex-spy in breach of the Official Secrets Act 1911, was a foretaste of difficulties to come in controlling the currency of information.[82] The book had been published abroad, but it was imported and became available in the UK despite injunctions issued by the courts.

In a different context, the trenchant criticism contained in the Scott Report (see above), which looked into the collapse of the Matrix Churchill case, signalled a change of approach in regard to Parliament. The previous assumption that information in the possession of public bodies could be routinely held back was fundamentally questioned in this report, and the codes of practice which applied to ministers and civil servants were modified subsequently.[83] Latterly, information placed in the public domain has proliferated exponentially through the internet, and this has, of course, transformed public expectations over the level of disclosure which is expected from public bodies.

On its return to power in 1997 after 18 years in opposition, the Labour Party was committed to introducing a Freedom of Information Act. Despite its shortcomings touched on below, the FOI Act 2000 is

---

[80] P Birkinshaw, 'Regulating Information' in J Jowell and C O'Cinneide (eds), *The Changing Constitution*, 9th edn (Oxford, Oxford University Press, 2019).
[81] P Wright, *Spycatcher* (New York, Viking, 1987).
[82] See *Attorney-General v Guardian Newspapers Ltd (No 2)* [1990] 1 AC 109.
[83] See Tomkins (n 61).

a ground-breaking constitutional measure. The Act, which came fully into force on 1 January 2005, provides under section 1 a general right of access to information held by public authorities, including government departments. It imposes an obligation to provide information within a limited time frame. As well as meeting the requirement under the Act to provide publication schemes, government, local government, and public authorities have responded to the new situation by making vast amounts of information available to the public, often on their websites.

Information which is exempt from disclosure is set out in Part II of the FOI Act 2000. The exempt categories fall into two classes, as the effect of the provisions differs depending on whether the sections confer absolute exemption, or qualified exemption subject to a prejudice test.[84] In essence, the areas which have an 'absolute exemption' are those where the need to balance the public interest in disclosure against the public interest in maintaining the exemption does not arise. This covers information relating to secret intelligence services, criminal intelligence matters, and national security.[85] There is limited scope for challenges before the Information Tribunal, but the grounds are very narrow.

For these categories, a certificate signed by a Cabinet minister, the Attorney General, the Attorney-General for Northern Ireland, or the Advocate General for Scotland certifying that the exemption is necessary is regarded as conclusive evidence but any such certificate issued by a minister overruling a judicial decision of the tribunal must be supported by valid reasons.[86]

For the second category of (qualified) exemptions, the application for information has to be balanced against the public interest in refusing disclosure. A test of *prejudice* has to be satisfied to justify non-disclosure. The areas that may be exempted are very wide ranging, as the following list illustrates: defence; communications with the royal family; all political advice; international relations; relations between the parliaments and assemblies of the UK, Scotland, Wales, and Northern Ireland; the economy; investigations by the police and customs and excise; court records; commercial information; health and safety; and all personal information and information provided to government in confidence. It will be apparent that this list includes any information relating to the formulation of government policy and investigations and proceedings carried out by

---

[84] P Birkinshaw and M Varney, *Government and Information Rights*, 5th edn (London, Bloomsbury Professional, 2019) 17ff.
[85] See FOI Act 2000, ss 23, 24.
[86] See *R (On the application of Evans) v Attorney General* [2015] UKSC 21.

a public authority. This exemption has been made subject to a prejudice test in order to deter public authorities from routinely suppressing such information.[87] It was argued that a higher threshold of *substantial prejudice* (as applies in Scotland) would have been more effective in encouraging disclosure.

Under the FOI Act 2000, the Information Commissioner performs an important function in overseeing the application of the Act.[88] Should a matter be contested, the Commissioner is empowered to rule that material should be made available in the public interest, and an enforcement notice can be issued, but the minister retains an ultimate veto over any such decision.[89]

An important test case concerned the freedom of information requests which were made to force the disclosure of the advice given to the PM by the Attorney General in March 2003 on the controversial matter of the legality of the second war against Iraq. Despite its initial argument that the advice from the Attorney General was protected by client privilege, the opinion was released by the government in May 2005. The Commissioner later served a single enforcement notice in May 2006 requiring the disclosure of some, but not all, of the information relating to the advice that had been requested under the Act. He also ruled, after balancing the issues by applying the prejudice test, that sufficient information had been disclosed by the government.[90]

E-Government Revolution

From cradle to grave, the encounter with information communication technology (ICT) and, in particular, the internet has become a significant and an increasing part of everyday experience. The new regime of openness under the FOI Act 2000, the introduction of publication schemes, and the sheer quantity of official information available on the internet have transformed public access to information, but equally these developments have implications for the accountability and accessibility of public bodies.[91]

---

[87] See eg FOI Act 2000, ss 26–29.
[88] The role of the Commissioner was extended to cover data protection under Part 5 of and Sch 12 to the Data Protection Act 2018.
[89] FOI Act 2000, s 53.
[90] See ICO press release at www.ico.gov.uk/sendICONewletters/newsletters/english.html#story15.
[91] Ward and Vedel (n 37) 212.

Computers are used universally to store, process, and communicate large amounts of data, and this technology is well suited to delivering many government services. The Cabinet Office launched a large-scale consultation on a policy for electronic democracy based on the premise that ICT can 'facilitate, broaden and deepen' participation.[92] As a result, computer technology is changing the ways in which services are delivered. For example, websites have been constructed allowing direct access to many services. The government gateway already allows many public services to be available online. It has been envisaged that the staged introduction of such technology as part of an evolutionary process might ultimately result in fully integrated online government, which, in turn, would require the radical modification of the structure and culture of administration to facilitate the introduction of this technology in the home. 'From the point of view of the citizen he or she would not be interacting with individual government departments any longer but with "Government" as a single entity.'[93]

A practical issue which is crucial to the general application of ICT concerns the extent of internet access. Before government bodies at central and local level can depend upon the internet, an even playing field is needed in the form of universal access to computers and a general capacity for citizens to connect online. It is estimated that 24 million UK households have access to the internet,[94] but the challenge is to overcome the difficulty of extending internet usage without introducing a form of social exclusion affecting disadvantaged groups (such as the poor, the elderly, and individuals with limited literacy), who may well be particularly reliant on government and local government services. As Morison states:

> Ideas of separation of powers, rule of law and basic principles of legality do not seem to have troubled the information systems engineers. From the standpoint of formal constitutional theory, not only are there issues over the penetration of the voluntary and private sector into government but also there should be concerns over the deployment of information gathered in one (public) context within another (private) one and vice versa ... [giving] rise to a whole host of other issues about privacy, data protection and confidentiality and human rights.[95]

---

[92] *In Service of Democracy: A Consultation Paper for Electronic Democracy* (2002).
[93] Morison (n 37) 177.
[94] www.statistics.gov.uk/downloads/theme_social/Social_Trends35/Social_Trends_35.pdf.
[95] Morison (n 37) 179.

The internet has impacted on public engagement with political protest and debate through social media. It presents the possibility of flash mobilisation of opinion, but equally this technology is capable of being subverted by organised crime, extremist parties, and terrorist organisations. Although the handling of personal data is controlled under the Data Protection Acts 1998 and 2018, the internet itself is largely self-regulated. Ofcom has a role in regulating competition but the internet is placed beyond the reach of the Communications Act 2003. Internet regulation consists mainly of a series of regimes of self-regulation, which have been developed to apply to the different technical layers of delivery.[96]

CONCLUSION

The failure of any single party to achieve decisive electoral success between 2010 and 2019 prompted a shift away from the executive dominance termed 'elective dictatorship' widely regarded as a central characteristic of the UK constitution. Particularly under the premiership of PM May, the PM was unable to control the parliamentary party through the power exercised by the party whips. Instead, the focus of debate shifted to the House of Commons as proposals put before it (particularly concerning Brexit) were questioned and voted down on numerous occasions. PM Johnson won a substantial overall majority in December 2019 and received a clear mandate giving the government the political capacity to pass the required legislation to deliver Brexit and other controversial measures.[97] Subsequently, the election of the Labour Party in 2024 led by PM Starmer with a massive majority once again returns to the situation where the executive is dominant and, at the same time, faced with a particularly weak and fragmented parliamentary opposition. In turn, this draws attention to familiar questions concerning the adequacy of current parliamentary, extra parliamentary, and judicial mechanisms designed to deliver executive scrutiny. This is especially the case when citizen rights are in danger of being eroded or constitutional reforms are likely to be enacted that promise to disturb the balance between the legislative, executive, and judicial branches.

---

[96] R Collins, 'Networks, Markets, Hierarchies: Governance and Regulation of the Internet' (2006) 59 *Parliamentary Affairs* 325.
[97] European Union (Withdrawal Agreement) Act 2020.

FURTHER READING

Birkinshaw P and Varney M, *Government and Information Rights*, 5th edn (London, Bloomsbury Professional, 2019).

Blick A and Jones G, *Premiership: The Development, Nature and Power of the Office of the British Prime Minister* (Exeter, Imprint Academic, 2010).

Brazier R, *Choosing a Prime Ministers: The Transfer of Power in Britain* (Oxford, Oxford University Press, 2020).

Davies A, 'Beyond New Public Management: Problems of Accountability in the Modern Administrative State' in N Bamforth and P Leyland (eds), *Accountability in the Contemporary Constitution* (Oxford, Oxford University Press, 2013).

Lord Hailsham, *The Dilemma of Democracy* (London, Fontana, 1978).

Harlow C and Rawlings R, *Law and Administration*, 4th edn (Cambridge, Cambridge University Press, 2022).

Hennessey P, *The Prime Minister: The Office and its Holders since 1945* (London, Penguin, 2001).

Hennessey P, *Whitehall*, 2nd edn (London, Pimlico, 2001).

House of Commons Political and Constitutional Reform Committee, *Role and Powers of the Prime Minister*, First Report of Session 2014–15, HC 351.

Marshall G, *Constitutional Conventions: The Rules and Forms of Political Accountability* (Oxford, Oxford University Press, 1984) ch 4.

Morison J, 'Models of Democracy: From Representation to Participation' in J Jowell J and D Oliver (eds), *The Changing Constitution*, 6th edn (Oxford, Oxford University Press, 2007).

Poole T, 'The Executive in Public Law' in J Jowell and C O'Cinneide (eds), *The Changing Constitution*, 9th edn (Oxford, Oxford University Press, 2019).

Seldon A, *The Impossible Office? The History of the British Prime Minister – Revised and Updated* (Cambridge, Cambridge University Press, 2024).

Tomkins A, *The Constitution after Scott: Government Unwrapped* (Oxford, Oxford University Press, 1998).

Woodhouse D, 'Ministerial Responsibility' in V Bogdanor (ed), *The British Constitution in the Twentieth Century* (Oxford, Oxford University Press, 2003).

7

The Constitutional Role of the Courts

Common Law – Statutory Interpretation – Supreme Court – Lord Chancellor – Red and Green Light Theory – Judicial Review – Public–Private Law Divide – Merits Issue – Human Rights – Wednesbury Unreasonableness – Proportionality

INTRODUCTION

THE PROFILE OF THE JUDICIARY has been a matter of increasing significance in recent years as the courts have been required to adjudicate in questions with far-reaching constitutional ramifications. In assessing the balance between the legislative, executive and judicial organs of the state we can observe that the *Miller* judgments stand as testimony to the greatly increased visibility of the courts on the constitutional stage. In *Miller 2*,[1] which concerned the Prime Minister (PM)'s advice to prorogue Parliament at a crucial time in the Brexit process, a fundamental issue of justiciability arose. Glancing back to the 1980s, the House of Lords in the *GCHQ* case[2] had been prepared to consider the PM's exercise of the prerogative power but, at the same time, high policy decisions, and the dissolution of Parliament in particular, were regarded by Lord Roskill as areas beyond the reach of the courts. In not following *GCHQ* and the High Court on the question of justiciability, we apparently encounter a marked shift in judicial policy. The PM on behalf of the government advises the Crown to exercise the power to prorogue Parliament, and according to the convention, the advice is followed without question.[3] The UK Supreme

---

[1] *R (on the application of Miller) v The Prime Minister* [2019] UKSC 41 (*Miller 2*).
[2] See *Council of Civil Service Unions v Minister for the Civil Service* [1985] AC 374 at 418 (referred to as the *GCHQ* case).
[3] The view has been questioned by some academic commentators. See S Theil, 'Unconstitutional prorogation of Parliament' [2020] PL 529.

Court (UKSC) recognised that the advice given to the Crown was inherently political in nature and that the way it is routinely exercised is not properly a legal question for the courts to adjudicate. But it held that the lawful limits of this power was a legal matter to be decided judicially. The UKSC was required to establish 'the standard which determines the limits of the power, marking the boundary between the prerogative power on the one hand, and the operation of the constitutional principles of the sovereignty of Parliament and responsible government on the other hand'.[4]

Having negotiated the obstacle of justiciability, the UKSC in *Miller 2* went on to consider whether the advice given to the Crown had been lawful. This was a question which hinged on whether there was reasonable justification for taking action which had an extreme effect at the very heart of democracy. Prorogation prevented the sitting of Parliament. The imposition of a five-week break for the preparation of the Queen's speech setting out the government's legislative programme was not accepted as a valid reason for the drastic curtailment of the democratic process at this crucial time. The UKSC was not only prepared to make a declaration to this effect, but also to quash the order in council (subordinate legislation) approving the prorogation.

The reasoning in this unanimous judgment by an 11 judge panel depends on stressing the importance of executive accountability to Parliament. The Court stated that: 'The decision to prorogue will be unlawful if the prorogation has the effect of frustrating or preventing, without reasonable justification, the ability of Parliament to carry out its constitutional functions as a legislature and as a body responsible for the supervision of the executive' (para [50]).[5] Certainly, ministerial (and Prime Ministerial) accountability to Parliament is a core convention of the UK constitution established at least since the Bill of Rights of 1689, as is the convention that the Crown acts upon the advice of her ministers. The problem is to reconcile the intervention here with the approach taken by the Supreme Court in the first *Miller* judgment. Lord Neuberger had stated unequivocally:

> Judges . . . are neither the parents nor the guardians of political conventions; they are merely observers. . . . [T]hey can recognise the operation of a political convention in the context of deciding a legal question but they cannot give legal rulings on its operation or scope, because those matters are determined within the political world.[6]

---

[4] *Miller 2*, para [52].
[5] *Miller 2*, para [50].
[6] *R (Miller) v SS for Exiting the European Union* [2017] UKSC 5 (*Miller 1*), para [146].

This reluctance to intervene applied to the so-called Sewel convention which has been set out clearly in statutory form (see Chapter 8). According to the language used in *Miller 2*, the court's acceptance of executive accountability was as an underlying constitutional principle standing behind the convention, not the convention itself. Given the lack of authority to support this finding, the distinction drawn between principle and convention is hardly convincing in legal terms.[7] In fact it has been suggested that '[t]he court has now moved from being a passive observer of political conventions to an active observer, indeed umpire, of political convention and etiquette'.[8] Many political decisions relating to the prerogative are routinely taken on a pragmatic basis. The court recognises that it has exercised a supervisory jurisdiction over the executive for centuries but if the executive is subject to this novel accountability principle in the way it exercises the prerogative, judicial intervention becomes possible on a routine basis.

This apparently heightened judicial profile should not be simply attributed to a deliberately interventionist policy by the judges.[9] The UKSC was called upon to adjudicate against a backdrop of extreme political conflict over Brexit that was also coincidental with the lack of a working majority in Parliament for the government. The prorogation in *Miller 2* concerned the obvious manipulation of the constitutional rules of the game which would otherwise have been placed beyond the rule of law and political scrutiny. The judicial fire brigade was called out to mediate, reflecting the British common law approach to addressing such problems. Rather, it might be concluded that such landmark cases expose a deeper constitutional malaise requiring a revised constitutional settlement: one that provides a clearer definition of the judicial role in resolving constitutional questions (see Chapter 10).

The first part of this chapter discusses the significance of the introduction of the UKSC to replace the Appellate Committee of the House of Lords before focusing upon the contribution of the common law and statutory interpretation in a constitutional context. Attention then turns to consider the implications of the modernisation of the historic office of the Lord Chancellor and the reform to the system of judicial appointments in establishing a principle of separation of powers and the protection of judicial independence. The second half of the chapter

---

[7] A Perry, 'Enforcing Principles, Enforcing Conventions', UK Const L Blog (3 December 2019).
[8] S Padijer, 'Miller No2: Orthodoxy as Heresy, Heresy as Orthodoxy', UK Const L Blog (7 October 2019).
[9] P Craig, 'The Supreme Court, prorogation and constitutional principle' [2020] *PL* 248.

considers the role of administrative law and, in particular, judicial review which has played an increasingly important part as a counter to the abuse of executive power by central and local government, as well as a range of other public bodies. Indeed, it will be apparent that the judicial profile was heightened with the enactment of the Human Rights Act 1998 (HRA 1998). The HRA 1998 provides a remedy in domestic courts for the infringement of rights under the European Convention on Human Rights (ECHR) by public authorities. The chapter concludes by reviewing the constitutional protection of rights and by evaluating the possible constitutional and legal consequences of attempting to replace the HRA 1998 with a British/UK Bill of Rights.

THE ROLE OF THE COURTS

A Supreme Court for the United Kingdom

In terms of court hierarchy, the Appellate Committee of the House of Lords was replaced by a Supreme Court in October 2009.[10] The UKSC has broadly similar appellate jurisdiction to its predecessor court and it was not designed as a constitutional court.[11] But, of course, it presides over cases (eg *Miller 1* and *2*) that raise constitutional issues. Furthermore, an important area of constitutional jurisdiction relates to the fact that the UKSC has taken over from the Judicial Committee of the Privy Council jurisdiction over 'devolution issues' arising from the Scotland Act 1998, Government of Wales Act 1998, and Northern Ireland Act 1998. While the courts frequently make judgments which develop the principles of the common law, the courts, and in particular the UKSC, do not have a general power of constitutional review. The panel of judges assigned initially to the court included the serving Lords of Appeal in Ordinary (Law Lords). As noted in Chapter 3, although the newly appointed Justices of the Supreme Court are given the title 'Lord' or 'Lady' they are not able to sit or vote in the House of Lords. At its head the new court has a President and a Deputy President.

---

[10] Constitutional Reform Act 2005, Part 3.
[11] For comparison with constitutional courts and supreme courts in other jurisdictions, see A Harding and P Leyland (eds), *Constitutional Courts: A Comparative Study* (London, Wildy, Simmonds and Hill, 2009); J Goldsworthy (ed), *Interpreting Constitutions: A Comparative Study* (Oxford, Oxford University Press, 2006); B Dickson (ed), *Judicial Activism in Common Law Supreme Courts* (Oxford, Oxford University Press, 2007).

For the appointment of judges to the UKSC a selection commission is specially convened for the purpose which must include the President and Deputy President of the Supreme Court and members of the Judicial Appointments Commissions for England, Scotland, and Northern Ireland.[12] To ensure that all parts of the UK have appropriate representation on the Supreme Court in terms of expertise concerning their jurisdictions, the Commission must consult the First Minister in Scotland, the Welsh Assembly (now Parliament), and the Secretary of State for Northern Ireland before making a recommendation of a suitably qualified person to the Lord Chancellor (LC). The LC has then to consult further with senior judges and representatives from the devolved parts of the UK before reaching a decision on the Commission's recommendation. If the LC approves of the Commission's choice, the LC can approve ('notify') the selection, which then goes on to be finally approved by the PM. At this point the LC also has the option, if certain specified grounds are satisfied, of rejecting the selection or requiring a reconsideration, but the LC has no power to choose an alternative candidate.

Common Law and Statutory Interpretation

It was pointed out in Chapters 1 and 2 that the common law is a recognised source of the constitution. Judges have the capacity to develop the law by setting precedents in the cases they decide. Some important areas of law, for example the law of contract and tort, have been largely created by judicial decisions. According to Chief Justice Coke writing in the seventeenth century: '[Cases] are not to be decided by natural reason, but by the artificial reason and judgment of law which requires long study and experience before that a man can attain cognizance of it.'[13] This principle recognises the collective wisdom of the judges refined over long periods and organised through precedents. An alternative, more critical, view would be to question any mystical notion of judicial omnipotence and would prefer to regard the common law as the creation of a professional elite of lawyers. The laws emanating from the courts have in the past tended to reflect many assumptions and prejudices of judges drawn from a narrow class.[14]

---

[12] Constitutional Reform Act 2005, ss 26 and 27.
[13] Coke, *Reports*, xii, 65, quoted from F Maitland, *The Constitutional History of England*, 10th edn (Cambridge, Cambridge University Press, 1946) 268–69.
[14] See J Griffith, *The Politics of the Judiciary*, 5th edn (London, Fontana, 1997) xv.

According to the doctrine of binding precedent, a decision made by a court in one case is binding on other courts of the same or lower status in subsequent cases involving similar facts. This rule is meant to ensure that similar cases will be decided in a similar manner. It relies on a system with a hierarchical appellate structure, and the principle depends on courts following the decisions of the courts above them.

The UKSC is the highest domestic appellate court and is generally bound by its previous decisions, but the UKSC can make changes to the law when it considers them necessary.[15] This relaxation of the rules of precedent provides scope at the highest domestic level to modify the law to bring it in line with changing circumstances and to avoid injustice. However, the need to weigh any considerations in favour of judicial innovation against the need for certainty and the danger of retrospective effect has meant that departures from precedent are rarely in evidence.

It has been generally acknowledged that the courts will not ignore or disapply statutes, and the courts were previously only able to question the legality of Acts of Parliament where matters of binding EU law arose.[16] However, the courts are responsible for the interpretation of statute law in cases that are brought before them. It is necessary for judges to perform this interpretative function when hearing cases at first instance or when deciding contested points of law on appeal. In other words, Parliament is supreme in passing laws, while judges have to decide what Parliament intended when it approved a particular piece of legislation. In situations where there is ambiguity the Interpretation Act 1978 and the common law rules of statutory interpretation (the literal rule, golden rule, and mischief rule, among others) are employed to assist the courts in performing this task. Moreover, the judgment in *Pepper v Hart*[17] confirmed that the courts could draw upon official reports of debates in Parliament to clarify Parliament's intentions in situations where legislation appears ambiguous or obscure.

Parliamentary sovereignty is, according to Dicey and other influential commentators, the fundamental rule of the constitution, which recognises that Parliament has the power to pass or repeal any law, including 'constitutional laws'.[18] This doctrine, as was noted in Chapter 3, not only makes the entrenchment of fundamental principle difficult but it also means that the will of Parliament predominates over that of the

---

[15] *Lord Chancellor's Practice Direction* [1966] 1 WLR 1234.
[16] *R v Secretary of State for Transport, ex p Factortame Ltd (No 2)* [1991] 1 AC 603.
[17] [1993] AC 593.
[18] See J Goldsworthy, *The Sovereignty of Parliament: History and Philosophy* (Oxford, Oxford University Press, 1999) ch 1.

courts. The position in the UK has often been contrasted with codified constitutions. It was also noted earlier that in the United States, the Federal Supreme Court has a constitutional review function. The decision in *Marbury v Madison*[19] in 1803 established the convention that the US Supreme Court could declare null and void as unconstitutional any statute or action of the federal or state governments which it considered conflicted with the supreme law of the constitution. This convention had the effect of establishing a principle of judicial sovereignty, giving the Court power to declare actions of other branches of government unconstitutional. Any such decision by the US Supreme Court will be binding on federal and state institutions. In exercising this function, there have been many occasions when the Court has been called upon to adjudicate at the centre of the political process. The US Supreme Court makes the final decision on the legality of contentious political issues ranging from racial segregation in schools,[20] women's abortion rights,[21] to the legitimacy of the presidential election process.[22]

Although the UK lacks a codified constitution with the introduction of so much legislation with constitutional implications, the position has changed in recent years. For example, the European Communities Act 1972 under sections 2 and 3 qualified the doctrine of sovereignty by recognising that a competing source of law was judicially enforceable in the courts. Up until UK withdrawal from the EU English courts were required to put into effect laws passed by EU institutions[23] even to the extent of suspending the provisions contained in domestic legislation. Moreover, the interpretative powers of the courts were extended by the adoption of a rule of construction approach, which holds that words in a statute should be read to have a meaning that was consistent with Community law, even if this involves a departure from the language used in the statute.[24] Of course under the Brexit Withdrawal legislation[25] the supremacy of EU law no longer applies prospectively but section 5(2) allows for the continuing supremacy of pre-existing EU law. The revised interpretative rules in the European Union (Withdrawal Agreement) Act 2020 allow Ministers of the Crown to issue regulations to any 'relevant court or tribunal' on how

---

[19] 5 US 137 (1803).
[20] *Brown v Board of Education of Topeka* 347 US 483 (1954).
[21] *Dobbs v Jackson Women's Health* 597 US 215 (2022).
[22] *Bush v Gore* 531 US 98 (2000).
[23] See *R v Secretary of State for Transport, ex parte Factortame (No 2)* [1991] 1 AC 603, discussed in Chapter 3.
[24] See Lord Diplock in *Garland v British Rail Engineering Ltd* [1983] 2 AC 751.
[25] European Union (Withdrawal Act) 2018, s 5.

to interpret and even to disapply EU retained case law as well as domestic case law which relates to EU retained case law.[26]

The HRA 1998 has modified the position of the courts by incorporating the ECHR into domestic law. Parliamentary sovereignty is not directly compromised by the HRA 1998, but the ECHR may be regarded as equivalent to a domestic Bill of Rights because, in effect, ECHR rights become part of domestic law by requiring public bodies to have regard to these rights in their dealings with members of the public (see section below). In yet another context, devolution has introduced a new kind of constitutional jurisdiction by requiring the courts to oversee the limits of the powers conferred as part of the devolution arrangements (see Chapter 8).

The Evolution of the Office of Lord Chancellor

In Chapter 3 it was observed that the ancient office of LC[27] conflicted with the idea of separation of powers.[28] The anachronistic position was clearly out of step with principles contained in the ECHR introduced into domestic law by the HRA 1998.[29] In consequence, the Constitutional Reform Act 2005 formally disqualifies the LC from sitting as a judge. The LC, also known as the Secretary of State for Justice,[30] is the cabinet minister with responsibility for the appointment of judges, the administration of the courts, the provision of legal aid, and (since 2007) for running the prison service. In common with all other ministers, the office holder must be a Member of Parliament, but there is no longer a requirement to be a member of the House of Lords.[31] Until the passage of the Constitutional Reform Act 2005 a legal background was considered essential, acknowledging a special nexus with the legal profession and ensuring that the views of judges and lawyers would be voiced with some authority at the cabinet table. In theory, the LC was capable of

---

[26] See European Union (Withdrawal Agreement Act) 2020. Section 26 introduces into s 6 of the European Union (Withdrawal) Act 2018 new subsections (5A) through (5D).

[27] Under the Constitutional Reform Act 2005 the Lord Chancellor is also Secretary of State for Justice.

[28] As head of the judiciary the incumbent retained until 2003 the right to sit on the highest appellate court while also serving as Speaker of the House of Lords and acting as a member of the cabinet. See D Woodhouse, *The Office of Lord Chancellor* (Oxford, Hart Publishing, 2001).

[29] European Convention on Human Rights, Art 6.

[30] The LC's ministerial role was revised from Lord Chancellor's Department, first to a Department of Constitutional Affairs (2003) and then to a Ministry of Justice (2007).

[31] Subsequent appointments to the office have remained MPs able to represent the Ministry of Justice in the House of Commons.

protecting the judicial branch from executive interference, particularly when it came to resource allocation (the extent to which this was true depended to a considerable degree on the personal authority of the office holder). After the 2005 reforms the LC must be 'qualified by experience' but a legal background is no longer a prerequisite.[32] Nevertheless, the Constitutional Reform Act 2005 requires the LC and all those involved in the administration of justice, including in the appointment of judges, to be under a duty to respect and maintain judicial independence.[33] The appointment of non-lawyers has attracted criticism, in part, because of a failure of some LCs to adequately support judicial independence in the face of personalised press criticism of individual judges. (See discussion of the first *Miller* case in Chapter 3.[34])

Appointing and Dismissing Judges

A crucial area that has been transformed by these changes concerns the role of the LC in relation to judicial appointments. The traditional system for judicial appointments that has now been replaced lacked transparency. This was because it was based on consulting existing judges to obtain informal recommendations. Nevertheless, it was accepted that the recommendations made by the LC for senior judicial appointments (or recommendations by the PM with respect to the Court of Appeal and House of Lords) went to the best-qualified individuals on the basis of their performance as barristers or solicitors rather than on the basis of any declared political affiliation.[35]

When it became clear that the judicial appointments system was going to be radically changed there was concern that the process could become politicised.[36] For example, it is quite common under codified constitutions for the executive to propose and the legislature to approve appointments to the higher judiciary.[37] There were very good reasons for not imitating

---

[32] Constitutional Reform Act 2005, s 2.
[33] Ibid, s 3.
[34] M Elliott, J Williams, and AL Young, 'The Miller Tale and Introduction' in M Elliott, J Williams, and AL Young (eds), *The Constitution after Miller: Brexit and Beyond* (Oxford, Hart Publishing, 2018) 12ff.
[35] Nevertheless, it has been argued that political bias is discernible in significant judicial decisions. See eg J Griffith, *Judicial Politics since 1920* (Oxford, Blackwell, 1993).
[36] For further discussion see M Tushnet, 'Judicial Accountability in Comparative Perspective' in N Bamforth and P Leyland (eds), *Accountability in the Contemporary Constitution* (Oxford, Oxford University Press, 2013).
[37] Art 104 of the Italian Constitution is one such example.

the procedure in the United States and involving Parliament actively in the appointment process. The Constitution of the United States was drafted to incorporate separation of powers as a core doctrine. In regard to the appointment of the most senior judges who sit on the US Supreme Court, the power to nominate candidates is given to the executive in the form of the President. On the other hand, the Senate, as part of the legislature, has the duty of confirming presidential nominations.[38] However, even though justices of the US Supreme Court once confirmed remain in place for their lifetime, this procedure has not been a guarantee of independence and political neutrality. In fact, the position has been exactly the reverse in regard to the US Supreme Court. The US Supreme Court exercises a constitutional review function and, unlike the UK courts, it has the power to oversee the constitution and to declare legislation invalid. This has projected the Court into the forefront of political controversy on many occasions.[39] Most obviously in recent times it was the US Supreme Court that finally had to decide the validity of the contested presidential election result in the year 2000 in the case of *Bush v Gore*.[40] The political dimension of the Supreme Court's role has resulted in deliberate attempts by US Presidents to select judicial candidates with views that appear to correspond to their own.[41] An obvious danger in making any such reform in the UK to the system of judicial appointments was introducing any form of political interference into the process.

The central objection made by Professor Griffith to the types of appointments to the judicial bench during the 1970s and 1980s concerned the elevation to the higher judiciary of a public school Oxbridge-educated elite section of society, nearly all of whom had experienced a similar legal training.[42] Influential commentators such as Lady Hale, former president of the UKSC, no longer view the problem mainly in terms of social class, but rather identify the need to appoint judges who are more representative of society as a whole.[43] LCs have increasingly recognised the importance of placing increasing emphasis on equality and diversity as well as the accepted

---

[38] Art II, s 2. The Senate will hold hearings to examine the suitability of candidates but presidential nominations are ratified unless there are blemishes to personal reputation: S Finer, *Five Constitutions* (London, Penguin, 1979).

[39] M Vile, *Politics in the USA* (London, Hutchinson, 1976) 242; R Denenberg, *Understanding American Politics*, 3rd edn (London, Fontana, 1992) ch 6.

[40] 531 US 98 (2000).

[41] M Tushnet, *The Constitution of the United States: A Contextual Analysis*, 2nd edn (Oxford, Hart Publishing, 2015) 128ff.

[42] Griffith (n 14) 18ff.

[43] Lady Hale, 'Equality in the Judiciary', Kuttan Menon Memorial Lecture, 21 February 2013; https://www.supremecourt.uk/docs/speech-130221.pdf.

qualities of integrity and judicial quality understood in terms of intellectual ability.[44] Despite the changes to the appointments system discussed below, and close monitoring of who is appointed, there is still an under-representation of women and ethnic minorities at the highest judicial levels.[45]

The task of selecting judges is now in the hands of a Judicial Appointments Commission (JAC) for England and Wales, which was established under the Constitutional Reform Act 2005 as an independent non-departmental body. This body is itself largely appointed by open competition and it is responsible for selecting judges up to and including High Court judges. It comprises 15 commissioners in total. There are five lay members, six judicial members, two professional members (one barrister and one solicitor), and one lay magistrate. The chair must be one of the lay members. Commissioners serve for between three and five years. The initial appointments to the Commission included seven women and two from ethnic minorities, one of whom chaired the Commission.

The weight attached to recommendations by the JAC for England and Wales is of central importance, especially for appointments to the higher judiciary. This issue comes down to whether the power to select that is given to the JAC can be undermined by the ratification process. For appointments up to and including those to the High Court, the Secretary of State will inform the JAC when a vacancy arises.[46] After the selection and interviewing process has been carried out by the JAC, a single name for each vacancy, together with reasons for the selection, will be forwarded to the appropriate authority, usually the Lord Chief Justice or Senior President of Tribunals but for some positions the LC. In the vast majority of cases the recommendation will be approved. However, if it appears that the evidence submitted does not demonstrate suitability further information may be requested. If the initial choice is rejected the matter goes back to the JAC. There is no scope for the recommending authority to substitute its own preferred candidate.

It will be remembered that the Act of Settlement 1701 is regarded as a significant step in securing judicial independence, as it introduced security of tenure for judges who have been appointed 'during good behaviour' ever since. In modern times judges have a retirement age (currently 75 for High Court, Appeal Court, and Supreme Court judges) but parliamentary

---

[44] See eg Lord Falconer, Lord Chancellor, Constitutional Reform Speech, University College London, 8 December 2003.
[45] K Malleson, 'Diversity in the Judiciary: The Case for Positive Action' (2009) 36 *Journal of Law and Society* 376.
[46] For the appointment of Heads of Division of courts and Appeal Court judges, the JAC must set up a selection panel which reports its selection to the Lord Chancellor.

action is necessary to remove senior judges, and no senior judges have been dismissed since the seventeenth century. In addition, the Constitutional Reform Act 2005 sets out procedures for exercising disciplinary powers over judges and for removing judges. At the same time as establishing a system of appointments and discipline, the 2005 Act introduces complaints procedures overseen by a judicial appointments ombudsman who must be a non-lawyer.

Taken together, these have been far-reaching reforms of great constitutional importance. In consequence, it remains crucial that, in practice, the safeguards set out in the Constitutional Reform Act 2005 are effective in underlining a necessary separation of powers and functions between the executive branch and the judicial branch.

ADMINISTRATIVE LAW AND JUDICIAL REVIEW

At a time when the executive has become extremely powerful through what in this book we have called 'elective dictatorship', many commentators believe that judicial review has now assumed particular importance as a counterbalance to executive power. In particular, it performs a crucial constitutional role in the absence of any other mechanism for legislative review (eg a constitutional court). While some kind of oversight function is desirable, the extent to which the courts are able to intervene in the routine processes of government is highly controversial. The courts have come to exercise what has been termed a supervisory jurisdiction, but in terms of actual practice the implementation of administrative law is carried out by central government, local government, and private organisations under contract, with reference to relevant statutory powers contained in primary and secondary legislation. A network of administrative tribunals deals with disputes and appeals against decisions taken by officials. In contrast, continental systems of administrative law, such as those in France, Italy, Germany, the Netherlands, and Spain tend to place much less emphasis on the role of courts (apart from administrative courts); rather, attention is concentrated on the nature of the administrative law (eg droit administratif in France) which provides the structure and functions of the public administration.[47]

---

[47] See W Wade and C Forsyth, *Administrative Law*, 11th edn (Oxford, Oxford University Press, 2014) as an exemplar of the UK court-centred approach, eg p 4: 'The primary purpose of administrative law . . . is to keep the powers of the government within their legal bounds'.

This part of the chapter will be in three sections. The first section sets out the well-known 'red light and green light theory' of administrative law, which helps to explain the historical context. The second section provides an overview of the current law of judicial review. The third section discusses the impact of the HRA 1998 on the regime of public law with particular reference to some important cases.

Red Light and Green Light Theory

In their influential study that begins by tracing the main trends in administrative law Harlow and Rawlings identify two contrasting models, which are termed 'red light' and 'green light'.[48] The former is more conservative and directed at control; the latter is more liberal/socialist in orientation and facilitative in nature. The two models developed in tandem with the emergence of the modern state and serve broadly to characterise competing approaches to administrative law from the late nineteenth century until the latter part of the twentieth century. In the current situation these polarities have been largely replaced by a continuum of overlapping assumptions, combining elements from red light at one end of the spectrum to green light at the other. It might be more accurate to claim that the lights now converge at amber.

The 'red light' view is traced back to Professor Dicey and a political tradition of nineteenth-century *laissez-faire* (minimal state) theory that embodied a strong suspicion of governmental power exercised by emerging state bureaucracy at central or local government level. Standing behind such a view was a desire to minimise the encroachment of the state on the rights (especially property rights) of individuals. Dicey maintained that the concept of *legal* sovereignty (we have already observed that this concept was regarded by him as *the* fundamental principle of the constitution) favours the supremacy of law. Parliament establishes a framework of general rules in society. Dicey's second principle, the rule of law, was of equal importance to his account of the constitution. For it was this concept that ensured that all public and private bodies, as well as individuals, would only act according to the law. The executive should govern strictly according to the rules set out by Parliament. The rule of law proposes that the law will operate to contain illegality and abuse, but without necessarily having, or needing, an explicit moral and

---

[48] C Harlow and R Rawlings, *Law and Administration*, 3rd edn (Cambridge, Cambridge University Press, 2009).

political foundation. Dicey did not elaborate any special guiding principles for law in general (or administrative law in particular, of which he was highly sceptical). The philosophy underpinning the common law was entirely one of pragmatism, that is, of adjustment to changing circumstances. At its most basic level in the context of judicial review, intervention by the courts is justified when public bodies (or any other body or individual) exceed their legal powers (that is, act ultra vires or abuse their powers) when exercising a public function. If unchecked, the bureaucratic and executive power of state institutions or mechanisms will threaten the liberty of us all. Such a view is closely allied to the idea of a 'self-correcting democracy', explained by Craig, in which law performs an important control function.[49] The courts come to be regarded as part of the constitutional system of 'checks and balances'. The grounds of judicial review that have been developed by the courts might be viewed as the response of the common law.

The modern state, and its attendant baggage of administrative procedures, guidance, and discretion, was established at the same time as the emergence of party government. From the outset there have been pronounced differences in ideological perspective between the main political parties as the state has evolved. For advocates of the 'red light' view, the judiciary was regarded as being autonomous and impartial and the common law was imbued with its own standards of independence and fairness. This meant that the courts could be relied upon as a kind of referee to adjudicate, not on the political or even the practical validity of any decision, but simply on the legality of executive action. Over time, judges have developed principles that have served to keep law at a step removed from politics; in other words, the courts should not be usurping the functions of public authorities on matters of fact, judgment, or policy. For example, we will soon see that *Wednesbury* unreasonableness[50] (also known as irrationality) establishes a high hurdle to overcome in judicial review cases, which are often challenging decisions of public bodies.[51]

The main function of the judiciary according to the 'red light' view is perceived as interpreting and applying the strict letter of the law. This conceptualisation of the role of the courts serves the needs of the legal

---

[49] P Craig, 'Dicey: Unitary, Self-correcting Democracy and Public Law' (1991) 106 *Law Quarterly Review* 105.

[50] *Associated Provincial Picture Houses Ltd v Wednesbury Corporation* [1948] 1 KB 223. See below under 'Grounds of Review'.

[51] M Taggart, 'Reinventing Administrative Law' in N Bamforth and P Leyland, *Public Law in a Multi-Layered Constitution* (Oxford, Hart Publishing, 2003) 323ff.

profession well by perpetuating a separation of law from policy issues, with the emphasis being placed on the strict construction of statutes or rules in isolation from their broader contextual framework. The problem is that the proposal that law *can* stand aside from politics and morality is strongly contested. Indeed, opponents of this view maintain that the ideological position of the judiciary is widely demonstrated by analysing crucial cases.[52]

The danger is now more accurately perceived as being that ministers and officials might tend to shelter behind a body of rules and delegated powers that have been created to facilitate the tasks of administration. Thus it is that, in a negative sense, judicial intervention becomes possible as a kind of safety-net, by taking up the democratic slack in those areas where parliamentary control is manifestly found wanting. Or by being activated during those periods when parliamentary opposition is regarded as being weak and ineffective.

Tribunals and the 'Green Light' View

The 'green light' perspective is based on an acceptance of a social democratic view of the state and regards law as an essential tool for the delivery of communitarian policy objectives. It originates from the utilitarian tradition of egalitarian and ameliorative social reform.[53] The introduction of policies extending public service provision was supported by green light theorists. For example, this approach is typified in the writings of Laski, Jennings, Robson, and Griffith from the London School of Economics and Political Science.[54] Statute law emanating from Parliament and resulting from the democratic process is regarded as *the* method for enabling the implementation of such policies. A statute is something concrete and can provide, in principle at least, the proper authority and framework with which to govern consensually. This position recognises that it is very much more difficult to achieve an adequate and sustainable provision of services without having the law on the side of the administration. Law comes to embody, in equal measure, both political legitimacy and moral

---

[52] Griffith (n 14).
[53] See eg S Webb and B Webb, *A Constitution for the Socialist Commonwealth of Great Britain* (London, Longmans, 1920).
[54] R Rawlings, 'Distinction and Diversity: Law and the LSE' in R Rawlings (ed), *Law, Society and Economy Centenary Essays for the London School of Economics and Political Science 1895–1995* (Oxford, Oxford University Press, 1997) 5ff; W Robson, *Justice and Administrative Law*, 3rd edn (London, Stevens, 1951).

persuasiveness. The contribution of the state is encouraged as the state bureaucracy is regarded as an effective means of facilitating the delivery of communitarian goals. It does this by assuming responsibility for at least basic minimum standards of provision, including housing, education, health, social security, and local services.

The emergence of a modern conception of administrative law not only coincides with the political and economic changes that have witnessed the development of the modern state, but it is inseparably linked to these changes. The expansion of the state has given rise to the centralisation of powers in some areas, for example, central government, the civil service, agencies (such as the Prisons Agency or the Benefits Agency), and quasi-government bodies; and the broad territorial diffusion of power in others, for example, the emergence of local government as an important focus of decision-taking and spending in the nineteenth and twentieth centuries (most recently marked by the emergence of a Parliament in Scotland and Assemblies in Northern Ireland and in Wales). In sum, power that is exercised by public bodies has greatly expanded; accordingly, the mechanisms for accountability have assumed a new importance, particularly since the 1960s.

It has been an equally important objective for advocates of what is termed the 'green light' view to establish organised institutions that are properly accountable, and at the same time capable of delivering these services effectively. The growth of bureaucracy in the public domain has meant a proliferation of delegated legislation, administrative rules, codes, and circulars. Some critics have argued that the emergence of strong party government (or 'elective dictatorship') has meant that Parliament no longer operates as anything like an adequate forum of accountability.[55] As will have been apparent from the discussion in Chapter 5, these shortcomings are largely because both Houses may fail to provide effective mechanisms for scrutiny of the executive. The question is whether citizens have sufficient rights in the face of omnipresent central and local government powers or, indeed, those powers exercised by bodies now in the private sector, for example, the privatised utilities.

The response from 'green lighters' to accountability issues has not been to rely primarily on the courts for redress but to build into the decision-making process certain rights, and a degree of participation by the citizen. We can see a reflection of this view in the growth of administrative

---

[55] See eg *Report on Ministers' Powers*, Cmnd 4060 (London, HMSO, 1932); *Report of the Hansard Society Commission on Parliamentary Scrutiny, The Challenge for Parliament. Making Government Accountable* (London, Hansard Society, 2001).

tribunals, introduction of ombudsmen and, perhaps to a lesser extent, in proposals centring on freedom of information, Citizen's Charter/'Service First', and the public sector benchmarking mechanism. The central concern has been to confer, for example, social welfare rights and a general empowerment of individuals in regard to the exercise of powers by public bodies. Equally, 'green light' advocates might wish to see the grounds of review in the courts developed to be more precisely focused on the detailed workings of particular administrative structures, for example, in the areas of social security or immigration control. Additional rights and powers to work through tribunals might be advocated, as these bodies can act as decision-makers/facilitators, as well as encouraging internal dispute resolution.

Tribunals might be regarded as the archetypical 'green light' remedy because of their ability to deal with a large throughput of cases relatively speedily and informally. Until recently, tribunals tended to be specialised bodies custom-designed by individual statutes to perform a particular adjudicative function in respect to an area of administration. Specific tribunals, by hearing a multiplicity of cases in crucial areas such as social security, employment, immigration, or mental health, kept the courts unburdened. However, following the implementation of the recommendations contained in the Leggatt Report there has been a complete overhaul of tribunals in the UK to create a single tribunal service which in some ways resemble administrative courts.[56] It consists of a generic first tier able to hear cases from any of the fields now incorporated as part of the service, and the Upper Tribunal which mainly has an appellate jurisdiction.[57] This change was partly in response to the ECHR's Article 6 requirements of fair trial, now incorporated under the HRA 1998. In order to provide a much clearer separation of powers tribunals are now independent of the departments which make the decisions under review, and tribunal judges have been made fully independent of the executive as they are appointed by the JAC.

The inhibitions on formal hearings imposed by the Covid-19 restrictions in 2020 undoubtedly accelerated an emerging trend towards online dispute resolution (ODR) for tribunals and courts. Against a tide flowing in the opposite direction ODR offers the potential of providing accessible, open, well-publicised remedies either without charge or at minimal cost.[58] The reforms involving the introduction of ODR were first adopted

---

[56] Sir Andrew Leggatt, *Tribunals for Users: One System, One Service* (HMSO, 2001).
[57] See the Tribunals Courts and Enforcement Act 2007.
[58] P Birkinshaw, *Grievances, Remedies and the State*, 2nd edn (London, Sweet & Maxwell, 1994), 285.

as an integral part of the Civil Courts Structural Review conducted by HMCTS.[59] The Public Accounts Committee of the House of Commons stated: 'Collectively, the planned changes to the courts and tribunal system are on a scale never before attempted anywhere in the world.'[60] The Chair of the Justice Committee of the House of Commons stated on the launch of an inquiry by the Justice Committee into the access to justice implications of the reforms that: 'There is no doubt that the HMCTS reforms represent a significant change in the delivery of justice across all areas of the system. . . . We are worried about the access to justice implications and will take this opportunity to put those at the heart of the inquiry.'[61] The cuts in legal aid in the UK have drawn attention to manifest gaps in the legal system. Individuals with savings of more than £8000 no longer qualify for legal aid.[62]

In *R(Cart) v Upper Tribunal*[63] the UKSC held that certain categories of decisions by the Upper Tribunal would not be subject to routine judicial oversight but cases would be amenable to review when raising an important point of principle. However, the Judicial Review and Courts Act 2022 removed this jurisdiction, despite the fact that it acted as a safeguard providing an extra level of judicial protection.[64] The upshot is that in the UK today there is an essentially self-contained tribunal service which bears more than a passing resemblance to the system of administrative courts found in continental systems.[65]

We can see that this 'green light' view implicitly challenges and corrects some of the misconceptions that may arise from the 'red light' view. It does this not by relying on the pragmatism which characterises the common law, but by adopting an instrumental approach (that is, it concentrates on the effectiveness of the measures in question). Administrative law becomes accepted as part of the total apparatus of government, not something largely distinct from it. It can be made to act as a regulator

---

[59] HM Courts and Tribunal Service (HMCTS) is the executive agency under the Ministry of Justice responsible for running the courts and tribunal service.

[60] 'Transforming courts and tribunals' Fifty-Sixth Report of Session 2017–19, *Public Accounts Committee*, 20 July 2018, HC 976.

[61] https://old.parliament.uk/business/committees/committees-a-z/commons-select/justice-committee/news-parliament-2017/court-and-tribunals-reform-launch-17-19/.

[62] Legal Aid, Sentencing and Punishment of Offenders Act 2012 impacted heavily on legal aid provision. See Sir Stanley Burnton, 'Delivering Justice in an Age of Austerity', *Justice*, April 2015.

[63] [2011] UKSC 28.

[64] Section 2 inserts section 11A to the Tribunals and Courts Act 2007 confirming the finality of Upper Tribunal decisions.

[65] L Brown and J Bell, *French Administrative Law*, 5th edn (Oxford: Oxford University Press, 1998).

and facilitator to enable social policy to be implemented effectively and fairly. The 'green light' approach continues to be manifested in the contribution of administrative tribunals and statutory regimes of regulation (eg applying to public utilities and railways).

In recent decades there has been a fundamental change affecting the nature of government, with a widespread tendency towards marketisation through the privatisation of many services that were once in the public sector and the development of public–private partnerships, and so on. Harlow and Rawlings recognised that by the 1980s in an era of reinvented government it was no longer accurate to see things in terms of a polarisation of 'red light' and 'green light' views. In the contemporary arena the clear ideological divide of right and left between the main political parties has virtually disappeared. The major parties have adopted the principles of market capitalism to various degrees. Despite the fact that some members of the higher judiciary may still be drawn from an Oxbridge elite, it is no longer clear that the affiliations of judges can be measured in terms of support for one political standpoint to the detriment of others, or one view of the constitution. Indeed, during the 1980s and 1990s under the Conservative governments of Margaret Thatcher and John Major, the courts were drawn into the political fray as a counterweight to government and a new jurisdiction under the HRA 1998 has added to this role. The result has been that a significant number of decisions have challenged controversial decisions and policies adopted by government (illustrated in the section on judicial review cases below).

Judicial Review as Remedy

As a procedure which developed to contain ultra vires action judicial review is not an appellate process concerned with the merits of particular decisions. Rather, the common law deployed a range of special prerogative remedies (now renamed: original names in italics) capable of containing an excess of legal authority quashing order (*certiorari*), prohibiting order (*prohibition*), mandating order (*mandamus*), which can apply as well as the equitable remedies of declaration and injunction, The effect is not necessarily to guarantee a particular final outcome. For example, a quashing order invalidates a decision and requires the decision-maker to take the decision again lawfully. On the other hand, the private law remedy of damages is rarely granted in judicial review proceedings. General exposure to financial compensation would have far-reaching implications for the funding of public bodies (see the discussion of liability of the Crown in contract and tort in Chapter 4).

Limiting Judicial Review: Ouster Clauses

A recurring question in determining the reach of the courts in curbing executive discretion has centred upon the validity of statutory ouster clauses. These clauses amount to a drafting formula expressly designed to prevent the intervention of the courts (shall not be questioned in any courts of law).[66] In *Anisminic v Foreign Compensation Commission*[67] it was held by the House of Lords that such statutory provisions appearing to limit the jurisdiction of the courts would be considered invalid and could not give blanket protection against a nullity or against jurisdictional error.[68] The same principle was confirmed much more recently by the Supreme Court in the *Privacy International Case*. Lord Carnwath explains

> I see a strong case for holding that, consistently with the rule of law, binding effect cannot be given to a clause which purports wholly to exclude the supervisory jurisdiction of the High Court to review a decision of an inferior court or tribunal, whether for excess or abuse of jurisdiction, or error of law. In all cases, regardless of the words used, it should remain ultimately a matter for the court to determine the extent to which such a clause should be upheld, having regard to its purpose and statutory context, and the nature and importance of the legal issue in question: and to determine the level of scrutiny required by the rule of law.[69]

In other words, this question is not merely a technical matter of how the courts interpret the precise wording and determine the application of each ouster clause, but it is also a constitutional issue of the highest importance because it concerns the capacity of the courts to consider cases and uphold the rule of law. This tension between the executive and the courts was recently highlighted after a successful judicial challenge by a group of asylum seekers[70] to the previous government's flagship Rwanda policy. The agreement reached with Rwanda would have allowed

---

[66] *Padfield v Minister for Agriculture, Fisheries and Food* [1968] AC 997.
[67] [1969] 2 AC 147.
[68] For further discussion, see Wade and Forsyth (n 47) 613ff.
[69] *R (On the application of Privacy Internation) v Investigatory Powers Tribunal* [2019] UKSC 22 at para 144.
[70] *R (On the application of AAA (Syria) and others) v SS for the Home Department* [2023] UKSC 42.

asylum claims to be considered in Rwanda rather than the United Kingdom, but the Supreme Court found that any such removal decisions would be in breach of the UK's obligations under international law and domestic human rights law as it denied protection from refoulement to the individuals concerned. The government responded to this decision by enacting the Safety of Rwanda (Asylum and Immigration) Act 2024, a piece of legislation which went to extraordinary lengths to oust the jurisdiction of the courts,[71] and, at the same time, disapplied the Human Rights Act[72] as well as conferring on ministers and officials a task that would otherwise have been regarded as a judicial role for the courts, namely, to oversee this sensitive area of rights protection.[73] The clash that might have arisen between the government and the courts failed to materialise as the Labour government elected in 2024 immediately scrapped the Rwanda policy. Nevertheless, this legislation remains on the statute book as a deliberate attempt to marginalise the judicial role in protecting rights and the upholding of the rule of law.[74]

Distinguishing Public Law from Private Law

A series of procedural innovations introduced in the late 1970s greatly simplified the process for applying (now claiming) for judicial review, and contributed to the increase in cases coming before the courts. The House of Lords decided unanimously in *O'Reilly v Mackman*[75] that the application for judicial review procedure[76] had been set up specifically to deal with public law issues and to impose, in the public interest, safeguards against, in Lord Diplock's words: 'groundless, unmeritorious or tardy attacks upon the validity of decisions made by public authorities in the field of public law'. The public interest was therefore given priority over the private. The normal route would be by way of judicial review procedure, with a number of limited exceptions being made to this general rule. A public law issue might be defined by reference to the authority making the decision: if it is a 'public' authority, then it should

---

[71] Section 2.
[72] Section 3.
[73] Section 4.
[74] P Leyland 'The UK's Rwanda Asylum Policy and the Courts: reflections on the Constitutional Consequences?' (2024) 2 *DPCE* 767–83.
[75] [1983] 2 AC 237.
[76] Introduced by Rules of the Supreme Court, Ord 53, later enacted under s 31 of the Supreme Court Act 1981 and revised under the Civil Procedure Rules, Part 54 (in 2000).

be subject to 'public' law regardless of the actual power being exercised. However, the exclusivity principle is subject to certain exceptions; for example, if the conduct of a public body impacts on private law rights as well as public law rights, an action can be brought in the ordinary civil courts.[77]

Apart from recognising that the judicial review procedure was directed at the control of public as opposed to private power, it has been necessary to find a method of distinguishing the public from the private – a task made more difficult by the increasing overlap between the two. For example, in what has been termed the 'contract state' not only has there been widespread privatisation and regulation, but also many governmental services, ranging from prisons to street cleaning and refuse disposal, are performed by private companies. The Court of Appeal in *R v Panel on Takeovers and Mergers, ex parte Datafin*[78] was faced with the dilemma of deciding whether it was the source of the powers of the organisation which was the crucial factor, or the nature of the body itself and the public consequences of its decisions. In this instance, the Panel on Takeovers and Mergers took the form of an entirely non-statutory, self-regulating association, set up by persons having a common interest, which had devised and operated a code of conduct to be observed in the takeovers and mergers of public companies. The court held that, bearing in mind that the panel did have government backing and was exercising public duties in the public interest, it should be subject to the control of public law. However, there has been a succession of cases where qualifications in the application of this functions test have seen charitable organisations, regulatory bodies, religious organisations, and political parties falling beyond the ambit of judicial review.[79]

The Requirements of Standing

In order to proceed with a claim for judicial review the claimant must have *standing*, which is defined as having 'sufficient interest' in the contested matter.[80] This hurdle has a useful function in that it deters frivolous or

---

[77] See eg *Roy v Kensington and Chelsea and Westminster Family Practitioner Committee* [1992] 1 AC 624.
[78] [1987] 1 All ER 564.
[79] See eg *R v Disciplinary Committee of the Jockey Club, ex parte Aga Khan* [1993] 2 All ER 853; *R (On the application of Tortoise Media Ltd) v Conservative and Unionist Party* [2025] EWCA Civ 673.
[80] Senior (formerly Supreme) Courts Act 1981, s 31(3).

vexatious claims, but if the rules are too narrowly drawn worthy cases might also be excluded. The extent to which standing has to be a direct personal interest has been a matter of discussion in a number of important cases. For example, in *Inland Revenue Commissioners v National Federation of Self-Employed and Small Businesses Ltd*,[81] the Federation objected to a decision taken by the tax authorities, who had reached a deal with a completely unconnected group of casual workers from the newspaper industry. Although it was held that this group representing small businesses did not have standing as ordinary taxpayers to mount a challenge, in an influential judgment Lord Diplock set out a more 'open' approach to standing:

> It would ... be a grave lacuna in our system of public law if a pressure group, like this federation, or even a public-spirited taxpayer, were prevented by outdated technical rules of locus standi [that is, standing] from bringing the matter to the attention of the court to vindicate the rule of law and get the unlawful conduct stopped.

Such an approach, which also recognises 'group' standing, has been in evidence in many subsequent cases. As Professor Harlow puts it: '[T]he legal process is transmut[ed] into a freeway [and is in danger of becoming] a free-for-all.'[82] Lastly, it is worth noting that the rules of standing under the HRA 1998 depend on a narrower 'victim' test[83] which entails that an action is open only to a person who is personally subject to a violation of rights. However, in practice, this requirement has not proved a significant impediment to claimants.

Grounds of Judicial Review

The basic principle is that a public authority cannot act outside the power (*ultra vires*) conferred on it or abuse that power. The power often derives from a statutory source; sometimes it is a prerogative power which is challenged,[84] and abuse of power through failure to adhere to procedural rules is another familiar ground in judicial review cases. If power is exceeded the courts have the capacity to intervene by awarding a

---

[81] [1982] AC 617.
[82] C Harlow, 'Public Law and Popular Justice' [2002] *MLR* 1 at 17.
[83] See HRA 1998, s 7.
[84] On the prerogative see earlier discussion of *R (on the application of Miller) v Secretary of State for Exiting the European Union* [2017] UKSC 5 and *R v Secretary of State for the Home Department, ex parte Fire Brigades Union* [1995] 2 AC 513.

remedy. For example, a quashing order will have the effect of invalidating a decision taken by a public body. The body concerned is required to act lawfully when taking the decision in the future. On the other hand, the courts should not intervene when public bodies are acting within their powers unless Parliament has specifically given them the authority so to do, usually by way of granting a statutory right of appeal, often to a tribunal. In *Associated Provincial Picture Houses v Wednesbury Corporation*[85] Lord Greene MR was concerned to emphasise that the courts only interfere with an act of an administrative authority if it has contravened the law. Even when the action is found to be ultra vires the court must not substitute itself for the decision-making authority. The court is acting in a supervisory capacity, not as an appellate body able to change the outcome.

The terminology used to describe the main grounds of review was explained by Lord Diplock in the *GCHQ* case:[86]

> The first ground I would call 'illegality', the second 'irrationality' and the third 'procedural impropriety' . . . By 'illegality', as a ground for judicial review, I mean that the decision maker must understand correctly the law that regulates his decision making power and give effect to it. Whether he had or not is *par excellence* a justiciable question to be decided, in the event of a dispute, by . . . the judges, by whom the judicial power of the State is exercisable. By 'irrationality' I mean what can now be succinctly referred to as '*Wednesbury* unreasonableness' . . . It applies to a decision which is so outrageous in its defiance of logic or of accepted moral standards that no sensible person who had applied his mind to the question to be decided could have arrived at it . . . I have described the third head as 'procedural impropriety' [which includes] failure to observe basic rules of natural justice or failure to act with procedural fairness towards the person who will be affected by the decision . . . this head covers also failure by an administrative tribunal to observe procedural rules that are expressly laid down in the legislative instrument by which its jurisdiction is conferred, even where such failure does not involve any denial of natural justice.

Additional sub-grounds of review exist under each of these main categories referred to by Lord Diplock.[87] Looking at the development and application of the grounds and sub-grounds under the common law, it

---

[85] [1948] 1 KB 223.
[86] *Council of Civil Service Unions v Minister for the Civil Service* [1985] AC 374 (known as the *GCHQ* case) at 410–11B.
[87] M Fordham, 'Surveying the Grounds: Key Themes in Judicial Intervention' in P Leyland and T Woods (eds), *Administrative Law Facing the Future: Old Constraints and New Horizons* (London, Blackstone, 1997).

becomes clear that for the decision-making process of public bodies to be lawful, it has to take place within a framework of rules. To take a few commonly occurring sub-categories associated with illegality (discussed above), improper purpose/motive is clearly related to exceeding lawful authority, since it refers to the fact that the decision-taker may have acted outside a statutory purpose, while the idea of relevance suggests that a body in exercising discretionary power must have regard only to legally relevant considerations. By the same token, it may have acted unlawfully by taking irrelevant considerations into account. Under the fettering principle, it can be unlawful for a decision-making body to form an over-rigid policy in advance which prevents it from exercising the discretion granted to it. Improper delegation occurs when a decision-making body acting under statutory authority gives away the power to act to another body.

A ministerial decision to grant aid to Malaysia for the Pergau Dam project under section 1 of the Overseas Development and Co-operation Act 1980 was successfully challenged as unlawful in *R v Secretary of State for Foreign Affairs, ex parte World Development Movement Ltd*.[88] It was held by Rose LJ that '[w]hatever the Secretary of State's intention or purpose may have been, it is ... a matter for the courts and not for the Secretary of State to determine whether, on the evidence before the court, the particular conduct was, or was not, within the statutory purpose'. The judge's reading of the statute identified an abuse of power, but it is arguable that the court has come close to interfering with ministerial discretion in the sensitive area of the formulation of foreign policy.

An equally important aspect of judicial review has been the recognition of procedural protection under the rules of fairness/natural justice, for example, the right to a fair hearing. Furthermore, legitimate expectation, which is closely related to the doctrine of legal certainty, has become an important part of domestic administrative law, both in a procedural sense, and as a matter of substantive law. In certain circumstances legitimate expectation has allowed a claimant to assert a substantive right. In the celebrated case of *R v North and East Devon Health Authority, ex p Coughlan*[89] a long-term quadriplegic patient who had been expressly promised a home for life by the health authority successfully challenged a subsequent decision to close the home. This breach of promise without prior consultation was held by the Court of Appeal to fall into a category of decisions which were so unfair as to amount to an abuse of power.

[88] [1995] 1 WLR 386.
[89] [2000] 2 WLR 622.

The danger in such cases is that the courts might have the potential to interfere with the rights of democratically elected public authorities to change their policies.

The Question of Merits

We have already noted that, according to the 'red light' view, the courts operating under the rule of law have, what we have called, a supervisory jurisdiction. They perform a control function but the scope of this jurisdiction is crucially important. Many writers have observed that even before the introduction of devolution and the HRA 1998 the reformulation of the grounds of judicial review coincided with a period of greater judicial activism.[90] The constitutional effect of widening the scope of judicial review represents a rebalancing of power between Parliament and the courts. *Roberts v Hopwood*[91] can be cited as an early twentieth-century case which demonstrates the implications of judicial intervention. Poplar Council had been empowered under the Metropolis Management Act 1855 to pay its employees such salaries and wages 'as . . . the council may think fit'. Although the statute appeared to confer a broad discretion, when a socialist local authority chose to use these wide discretionary powers to pay female and male workers equally and also a wage above the market rate, its policy was deemed to be unlawful by the House of Lords.

Looking back to the post-World War II period, it is clear from Lord Greene's landmark judgment in *Associated Provincial Picture Houses v Wednesbury Corporation*[92] that a restricted role for the courts was envisaged. To keep the courts a step removed from political decision-making, the concept of *Wednesbury* unreasonableness/irrationality deliberately erects a high hurdle to overcome before intervention will be possible. An authority operating within its statutory remit would have to have 'come to a conclusion so unreasonable that no reasonable authority could ever have come to it'. His Lordship cited the example of a red-haired teacher dismissed for no other reason than the colour of her hair to illustrate this. Judicial reluctance to intervene when the flagship policies of central government were at stake was evident in *Nottingham City Council v*

---

[90] See eg S Sedley, 'Sounds of Silence: Constitutional Law without a Constitution' (1994) 110 *LQR* 270.
[91] [1925] AC 578.
[92] [1948] 1 KB 223.

Secretary of State for the Environment.[93] Nottingham CC sought to challenge what appeared to be a manifestly unfair government policy directed at city councils that imposed crippling financial penalties (rate capping) for overspending. For a remedy to be granted Lord Scarman stated that the decision of the minister would have to have been so absurd that he must have taken leave of his senses. In other words, an even higher hurdle would need to be overcome in such cases. On the other hand, as will be apparent when discussing the HRA 1998 below, a lower threshold will apply in cases concerning the infringement of human rights.

Particularly since the 1980s there have been important decisions which demonstrate a greater judicial willingness than was previously discernible in overseeing the activities of central and local government, often with controversial results. In *Bromley v Greater London Council*[94] the courts were called upon to decide on the legality of a policy decision by the Greater London Council (GLC) (later abolished). In line with a local election commitment the Council wanted to reduce fares on London transport. The Transport (London) Act 1969 placed the authority under a duty to develop policies, and to encourage, organise and, where appropriate, to carry out efficient and economic transport facilities and services for Greater London. This section of the Act appeared to give the GLC considerable discretion in the way it chose to run the transport system and allocate resources, but on final appeal to the House of Lords, it was held that the new policy was unlawful. The fiduciary duty owed to ratepayers (local taxpayers) had not sufficiently been taken into account when making the decision. The word 'economy' used in the Act was given a narrow interpretation in the House of Lords. The council was not acting irrationally, and an alternative approach to interpreting the statute would have recognised that the GLC had the scope to reallocate funding in the form of grants to underpin its reduced fares policy.

The Impact of Judicial Review

By requiring public bodies to act lawfully, judicial review imposes legal limits to decision-making in the public domain. The grant of judicial review is discretionary and in two stages. Claims (formerly called applications) for judicial review are assessed by a judge who will consider whether they are sufficiently well founded to proceed. This remedy is

[93] [1986] AC 240.
[94] [1983] 1 AC 768.

available only to a claimant who has exhausted all other avenues of redress such as informal complaints procedures, ombudsmen, statutory rights of appeal, and so on. And it must normally be sought within a strict time limit that requires that an application be made *promptly* and in any event within three months from the time the decision was taken.

The growing importance of judicial review has been partly reflected by the increase in the number of cases coming before the courts.[95] For example, between 1982 and 2005 the number of (first stage) permissions for leave for judicial review increased from 685 to over 5,000. In the next ten years the number of permissions increased spectacularly again, peaking at 15,500 in 2013 before declining to a more constant annual figure for the next 10 years of around 4,000 cases a year.[96] However, this exponential rise in the number of permissions from the 1980s and the subsequent decline requires further qualification. First, this is because, in order to filter out unmeritorious cases, judicial review is, as mentioned above, a two-stage process, and only a small proportion of claims reach the final substantive stage in the form of a full court hearing. (For example, a public authority may prefer to settle and reconsider its decision or a claimant may withdraw if faced with the prospect of losing at the hearing.) Second, rather than showing an even distribution across the entire spectrum of government activity, the statistics reveal that a large percentage of applications were previously concerned with immigration and asylum cases. The overall number of permissions decreased spectacularly once the bulk of immigration and asylum cases were diverted to the Upper Tribunal. Currently, there are approximately the same numbers of claims concerning central government and local government. Third, while the number of cases has increased the caseload represents only a tiny fraction of decisions taken by public bodies (well under 1 per cent). However, since the 1980s civil servants and local government officers have been issued with an internal publication entitled *The Judge over Your Shoulder* stressing the importance of good decision-making and the susceptibility of decisions incorrectly taken to JR challenges.[97] It might be concluded at this point that there is uneven access to judicial review, and that, if government administration is taken as a whole, its impact might appear of marginal importance. On the other hand, the

---

[95] For in depth evaluation see C Harlow and R Rawlings, *Law and Administration*, 4th edn (Cambridge, Cambridge University Press, 2022) chapter 19.

[96] Civil Justice Stats, main tables Apr–Jun 2017, www.data.gov.uk/dataset/163c7366-0988-44f8-9803-6d3124311716/civil-justice-statistics. Only a fraction of these applications proceed to a full hearing.

[97] 'The Judge Over Your Shoulder', *Government Legal Department*, 6th edn, 2022.

possibility of judicial review lurking in the background almost certainly has a deterrent effect and encourages decision-making bodies to act lawfully.

THE CONSTITUTIONAL PROTECTION OF RIGHTS AND THE HUMAN RIGHTS ACT 1998

As we noted in Chapter 2 the idea of positive rights was not part of the Diceyan constitution outlined in 1885. The rule of law operated on the basis that all conduct would be regarded as lawful unless it happened to conflict with a particular law. For example, UK citizens have enjoyed freedom of speech to the extent that what they uttered did not defame the reputation of another citizen contrary to the laws of libel and slander, divulge an official secret contrary to the Official Secrets Act 1989, or incite a person to racial hatred contrary to the Public Order Act 1986, and so on. In a liberal democracy, as defined in Chapter 1, it is axiomatic that in a practical sense civil liberties and human rights are a prerequisite and are of central importance to the security and well-being of all ordinary citizens.

Certain rights that were contested over many generations such as the universal right to vote may now appear relatively secure but the continuance of crucial rights may be under threat at any time. As the nation celebrated the 800th anniversary of Magna Carta in 2015, many judges, lawyers, and academic commentators[98] pointed to an impending crisis in the criminal and civil justice system that presents a direct threat to the spirit of the famous Article 39:

> No free man shall be seized or imprisoned or stripped of his rights or possessions, or outlawed or exiled or deprived of his standing in any other way, nor will we proceed with force against him or send others to do so except by the lawful judgment of his peers or by the law of the land.[99]

The imposition of courts fees in criminal cases and government cuts to the legal aid budget which were justified as a money saving exercise are not only having an impact on the sustainability of sections of the legal profession but they represent an assault on the rights to a fair trial of ordinary citizens lacking the means to obtain legal representation. The

---

[98] See eg F Wilmot-Smith, 'Necessity or Ideology' (2014) 36(4) *London Review of Books*, 6 November.
[99] A Arlidge and I Judge, *Magna Carta Uncovered* (Oxford, Hart Publishing, 2014) 59ff.

Legal Aid, Sentencing and Punishment of Offenders Act 2012 came into force in April 2014. This piece of legislation deprives many citizens of basic access to justice. To be granted a legal aid certificate, applicants must cross three hurdles. They must first prove that their claim belongs in a category of law that is eligible for funding. Second, they must pass a 'merits' test by demonstrating that their case is serious. Third, a 'means' test assesses income and capital. In most cases, this must be less than £2,657 gross monthly income. The upshot is that legal representation has been radically curtailed. And it is now only available in family law cases where there is evidence of domestic violence. This demonstrates that the erosion of rights is ongoing as part of political disagreement over such rights, and attacks on such rights need to be constantly resisted.

Of course, the HRA approach requires a marked change in legal culture.[100] This is because public authorities have been forced to comply with the Act from the time it came into force in October 2000. Any action by government or other public bodies that does not comply with the ECHR can be challenged as being unlawful. At the same time the HRA 1998 was a new departure for the UK constitution because it has the effect of incorporating the ECHR into domestic law. Prior to the enactment of the HRA 1998, the ECHR enjoyed the status of an international treaty. In the absence of any statute or domestic authority to the contrary, the courts endeavoured to interpret domestic law in a way that was consistent with the ECHR, but, in general, a citizen who considered that his or her Convention rights had been breached had to take the case to the Court of Human Rights in Strasbourg for resolution, and this process often took in excess of five years. In contrast, the rights set out in the Convention might now be regarded as being equivalent to a domestic Bill of Rights. Since the Act came into force it is unlawful for a public authority to disregard an individual's Convention rights. (The ECHR includes rights to life; freedom from torture; freedom from slavery; freedom of thought, conscience, and religion; privacy; freedom of expression; and freedom of peaceful assembly and association.)

It is stressed once again that the HRA 1998 seeks to prevent judicial supremacy from replacing parliamentary supremacy. If the courts are called upon to determine whether primary or subordinate legislation is in incompatible with Convention rights, section 3 provides: 'So far as it is possible to do so, primary legislation and subordinate legislation must be read and given effect in a way which is compatible with the

---

[100] See A Kavanagh, *Constitutional Review under the UK Human Rights Act* (Cambridge, Cambridge University Press, 2009).

Convention rights.' This section confers an interpretative power which allows the courts to consider legislation and transform it by stretching its meaning, where it is possible to do so, in order to achieve Convention compatibility. This interpretative power under section 3 marks a significant shift of power from Parliament to judges, since the courts are able to rewrite sections of acts by reading into them words that are not there, and by doing so, remove potential conflicts with the Convention. For example in *Ghaidan v Godin-Mendoza*[101] the House of Lords interpreted the term 'spouse' under schedule 1 of the Rent Act 1977 to allow surviving same-sex partners to enjoy equal tenancy rights to heterosexual couples. The majority of their Lordships were mindful of achieving a correct separation between the courts and Parliament in fulfilling their interpretative obligation, and it is possible to view this case as acceptable judicial legislation:

> [T]he courts were interpreting existing statutory words as opposed to filling in gaps, no procedural modifications were required, there were no wide-ranging practical ramifications of the Convention compatible interpretation and the modification was an incremental addition to previous legislative amendments.[102]

The courts are not given power to invalidate primary legislation. If they find it impossible to interpret legislation in a Convention-friendly way, they can issue a declaration of incompatibility under section 4. As will be apparent in the so-called *Belmarsh* case[103] discussed below this does 'not affect the validity, continuing operation or enforcement' of the Act in question. The effect of a declaration of incompatibility is to refer the matter back to Parliament. The Act introduces a fast-track procedure for the purpose of amending any offending legislation (there have been examples of this procedure being used). After a declaration of incompatibility has been issued, section 6(2) stipulates that until such time as any offending legislation is amended it will not be unlawful for a public authority to act in a way which is incompatible with the Convention. To achieve the compatibility of prospective legislation there is a procedure at the drafting stage under section 19 requiring the relevant minister to 'make a statement of compatibility'. Further, under section 2 of the HRA courts in the UK are required to take into account Strasbourg jurisprudence but they are not bound by it. This requirement suggests that a

---

[101] [2004] UKHL 30; [2004] 3 All ER 411.
[102] A Young, '*Ghaidan v Godin-Mendoza*: avoiding the deference trap' [2005] *PL* 23, at 27.
[103] *A and Others v Secretary of State for the Home Department* [2004] UKHL 56.

court, unless it has good reason for doing so, will keep pace with Strasbourg case law and will not dilute or weaken its effect. On the other hand, the scope for UK judges to develop interpretation has also been recognised.[104]

Vertical or Horizontal Effect

The HRA 1998 has a 'vertical' effect by requiring *public* bodies such as government, local government, the courts, and the police in their dealings with the public to adhere to the Convention. The courts are required to determine what constitutes public functions for these purposes, and, since the Act has been in force, it has been necessary to determine how far its provisions extend. This task is complicated by the fact that the *private* sector frequently carry out high-profile *governmental* services that are publicly funded (eg in the realms of health, education, housing, prisons, etc). It would appear that ECHR rights are not only directly enforceable against public bodies in respect of *all* of their activities, but may also be directly enforceable against some private companies and organisations in respect of their *public* functions.[105] In determining the extent to which the Act can be applied the courts have given a narrow definition to what constitutes a public body. For instance, the House of Lords held in YL *v Birmingham City Council*[106] that Article 8 would not be available to a claimant as the nursing care provision depended on a private contractual relationship between the provider and the public authority. This limitation was later removed by legislation.[107] Section 6 of the HRA 1998 is directed primarily at public authorities, but it is clear that there are ways in which Convention rights apply 'horizontally' under the Act. The HRA 1998 gives no direct right to sue in the civil courts for an alleged breach of a Convention right by another individual or private company, but the courts are a public body to which the Act applies. Therefore, if an action is taken to sue in the courts on a private law matter which involves interpreting a statute affecting Convention rights, the courts are now required to interpret that statute according to section 3 in a way that is compatible with Convention rights. The same obligation attaches to

---

[104] D Irvine, 'A British Interpretation of Convention Rights' [2012] *PL* 237. See eg *Manchester CC v Pinnock* [2010] UKSC 45.
[105] See HRA 1998, s 6(3)(b).
[106] [2007] UKHL 27.
[107] Section 145 of the Health and Social Care Act 2008.

the common law, which must be interpreted in a compatible manner.[108] In sum, the HRA 1998 places no *direct* obligations in regard to the conduct of private citizens and private organisations.

Proportionality Review

It is clear that the HRA 1998 establishes a new statutory type of illegality by requiring ministers and public officials at all levels to exercise their powers in ways that are compatible with Convention rights. Judicial review proceedings may be taken by victims to contest any violation of Convention rights by a public authority. The standard of review which is applied in cases involving Convention rights is proportionality (rather than *Wednesbury* unreasonableness/ irrationality). In essence, the administrative court has to determine whether the interference with Convention rights has been proportionate. In the first place, the proportionality test is a *balancing* exercise, which usually ends up deciding whether the means employed, involving interference with fundamental rights, are justified by the end, which is nearly always associated with considerations such as pressing social need, public policy, national security, or public good. Second, the court decides between competing interests (often those of an individual against those of a public authority). Therefore, it would appear that there is a danger of the court being sucked into the decision-making process itself, which should be regarded as the province of the executive (see discussion of the *Prolife Alliance* case below, and the divergence of views between the Court of Appeal and House of Lords). However, it might be argued that this question of proportionality is decided as a question of law, just as matters are determined under the ultra vires principle. The court decides the boundaries of discretion according to familiar grounds of judicial review; similarly, under proportionality the central issue is not the correctness of the decision or action taken by the executive branch, but simply whether the decision-maker is operating within the bounds set by the ECHR and the HRA 1998. A further point is that the approach of the courts will vary according to the ECHR Articles which are at issue, since the intensity of review will depend upon the subject matter in hand. Certain Convention

---

[108] See *Douglas v Hello! Ltd* [2001] 2 WLR 992 and *Campbell v MGN* [2004] 2 WLR 1232. For example, Baroness Hale said in *Campbell* that the courts could not invent a new cause of action to cover types of activity not previously covered. But where there is a cause of action, the court, as a public authority, must act compatibly with both parties' Convention rights.

rights are set out in absolute terms with no exceptions and cannot be balanced against a public interest. These are Article 2 (right to life), Article 3 (prohibition of torture), Article 4(1) (prohibition of slavery), and Article 7 (no punishment without law). On the other hand, the rights in Article 4(2), Article 4(3) (forced labour), and Article 5 (liberty and security) are subject to a long list of exceptions, while Articles 8–11 and the First Protocol of the ECHR permit a public authority to claim that the interference was necessary in the interests of a democratic society.

The House of Lords confirmed that the proportionality test would apply in cases related to HRA 1998 in *R v Secretary of State for the Home Department, ex parte Daly*.[109] It was held that new prison rules under the Prison Act 1952 permitting staff to read the correspondence of prisoners when searching cells without the prisoner being present constituted a breach of Article 8 ECHR. The rule constituted a disproportionate breach of the Convention. Lord Steyn stated that the proportionality test should now be used in cases of this type as the differences in approach between the traditional grounds of review based on the Wednesbury standard and proportionality may sometimes lead to different results:

> The starting point is that there is an overlap between the traditional grounds of review and the approach of proportionality. Most cases would be decided in the same way whichever approach is adopted. But the intensity of review is somewhat greater under the proportionality approach.

Proportionality operates as 'a *balancing* exercise':

(1) it usually ends up deciding whether the means employed, involving interference with fundamental rights, are justified by the end, which is nearly always associated with considerations such as pressing social need, public policy, national security, or public good;

(2) the court decides between competing interests (often those of an individual against those of a public authority).

Significant Cases Under the Human Rights Act 1998

In the section that follows we will look more closely at a selection of cases decided under the HRA 1998 in order to consider its wider impact. Although concerning different rights and diverse policy areas such decisions demonstrate a greatly increased judicial profile in ensuring that

---

[109] [2001] 3 All ER 433.

the decision-making of government and other public bodies achieves an appropriate balance between legitimate public interests and the rights set out under the ECHR.

The so-called *Belmarsh* case[110] was a landmark decision[111] considered by a nine-judge panel which illustrated the potential and, at the same time, the limits of the HRA 1998. Set against the response to a perceived threat presented by international terrorism successive governments have introduced increasingly draconian legislation which has had the effect of eroding citizen rights. The Anti-Terrorism, Crime and Security Act in 2001[112] permitted the indefinite detention of foreign nationals suspected of terrorism without trial. A group of Algerian suspects challenged their detention in Belmarsh prison. The court had to consider whether there had been a lawful derogation under Article 15 from their Article 5 right to liberty and security. A derogation requires proof of a public emergency threatening the life of the nation. The court was prepared to accept that the Home Secretary (as cabinet minister responsible) with access to security information was in a position to make a political assessment relating to the severity of the terrorist threat.

But under the 2001 Act these Algerian detainees were treated as foreign nationals. The House of Lords rejected the government's contention that the discrimination in their treatment was a matter of immigration law beyond the reach of the courts. Rather, their detention was regarded as a matter of state security. The detainees were treated differently from British citizens, or others with a right of abode in the UK, who might be suspected terrorists. It came down to whether persons in a similar situation to the detainees were subject to preferential treatment without objective justification, and the difference of treatment was on grounds of nationality or immigration status (which are proscribed grounds under Article 14). Moreover, indefinite detention without trial was regarded by the court as a wholly disproportionate response to the problem.

In reaching this conclusion the House of Lords was, in effect, required to consider the limits of judicial deference. Lord Bingham (the senior Law Lord) assessed the respective roles of Parliament, the executive, and the judiciary and decisively rejected a distinction that the Attorney-General

---

[110] *A and Others v Secretary of State for the Home Department* [2004] UKHL 56.

[111] R Clayton, 'A v Secretary of State for the Home Department [2005]: The Belmarsh Case' in S Juss and M Sunkin (eds), *Landmark Cases in Public Law* (Oxford, Hart Publishing, 2017) 161ff.

[112] See A Tomkins, 'Legislating Against Terror: The Anti-Terrorism, Crime and Security Act 2001' [2002] *PL* 205.

had attempted to draw between democratic institutions such as the Immigration Service and the courts. It was

> wrong to stigmatise judicial decision-making as in some way undemocratic. It is particularly inappropriate in a case such as the present in which Parliament has expressly legislated in section 6 of the 1998 Act to render unlawful any act of a public authority . . . incompatible with a Convention right.

Moreover, he stated:

> [T]he greater the legal content of any issue, the greater the potential role of the court, because under our constitution and subject to the sovereign power of parliament it is the function of the courts and not of political bodies to resolve legal questions.

The court issued a declaration of incompatibility under section 4 of the HRA 1998 but this, of course, could not nullify the legislation directly. The suspects remained in prison. However, the judicial condemnation of the legislation in such comprehensive terms prompted the government to respond. It was persuaded to replace the incompatible provisions of the Anti-Terrorism, Crime and Security Act 2001 with a revised approach to controlling terrorist suspects under the Prevention of Terrorism Act 2005 involving arguably less draconian 'non-derogating control orders' and 'derogating control orders' issued by the Secretary of State under judicial supervision.

Turning next to a decision concerning freedom of speech, the *Prolife Alliance* case[113] provides a good example of two distinct conceptions of the judicial role. The claim involved a challenge to a decision by the BBC and other broadcasters not to transmit in Wales a party election broadcast which had been made by the Prolife Alliance. The Alliance contended that this was in breach of its Convention rights to free speech under Article 10 ECHR. The broadcast used material that the broadcasters considered to be sensational and disturbing. Prior to this refusal it had been pointed out to the Prolife Alliance (as would be the case with others proposing to make election broadcasts) that a significant proportion of their programme would not comply with the relevant provisions of the Producers' Guidelines of the BBC and the Programme Code of the Independent Television Commission in respect of matters of taste and decency.

The majority in the House of Lords rejected the view expressed in the Court of Appeal that the courts owed a special responsibility to the

---

[113] *R v British Broadcasting Corporation, ex parte Prolife Alliance* [2003] UKHL 23.

public as the constitutional guardian of the freedom of political debate, holding that the court had taken on the role Parliament had given to broadcasters. Lord Nicholls pointed out that 'in effect [the Court of Appeal] carried out its own balancing exercise between the requirements of freedom of political speech and the protection of the public from being unduly distressed in their own homes'. Such a decision comes close to a merits review, with the court, rather than the statutory body/regulatory authority, deciding what was fit for transmission. There was nothing to indicate that the BBC had applied an inappropriate standard in assessing whether the broadcast was offensive. Their Lordships held that the decision had been taken in a responsible manner with account taken of the implications for freedom of speech. This judgment would appear to place limits on the capacity of the courts to intervene where Parliament has set out a clear statutory framework for the determination of such issues.[114]

A prominent decision involving the extent of religious freedom, also raised the issue of the respective roles of courts and other decision-makers in the public domain. In *R (on the application of SB) v Head teacher and Governors of Denbigh High School*[115] an Islamic student challenged the particular school dress code for Muslim girls at a state school as a violation of her right to manifest her religious beliefs under Article 9 ECHR. The court found that in situations of this kind, it is the practical outcome that matters, not the type of the decision-making process that led to it. The school in laying down its rules, which were acceptable to and developed in consultation with mainstream Muslim opinion, had acted in an 'inclusive, unthreatening and uncompetitive' way.[116] From a constitutional standpoint a contrast can be drawn between a policy approach in the UK accepting multiculturalism manifested in school dress codes which is confirmed in such judicial decisions as the *Begum* case and the position in France, which has a secular state under Article 2 of the constitution. This provision allowed a controversial law to be introduced in 2004 banning the wearing of headscarves and other conspicuous religious symbols in French state schools.[117]

---

[114] On the HRA and the limits of free speech see also *R v Shaylor* [2002] UKHL 11.
[115] [2005] EWCA Civ 199; [2006] UKHL 15; see T Poole, 'Of Headscarves and Heresies: The Denbigh High School Case and Public Authority Decision-making under the Human Rights Act' [2005] *PL* 685.
[116] Some doubts over aspects of the policy were expressed in a thoughtful partly dissenting judgment by Baroness Hale.
[117] Loi no 2004-228 of 15 March 2004.

In another context, the right to life under Article 2 of the ECHR arose on the vexed question of resource allocation. In *R (on the application of Rogers) v Swindon NHS Primary Care Trust and Sec of State for Health*[118] the backdrop was a challenge to the denial of a very expensive drug treatment for breast cancer by a public authority set against the needs of an individual patient. Also, the case involved alleged discrimination as there was evidence that availability of this drug under the NHS varied according to locality, which amounted to a so-called 'postcode lottery'. The Court of Appeal held that the prioritisation of funding for treatment which provided for exceptions in unidentified circumstance was not in itself unlawful. However, they declared that the policy was unlawful in this case because the decision-maker, that is the Primary Care Trust, had not specified what the exceptional circumstances would be and they were therefore unable to justify such a policy in clinical terms. This decision calls into question the use of the HRA 1998 by private individuals in such circumstances. The courts are called upon to look at the question from the perspective of the private right to be treated while the health service managers with finite budgets have to balance the rights of the many different patients that require treatment.[119]

What has been the impact of the HRA 1998? The practice of public authorities has been affected by the imposition of a duty under section 6 of the HRA 1998, which requires them to conform with the ECHR. Public bodies, including the police, prison service, Immigration Service, and the courts, have been forced to modify many of their procedures to make sure that they perform their duties in a manner which is compliant with Convention rights. Turning to the courts, the proportionality principle gives judges a more sensitive tool to consider whether the restriction of a right can be justified (are the means used to impair the right or freedom no more than is necessary to accomplish the objective?). In cases such as *Prolife Alliance* and *Denbigh High School* the courts have been cautious about straying into the territory of administrative decision-making by public authorities. However, in the *Belmarsh Detainees* case (discussed above) the House of Lords was willing to issue a declaration of incompatibility in a situation where it considered that fundamental rights had been contravened in a disproportionate manner.[120] Parliament

---

[118] [2006] EWCA Civ 392.

[119] K Syrett, 'Opening Eyes to the Reality of Scarce Health Care Resources?' [2006] PL 664.

[120] *A and Others v Secretary of State for the Home Department* [2004] UKHL 56.

responded by amending the offending legislation. In a period where there is a perceived increase in the threat of terrorism, the HRA 1998 has not prevented repressive legislation from reaching the statute book. For example, the Prevention of Terrorism Act 2005 allowed the detention of terrorist suspects without trial for periods of up to 28 days.[121]

Reforming the Human Rights Act or Replacing it with a British Bill of Rights?

Many constitutional commentators and public law practitioners would now acknowledge that in the absence of a codified constitution the incorporation of the ECHR into domestic law under the HRA 1998 has served as an effective method for enforcing citizen rights and minority rights without handing over too much power to the judiciary.[122] Nevertheless, the Act has also attracted criticism: particular reference has been made to individual cases featured in the media where suspected terrorists, asylum seekers, or sex offenders have appeared to use the law, sometimes at considerable public expense, as a shield from justice.[123] Moreover, on the vexed question of the blanket denial of prisoner voting rights[124] vigorous opposition has been voiced within Parliament and expressed more generally in the press in response to Strasbourg judgments which require changes to UK domestic law to achieve conformity with the convention under Article 46.[125] At the same time, Brexit has resulted in further uncertainty over rights protection, as a result of UK withdrawal from the European Charter of Fundamental Rights.[126]

Since 2010 the Conservative Party has made several attempts to repeal the HRA 1998 and introduce a British/UK Bill of Rights as a substitute.

---

[121] The Patriot Act 2001 in the United States gives enormous powers to the authorities to combat terrorism, effectively suspending important rights under the Constitution.

[122] See eg T Bingham, *The Rule of Law* (London, Allen Lane, 2010) 66ff.

[123] For example, the litigation concerning Mustafa Kamal Mustafa (Abu Hamza) which continued for eight years following an extradition request in 2004 by the USA.

[124] See S Fredman, 'From Dialogue to Deliberation: Human Rights Adjudication and Prisoner's Right to Vote' in M Hunt, H Hooper, and P Yowell (eds), *Parliament and Human Rights: Redressing the Democratic Deficit* (Oxford, Hart Publishing, 2015) 447; *Hirst v United Kingdom*, Application no 74025/01, 6 October 2005 and *R (Chester) v Secretary of State for Justice and McGeoch v The Lord President of the Council* [2013] UKSC 63.

[125] A Horne and H Tyrell, 'Sovereignty, Privilege and the ECHR' in A Horne and A Le Sueur (eds), *Parliament Legislation and Accountability* (Oxford, Hart Publishing, 2016) 271ff.

[126] M Markakis, 'Brexit and the EU Charter of Fundamental Rights' [2019] *PL* 82, 93.

For example, most recently in 2022 a Bill of Rights bill was introduced by the then government (later dropped) which would have retained the protection of convention rights and their enforcement in domestic courts, but the obligation to interpret legislation compatibly with convention rights and the duty to consider Strasbourg jurisprudence would have been removed.[127] Such changes would almost certainly have reduced the level of rights protection available to vulnerable members of society. The problem in replacing the HRA remains as no consensus over a replacement has actually emerged. Indeed, the wide divergence of views expressed by the independent Commission on a Bill of Rights set up by the Conservative/Liberal government which reported in December 2012[128] mirror the disagreements over rights protection across the wider community, and also within the main political parties.[129] A majority of this Commission were prepared to support the principle of a British Bill of Rights. The assumption being that this charter of rights would incorporate and build on all of the UK's obligations under the ECHR. The majority report concluded that the ECHR would still be at the core of rights protection, it provides remarkably little detail on the nature of the rights that might be covered beyond existing ones. Presumably the charter would embody some general principles, including a commitment to the rule of law, an impartial judiciary and the recognition of some general values: liberty, democracy, fairness, and perhaps civic duty. Without making significant substantive changes there was some support for cosmetic redrafting of existing Convention rights in contemporary language and a novel element would be to introduce a link between citizen responsibilities and rights.[130]

On the other hand, minority views from the Commission favoured the adoption of a free-standing British Bill of Rights and this could include taking the radical step of withdrawing from the ECHR. This approach reminds us that the key question from a technical legal standpoint is whether a British Bill of Rights would remain compatible with the Convention and therefore allow the UK to continue with its international treaty obligations. For example, would it be possible to amend

---

[127] This would involve the repeal and replacement of section 3 and section 2 of the Human Rights Act 1998.

[128] The Commission on a Bill of Rights, 'A UK Bill of Rights? – The Choice Before Us', 18 December 2012.

[129] D Grieve, 'Why Human Rights Should Matter to Conservatives' (2015) 86(1) *Political Quarterly* 62.

[130] See S Dimelow and A Young, '"Common Sense" or Confusion? The Human Rights Act and the Conservative Party', *The Constitution Society*, 2015.

section 2 of the HRA 1998 that requires a court or tribunal to take into account ECHR jurisprudence whenever it is relevant.[131] Lord Neuberger explained the current approach:

> This court is not bound to follow every decision of the European court. Not only would it be impractical to do so: it would sometimes be inappropriate, as it would destroy the ability . . . to engage in the constructive dialogue with the European court . . . Where, however, there is a clear and constant line of decisions whose effect is not inconsistent with some fundamental substantive or procedural aspect of our law, and whose reasoning does not appear to overlook or misunderstand some argument or point of principle, . . . it would be wrong for this court not to follow that line.[132]

Additional obstacles encountered by attempting to replace the HRA 1998 would relate to the impact of any such changes on devolution. From a legal standpoint, the ECHR is directly incorporated by the 1998 devolution legislation as part of the devolution arrangements. The HRA 1998 applies in the sense that conformity with the Convention limits the legislative competence of the devolved legislatures.[133] In consequence, securing changes to the HRA 1998 would require amendment of the original devolution legislation and therefore the agreement of the devolved Scottish and Welsh parliaments and the Northern Ireland Assembly. But there have been indications that a British/UK Bill of Rights would be widely opposed in Scotland, Wales, and Northern Ireland. Any change embarked upon without agreement carries with it far-reaching political implications. The Scottish Nationalist party not only objects to any watering down of rights protection, but also, shows no sign of consenting to the imposition of a charter of rights drafted by a Conservative Government at Westminster. At the same time, the Belfast peace agreement in Northern Ireland, already showing signs of fragility, is founded upon the incorporation of the ECHR and the availability of remedies for any breach of the Convention. No detailed proposals for replacement or reform of the HRA 1998 have been forthcoming since the 2012 Commission reported. However, in December 2020 the government set up an independent review of the HRA 1998 which will consider how the Act is working in practice and whether any change to it is needed.[134]

---

[131] See Lord Irvine of Lairg, 'A British Interpretation of Convention Rights' UCL, Bingham Centre, 14 December 2011 and 'Lord Irvine: human rights law developed on a false premise', *The Guardian*, 14 December 2011.
[132] *Manchester CC v Pinnock* [2010] UKSC 45 at para [48].
[133] See Scotland Act 1998, s 29(2)(d).
[134] The Conservative Party election manifesto in 2019 proposed only 'to update the Human Rights Act' (47). www.gov.uk/guidance/independent-human-rights-act-review.

Further, it should be clear that the domestic courts employing the proportionality principle under the HRA 1998 have developed an impressive body of jurisprudence concerned with rights protection alongside the common law. The upshot is that no credible replacement whether a British or UK Bill of Rights could simply revert to the pre-HRA 1998 era without profound consequences. Rather, the challenge is to extend protection in the face of contemporary threats to citizen rights. Certainly, any attempt to withdraw from the convention would undermine the UK's international reputation and single the country out in Western Europe as a pariah nation.

CONCLUSION

Against a backdrop of the manifest limitations in parliamentary scrutiny of primary legislation and delegated legislation and the ever-increasing powers handed over to the executive, we have seen in this chapter that judicial review and human rights protection has emerged as one important counterweight to executive dominance, with a growing recognition of the role of the courts. The jurisdiction under the HRA 1998 and the devolution legislation represent a further shift of power to the judiciary, who must now adjudicate on alleged breaches of Convention rights, inter-governmental disputes, and the validity of legislation emanating from the Scottish and Welsh parliaments and the Northern Ireland Assembly. In turn, this much increased judicial profile raises a number of further and, as yet, unresolved issues about the role of the courts at the highest level. Senior judges have made statements suggesting that:

> [I]t is not unthinkable that circumstances could arise where the courts may have to qualify a principle established on a different hypothesis of constitutionalism. In exceptional circumstances involving an attempt to abolish judicial review or the ordinary role of the courts, the Appellate Committee of the House of Lords or a new Supreme Court may have to consider whether this is a constitutional fundamental which even a sovereign Parliament acting at the behest of a complaisant House of Commons cannot abolish.[135]

While it may be widely accepted that the developments over the last 50 years or so have resulted in a significant trend to constitutionalise public law, there is much less agreement on whether the UKSC should also act as a constitutional court, in the sense of determining the limits of powers

---

[135] Lord Steyn, in *Jackson v A-G* [2005] UKHL 56 at [102]; see also Lord Woolf, 'Droit Public English Style' [1995] *PL* 57 at 68; T Allan, *Law, Liberty and Justice: The Legal Foundations of British Constitutionalism* (Oxford, Clarendon, 1993) 286.

under the constitution. Certainly, it would be a drastic step to dispense with the core principle of parliamentary sovereignty and allow the courts to invalidate legislation. The courts are not directly accountable, except through the appellate process. This would mean that unelected judges would have the capacity to undermine the legitimacy of decisions made by democratically elected politicians. Finally, it is doubtful whether members of a judiciary schooled in specialist areas of law have the training and background to equip them to act as guardians and regulators of an uncodified constitution (see also Chapter 10 for debates relating to codification of the constitution and the possible impact on the role of the courts).

FURTHER READING

Introduction to Common Law and the Courts System

Griffith J, *The Politics of the Judiciary*, 5th edn (London, Fontana, 1997).
Le Sueur A, 'The Foundations of Justice' in J Jowell and C O'Cinneide (eds), *The Changing Constitution*, 9th edn (Oxford, Oxford University Press, 2019).
Leyland P, 'English Common Law: A Matter of Interpretation' in G Tieghi (ed), *Comparative Law and Global English for Legal Studies* (Naples, Jovene Editore, 2024).
Malleson K, 'The Evolving Role of the UK Supreme Court' [2011] *PL* 754.
Partington M, *Introduction to the English Legal System 2015–2016* (Oxford, Oxford University Press, 2015).
Twining W and Miers D, *How to Do Things with Rules*, 5th edn (Cambridge, Cambridge University Press, 2010).

Judicial Review and Administrative Law

Bamforth N, 'Courts in a Multi-Layered Constitution' in N Bamforth and P Leyland (eds), *Public Law in a Multi-Layered Constitution* (Oxford, Hart Publishing, 2003).
Craig P, *Administrative Law*, 10th edn (London, Sweet & Maxwell, 2025).
Elliott M, 'Ombudsmen, Tribunals, Inquiries: Refashioning Accountability Beyond the Courts' in N Bamforth and P Leyland (eds), *Accountability in the Contemporary Constitution* (Oxford, Oxford University Press, 2013).
Harlow C and Rawlings R, *Law and Administration*, 4th edn (Cambridge, Cambridge University Press 2022).
Leyland P and Anthony G, *Textbook on Administrative Law*, 8th edn (Oxford, Oxford University Press, 2016).

Civil Liberties and the Human Rights Act 1998

Amos M, *Human Rights Law*, 3rd edn (Oxford, Bloomsbury Publishing, 2021).

O'Cinneide C, 'Human Rights and the UK Constitution' in J Jowell and C O'Cinneide (eds), *The Changing Constitution*, 9th edn (Oxford, Oxford University Press, 2019).

Wadham J, *Blackstone's Guide to the Human Rights Act 1998*, 8th edn (Oxford, Oxford University Press, 2024).

Young AL, 'Accountability, Human Rights Adjudication and the Human Rights Act 1998' in N Bamforth and P Leyland (eds), *Accountability in the Contemporary Constitution* (Oxford, Oxford University Press, 2013).

8

Devolution

Scottish Parliament – Welsh Parliament – Northern Ireland Assembly – Additional Member System of Elections – Single Transferrable Vote – Power Sharing – Block Grant Barnett Formula – Brexit and Devolution – West Lothian Question – Devolution and the Courts – Intergovernmental Relations – Concordats – The Sewel Convention – Legislative Consent Motion – Scottish Referendum – Federal

INTRODUCTION

THIS CHAPTER EXAMINES the evolving relationship between central government and devolved government. Until the introduction of devolution the UK was frequently regarded by constitutional commentators as a centralised unitary state. However, the devolution legislation, which was introduced in 1998, gave varying degrees of decision-making authority to Scotland, Wales, and Northern Ireland.[1] The effect of these changes was to establish a new set of democratically elected bodies and to confer substantial powers on devolved legislatures and executives. It will soon be apparent, as the extent and implications of these reforms are discussed, that the constitutional balance between central government and the regions has been significantly modified. As well as setting out the main characteristics of devolution this chapter will reveal an underlying tension between the devolution of power and the centralisation of power. Viewed from a wider European angle the UK trend in establishing devolution in the late 1990s might be regarded as consistent with the principle of subsidiarity set out in the consolidated version of the Treaty on European Union (TEU). This was an initiative designed to encourage decentralisation and regionalism.[2] Varying degrees of power have been conferred on the devolved institutions in

---

[1] A Mayor and Assembly for London was also introduced, discussed further in Chapter 9.
[2] See Article 5.3 TEU.

Scotland, Wales, and Northern Ireland as part of devolution; however, the continuing role of central government should not be underestimated. In a formal sense the Westminster Parliament has retained sovereignty and, it still partly controls the financial parameters of devolution by means of a block grant formula (see below).

HISTORICAL BACKDROP

Devolution was not part of a grand constitutional design; rather, the approach in each case needs to be understood in relation to the distinct history of each nation. Turning first to Scotland, the Crowns were united when James VI of Scotland succeeded to the English throne in 1603 as James I of England. The parliaments of England and Scotland were combined just over century later with each agreeing to an Act of Union in 1707. In legal terms the Kingdoms of England and Scotland were replaced by a United Kingdom of Great Britain. Although Scotland was represented in the Westminster Parliament, important aspects of the Scottish system were never integrated with England. For instance, Scotland retained its distinctive legal and educational system and separate Presbyterian church. In contrast, Wales has been closely linked to England from medieval times. The application of English law and administration in Wales, Welsh representation in Parliament, and the use of English as the official language were included in the so-called Act of Union of 1536; nevertheless, Wales retained its strong Welsh cultural identity and Welsh remained a living language.

From 1800 Ireland was represented at Westminster as part of the Union but in the period during and immediately after World War I there was a prolonged campaign for Irish home rule conducted by Irish nationalists.[3] Notwithstanding a treaty of 1921 approved by the Westminster Parliament and the Dial (Irish Parliament) it was only after a civil war ending in 1923 that an Irish Free State within the commonwealth came into existence in the South. This later became the fully independent Irish Republic in 1937.[4] As part of the settlement to the civil war in the early 1920s a self-governing province of Ulster's six counties, now Northern Ireland, remained part of the UK.[5] In essence, the brand of devolved government in Northern Ireland was fashioned to reconcile the conflicting Ulster protestant and Irish Roman Catholic traditions. From

---

[3] Irish Republican Army (IRA) formed the military wing.
[4] A Taylor, *English History 1914–1945* (London, Penguin, 1970) 206ff.
[5] The Irish Republic was eventually formed from the remaining three counties.

the outset the devolution legislation resulted in an asymmetrical distribution of powers, not only because the extent of the powers given to the Scottish Parliament and the Assemblies in Wales and Northern Ireland were different, but also because neither England nor its various regions acquired an equivalent level of government.

Support for the Scottish Nationalist Party (SNP) had risen between 1964 and 1974, and the Welsh Nationalist Party also emerged as a force in domestic politics. In the wake of the discovery of reserves of oil and gas offshore in the 1960s, nationalists in the 1970s maintained that Scotland could claim economic self-sufficiency. The cause of nationalism was further reinforced by UK membership of the EU. The Kilbrandon Commission, which reported in 1973, recognised that the system of government was over-centralised and recommended an elected assembly for Scotland and a lesser form of legislative devolution for Wales. The original devolution legislation for Scotland and Wales introduced by the Labour government of 1974–79 failed to attract the popular support in referendums that would have been required for its implementation.

During the Thatcher/Major period (1979–97) government in the UK had become highly centralised and political power tended to be concentrated at Westminster. The central government departments with responsibility for Scotland and Wales were based in Whitehall. The decline of traditional industries and relatively high rates of unemployment had added to a build-up of pressure for change. While London and some parts of England boomed economically, this prosperity was perceived to be at the expense of Scotland, Wales, Northern Ireland, and also some parts of mainly northern England. This contributed to the re-emergence of Scottish and Welsh national parties and a spectacular decline in political support for the Conservatives in Scotland and Wales. The Conservative party failed to win a single Scottish or Welsh parliamentary seat at Westminster in the 1997 General Election. In the same election the Labour Party, as well as being the dominant party in Scotland and Wales, was elected with a large majority to form a government at Westminster. The Labour leadership were keen to use the political momentum of victory to negotiate a settlement in Northern Ireland and the Party had a manifesto commitment to introduce devolution for Scotland and Wales.

INSTITUTIONAL FEATURES: SCOTLAND AND WALES

UK devolution in its current form was established by statute in Scotland, Wales, and Northern Ireland in 1999, creating an additional layer of elected government. From the outset the distribution of powers and functions was uneven.[6] The basic framework in each case represented a pragmatic response to the distinct political situation in each part of the nation and particularly the perceived differences in enthusiasm for devolved government.[7] Turning first to Scotland and Wales, this approach meant that Scotland, with a stronger nationalist voice, was provided with a Scottish Parliament empowered to pass primary laws, albeit confined to matters under the scope of its legislative competence. The Scottish Parliament also had limited tax-raising powers. On the other hand, what was initially termed 'executive' devolution in Wales featured an elected Assembly without any primary law-making capacity or any tax-raising powers. The Assembly simply formed a government responsible for the administration of Welsh ministerial departments and quangos.[8] Following legislative intervention the respective systems in Scotland and Wales have fundamental characteristics in common.[9] The Government of Wales Act 2006 (GWA 2006) which followed the report of the Richard Commission eventually provided the Assembly (now Senedd) with full law-making capacity but this major change in status required approval in a referendum held in 2011. In having the capacity to pass laws in their own right the devolved parliaments and assemblies have become co-equals.

The handover of power from central government Whitehall departments to the devolved executives in 1999 was relatively straightforward. The smooth transition was possible because, for the most part, the functions previously administered by the Scottish Office, Welsh Office, and Northern Ireland Office (central government departments) were conferred on the devolved executives, and the civil servants from central government formed the core administration as part of the new scheme. Moreover, the mechanisms of accountability that have been set in place as part of devolution are in several ways different from those at Westminster.

Further, Scottish devolution in its original form was to some extent comparable to federal systems since it adopted a reserved powers model involving a range of powers and functions which were transferred to the

---

[6] See N Burrows, *Devolution* (London, Sweet & Maxwell 2000) 3ff.
[7] In the 1999 Welsh referendum needed to trigger devolution only 50.01 per cent of the electorate voted in favour.
[8] These are non-departmental governmental organisations, funded and appointed by government, eg Welsh Health authorities, the Welsh Tourist Board.
[9] R Rawlings, 'The Welsh Way' in J Jowell and C O'Cinneide (eds), *The Changing Constitution*, 9th edn (Oxford, Oxford University Press, 2019).

Scottish Parliament and Executive[10] but with other powers and functions reserved for the Westminster Parliament.[11] There was no exact alignment between the two systems in terms of devolved functions,[12] but once again, in line with its Scottish counterpart Welsh devolution has been turned into a reserved powers model.[13] This is an approach which arguably provides a clearer separation of powers between what is devolved and what remains. For example, it enables the Senedd to legislate using a specified test except on those subjects reserved for Westminster.[14]

Turning next to elections, the Labour government sought to bring democracy closer to the people in the devolved parts of the UK, and the Additional Member System (AMS) adopted initially in both Scotland and Wales introduced a proportional element to the electoral process. Elections are held every five years. AMS works on a top-up basis, entitling each elector to two votes. One vote is awarded to a constituency candidate and the other for a regional candidate from a party list. In Scotland 73 constituency members of the Scottish Parliament are elected on the basis of first-past-the-post, with 56 additional regional members elected proportionately from party lists.[15] The top-up allows a party that has won disproportionately fewer seats in relation to their overall level of support to be allocated additional seats from regional party lists of candidates.

The voting system for the Senedd Cymru (or Welsh Parliament) (formerly referred to as the Assembly) has been radically changed to a closed party list system of proportional representation, based on 16 area multi-member constituencies elected by the D'Hondt formula. Each constituency from 2026 onwards will elect six candidates. This change also expands the Senedd's membership from 60 to 96.[16]

---

[10] Scotland Act 1998, Sch 5.
[11] See *The UK Withdrawal from the European Union (Legal Continuity) (Scotland) Bill* [2018] UKSC 64 at para [41]: '... in contrast to a federal model, a devolved system preserves the powers of the central legislature of the state in relation to all matters, whether devolved or reserved'.
[12] Functions devolved to Scotland and Wales from 1999: agriculture, fisheries, education, economic development, employment, environment, health and social care, housing, local government, passenger and road transport, planning, sport and the arts, tourism, transport. Some notable differences in the first wave of devolution, eg justice and judicial appointments, were devolved in Scotland but not in Wales and Northern Ireland.
[13] Rawlings (n 9) 304ff.
[14] Wales Act 2017, s 3 and Sch 1.
[15] Scotland Act 1998, ss 5–8.
[16] https://senedd.wales/senedd-now/senedd-blog/how-will-the-new-voting-system-work-at-the-next-senedd-election/.

The introduction of a proportional element to the electoral systems makes it more difficult for any single party to obtain an overall majority in the Scottish Parliament or Welsh Parliament. Elections are not triggered by a defeat for a bill introduced in the legislature, which allows more freedom for individual members dissatisfied with proposals to vote against them.

The formation of a government following an election involves a similar procedure in both Scotland and Wales. For instance, following an election to the Scottish Parliament, a government is formed after Parliament has nominated a Scottish First Minister.[17] If Members of the Scottish Parliament (MSPs) cannot agree on a suitable candidate as First Minister, the Parliament's Presiding Officer is required to enter into negotiations with the parties to facilitate the selection of a candidate. After a nomination has been accepted the First Minister is empowered to appoint ministers from the MSPs to form a Scottish Executive. The executive is roughly equivalent to the Cabinet, and the ministerial appointments are made subject to formal approval by the Queen. The First Minister and Scottish Executive are directly accountable to the Scottish Parliament for the policies pursued by the devolved administration.

The Scotland Act 2016 and the Wales Act 2017 recognise the devolved parliaments and governments as a permanent feature of the UK's constitutional arrangements that cannot be abolished without a referendum.[18] Such a commitment might be regarded as a robust consolidation of an enhanced form of devolution. Some commentators view this trend as representing a step towards the creation of a new kind of federal constitution marked by a clearer division of power.[19] Nevertheless, constitutional orthodoxy founded on Dicey's definition of legal sovereignty places overwhelming emphasis on the legal omnipotence of the Westminster Parliament. In legal terms we find that the Scottish Parliament, Welsh Parliament, and Northern Ireland Assembly can pass legislation only in areas within their legislative remits. All bills are subject to a process of pre-legislative and post-legislative scrutiny to ensure that they remain within devolved competence.[20] Prior to bringing legislation before the

---

[17] Scotland Act 1998, ss 45 and 46.
[18] See Scotland Act 2016, s 1 and Wales Act 2017. By contrast devolution in Northern Ireland envisages the possibility of a referendum on Irish unity.
[19] S Tierney, 'Drifting Towards Federalism' in R Schütze and S Tierney (eds), *The United Kingdom and the Federal Idea* (Oxford, Hart Publishing, 2018) 113ff; R Schütze, 'Introduction' in R Schütze and S Tierney (eds), *The United Kingdom and the Federal Idea* (Oxford, Hart Publishing, 2018) 22.
[20] See eg Scotland Act 1998, ss 31, 32.

Scottish Parliament, its Presiding Officer is under a duty to ensure that legislative proposals fall within legislative competence.[21] Following Parliamentary approval, but before the royal assent is given, there is a four-week delay to allow the Scottish law officers, if they consider it necessary, to send a bill to the UK Supreme Court (UKSC) to determine whether the bill in its amended form falls within the legislative competence of the Parliament. The law officers (that is, the Advocate General, the Lord Advocate, and the Attorney-General) have an important role in making sure that this function is properly discharged.[22] In practice, notwithstanding these procedural safeguards this conferral of legislative powers on the devolved legislatures amounts to a significant qualification of the sovereignty of the Westminster Parliament.[23] In the absence of a legislative consent (Sewel) motion (discussed below) the Scottish and Welsh Parliaments and Northern Ireland Assembly legislate routinely over devolved matters.

A NEW FORM OF DEVOLUTION FOR NORTHERN IRELAND

For the six counties in Northern Ireland the Stormont Parliamentary system of devolved government was set up by the Government of Ireland Act 1920 in order to avoid direct rule from Westminster. The arrangements conferred considerable powers to the Parliament and Executive, but the method of government formation resulted in a permanent Unionist majority. The devolved government at Stormont pursued policies which were regarded as discriminatory by the Nationalist minority, and the flaws in the system, particularly the under-representation of the largely Roman Catholic nationalist community, contributed to the upsurge in violence by paramilitary groups during 'the Troubles' of the 1970s and 1980s. Stormont was suspended in 1972, and Northern Ireland was governed directly from Westminster, with executive functions being performed by the Secretary of State, Ministers of State, and officials at the Northern Ireland Office.

The Northern Ireland Act 1998 (NIA 1998) was designed to restore devolved government in a radically different form.[24] The legislation

---

[21] Similar provisions apply in Wales and Northern Ireland. See eg Wales Act 2017, s 3 which amends the GWA 2006; and NIA 1998, ss 10 and 11.
[22] Scotland Act 1998, s 33.
[23] See eg D McCrone and M Keating 'Questions of Sovereignty: Redefining Politics in Scotland' (2021) 92(1) *Political Quarterly*.
[24] B Dickson, 'Devolution in Northern Ireland' in J Jowell and O'Cinneide (eds), *The Changing Constitution*, 9th edn (Oxford, Oxford University Press, 2019) 247ff.

resulted from protracted negotiations between the UK and Irish governments and the main political parties which in 1998 led to the Belfast Agreement (also known as the Good Friday Agreement). The elements of a permanent power-sharing settlement were agreed by the parties, but the controversial question of disarmament of paramilitary elements (alluded to below) was set to one side as a separate process to be realised in stages.

A directly elected Assembly was established in Northern Ireland consisting of 108 members (now reduced to 90 members) elected every four years.[25] These members are elected by single transferable vote (STV) from multi-member constituencies. The Assembly is given competence to exercise legislative authority[26] over those matters falling under the responsibility of the First and Deputy First Minister (who preside over a shared set of functions) and the nine Northern Ireland government departments (posts shared between Unionists and Nationalists).[27] In common with Scotland and Wales the Presiding Officer of the Assembly examines proposed legislation to ensure it falls within the legislative scope of the Assembly. Legislation passed by the Assembly requires the royal assent,[28] and the NIA 1998 further provides that this law-making power should not affect the sovereignty of the UK Parliament.[29] Although the Northern Ireland Assembly is empowered to pass legislation it currently has no independent tax-raising powers.[30]

The NIA 1998 has created a unique system of compulsory power-sharing at every level of decision-making to ensure joint participation by both communities in the processes of government. From First Minister to Deputy First Minister, executive posts are shared on a proportionally elected basis between Unionists and Nationalists forming the Cabinet and holding all ministerial posts. These provisions for permanent coalition government not only prevent any single party from ruling alone

---

[25] See Northern Ireland (Elections) Act 1998, s 1, and NIA 1998, Part II. www.legislation.gov.uk/nia/2016/29/contents.

[26] See G Anthony and J Morison, 'Here, There and (Maybe) Here Again: The Story of Law Making for Post-1998 Northern Ireland' in R Hazell and R Rawlings (eds), *Devolution, Law Making and the Constitution* (Exeter, Imprint Academic, 2005).

[27] The Northern Ireland Executive departments are: The Executive Office, Finance, Economy, Justice, Infrastructure, Health, Education, Communities, Agriculture, Environment and Rural Affairs.

[28] NIA 1998, s 5(2).

[29] NIA 1998, s 5(6).

[30] If activated the Corporation Tax (Northern Ireland) Act 2015 allows the Assembly to set the rate of corporation tax.

but further require cross-community support for policy initiatives and legislation.[31]

As well as establishing a system of devolved government, the main objective in Northern Ireland was to accommodate the deep-seated political differences between Unionist and Nationalist communities. To this end, specialist watchdog bodies were designed to oversee the wider process of reconciliation. For instance, a Northern Ireland Human Rights Commission was set up under section 68 of the NIA 1998 to promote awareness of the importance of human rights in Northern Ireland. At the same time, the Equality Commission for Northern Ireland was established under section 73 of the NIA 1998 as an independent public body responsible for the elimination of discrimination, and for promoting good relations between different racial groups.

Further, as should be apparent from the earlier discussion of EU membership the Brexit agreement has had a significant impact, with the need for a Northern Ireland 'Backstop' to preserve an open border between North and South, now modified under the Windsor Framework (see below and Chapters 1, 2, and 10). Moreover, the continuation of supra-national dimension to the original settlement is of crucial importance. In order to accommodate Nationalist aspirations for a united Ireland, the system of government is linked to that of the Irish Republic. To satisfy Unionists' fears that the union could be severed without consent there are links with the UK. The North–South Ministerial Council brings together members of the executive of the Northern Ireland Assembly and representatives of the Irish government for the purposes of co-operation on issues of common interest. The British–Irish Council is a body to consider broader mutual interests between the Irish Republic and the UK. It consists of representatives from the UK government, Irish government, Scottish Parliament, Welsh Parliament, the Channel Islands, and the Isle of Man. To satisfy nationalist aspirations the need for ongoing consent for Northern Ireland to remain part of the UK is built into the legislation.

The repeated breakdown of power sharing has exposed the fragility of the peace settlement. On six occasions between 1999 and 2024 Northern Irish devolution has been suspended. Until 2007 these interruptions were caused by a lack of progress with the disarmament process by paramilitary groups. Latterly, the suspensions have been triggered by issues relating to Brexit, political scandals affecting Northern Ireland Assembly

---

[31] NIA 1998, ss 16, 16A–16C (as amended by Northern Ireland (St Andrews Agreement) Act 2006), 17, 18.

members and difficulties reaching agreement between the main parties over the formation of a government following the 2022 election. On these occasions the Northern Ireland Executive has been run by civil servants operating from the Northern Ireland Office.[32]

INTERGOVERNMENTAL RELATIONS: A REVISED APPROACH

Legislating

The devolution initiative established parliaments and assemblies with limited law-making capacity for the respective parts of the United Kingdom. This meant that significant legislative overlap arises, and, in addition, that the Westminster Parliament retained the ultimate capacity to legislate over devolved matters.[33] The retention of this power by the central authority has the potential to challenge the entire concept of devolution. The Sewel convention however recognises the respective legislative competencies of the devolved legislatures and the Westminster Parliament. The UKSC acknowledged that the purpose of current legislative recognition of Sewel[34] was to entrench a practice 'normally' involving consultation between legislatures but only as a convention acting as a political restriction not as a legally enforceable rule upheld by the courts stating that 'Judges . . . are neither the parents nor the guardians of political conventions; they are merely observers'.[35] The upshot was confirmation that legislative consent motions cannot be employed as a form of veto exercisable by the devolved legislatures. Rather, they are an integral part of the established procedure to allow for consultation between the two layers of governance.

Although not originally set out in legal form, Lord Sewel had stated, as the responsible minister during the passage of the Scotland Bill in the House of Lords, that Parliament would not normally legislate in areas devolved to Scotland (this also applies to Northern Ireland and Wales) without the consent of the devolved legislature.[36] This protocol between

---

[32] See D Torrance, 'Direct Rule in Northern Ireland' House of Commons Library CBP 8638, 28 July 2025.

[33] See s 28(7) Scotland Act 1998.

[34] Scotland Act 2016, s 2 and the Wales Act 2017, s 2 refer specifically to the Sewel convention: 'but it is recognized that the Parliament of the United Kingdom will not normally legislate with regard to devolved matters without the consent of the Parliament/Assembly'.

[35] *R (On the application of Miller) v SS for Exiting the EU* [2017] UKSC 5, paras [146], [149], and [150].

[36] The same convention applies to the Northern Ireland Assembly and the Welsh Senedd.

legislatures in the form of a legislative consent motion (LCM) was considered crucial to prevent the role of the devolved legislatures from being undermined by the Westminster Parliament. In practice, where there is overlap a process of consultation should take place before the Westminster Parliament proceeds with its legislation. As Labour was the dominant party at Westminster and in Scotland and Wales during the first phase of devolution until 2010 the situation did not operate as originally envisaged.[37] This is because following the consultative process the devolved legislatures usually consented to the Westminster Parliament legislating on many devolved matters.[38] Despite recent trends Westminster legislation has continued to be of importance in relation to some devolved areas of competence[39] and the statistics also show that notwithstanding the high number of Sewel consent motions, the devolved legislatures have produced a substantial amount of home-grown legislation.[40] This convention has been regarded as crucial to the spirit of devolution because it recognises the need for collaboration between the respective parliaments and the levels of government. The fact that from 1997 until 2019 there were less than 10 occasions when LCMs were refused might be taken as a positive indication of consultation, co-operation, and ultimately consent with respect to legislative initiatives, but it is significant that recent instances of withholding consent have increased very significantly. Since 2019 13 LCMs were withheld by the Scottish Parliament and 14 by the Senedd.

A high proportion of these instances concerned the Brexit process where conflicting objectives between the Westminster government and the devolved administrations have come to the fore. Brexit has had a direct impact on devolution as a substantial body of EU law relates to functions that have been devolved.[41] In particular, the withdrawal legislation deals with transferred matters and makes changes to the powers of devolved Ministers and of the devolved legislatures. In other words, UK

---

[37] A Page and A Batey, 'Scotland's Other Parliament: Westminster Legislation about Devolved Matters in Scotland since Devolution' [2002] *PL* 501.

[38] Between 1999–2019 in respect to 202 Westminster bills referred to them, the devolved legislatures have only withheld LCMs on 10 occasions.

[39] www.instituteforgovernment.org.uk/publication/devolution-at-20/westminster-and-whitehall.

[40] Between 1999 and 2018, 282 Acts of the Scottish Parliament, 173 Acts of the Northern Ireland Assembly; 37 Acts in Wales 2011–2018 since the Assembly (now Parliament) gained full legislative powers.

[41] Withdrawal from the EU deprives the devolved legislatures of their statutory obligation to respect EU law. In turn, this called for modifications to devolution legislation and thus required legislative consent motions.

withdrawal from the EU affects the scope of devolved matters. Without further legislation, it enlarges them. This is because the devolved legislatures are no longer constrained by EU law in relation to transferred matters. Given that the Brexit withdrawal legislation transposes EU law on these devolved matters, the withdrawal legislation by the Westminster Parliament obviously required legislative consent motions.[42] In view of its impact on the devolved parts of the UK the UK Internal Markets Act 2020, designed to establish and enforce uniform trading conditions across the UK, exemplifies this pull to uniformity across the nation.[43] LCMs were refused here but also the Scottish and Welsh governments have interpreted a repeated willingness of the Westminster government in recent years to override their input by going ahead with such legislation without Sewel LCM motions as a deliberate strategy to recentralise powers.[44] To overcome this trend and also provide greater legislative and executive autonomy, it has been proposed since the 2024 election that the consolidation of devolution requires a statutory reformulation of the Sewel Convention to make the procedure formally legally binding, or to replace it with an altogether more robust legal provision.[45] The Brown Report had advocated that any such guarantee of devolved autonomy should be rated as a protected category of constitutional law.[46] However, giving this convention legal force runs the risk of dragging the courts into the resolution of what are essentially political questions.[47]

Policy Co-ordination

The co-ordination of policy between central and devolved government has been managed to a large extent without resort to litigation, but by

---

[42] B Allen, G Byrne, and A Paun 'The Sewel Convention in Practice: Five Case Studies from the 2019–24 Parliament' *Institute for Government* 2024.

[43] P Leyland, 'Navigating the Constitutional Path to English Devolution: How Not to Crack an Old Chestnut in a Disunited Kingdom' (2023) 3 *Istituzioni Del Federalismo* 571.

[44] 'The Governance of the Union: Consultation, Co-operation and Legislative Consent, 1st Report of Session 2024–25 House of Lords, Select Committee on the Constitution, HL Paper 13, 17 para 42.

[45] See 'Inter-governmental relations in the United Kingdom' *House of Lords, Select Committee on the Constitution*, 11th Report of Session 2014–15, HL Paper 146, 64.

[46] 'A New Britain: Renewing our Democracy and Rebuilding our Economy' (Commission on the UK's Future, Labour, 2022), Chaired by former PM Gordon Brown and hereafter referred to as the Brown Report, 103.

[47] 'The Governance of the Union: Consultation, Co-operation and Legislative Consent, 1st Report of Session 2024–25 House of Lords, Select Committee on the Constitution, HL Paper 13, 66.

means of a series of informal agreements, termed 'concordats'.[48] At an administrative level, intergovernmental relations have required a distinct approach and devolution has been incorporated into the existing uncodified constitutional arrangements in an unsystematic and informal fashion.

Initially, the process was managed by mechanisms that operated outside the main legislative framework. A general Memorandum of Understanding (MOU) contained a set of principles. These included: good communication and information sharing, early warning of policy proposals, co-operation on matters of mutual interest, and rules of confidentiality to be applied within the workings of the post-devolutionary system of government. At the same time, non-legally enforceable bi-lateral and multi-lateral concordats between administrations were drawn up behind the scenes by senior departmental officials amounting to a form of soft law operating between central and devolved government. A Joint Ministerial Committee (JMC) comprising the political heads from the devolved governments and Westminster government, chaired by the Prime Minister was tasked with acting as the final arbiter in dispute resolution. There were several drawbacks which undermined effectiveness. For example, the concordats were drawn up in a way that has contributed to a lack of openness and transparency reinforcing an unequal partnership by allowing domination by Whitehall, and this, in turn, raised issues of political accountability.[49] The shortcomings of the system were amplified by the extreme divergence of approaches to the Brexit process. Sporadic meetings of the JMC were held but not able to resolve the conflicting interests and policies that arose through UK withdrawal.[50]

Since Brexit a review of intergovernmental relations has resulted in the overhaul of the co-ordination machinery at every level. The promotion of positive engagement has been preferred to placing the entire system on a statutory footing. The revised scheme introduced in 2022 adopts a fresh set of principles with a particular emphasis on transparency, maintaining trust, promoting understanding, and particularly on effective dispute resolution. The first tier commits the respective governments to regular portfolio-level engagement on areas of mutual interest through formal Interministerial Groups. An intermediate (middle) tier comprises an Interministerial Standing Committee established to consider cross-cutting

---

[48] R Rawlings, 'Concordats of the Constitution' (2000) 116(Apr) *Law Quarterly Review* 257–86.
[49] R Rawlings, 'Brexit and Territorial Constitution: Devolution, Reregulation and Intergovernmental Relations', *The Constitution Society* 2017, 6ff.
[50] Ibid; See also Report of the Joint Ministerial Committee 2015–18.

strategic issues. At the summit a council consisting of the Prime Minister and Heads of Devolved Governments oversees the entire system of intergovernmental relations.[51] At the same time, the new framework is supported by its own secretariat and a Minister for Intergovernmental Relations based in the Cabinet Office who is responsible for leading the co-ordination of relations between the devolved governments. Furthermore, the Labour government is committed to developing co-operation further by establishing a Council of the Nations and Regions comprising the Prime Minister and the heads of devolved government.[52]

DEVOLUTION AND THE COURTS

The courts are required to oversee the limits of the powers conferred to devolved legislatures and executives as part of the devolution arrangements. From the standpoint of the UK, Acts of the devolved legislatures might be regarded as subordinate legislation but the devolution statutes confer the right to pass a form of primary legislation in the areas falling under devolved competence. We have already noted above that strong safeguards are in place to prevent from reaching the statute book legislation and delegated legislation which exceeds the powers granted. In part, the job of policing the boundaries of the devolution legislation is given to the courts. The introduction of new procedures involves handing over a new kind of constitutional jurisdiction to judges which, in turn, has important political, as well as legal implications. As well as the law officers (see above) any person or body with *locus standi* can apply to the court for judicial review to determine 'a devolution issue', and this may involve the court declaring an Act of the Scottish Parliament to be invalid. The court performs this statutory role with the assistance of new interpretative rules which place judges under an obligation to read Scottish legislation and subordinate legislation so as to render any measure under consideration *within* the legislative competence of the Scottish Parliament. Matters reserved for Westminster are listed in some detail in the 1998 Act. This provision means that the interpretation of the Scotland Act 1998 under section 29(2)(b) is important constitutionally, since it provides that a matter is outside the competence of the Scottish

---

[51] See 'Inter-governmental relations in the United Kingdom' *House of Lords, Select Committee on the Constitution*, 11th Report of Session 2014–15, HL Paper 146.
[52] Kings Speech, 17 July 2024; S Torrance, 'The Council of Nations and Regions' *House of Commons Library*, 12 September 2024.

Parliament if it relates to any of these reserved matters. If this section were to be given a narrow definition, it would restrict the Scottish Parliament's legislative capacity.[53]

'Devolution issues' concern the legislative competence of the Scottish Parliament and the extent of the functions of the devolved Scottish Executive. There is a similar provision for the judicial resolution of devolution issues under the Government of Wales Act 1998 (GWA 1998) and the NIA 1998. In Wales the Attorney-General can institute proceedings, for example, to determine whether a function is exercisable by the Assembly (now Parliament) and comes within its powers, or whether the Assembly has failed to comply with a duty imposed on it.

Challenges to Acts of the Scottish Executive or legislation passed by the Scottish Parliament can be mounted on the basis of incompatibility with the European Convention on Human Rights (ECHR) (as well as that of being beyond the executive's competence). We observed earlier that in respect of English legislation the Human Rights Act 1998 recognises the sovereignty of the Westminster Parliament and only gives the courts the right to issue a declaration of incompatibility if a provision is not Convention-compliant, but any action of the Scottish Executive or legislation from the Scottish Parliament in breach of the ECHR may be invalidated. For example, not long after the Scotland Act 1998 came into force the independence of Scottish sheriffs[54] was successfully challenged in Scotland as a 'devolution issue' in *Starrs and Chalmers v Procurator Fiscal, Linlithgow*.[55] This was because it was successfully argued that the Lord Advocate's role in the appointment process of temporary sheriffs (junior judges) was in breach of Article 6 of the ECHR as he was appointed as member of the Scottish Executive under section 44 of the SA.

Legal proceedings in Scotland concerning devolution issues have mainly been by way of judicial review in the (Scottish) Court of Session, but in certain circumstances the Scotland Act 1998 allows devolution cases to be resolved by direct reference to the courts.[56] For example, in *Anderson, Reid and Doherty v Scottish Ministers*[57] patients at a mental

---

[53] A McHarg, 'Devolution in Scotland' in J Jowell and C O'Cinneide (eds), *The Changing Constitution* (Oxford, Oxford University Press, 2019) 284ff.
[54] Sheriffs perform a judicial function in the lower courts in Scotland, roughly equivalent to that of magistrates in England.
[55] [2000] HRLR 191.
[56] Before the UKSC was established in 2009 the Judicial Committee of the Privy Council exercised this jurisdiction. See the Constitutional Reform Act 2005, s 40 and Sch 9.
[57] [2001] UKPC D5, [2002] HRLR 6.

hospital challenged section 1 of the Mental Health (Public Safety and Appeals) (Scotland) Act 1999 on the grounds that the legislation passed by the Scottish Parliament was incompatible with Article 5 of the ECHR. Any such Convention-incompatible legislation would have fallen outside the Parliament's legislative competence and could therefore be declared invalid. After considering the relevant Convention jurisprudence the court held that section 1 of the Scottish Mental Health Act did not infringe the claimant's rights under Article 5 of the ECHR, and the Act remained in force.[58]

The legislative competence of the Welsh Assembly has been contested successfully in the courts. In *Recovery of Medical Costs for Asbestos Diseases (Wales) Bill: Reference by the Counsel General For Wales*[59] the UKSC held that provisions in a bill which would have made insurers liable to a charge payable to the Welsh government were not 'concerned with the organisation and funding' of the National Health Service as required under section 108(4) of the GWA 2006 and therefore that they fell outside the devolved competence of the Welsh Assembly. A further example of the courts determining the limits of a devolved competence under the GWA 1998 was in *R (on the application of South Wales Sea Fisheries) v National Assembly for Wales*.[60] On this occasion the devolution issue was in regard to subordinate legislation. It was held that the South Wales Sea Fisheries (Variation) Order 2001[61] was unlawful, because it not only set the precise amounts of contributions by South Wales Sea Fisheries, but also imposed restrictions on this body's discretionary powers. In essence, by adopting this Order the Assembly had been misdirected in law concerning both the membership and the funding of sea fisheries committees, and, accordingly, the Order was quashed so that the Assembly could reconsider its position. Under the GWA 2006, proposed Orders in Council can be referred by the Attorney-General for scrutiny by the UKSC.[62]

The *Robinson* case[63] drew attention to the exposed political role of the courts under the new constitutional arrangements. It concerned the

---

[58] The distinction between reserved and devolved powers was considered by the UKSC in *Martin v HM Advocate* [2010] UKSC 10.

[59] [2015] UKSC 3.

[60] [2001] EWHC Admin 1162, [2002] RVR 134.

[61] SI 2001/1338.

[62] See GWA 2006, s 95.

[63] *Robinson v Secretary of State for Northern Ireland* [2002] UKHL 32. See also B Hadfield, 'Does Northern Ireland Need an Independent Judicial System Arbiter?' in N Bamforth and P Leyland (eds), *Public Law in a Multi-layered Constitution* (Oxford, Hart Publishing, 2003) 184ff.

validity of the election of the Northern Ireland leader and deputy leader in 2002 required to re-launch the Assembly but conducted outside a time frame specified by the NIA 1998. In having to finally determine the meaning of the 1998 Act the court reached a decision which would have a direct bearing on the political process whichever way it was decided. The purposive interpretation arrived at by the majority of the judges in the House of Lords (the UK's top court before it became the UKSC) offered the possibility of keeping the Assembly and Executive operating. On the other hand, a literal reading would have prompted immediate elections at a moment that could have been fatal for the peace process.

The courts have been called upon to consider the limits of the discretion exercised by officials during the period when the Northern Ireland Assembly was not sitting for political reasons between 2017 and January 2020. The Court of Appeal of Northern Ireland ruled in *Buick* that civil servants in Northern Ireland did not have the power to take certain decisions in the absence of a minister.[64] This was because the decision in question was not under the discretion and control of a Northern Ireland minister. It was held that under the Belfast Agreement the grant of a major planning application for a waste management centre was a cross-cutting issue which needed to be taken by the executive as a whole. This matter was not resolved by the UKSC but by the passage of temporary legislation at Westminster to enable officials to take decisions on behalf of Northern Ireland ministers.[65]

In relation to the response to Brexit, the *Legal Continuity Scotland Bill*[66] case tested the legal limits of co-operation reflected in the devolved legislative process.[67] The complexity of the Brexit process was compounded by intense political disagreement over the approach to Brexit between the objectives of the then Conservative government at Westminster, and the Scottish and Welsh national parties, as well as other parties in represented in the devolved legislatures. As a result, the Scottish Parliament introduced its own Brexit Bill but did it fall within legislative competence? On referral by the UK law officers the UKSC held on the crucial issue of sovereignty that this proposed bill would have prevented under section 17 subordinate legislation from the UK Parliament from having legal effect post Brexit. In turn, limiting the sovereign powers of the UK Parliament

---

[64] *Buick's (Colin) Application* [2018] NICA 26.
[65] See Northern Ireland (Executive Formation and Exercise of Functions) Act 2018.
[66] *UK Withdrawal from the European Union (Legal Continuity) (Scotland) Bill – A Reference by the AG and Advocate General for Scotland* [2018] UK SC 64.
[67] The referral by the A-G relating to legislative competence was under Section 33(2) of the Scotland Act 1998.

by modifying section 28(7) of the Scotland Act. This provision was therefore declared to be invalid and the bill subsequently dropped.[68]

The scope for challenge by way of judicial review of Acts of the Scottish Parliament was considered by the Inner House of the Scottish Court of Session in *AXA General Insurance, Petitioners*[69] and subsequently by the UKSC. After the House of Lords had ruled in English appeals that damages would not be recoverable for asbestos-related conditions the Scottish Parliament passed the Damages (Asbestos-related Conditions) (Scotland) Act 2009 to allow damages to be claimed in Scotland. In this case the validity of this legislation was called into question. The Inner House accepted that section 29 of the Scotland Act 1998 should not be interpreted as setting out an exhaustive list of the grounds of review. On final appeal the UKSC set a very high threshold holding that the ground of irrationality would not be enough to justify review. Lord Reed confirmed that nothing less than a deliberate misuse of power involving, for example, the abrogation of human rights or violation of the rule of law would be sufficient to satisfy the threshold of intervention given the democratic legitimacy of the Scottish Parliament to pass laws at devolved level.[70]

THE SCOTTISH REFERENDUM 2014 AND SCOTTISH DEVOLUTION MARK II

In the elections for the Scottish Parliament held in May 2011 the Scottish Nationalists won an overall majority.[71] This result changed the political landscape in Scotland and at Westminster, not only because it revealed the growing unpopularity of the other parties at the ballot box, but also because in Scotland's unicameral system, the SNP was left in a dominant position in the Scottish Parliament. The dominance of the SNP also created an interesting dilemma for the party over its quest for independent statehood. Polls indicated that there was no majority support for independence but since the SNP is committed to secession from the UK, the Scottish First Minister demanded a referendum on independence at the first opportunity. The prospect of holding one seemed unlikely

---

[68] For detailed analysis of this case see G Anthony, 'Brexit and Devolution' in S Kadelbach (ed), *Brexit – And What It Means* (Baden Baden, Nomos, 2019) 68ff.

[69] [2011] CSIH 31.

[70] *AXA General Insurance Limited v The Lord Advocate* [2011] UKSC 46. See eg Lord Reed's judgment, para [153].

[71] J Curtice, 'The 2011 Scottish Election: Records Tumble, Barriers Breached' (2011) 76(1) *Scottish Affairs* 51.

as under the Scotland Act 1998 the right to call a binding referendum on independence lay with the Westminster government.[72] Nevertheless, it was this electoral success by the SNP, indicating a clear mandate in Scotland for an independence referendum, that prompted the UK government to enter into direct negotiations with the Scottish Government on the holding of such a referendum. The principle of a binding Scottish referendum was conceded by the Prime Minister (PM) Cameron on behalf of the Westminster coalition government. The economic case for independence has always been fraught with difficulties, and incidentally, remains so post Brexit. Would an independent Scotland be able to retain the pound? What remaining oil revenue would be available to a Scottish Exchequer after independence? The SNP were keen on leaving the UK but were intent on joining the EU as an independent nation state without any assurance that this would be possible. Furthermore, there was no consensus amongst those in favour of independence about what independence should amount to in practice. For example, would an independent Scotland keep the King as head of state and maintain the same defence arrangements as the UK? The vote for or against independence exposed the nation to the genuine risk of constitutional disintegration but equally, despite the electoral success of the SNP, surveys repeatedly suggested that there was no majority in Scotland in support of independence. From PM Cameron's standpoint a decisive rejection after a full debate offered the prospect of stemming the incoming tide of nationalism.[73]

At the 2014 referendum the electorate were asked: 'should Scotland be an independent country?' In statistical terms, 2,001,926 (55.3 per cent) voted to remain part of the Union by registering a 'No' vote, while 1,617,989 (44.7 per cent) voted in support of independence with a 'Yes' vote. The turnout of 3.6 million comprising 84.6 per cent of the electorate was very high by UK standards and it included many 16 and 17 year olds who were able to vote for the first time. Against a backdrop of falling participation in elections the referendum was viewed by many commentators as a celebration of the democratic process because of the high turnout and the sophistication of the debate. Before the Brexit issue was on the agenda both defenders of the union and nationalists shared a belief in Scotland's nationhood but Unionists clung, for the time being at least, to the idea that national aspirations could be reached within the UK.

---

[72] See Scotland Act 1998, Sch 5.
[73] See also P Leyland, 'Referendums, Popular Sovereignty, and the Territorial Constitution' in R Rawlings, P Leyland, and A Young (eds), *Sovereignty and the Law* (Oxford, Oxford University Press, 2013) 153ff.

The result did not, however, fully reflect the popular mood of the campaign which had demonstrated a general desire in Scotland for greater autonomy. As the campaign progressed mainstream politicians from all three major national parties signed up to 'The Vow' – a widely advertised promise of additional powers for the Scottish Parliament and Executive. In the immediate aftermath of the vote the all-party Smith Commission was set up to assist in its implementation by way of legislation in the form of the Scotland Act 2016.[74] The number of competences devolved to the Scottish Parliament were expanded significantly.[75] The supplementary list is headed in importance by the devolution of welfare benefits which means the Scottish Parliament has autonomy in determining the structure and value of existing benefits or of any new benefits which might replace them. Further, the Scottish Parliament has taken over responsibility for the support for the unemployed. The Scottish Parliament assumes all powers in relation to the holding of elections at devolved level and for local government in Scotland. Also, certain powers in relation to energy efficiency and fuel poverty have been transferred to Scotland. In the domain of broadcasting the Scottish Government and Scottish Parliament has a formal consultative role reviewing the Charter under which the BBC operates and in appointments to and the setting of strategic priorities for the broadcasting regulator OFCOM. Other areas where additional powers have been devolved include consumer advice and advocacy, rail franchising, roads, and onshore oil and gas extraction.[76]

The outcome included a formidable combination of tax-raising powers discussed below (which had already been partly set in place by earlier legislation) taken together with the legal recognition of the permanence of devolution and the conferral of many additional functions. In effect, the referendum heralded a new phase of devolved government for Scotland.

FINANCE AND TAX-RAISING

In its original form devolution failed to link spending with the degree of revenue-raising at the devolved level. The conferment of tax-raising powers on a Scottish Parliament had featured prominently in the discussion

---

[74] For a wider overview see: 'Proposals for the devolution of further powers to Scotland', *House of Lords, Select Committee on the Constitution*, 10th Report of Session 2014–15, 24 March 2015.

[75] See Scotland Act 2016.

[76] See *Scotland in the United Kingdom: An enduring settlement*, January 2015, Cm 8990.

that preceded the introduction of the original legislation. The 1999 referendum in Scotland to approve devolution had a second question asking for the endorsement of a Parliament with tax-raising powers. Despite the attention devoted to this issue when devolution was under discussion, the financial powers actually conferred by the Scotland Act 1998 were limited, never used, and then abolished.[77] The overall budget allocated by Westminster in 1998 was calculated under the block grant 'Barnett' formula which takes account of equivalent spending levels in England for the individual functions devolved.[78] Under the formula a higher percentage was allocated to Scottish and Welsh citizens for each of the devolved policy areas in order to allow for the prevailing economic circumstances. Calculated on this basis, devolved governments were handed a financial sum that they were free to allocate between spending departments but, in addition to lacking transparency, the entire block grant system fails to take account of need in each part of the UK and it makes no adjustment to allow for the removal of EU funding post Brexit. As a feature of the evolution of devolved government in the UK the Scottish Parliament and Welsh Senedd have been granted powers to set the income tax rates for Scottish and Welsh taxpayers and the Scottish Parliament has additional financial powers allowing it to borrow money, raise revenue via other local taxes (eg, airport tax), and keep receipts from value added tax collected in Scotland. Crucially, these changes introduce a link between spending and revenue-raising which was previously absent.[79] Scotland and Wales continues to receive a block grant from Westminster but this is adjusted to take account of revenue raised through local taxes.[80]

In sum, the revised form of Scottish devolution amounts to a formidable catalogue of powers and functions. The devolved institutions in Scotland have acquired a greater degree of autonomy, particularly in relation to finance, than is evident in many federal systems. Over the same period Wales has acquired a conferred powers model of devolution and it has been granted some tax-raising powers.[81] Additional competences have been given to the Senedd in significant policy areas,[82] but, in

---

[77] See Part IV, Scotland Act 1998 and the Scotland Act 2012 which sets out a new legislative framework repealing the Scottish Variable Rate.
[78] Joel Barnett, first Secretary to the Treasury in 1976 adopted the method for calculating the amount allocated to Scotland, Wales and Northern Ireland.
[79] See the Wales Act 2014 and Scotland Act 2016.
[80] M Keep, 'The Barnett Formula and Fiscal Devolution' July 2025, House of Commons Library 7386, 25ff.
[81] Wales Act 2017, ss 17, 18.
[82] Wales Act 2017, ss 23–44.

contrast to Scotland, there is limited capacity for the legal divergence of Welsh institutions from those in England.[83]

BREXIT AND THE STATE OF THE UNION

Scotland

The break-up of the UK as a nation state was viewed by some commentators after the Brexit referendum as a likely consequence of UK withdrawal from the European Union. As will be apparent from this discussion there has been a consolidation and extension of Welsh devolution[84] without any likely prospect of independence. On the other hand, Scotland shares certain characteristics with the Republic of Ireland and other nations of comparable population within the EU but the case for Scottish independence nevertheless remains challenging. For instance, an independent Scotland might be left with a hard border with England, by far her largest market and exclusion from the internal market of the rest of the UK. Furthermore, if Scotland retained the pound its monetary policy would be determined from London.[85] The Covid-19 crisis 2020–22 drew attention to the likely exposure of the economy to intense economic uncertainty. The UK government met the added cost of managing the economic consequences. An independent Scotland, with a limited base of taxpayers and falling oil revenues, would face the conundrum of how to maintain a traditionally strong commitment to public services. In the aftermath of the Brexit referendum the then Scottish First Minister, Nicola Sturgeon (2014–2023) representing the Scottish National Party campaigned for a second vote on Scottish independence. However, popular support for the SNP and for independence has fluctuated since 2016 and has settled below the 50 per cent threshold.[86] In addition, there have been setbacks to the political fortunes of the SNP with a drop in its support. In the 2024 General Election the SNP polled 30 per cent of the popular vote in Scotland compared with 45 per cent in the 2019 election, and was left with nine seats at Westminster compared to 48 after the previous election. At the time of writing there is no immediate prospect of a second independence referendum, but of course, whether any such

---

[83] Rawlings (n 9) 304 ff.
[84] R Rawlings, 'The Strange Reconstitution of Wales' [2018] *Public Law* 62–83.
[85] V Bogdanor, *Beyond Brexit: Towards a British Constitution* (London, IB Tauris, 2019) 209.
[86] www.instituteforgovernment.org.uk/explainer/scottish-independence.

future vote is held will depend on the prevailing political and economic circumstances in Scotland and the remainder of the UK.[87]

Northern Ireland

The status of Northern Ireland within the UK might be called into question for different reasons. While there is no immediate prospect of a united Ireland, the NIA 1998 makes provision for a binding referendum on unification if the Secretary of State for Northern Ireland believes that it would have a reasonable chance of success. Analysis of the demographics suggests that the nationalist community will overtake the Unionists as a proportion of the Northern Ireland population. Already, in the Assembly election held in Northern Ireland Sinn Fein have been confirmed as the largest party with its leader, Michelle O'Neill, emerging as First Minister. Such a trend makes a vote to test support for unification more likely in the medium term, but whether unification would achieve majority support would not only depend on an assessment of economic benefits of unification, but also on the likelihood of a militant reaction by hardcore Unionists.

Even with the UK remaining as it is, the Brexit withdrawal process has impacted heavily on the functioning of devolved government. For Northern Ireland it has immediate implications which threaten the fundamentals of the peace settlement. Despite a Democratic Unionist Party (DUP) campaign in favour of Brexit, 56 per cent of the Northern Irish electorate voted in favour of 'remain' in the 2016 referendum. Under the Belfast/Good Friday Agreement the UK and Irish governments are jointly placed under an obligation to implement and protect the terms of the Accord. Clearly, it was negotiated when the UK and the Republic of Ireland were both members of the EU. In consequence, the free movement of people and goods across two sovereign states was taken for granted and central to the reconciliation of both communities. A commitment is included in both the protocol and EU (Withdrawal Agreement) Act 2020 to ensure that there is no diminution of rights, safeguards, or equality of opportunity as set out in the 1998 Agreement. For example, in regard to citizenship, under the Belfast Agreement nationalist aspirations were partly accommodated through the recognition of Irish identity. Any permanent resident of Northern Ireland has the right

---

[87] C Martin, 'The Union and the State: Contested Visions of the UK's Future, Institute for Government', Bennett Institute for Public Policy, February 2024.

to hold dual citizenship. Citizens of Northern Ireland opting to apply for an Irish passport are entitled to EU citizenship and post Brexit this provision remains in place.[88]

The so-called 'Irish backstop' question was of fundamental importance to the entire Brexit process and continues to raise controversial questions. The dilemma here concerned how to reconcile a desire to maintain an open border between Northern Ireland and the Republic with a Brexit deal which places the UK outside the EU's Customs Union. The election of a majority Conservative government in December 2019 avoided the spectre of a 'no deal Brexit'. The backstop arrangement negotiated by the government of PM Johnson as part of the final Withdrawal Agreement avoided the introduction of a hard border. In order to allow Northern Irish businesses and citizens to retain unfettered access to the UK market but at the same time protect the EU's single market, a complex protocol[89] was agreed between the UK and Europe. This facilitates regulatory alignment and enables tariffs to be collected on goods at risk of entering the EU's single market at ports of entry, rather than at the land border that is the legal boundary between the UK and EU's customs territories. In effect, it resulted in the UK authorities applying EU customs rules to goods entering Northern Ireland. However, this original agreement created a bottleneck of 'red tape' and was the source of 'acute political, economic and societal difficulties'. In particular, it was found to be unworkable by businesses in Northern Ireland. This breakdown also resulted in a further suspension of the Northern Ireland Assembly in February 2022. To overcome these difficulties the 'Windsor Framework' was negotiated in 2023 with the EU by PM Rishi Sunak to amend the offending sections of the protocol and it introduces a revised form of dual regulation.[90] Apart from streamlining the procedures to allow the free flow of trade, it also includes a new Stormont Brake to address a democratic deficit and, at least to some extent, alleviate the fears of Unionists. This provision restricts the application of EU law within Northern Ireland and it empowers the UK government if certain conditions are met to veto the application of any new EU laws. Despite resistance from hardline Unionists the resumption of devolved government in February 2024 was eventually agreed following the endorsement of the Windsor agreement. Furthermore, a House of Lords NI scrutiny

---

[88] Bogdanor (n 85) 195. Obviously the benefits of the EU's Charter of fundamental rights and other EU rights will not be enforceable in Northern Ireland post Brexit.
[89] 'The UK's Approach to the Northern Ireland Protocol', Cabinet Office, May 2020, CP225.
[90] 'The Windsor Framework: A New Way Forward', February 2023, CP 806.

committee to oversee the implementation of the Northern Ireland Protocol and the Windsor Framework was established in 2024.

Devolution and England

Devolution has changed the nature of domestic politics, but it has also reshaped the constitution by a substantial re-distribution of powers away from Westminster and by the introduction of new political and administrative institutions. In considering how much power has been given away, it will be evident that Scotland came closest to having the powers which are often conferred under federal constitutions. The Scottish Parliament, apart from presiding over an increasing number of policy areas, passes a form of primary legislation and a significant proportion of its funding is supplied by taxes raised locally. The Welsh Parliament and Northern Ireland Assembly enjoy similar law-making powers but depend less on local tax-raising. At this point we will consider how devolution brings in its wake a number of implications for England, which is not as well served by current arrangements as Scotland, Wales, and Northern Ireland. Its citizens lack a comparable level of political representation, England receives less generous funding for as long as the Barnett formula continues to apply, and devolution has an impact on pre-existing governmental and administrative organisation. In 2015 the all party House of Lords Constitution committee put on record their astonishment

> that the UK Government do not appear to have considered the wider implications for the United Kingdom of the proposals set out in Scotland in the United Kingdom. We do not consider that it is appropriate or sustainable, to address the issue of additional powers for Scotland alone without also considering the knock-on consequences for the wider UK constitution.[91]

From a constitutional standpoint, asymmetrical devolution has produced an inequality of political representation at Westminster, an issue sometimes referred to as the 'West Lothian question'.[92] The introduction of a Scottish Parliament and Executive with considerable power together with equivalent bodies in Wales and Northern Ireland undermines the

---

[91] 'Proposals for the devolution of further powers to Scotland', House of Lords, Select Committee on the Constitution, 10th Report of Session 2014–15, 24 March 2015, para 22.
[92] Tam Dalyell, the Westminster MP representing the Scottish constituency of West Lothian, raised this issue as a question in a debate in the House of Commons on 14 November 1977, and it has since been referred to as the 'West Lothian question'. See O Gay, H Holden, and P Bowers, 'The West Lothian Question' SN/PC/02586, 23 March 2011.

previously accepted notion of representative government in the UK. Since devolution, MPs representing English constituencies are no longer able to vote on matters devolved to Scotland, Wales, and Northern Ireland, but Scottish, Welsh, and Northern Irish MPs at Westminster retained the right to vote on domestic policy for the rest of the UK. Furthermore, by the transfer of many domestic functions to the devolved legislatures, Scottish, Welsh, and Northern Irish MPs at Westminster have a greatly reduced role to play in relation to their constituents. The obvious line of accountability for the devolved areas of domestic policy is through the Scottish, Welsh, or Northern Irish members of the devolved legislatures.

In the event, as we saw in Chapter 5, the position was temporarily addressed by introducing the English Votes for English Laws (EVEL) procedure in the House of Commons, which while in place sought to limit the voting rights over English legislation of MPs representing Scottish, Welsh, and Northern Irish constituencies. The EVEL procedure as a response to the West Lothian question was deficient in obvious ways, as it presented a negative veto to English MPs, thus calling into question the role of Westminster as a national parliament.[93]

A radical option to correct this anomaly would be to introduce a fully federal system.[94] The case has not been presented convincingly for the introduction of an English Parliament.[95] Proposals for an equivalent body to the Scottish Parliament might appear to have some justification, since setting up a Parliament for England could provide the basis for addressing the glaring asymmetries relating to representation, accountability, and administration which have been raised by devolution. However, any proposal to create a federation would not be a good fit in constitutional terms and potentially has important shortcomings. The Parliament for England would represent more than 80 per cent of the UK population. Assuming that it had equivalent powers to the Scottish Parliament, it would be dominant in relation to its Scottish, Welsh, and Northern Irish counterparts, and it would be a strong competitor to the Westminster Parliament, which would no longer have a pivotal role in relation to domestic issues. Also, an English Parliament as an additional elected political body would be expensive to introduce. As there is a lack

---

[93] L Laurence Smyth, 'English Votes for English Laws' in A Horne and G Drewry (eds), *Parliament and the Law*, 2nd edn (London, Bloomsbury, 2018) 207ff.

[94] See R Schütze, 'Introduction' in R Schütze and S Tierney (eds), *The United Kingdom and the Federal Idea* (Oxford, Hart Publishing, 2018).

[95] In some respects devolution has turned the Westminster Parliament into a mainly English Parliament by default as most domestic policy matters in Scotland, Wales, and Northern Ireland fall under the remit of the devolved legislatures.

of the necessary support within any of the mainstream political parties, or more widely among the English electorate, an English Parliament operating alongside the Westminster Parliament is unlikely to be introduced in the foreseeable future.[96]

On the question of reform, the anachronistic composition of the House of Lords is also worthy of mention (see also Chapter 5). In its current form the upper house has been strongly criticised, for both being unrepresentative and for having far too many members, but it continues to perform some useful constitutional functions.[97] In recent years there have been calls for its replacement with a regional second chamber of some kind. The proposal in the Brown Report for a Senate of the Regions to replace the existing House of Lords with a second chamber set up to be more representative of the nations and regions approaches the lack of equal representation across the nation from a different perspective.[98] The transformation of the House of Lords to a chamber elected on a regional basis would add to its democratic legitimacy and give politicians from the nations and regions a relatively greater say in policy-making. Thus, it would move some way towards rebalancing the national parliament to take account of the asymmetry of devolution. However, the attempt to create an elected body with sufficient representative credibility almost inevitably raises questions about how to avoid the second chamber becoming a competitor to the elected House of Commons.

It is also relevant to note that except for an interruption between 1985–1999, London has had in place a strategic level of elected subnational government (see Chapter 9), and also that a form of elected English regional government between central and local government was trialled unsuccessfully as a belated response to devolution for England by the Labour government (2001–05).[99] Finally, in Chapter 9 there is discussion of current plans published by the Labour government in 2024 for extending a distinct form of devolution for England based on Mayoral strategic authorities.[100]

---

[96] Shütze (n 94) 21ff; A Tomkins, 'Shared Rule: What the UK Could Learn from Federalism' in R Schütze and S Tierney (eds), *The United Kingdom and the Federal Idea* (Oxford, Hart Publishing, 2018).
[97] M Russell, *The Contemporary House of Lords: Westminster Bicameralism Revived* (Oxford: Oxford University Press, 2013) 228ff.
[98] The Brown Report (n 46)138ff.
[99] Your region, Your choice: Revitalising the English regions, CM 5511 (2002).
[100] English Devolution: White Paper, Power and Partnership, Foundations for Growth, December 2024 CP 1218.

CONCLUSION

The reconfiguration of territorial governance can be considered as an evolutionary journey without a clear destination. Certainly, since 1999 devolution has been a dynamic feature of the constitution, generating further change in response to the prevailing political climate. On the one hand, a vast range of functions and powers have been devolved to Scotland, Wales, and Northern Ireland. The upshot is that it has become difficult for any government acting through the Westminster Parliament to ignore the democratic mandate for policies adopted and legislated at devolved level. Perhaps most vividly, the referendum for Scottish independence in 2014, despite recording a pro-union 'No' vote, provided a demonstration of the political forces which have been unleashed. While a second independence referendum is not imminent, the conferral of many additional powers and functions to the Scottish Parliament has not dimmed the aspirations of many nationalists for achieving secession.

On the other hand, more than 25 years after the introduction of devolution ultimate control remains legally with the Westminster Parliament. Devolved bodies must operate within their devolved legal competence. In what some have viewed as a partial re-assertion of sovereignty the process for the repatriation of EU law, which fell squarely within the remit of central government, resulted in the Westminster Parliament proceeding with withdrawal legislation impacting on the devolved parts of the UK despite strong political opposition at devolved level. From the standpoint of the Westminster government, this policy achieved a consistent UK-based approach to the complex uncoupling process, involving as it does a myriad of rules and regulations. On yet another front, the consequences of policy divergence and the obvious lack of policy co-ordination were highlighted by the varied response to the Covid-19 crisis in 2020–22. Finally, the stability of the Northern Ireland peace process post Brexit depends on the implementation of the withdrawal agreement with the EU, now based on the Windsor Framework which guarantees an open border between the Irish Republic and Northern Ireland.

FURTHER READING

Birrell D, Carmichael P, and Heenan D, *Devolution in the UK: Politics, Powers and Policies* (London, Bloomsbury Academic, 2023).

Bogdanor V, *Devolution in the United Kingdom* (Oxford, Oxford University Press, 1999).

Further reading

Hazell R (ed), *The English Question* (Manchester, Manchester University Press, 2006).

Himsworth C and O'Neill M, *Scotland's Constitution: Law and Practice*, 3rd edn (Edinburgh, Lexis Nexis, 2015).

Leyland P, 'The Multifaceted Constitutional Dynamics of UK Devolution' (2011) 9(1) *I-CON* 251.

Martinelli C, *Brexit and the British Constitution* (London, Routledge, 2025).

McEldowney J, 'Federalism' in J Jowell and C O'Cinneide (eds), *The Changing Constitution*, 9th edn (Oxford, Oxford University Press, 2019).

McEvoy K, Bryson A, and Kramer A, 'The Empire Strikes Back: Brexit, The Irish Peace Process, and the Limitations of the Law' (2019) 43(3) *Fordham International Law Journal* 609.

McHarg A, 'Devolution in Scotland' in J Jowell and C O'Cinneide (eds), *The Changing Constitution*, 9th edn (Oxford, Oxford University Press, 2019).

Rawlings R, 'The Strange Reconstitution of Wales' [2018] *Public Law* 62–83.

Rawlings R, 'The Welsh Way' in J Jowell and C O'Cinneide (eds), *The Changing Constitution*, 9th edn (Oxford, Oxford University Press, 2019).

Schütze R and Tierney S, *The United Kingdom and the Federal Idea* (Oxford, Hart Publishing, 2018).

9

Local Government

Mayor of London – English Devolution – Greater London Authority – Mayor – City-Region – Referendums – Participation – Rate Capping – Stakeholders – Competitive Tendering – Best Value – Accountability Mechanisms – The Big Society – Local Referendums

INTRODUCTION

THIS CHAPTER EXAMINES the layers of city-wide government and local government responsible for providing services at a local level. In common with devolution, local government is elected and operates under powers granted by Parliament under statute but local authorities cannot pass legislation in their own right. Far from extending the autonomy of local authorities, legislation has been introduced by both Conservative and Labour governments to constrain the activities of local authorities and to reign back their spending powers. The effect of these policies over the years has been to concentrate power at the centre. Although several types of sub-national government remain responsible for the delivery of many services the relatively autonomous local government built up in the Victorian era has been in decline, particularly if considered in terms of public participation supporting local democracy. The tendency is reflected in reduced turnouts in elections for local councils.[1] And over the same timeframe, deep cuts in funding and control of spending imposed by central government have impacted on the front-line services provided by government at local level. Under the Labour administration of Prime Minister (PM) Blair the Local Government Act 2000 sought to transform the operation of local democracy both by providing greater efficiency, transparency, and accountability for local authorities

---

[1] E Uberoi, 'Turnout at Election', *House of Commons Library*, Number 8060, 10 January 2023, 17ff.

and by introducing elected mayors for the largest cities and setting out new political management structures. One of the effects was to create a new decision-making framework which separates the decision-making from the scrutiny of decisions by new committees.[2] The Localism Act 2011 championed by the coalition government of PM Cameron was aimed at reinvigorating local democracy by extending some of the powers of local authorities but also by encouraging wider citizen involvement in the formation and implementation of policy by local authorities. Its supporters saw it as an attempt to place the initiative at grass-roots level by promoting people-power. In part, by breaking state monopolies and by encouraging charities, social enterprises, and companies to provide public services. To take one example, by allowing free schools to be set up outside of local government by parents, communities, faith groups, charities, businesses, and universities. The overall objective was to reduce the size of the state.[3] Viewed retrospectively, the Localism initiative seems only to have had marginal impact on citizen involvement and the pivotal role of the state locally is largely undiminished.[4] Mindful of these trends, it is noteworthy that the Labour Government elected in 2024 has a strong commitment to combatting the perceived over-centralisation of power,[5] and as discussed below, is seeking to deliver a re-branded form of 'English Devolution and Community Empowerment'.[6]

Viewed from a historical perspective, the Westminster Parliament has introduced a succession of statutes which set the parameters for the structure and operation of local government, mainly since the Municipal Corporation Act 1835 established the modern principle of introducing democratically elected government at a local level (see eg the Local Government Acts 1888, 1894, 1933, and 1972). The effect has been to introduce locally elected bodies responsible for a range of different functions. The Westminster Parliament retains this power to establish, modify, and even to abolish layers of local government. In fact, Parliament has,

---

[2] LGA 2000, s 21.

[3] D Cameron, 'Our Big Society Plan' (2010); C Pattie and R Johnston, 'How Big Is the Big Society?' (2011) 64 *Parliamentary Affairs* 403.

[4] See eg J Stanton, 'Decentralisation and Empowerment under the Coalition Government: An Empirical Study of Local Councils in London' (2015) 9 *Journal of Planning and Environment Law* 978–93.

[5] 'A New Britain: Renewing our Democracy and Rebuilding our Economy' (Commission on the UK's Future, Labour, 2022), Chaired by former PM Gordon Brown and hereafter referred to as the Brown Report, chapter 3, chapter 7.

[6] English Devolution: White Paper, Power and Partnership, Foundations for Growth, December 2024, CP 1218.

on a number of occasions, re-organised local government. For example, a layer of local government comprising the Metropolitan Councils, and including the Greater London Council, was dispensed with by the Local Government Act 1985. It is also important to remember that central government through the passage of legislation has frequently imposed important statutory duties and limitations on local authorities. For example, the Education Act 1944 required the appropriate authority to ensure that there are sufficient schools in its locality; the Housing Act 1985 imposed a duty on local authorities to maintain council housing in their areas, while the Housing Act 1985, Part III imposed a duty to accommodate certain limited categories of homeless persons. Local authorities are the elected bodies which perform the majority of essential everyday governmental functions, and in a number of policy areas local government has become the means for the implementation of policy by central government at local level.

London and City Regions: 'English Devolution' and Strategic Governance?

In the previous chapter it was pointed out that England does not have a nationwide intermediate layer of government comparable to that established in Scotland, Wales, and Northern Ireland with its own parliament. Nevertheless, the initiatives in local democracy relating to city regions promoted by both Conservative and Labour governments launched since 1999 frequently employ the language of devolution, and have meant that at least some additional powers have been devolved down to a strategic level of government. Accordingly, these so-called English devolution policies while not equivalent to the systems in place in Edinburgh, Cardiff, and Belfast might be regarded as an indirect response from Westminster as they seek to address the concentration of power at the core of the polity.

Most obviously, London-wide government introduced in 2000 to provide a more accountable method for governing the largest urban conurbation in Western Europe has some affinities with devolution. After the abolition of the Greater London Council in the mid-1980s, it was recognised that London lacked a crucial layer of government which was necessary both to provide democratic accountability and to co-ordinate strategic aspects of administration that cut across the remit of the inner and outer London boroughs. The Greater London Authority Act 1999 introduced a Mayor and Assembly for London. The first elections by an additional member system were held in 2000 after a referendum in 1999 approving the principle.

The Greater London Authority Act 1999 restored democracy and accountability for many services and bodies by putting the police, the fire service, and a number of non-departmental bodies under democratic control. The main areas coming under the Mayor and Greater London Authority (GLA) are: transport (ie integrated strategy for London, traffic management, and regulation); economic development (responsibility for London Development Agency); police (creating a new Metropolitan Police Authority, and Fire and Emergency Services); planning (required to develop a land use strategy for London); environment (eg air quality and waste); culture (eg museums, library services, and the arts).

The Mayor is placed at the head of the executive and is responsible for the policies that are adopted.[7] In terms of structure a separation of powers is built into the system. The Assembly, comprising full-time salaried politicians, is responsible for holding the Mayor to account for policies and proposals by public scrutiny and criticism. In addition, the Assembly is able to question the Mayor and the Mayor's staff, to hold public hearings on issues of importance, and to have access to relevant people, papers, and technical expertise. It also has powers to secure amendments to the Mayor's budget proposals.

In recent years a brand of personality politics has developed around the character and style of the candidates seeking mayoral office in London, city regions and cities with directly elected mayors. The office of London Mayor is not only directly elected and thus given a mandate by the London electorate but also professionalised along North American lines with a fully remunerated office holder and a trimmed-down executive.

Before discussing Metro Mayors it is worth stressing that transport not only takes up by far the highest proportion of the Mayor's budget but this area is clearly of enormous strategic importance for London and for the nation. Transport for London (TfL) is a body corporate established under the GLA Act which implements the Mayor's transport strategy, including the setting of fares on London Transport. TfL is headed by a Transport Commissioner appointed by the Mayor.[8] Finally, it is worth noting that in relation to the powers which have been granted to the Mayor conflicts have arisen between the Mayor and central government

---

[7] White Paper, *A Major and Assembly for London*, Cm3897 (London, HMSO, 1998) para 3.16.

[8] Greater London Authority Act 1999, ss 154 and 155.

over annual budget allocations and the management of policy, particularly in the field of transport policy.[9]

In order to reorganise the devolution of power on a regional basis to other major conurbations, the Conservative government elected in 2015 devised a city based form of strategic local governance which adapts the London model.[10] The blueprint for what it called the 'Northern Powerhouse strategy' was a 'Metro Mayor' elected for the first time in 2017 representing Manchester and its neighbouring towns.[11] Primarily, the office holder was granted control over a devolved consolidated regional transport budget with a multi-year settlement, but in addition given responsibility for other matters such as strategic planning and control, devolved support budgets, and control of apprenticeship grants.[12] Under powers contained in the Cities and Local Government Devolution Act 2016 city region conurbation-wide Metro Mayors, each based on an individual agreement with the Secretary of State, have been elected for a series of city/regions of comparable size to Manchester.[13] Since their introduction the Metro Mayors have had a notable political impact by installing elected personalities with some kudos representing these regions in a variety of fora, but the approach outlined has manifest shortcomings if assessed in terms of its constitutional outcome as a decentralising measure.[14] In particular, the Secretary of State for Housing, Communities and Local Government representing the Westminster government exercised control over each of the individual agreements reached, approved the allocation of 'ring fenced' financial budgets, and determined the specific powers granted to the Metro Mayors. Moreover, in gauging the impact of this layer of governance it will be apparent that these Metro Mayors have a narrow but also variable portfolio of competences which fall a long way short of those granted to the executives in Scotland, Wales, and Northern Ireland and also in comparison to the London Mayor. Further, each Metro Mayor is answerable on an

---

[9] See C Harlow and R Rawlings, *Law and Administration*, 3rd edn (Cambridge, Cambridge University Press, 2009) 425ff.
[10] The towns and cities of Greater Manchester consist of: Bolton, Bury, Manchester, Oldham, Rochdale, Salford, Tameside, Trafford, and Wigan.
[11] See 'The Northern Powerhouse strategy' HM government November 2016, www.gov.uk/government/publications/northern-powerhouse-strategy.
[12] R Lupton, C Hughes, and S Peake-Jones 'City Region Devolution in England' SPDO Research Paper 2, LSE, November 2018.
[13] This includes: Birmingham/West Midlands, East Midlands, Liverpool City Region, South Yorkshire, West Yorkshire, Tees Valley, West of England/Bristol.
[14] P Leyland, 'England Unincorporated: Reflections on the Constitutional Way Ahead Post Devolution' (2022) 10 *federalisimi.it* 184ff.

occasional basis to elected representatives from existing councils rather than routinely to a separately elected authority (as is the case with the London Mayor). But perhaps the most serious deficiency is the fact that this level of strategic governance based on Metro Mayors only applies to around half of England's population.[15]

The Labour government has targeted the transformation of territorial governance as a priority concern regarded as essential to facilitate the elimination of inequality and to encourage economic development. Following its general election win in 2024 the reforms published by the government that are to be enacted in the English Devolution and Community Empowerment Bill place strong emphasis on what is again termed English devolution,[16] and in important respects the approach adopted responds to some of the criticisms detailed above. First, the new devolution structures partly build on the strategic authorities already in place[17] but rather than approach the task of extending a new form of governance in a haphazard fashion on an incremental basis by setting up regional mayors in response to individual bids, the objective is to cover the entire map of England by establishing different categories of strategic authorities with the functions varying according to local conditions.[18] At the same time, the implementation is to be linked to the re-organisation of local government to combine previous tiers in favour of a universal national standard of two-tier authorities (for example, each citizen will have a city, county, or town council at base level and strategic authority of some kind above that).[19] Second, in terms of the range of integration across policy areas the list of functions has been expanded very significantly. As well as integrated transport it now includes: skills and employment; housing and planning requiring a spatial development strategy; economic development and regeneration; environment and climate change; health and wellbeing; public service reform; health and safety. In other words the scope of this devolution scheme has been widened to include the entire

---

[15] P Silk, 'Devolution and the UK Parliament' in A Horne and G Drewry (eds), *Parliament and the Law*, 2nd edn (Oxford, Hart Publishing, 2018) 194ff.

[16] M Sandford, 'English devolution: Mayoral strategic authorities', *House of Commons Library*, 14 February 2025, number 10194.

[17] English Devolution: White Paper, Power and Partnership, Foundations for Growth, December 2024, CP 1218. www.gov.uk/government/publications/english-devolution-white-paper-power-and-partnership-foundations-for-growth/english-devolution-white-paper#upgrading-the-systems.

[18] Identified as Foundational Strategic Authorities, Mayoral Strategic Authorities, Established Mayoral Strategic Authorities.

[19] www.instituteforgovernment.org.uk/comment/labours-devolution-priority-programme-welcome.

nation and deepened to encourage policy co-ordination across a greater range of policy fields. To cite some examples: glancing ahead mayoral authorities will be placed under a statutory duty to produce local growth plans but also forced to consider their impact on climate change; they will be required to tackle economic inactivity through the adoption of a national approach in the domain of education and training; the task of having to address health and health inequalities in the region opens up a new field for this tier of English regional governance. Given the resource implications which will arise there will undoubtedly be severe challenges to overcome in the implementation of this policy. Another key issue will be ensuring that the institutional framework provides sufficient democratic oversight. For example it has been stated that integrated financial settlements will have greater flexibility to allow funding to be allocated across different policy areas, with what is described as a 'streamlined overarching single accountability process'. This process will be conducted in house by the department, with a strong emphasis on achieving value for money, but it appears that no systematic democratic scrutiny will be provided over policy initiatives and budgetary matters under the revised system.

In sum, these proposals do not seek to mimic the devolved institutional framework operating in Edinburgh, Cardiff, and Belfast but the changes in prospect are likely to result in a more extensive devolution of powers on a regional basis throughout the whole of England.

TYPES OF LOCAL GOVERNMENT: COUNTIES, CITIES, TOWNS

Local authorities share with Parliament the characteristic of being elected, and in this sense they are representative bodies of the communities on behalf of which they administer services. Councillors represent territorial units called wards, and they normally face re-election every four years, which means that the composition of the authority changes with elections, but the Local Government Act 1972 lays down that each authority is a body corporate that exists in perpetuity. This provision means that authorities are distinct legal entities able to acquire property, enter contracts, and be party to private legal proceedings. Local councillors do not generally receive a salary, but they are entitled to claim expenses incurred while performing council business.

The main form of the current arrangements was established in outline by the Local Government Act 1972, which came into force in April 1974. This framework has been subject to ongoing review since 1997.

In rural areas the 1972 Act provides a two-tier division of the main powers between county councils as the upper layer and district councils as the lower layer. In addition, parish councils have responsibility for a very limited number of minor matters. The Act originally created 39 county councils, responsible for education, strategic planning, personal social services, major highways, public transport, consumer protection, and fire and police services (although fire and police services may spread over more than one authority). The county areas were subdivided into 296 non-metropolitan district councils, with responsibility for housing, environmental health, public health and sanitation, and refuse collection. Responsibility for town and country planning is shared with district councils. The Localism Act 2011 increased the presidential style politics of directly elected mayors accountable to an elected assembly for 12 major English cities but first required a referendum in each city to ascertain whether there was support for the change to an elected mayor.[20]

The Local Government Act 1992, section 13(1) empowered the Local Government Commission to recommend boundary, structural, or electoral changes 'having regard to the need: (a) to reflect the identities and interests of local communities, and (b) to secure effective and convenient local government'. This re-organisation was essentially completed by 1997 and it resulted in many two-tier authorities becoming single-tier 'unitary' authorities. In much the same way, the Local Government (Wales) Act 1994 provided a new unitary structure for local government in Wales. The previously existing counties and districts were abolished and replaced by 22 unitary authorities, known as 'principal councils'. In Scotland the Local Government (Scotland) Act 1994 provided for the creation of 32 single-tier authorities. In Northern Ireland local government comprises 26 district councils and nine area boards. Responsibility for local government comes under the devolved governments established in 1999.

The situation in the main cities has always been different. The position was modified significantly by the Local Government Act 1985 which (as mentioned above) abolished the Greater London Council and the six metropolitan area councils. This reform left the 32 London boroughs and 36 metropolitan district councils as a single tier of local government in urban areas. These councils are now typically responsible for providing education (with the exception of those schools opting out),

---

[20] I Leigh, 'The Changing Nature of Local and Regional Democracy' in J Jowell and D Oliver (eds), *The Changing Constitution*, 7th edn (Oxford, Oxford University Press, 2011) 246ff.

personal social services, highways and transportation, refuse disposal, town and country planning, consumer protection, parks and recreations, and libraries.

It has already been stated that the main powers of local authorities are defined by legislation, and section 101 of the Local Government Act 1972 provides that many decision-making powers can be delegated by an authority to council committees, sub-committees, or officers of the authority. However, delegation to individual council members, including committee chairpersons, is unlawful. The title of these committees will correspond to the nature of the functions for which each is responsible. These committees used to draw up and discuss the more detailed questions of policy formation, and their recommendations were usually presented to the main body of the council for ratification, but since the Local Government Act 2000 decision-making is in the hands of the leader/mayor and a cabinet. Once policy is formed, the power to implement it at a local level is by officers of the council. The power under which the officers act is not usually by direct means, but rather through specific forms of statutory provision, by-laws, and compulsory purchase orders.

LOCAL GOVERNMENT FINANCE AND SERVICE DELIVERY

Another reason why local government has limited autonomy is because of its financial dependency on Westminster. (In Scotland and Wales it is the devolved executive which allocates funding to local government. This funding has been made available to the executives under calculations made according to the Barnett formula discussed in Chapter 8.) The main slice of local government revenue comes from central government grants (about 60 per cent of total revenue) with a proportion of this revenue targeted for particular services, for example the fire brigade and police. In addition, central government makes a general contribution to local government funding, which can be allocated by an authority between budget heads. Local authorities make up the remainder of their budget requirements by raising revenue locally. The major component of their income comes from council tax, which is a tax paid on all properties in an area.[21] It is a banded tax calculated according to the market value of the property concerned. As well as taxation, local authorities are allowed to charge for the provision of certain services ranging from rents and

---

[21] See the Local Government Finance Act 1992.

repairs, the sale of council houses, recreational facilities, pest control, etc. Finally, local authorities can borrow money by issuing bonds, but this is subject to strict conditions imposed by the Treasury.

Since the early 1980s there have been repeated attempts by central government to impose strict cash limits by 'capping' local government spending.[22] These capping measures were the product of bitter political controversy between central government and the local authorities (often in different political hands) during the 1980s, and the legality of the schemes was challenged in the courts (mainly unsuccessfully). The imposition of such rigid financial constraints has reduced direct accountability to the local electorate, since many councils have found it necessary to cut their services to meet government financial targets without regard to electoral commitments to continue with them or expand them.

Another prominent feature introduced to promote economy throughout the sector was the revision of the manner of delivery of many local government services.[23] The market driven policies adopted since the 1980s under the Thatcher Government (1979–90) have required the contracting out of local services by local authorities to private companies and to independent charitable organisations. These services range from refuse collection and street cleaning to the provision of care for the elderly.[24] The legislation has been refined to deliver what is termed 'best value', understood as not only improved efficiency and effectiveness in the use of resources, but also to take account of the quality of the service delivery delivered to the citizen.

THE ACCOUNTABILITY OF LOCAL GOVERNMENT

In order to improve the public perception of local government and local councillors, Part III of the Local Government Act 2000 established a new ethical framework, which included the introduction of statutory codes of conduct, with a requirement for every council to adopt a code covering the behaviour of elected members and of officers, and the creation of a standards committee for each authority. This approach has many

---

[22] M Loughlin, *Legality and Locality: The Role of Law in Central-Local Government Relations* (Oxford, Clarendon Press, 1996).

[23] I Leigh, 'The Changing Nature of the Local State' in J Jowell, D Oliver and C O'Cinneide (eds), *The Changing Constitution*, 8th edn (Oxford, Oxford University Press, 2015).

[24] See the Local Government Act 1988 under the Conservatives and the Local Government Act 1999 under Labour.

characteristics in common with the Westminster regime for parliamentary standards. However, the standards board introduced in 2004 to root out corruption in local government was abolished by the Localism Act 2011 but the same legislation seeks to increase transparency by introducing a requirement to publish the salaries of senior staff.

The Local Government Act 1972, section 151 provides that councils must ensure the proper administration of their financial affairs, and the Local Government Finance Act 1982 set in place the mechanism for external audits by an Audit Commission for local authorities in England and Wales. This introduced commercial accounting methods to the local government sector. (For the auditors' current powers, see the Audit Commission Act 1998.) The district auditor has the duty to see that public money is spent according to the law. If it is found that there has been unlawful expenditure by the authority in the discharge of its public duties, the auditor has the power to enforce financial penalties against named councillors or officials.[25] Further, the Local Government Act 1974, Part III allows a local government ombudsman to investigate complaints concerning questions of local maladministration. These matters are referred to the local government ombudsman directly or through a local councillor.

As mentioned earlier the Localism Act 2011 experimented with direct democracy as it introduces referendums as a form of accountability to the voters in the locality.[26] For example, a petition signed by 5 per cent or more citizens might trigger a consultative referendum on local issues. In a different sense, the Act also empowered the Secretary of State to insist on a binding referendum as a means of controlling expenditure by providing that any rise in council tax above a given threshold set by her or him must be approved by voters.[27] This provision should however be regarded as an expensive and time consuming last resort that will only apply if negotiations between the authority and Secretary of State prove to be unsuccessful.[28] None of the initiatives adopted by central government overcome the question at the heart of the problem, namely, that all forms of local government continue to be largely financially dependent on central government.[29]

---

[25] See *Porter v Magill* [2001] UKHL 67.

[26] See Localism Act, Schedule 5.

[27] M Sandford 'Council tax: local referendums' *House of Commons Library*, 3 February 2025, Number 05682.

[28] In fact only one referendum has been held under these provisions in Bedfordshire in 2014–15. See M Sandford, 'Local Government: Polls and Referendums' Briefing Paper, Number 03409, 2 March 2016, House of Commons Library, 13.

[29] Lowndes V and Pratchett L, 'Local governance under the coalition government: Austerity, localism and "The Big Society"' (2012) 38(1) *Local Government Studies* 21.

CONCLUSION

The primary reason for setting up modern forms of local government was to vest elected authorities with broad enabling powers, permitting them to respond flexibly to new challenges without being unduly constrained by the fear of legal intervention. As a result, local government in its original form was afforded considerable discretion in its ability to respond to local needs and it is worth remembering that the Covid 19 pandemic (2020–22) once again drew attention to the crucial role of local authorities in maintaining public services. However, the predominant concern of central government in recent years has been to strictly control public expenditure. The Conservatives while in power in 1979–97 were set on a course of reducing the role of local government by privatising services, establishing housing trusts, and introducing private sector funding. But while it was clear that the Labour government (1997–2010) was also intent on controlling public expenditure by imposing tight restrictions on the spending of local authorities, it was less ideologically driven than its Conservative predecessor, and while it retained a commitment to public–private partnerships and privatisation in general, it also relaxed controls and extended certain additional powers of local government. Winding the clock forward to the present, the current emphasis on local government reform in England is in part generated by the constitutional imbalance caused by the introduction of the devolved systems of government in Scotland, Wales, and Northern Ireland and the widely recognised relative economic decline beyond the South East sector of England. It will be apparent from this discussion that the latest version of devolution for England under the Labour government seeks to counteract the concentration of power at the centre by establishing a nationwide strategic level of government that builds upon and extends the existing network of elected Metro Mayors.[30]

FURTHER READING

Bailey S and Elliott M, 'Taking Local Government Seriously: Democracy, Autonomy and the Constitution' [2009] *Cambridge Law Journal* 436.

Beel D, Jones M, and Rees Jones I, *City Regions and Devolution in the UK: The Politics of Representation* (Bristol, Bristol University Press, 2021).

---

[30] English Devolution: White Paper, Power and Partnership, Foundations for Growth, December 2024, CP 1218.

Leigh I, 'The Changing Nature of Local and Regional Democracy' in J Jowell, D Oliver, and C O'Cinneide (eds), *The Changing Constitution*, 8th edn (Oxford, Oxford University Press, 2015).

Leigh I, *Law, Politics and Democracy* (Oxford, Oxford University Press, 2000).

Loughlin M, 'The Demise of Local Government' in V Bogdanor, *The British Constitution in the Twentieth Century* (Oxford, Oxford University Press, 2003).

Loughlin M, *Legality and Locality: The Role of Law in Central-Local Government Relations* (Oxford, Clarendon Press, 1996).

Lupton R, Hughes C, Peak-Jones S, and Cooper K, *City-region devolution in England*, London School of Economics, SPDO research paper 2, November 2018.

10

The UK Constitution
The Way Ahead?

Parliament – Ministerial Briefings – Parliamentary Scrutiny – Challenge to International Treaty Obligation in Breach of the Rule of Law – Civil Service Appointments and Dismissals – United Kingdom as Nation State – Codification of the Constitution

INTRODUCTION

THE BRIEF FOR THIS STUDY does not extend to considering the wider politics nationally or internationally, but many observers believe that the constitutional climate has radically changed because we are experiencing a period of social, political, and economic upheaval unmatched since the Second World War, and on the political front these developments have been accompanied by a rise of different forms of populism in the UK, Europe, the USA, and beyond.[1] A shared common denominator of the emergent politics has been the contestation of fundamental aspects of the accepted institutional framework relating to the entire system of government.[2] How well have the existing structures here stood up to what must be regarded as a major change in the constitutional climate? In reaching an overall assessment of any liberal democratic constitution, regardless as to whether it is unwritten as in the UK or in a single formal document as applies to nearly every other constitution, it might be argued that the extent to which it embeds accountable institutions at all levels of government must be a fundamental consideration.

---

[1] J Muller, *What Is Populism?* (London, Penguin Books, 2017).
[2] R Bellamy, 'Political Constitutionalism and Populism' (2023) 50(1) *Journal of Law and Society* Part 2.

This discussion explains that the historical constitution of the UK reflects the gradual transition from absolute monarchy to modern democracy. It has relied heavily on the twin concepts of parliamentary sovereignty qualified by the rule of law, but it is also supported by key conventions imposing restraints on constitutional practice, and placing limits on the respective powers of the main constitutional actors.[3] Some years have passed since Brexit and then Covid 19 came as unexpected force 10 cyclones testing constitutional principles and established conventions to their limits, but if we continue to adopt the climate metaphor the examples cited below suggest that unsettled and often stormy conditions persist in many areas.[4] The discussion concludes by considering whether the antidote might lie with the adoption of a codified constitution.

PARLIAMENT AND CIVIL SERVICE: CHALLENGES TO CORE INSTITUTIONS

First, there is evidence to suggest that Parliament faces the prospect of marginalisation as the UK's core democratic institution. There has been an obvious failure to make this pivotal institution more representative by introducing a proportional element to the electoral system and by reforming the House of Lords to provide a counterbalance to the Commons; rather, Parliament has been neglected under recent governments as the main sounding board of democracy and site for establishing executive accountability.[5] For instance, during the Covid pandemic (2020–22) the general public were briefed on live TV by the Prime Minister (PM), other Cabinet ministers, and senior health officials on the implementation of policy. At the same time Parliament was inundated with emergency Covid-19 regulations as well as Brexit-related statutory instruments.[6] The Speaker of the House of Commons was concerned over the absence of scrutiny for these far-reaching measures and issued an unprecedented statement accusing the government of showing contempt for the House of Commons, stating that 'important statutory instruments have been published a matter of hours before they come into force, and some

---

[3] See eg J Sharpe, 'Parliamentary Conventions', *The Constitution Society*, 2020.
[4] A Blick, *Stretching the Constitution: The Brexit Shock in Historic Perspective* (Oxford, Hart Publishing, 2019) 299ff.
[5] AL Young, *Unchecked Power: How Recent Constitutional Reforms are Threatening UK Democracy* (Bristol, Bristol University Press, 2024) 76ff.
[6] R Fox and B Fowler, 'Coronavirus and EU exit have exposed the unacceptable scrutiny regime governing delegated legislation' (2020) *Prospect*, 11 September.

explanations why important measures have come into effect before they can be laid before this House have been unconvincing'.[7] Legislation continues to be enacted and secondary legislation introduced with inadequate parliamentary scrutiny.[8]

Concerns have been raised over the commitment to basic rule of law values of successive governments. For example, the UK Internal Market Act 2020 was introduced post Brexit ostensibly to agree consistent regulatory standards throughout the UK. The need for a common national regulatory framework was an important objective given the repatriation of EU laws. Nevertheless, the published bill as placed before Parliament during the final stages of negotiations for a post Brexit trade agreement with the EU was set to have profound consequences for the rule of law and international law. In particular, it proposed far-reaching delegated powers that the government acknowledged conflicted with the EU Withdrawal Agreement and the Northern Ireland Protocol. In consequence, the legislation if approved in this state would have been in breach of international law. The House of Lords Constitutional Committee in a highly critical report stressed that:

> The rule of law requires that everyone – from government ministers to the person on the street – be bound by, and entitled to the benefit of, the law. . . . The rule of law also includes compliance with international law; treaty obligations are binding on nation states as matter of international law once they are ratified.[9]

In response to its highly critical reception the most egregious of the offending clauses were dropped from the final bill.[10] As with the Rwanda policy discussed below, the willingness by government to contemplate using legislation in flagrant breach of international obligations is singled out here as an alarming departure from previous practice.[11]

Second, the constitutional mechanisms relied upon to achieve executive accountability at the heart of government have been increasingly called into question by the centralisation of power in the hands of the

---

[7] Sir Lindsay Hoyle, 30 September 2020, Hansard, Vol 681, col 331.
[8] M Russell, 'Should We Be Worried by the Decline of Parliamentary Scrutiny?' [2025] *Public Law* 31–57.
[9] United Kingdom Internal Markets Bill, *HL Select Committee on the Constitution*, 17th Report of Session 2019–21, 16 October 2020, HL Paper 151.
[10] Clauses 44, 45, and 47 were removed from the final bill. See Legislative Scrutiny: The United Kingdom Internal Market Bill: The Government response to the House of Lords Constitution Committee, Seventh Report of Session 2019–21. https://committees.parliament.uk/publications/4256/documents/43295/default/.
[11] S Wallace, 'A Triple Threat to the Rule of Law', UK Const L Blog (27 October 2020).

PM and the Policy Unit based at 10 Downing Street.[12] Amongst the many examples that have arisen, the neutrality of the civil service has been called into question. The increasing dependence on special advisers (SPADS) in policy formation was observed when discussing the executive (Chapter 6) but also there has been an unprecedented number of senior officials heading departments (Permanent Secretaries) forced into resignation because they were considered to be out of tune with the policy of the government elected. The trend established after the election of PM Johnson in 2019 was replicated by the high profile sacking of Tom Scholar as Treasury Permanent Secretary soon after Liz Truss's premiership began. Given the financial crisis that unfolded subsequently, it is ironic that the removal was deemed necessary because the incumbent head was associated with the caution associated with Treasury orthodoxy.[13] Senior officials have been replaced by appointees perceived (in the words of ex PM Mrs Thatcher) as 'one of us' by the PM or the respective departmental Secretary of State. A relatively uncritical loyalty and receptivity to change is perhaps part of the allegiance associated with these preferments, but such political intervention undermines the established principles of permanence and continuity which lend stability to the system of governance.

Turning to the subject of policy implementation, rather than the Secretary of State assuming full responsibility before Parliament for serious policy shortcomings, senior officials have been personally identified and scapegoated for policy shortcomings.[14] On the other hand, the PM, senior ministers, and appointed special advisers acting in clear breach of criminal law and/or ministerial codes of practice failed to resign for their personal conduct.[15] A revised Ministerial Code supported by a newly appointed advisor on ministerial interests was adopted in 2024 but no Ethics and Integrity Commission has yet been established and the procedures in place to curb abuse under the Labour Ministerial Code still rely on the PM as the ultimate 'guardian of the constitution'. He or she must accept any disciplinary recommendations concerning the conduct of government ministers. In response to allegations of sleaze and corruption at the heart of politics no plans have been published to

---

[12] S Payne and G Parker, 'The Smashing of the British State' (2020) *FT Magazine*, 10/11 October.
[13] A Seldon, *Truss at 10: How Not to Be Prime Minister* (London, Atlantic Books, 2025) 112ff.
[14] R Brazier, 'Contempt for the Constitution?', UK Const L Blog (6 October 2020).
[15] M Gordon, 'Dominic Cummings and the Accountability of Special Advisers', UK Const L Blog (3 June 2020).

restore trust in political institutions, for example by the regulation of the covert overseas funding of political parties.[16] PM Starmer is committed to improving civil service efficiency by promoting joined-up government through the complete internal re-wiring of the modern state.[17]

THE PROTECTION OF CITIZEN RIGHTS

There is mounting evidence of the erosion of democratic values and citizen rights recognised under common law given statutory protection or protected under international law. While the momentum behind attempts to repeal the Human Rights Act 1998 and replace it with a British Bill of Rights has subsided with the change of government in 2024, the sum of other recent developments in a wide range of areas has cumulative effect. To take some prominent examples, there has been a pervasive use of AI and automated decision-making by public authorities at central, devolved, and local government level without debate and often without adequate safeguards.[18]

In addition, with the rationing of legal aid limiting general access to the courts[19] and restrictions on judicial review noted in Chapter 7, the possibility looms of a dilution of what has been widely perceived as a fundamental constitutional right, namely, the right to opt for jury trial even for relatively minor criminal offences. Following a report by a senior judge[20] this entitlement could be sacrificed in order to tackle chronic delays in the criminal justice system.[21]

Significant qualifications to the right to peaceful protest, once again a right long recognised as a cornerstone of British democracy, have been introduced.[22] Faced with the inconvenience of disruptive but peaceful protests (for example, from 'Stop Oil' environmentalists opposed to fossil fuels causing traffic chaos in central London) new offences have

---

[16] Cheques and Balances: Countering the Influence of Big Money in Politics, Transparency International Ltd, 2024.
[17] www.instituteforgovernment.org.uk/comment/new-take-how-rewire-state.
[18] See eg E Sarid and O Ben-Zvi, 'Machine Learning and the Re-enchantment of the Administrative State' (2024) 87(2) *Modern Law Review* 371–97.
[19] https://consult.justice.gov.uk/digital-communications/legal-aid-eligibility-and-universal-credit/supporting_documents/annexcsummaryofcurrentlegalaidfinancialeligibilityrules.pdf.
[20] Independent Review of the Courts, Part I, Sir Brian Leveson, 2025.
[21] A Benn, 'In Crisis: the Constitutional Right to Jury Trial' Constitutional Law Association Blog (18 July 2025).
[22] 'Legislative Scrutiny: Public Order Bill, Joint Committee on Human Rights, First Report of Session 2022–23, 17 June 2022, HC 351.

been enacted criminalising disruptive conduct and granting the police additional executive powers allowing a senior officer to place conditions on what she or he considers to be disruptive protest.[23] Further, in relation to protests against the military action in Palestine by Israel resulting in multiple civilian casualties, anti-terrorism legislation has been used by the Home Secretary to proscribe peaceful demonstration against the Israeli action. What amounts to a blanket ban is then justified because the protest happens to be supported by one or more groups proscribed as a terrorist organisation committed to violence.[24]

Further still, the legislation pushed through Parliament by the Conservative government in 2024 to activate its Rwanda policy set a dangerous precedent by not only flouting the UKs obligations under international law, but by ousting the jurisdiction of the courts. If this measure is ever activated it replaces any right to judicial protection under judicial review, the Human Rights Act 1998 or international law with unqualified executive discretion (see Chapter 7).[25]

THE CONFIGURATION OF THE UK AS NATION STATE POST BREXIT

In respect to the UK as nation state, many of the unresolved questions concerning the running of territorial governance and Brexit have already been discussed (see Chapters 8 and 9).[26] Nevertheless, the following points are worth highlighting as we glance towards the future. A modified agreement was negotiated between the EU and the British government in May 2025 which appears to herald a new phase of closer and more friendly co-operation in trading relations and includes a planned easing of travel between the UK and the EU.[27]

Turning to devolution, for the time being at least, the tide of support in Scotland for secession has receded, and a referendum for a united Ireland under the Northern Ireland Act 1998 is not on the immediate horizon. The Windsor agreement linked to the backstop protocol has been crucial

---

[23] See the Police, Crime, Sentencing and Courts Act 2022, Public Order Act 2023.

[24] 'Gross abuse of state power' defiance grows over UK Ban on Palestine protest group', *The Guardian* 9 August 2025.

[25] P Leyland, 'The UK's Rwanda Asylum Policy and the Courts: reflections on the Constitutional Consequences?' (2024) 2 *DPCE* 767–83.

[26] R Shütze, 'Introduction' in R Shütze and S Tierney (eds), *The United Kingdom and the Federal Idea* (Oxford, Hart Publishing, 2018).

[27] www.instituteforgovernment.org.uk/comment/keir-starmers-uk-eu-reset.

in permitting the resumption of devolved power sharing at Stormont, with the Sinn Fein leader as First Minister, and Nationalist parties now forming the largest grouping in the Assembly. Despite the streamlining of procedures and the safeguard of a brake preventing inadvertent further Europeanisation Northern Ireland has remained, in effect, within the EU single market. Further, NI citizens can take advantage of an entitlement under the Irish constitution to apply for Irish citizenship and passports giving them the full status as EU citizens. Without specifically mentioning unification, the Irish government elected in November 2024 is committed to securing Ireland's future by further strengthening relations with the UK, while also encouraging reconciliation and lasting peace within Ireland. Further, Ireland is actively supporting greater integration, for example with the improvement of transport links throughout Ireland.[28]

The measures introduced in 2022 to reform inter-governmental relations at devolved level coupled with the more sensitive application of the Sewel Convention can be contrasted with the abrasive and confrontational relationship between central government at Westminster and the devolved governments in Edinburgh, Cardiff, and Belfast during the period of withdrawal from the European Union. Lastly, in order to address the concentration of power at the centre the present Labour government is introducing a revised and more comprehensive version of devolution for the whole of England based on the existing network of Metro Mayors (see Chapter 9).

IS THERE A CASE FOR THE INTRODUCTION OF A CODIFIED CONSTITUTION?

The radical constitutional reforms embarked upon by the Labour government elected in 1997 (eg devolution, Human Rights Act) changed the complexion of the UK constitution. In some areas it resembles a codified constitution with a collection of landmark 'constitutional statutes' dealing with fundamental constitutional questions.[29] The trend towards progressively codifying key aspects of the constitution has it seems redefined the relationship between Parliament, the executive, and the courts in a wide range of different contexts. As just mentioned the concept of

---

[28] 'Shared Ireland Initiative', *The Government of Ireland*, March 2025.
[29] Eg devolution, Human Rights Act, Freedom of Information Act, introduction of UK Supreme Court. See J Laws, 'The Miller Case and Constitutional Statutes' in M Elliott, J Williams, and AL Young (eds), *The Constitution after Miller: Brexit and Beyond* (Oxford, Hart Publishing, 2018).

'elective dictatorship' used in this book draws attention to shortcomings in the accountability of government before Parliament. The overall impact of these uncoordinated reforms is now linked to the constitutional implications of Brexit, the rise of populism, and the uncertainties related to the present unsettled constitutional climate.[30] Some influential commentators believe that the time has come to complete the task with the adoption of a codified constitution.[31] As Ferdinand Mount observes recasting the constitution might: 'animate society with a sense of what is right and instil into government an understanding of the proper limits to the exercise of power; above all it can inform the conversation of politics with a sense of dispersed responsibility'.[32] Moreover, codification promises to offer the advantage of 'attaining greater clarity, wider and deeper dispersal of power, and a firmer more enforceable set of principles and rules'.[33]

To take one example, the blueprint for a written constitution set out by Richard Gordon is founded on principles of representative democracy and based on popular sovereignty.[34] If such a constitution were to be accepted by referendum it would have a claim to legitimacy by deriving its authority from the people. Equally, it would offer the advantages of entrenching the rights contained therein. However, this constitution goes well beyond repeating the rights under the European Convention on Human Rights incorporated by the Human Rights Act 1998. It contains a redrafted domestic bill of rights, which is extended to social and economic rights. These include: an adequate standard of living; access to sufficient food, water, clothing, and housing; social security; appropriate health and social care services free at the point of delivery; and the right to education. International experience of constitution-making has demonstrated that the elaboration of such rights is not, in itself, a guarantee that all citizens will be entitled to at least the minimum standards of life, particularly in tight economic times. The problem is that either such rights come to be regarded as no more than non-justiciable directives of

---

[30] A Blick and P Hennessy *Could it happen here? The Day a Prime Minister Refuses to Resign* (London, Haus Publishing, 2025).

[31] V Bogdanor, *Beyond Brexit: Towards a British Constitution* (London, Tauris, 2019), 276.

[32] F Mount, *The British Constitution Now* (London, Mandarin, 1993) 266.

[33] A Blick *Beyond Magna Carta: A Constitution for the United Kingdom* (Oxford, Hart Publishing, 2015). More detailed discussion of the arguments for and against can be found at https://publications.parliament.uk/pa/cm201213/cmselect/cmpolcon/writev/mapping/cde02.htm.

[34] R Gordon, *Repairing British Politics: A Blueprint for Constitutional Change* (Oxford: Hart Publishing 2010) 27. See also V Bogdanor and S Vogenauer, 'Enacting a British Constitution: Some Problems' [2008] *Public Law* 38–57.

state policy, or alternatively, the UK Supreme Court, or any other court having responsibility for the interpretation of the constitution, is called upon as the mechanism for achieving delivery. As well as recognising that this raises questions of institutional competence, former South African Constitutional Court Justice Albie Sachs explains the dilemma with admirable clarity: '[S]hould the Constitution be read as handing over to each judge in each court the right and duty to decide who should have priority access to social goods in short supply?' It is inherently unfair if the granting of a constitutional right to a home/water, etc, is related to the capacity of any individual citizen to litigate. The South African court held that the guiding principle with any provision on access to adequate resources was not for the court to come to the assistance of an individual but the recognition of the obligation on the state (given the provisions in the constitution) to take reasonable legislative steps and other measures progressively to realise the right. This acknowledges the special expertise of government rather than judges in developing ways to ration the allocation of scarce resources.[35]

By way of contrast, Adam Tomkins, on the basis of a wide historical analysis, sets out 'Our Republican Constitution'. In order to achieve popular sovereignty, it is crucial, he believes, to start at the bottom with the people and not with the monarchy. The objective is to encourage self-government through processes of informed, public-spirited deliberation. There is an underlying assumption that material inequality has to be addressed so that the poor are not dominated by the wealthy. The conception of freedom based on non-domination requires that political decisions are taken in the public interest. Moreover, the idea that the common law courtroom should be preferred over Parliament to resolve highly sensitive questions where personal opinion is deeply divided is rejected. Rather, the challenge in terms of institutional design is to develop a structure that delivers appropriate forms of accountability to the wider citizenry.[36]

Over the last 50 years or so, the courts have emerged as a counterbalance to the increase in the powers of government, but also they have been required to intervene to protect citizen rights and to resolve devolution issues.[37] Some advocates of constitutional codification (or partial codification) would seek to recalibrate the distribution of constitutional power in favour of the courts as part of a written constitution with a

---

[35] A Sachs, *The Strange Alchemy of Life and Law* (Oxford, Oxford University Press, 2009) 177.
[36] A Tomkins, *Our Republican Constitution* (Oxford, Hart Publishing, 2005) 5, 31, 61.
[37] R Stevens, 'Government and the Judiciary' in V Bogdanor (ed), *The British Constitution in the Twentieth Century* (Oxford, Oxford University Press, 2003) 350ff.

constitutional court.[38] This is justified because '[a] political constitutionalism that diminishes judicial review, rejecting the implications of a moral understanding of law and legality, undermines democracy rather than promoting it'.[39] Such an approach rests on the questionable assumption that political questions can be, and should be, separated from legal questions. While not denying the vital necessity of democratic institutions of government state powers and individual rights would be ultimately limited by principles of legality laid down by judges as higher order law.[40] Whether or not the courts should perform an increased role in upholding the rule of law and safeguarding constitutional rights remains highly controversial (Chapter 7). There are academic and judicial critics of judicial review who have argued that senior judges in the UK Supreme Court and the Court of Appeal have deliberately adopted an interventionist agenda and this higher judicial profile inhibits the accepted role of government.[41] To the contrary, it has been observed by others that Parliament has been at least partly responsible for an enhanced judicial role through the passage of key legislation, including the Human Rights Act 1998 and devolution statutes.[42] In previous chapters (Chapters 3 and 7) it has been stressed that under the Diceyan conception of the rule of law, as developed by the courts as part of judicial review, judicial oversight has been crucial to ensure that the executive performs its legal obligations and that it obeys the law.[43]

Some commentators opposing legal constitutionalism maintain that '[t]he judicial constraint of democracy weakens its constitutional attributes, putting inferior mechanisms in their place'.[44] At the same time, the idea that the courts can be relied upon as impartial guardians of the law is rejected.[45] Judges are not politically accountable and this

---

[38] J Jowell, 'The Rule of Law and its Underlying Values' in J Jowell and C O'Cinneide (eds), *The Changing Constitution*, 9th edn (Oxford, Oxford University Press 2019) 27ff.

[39] T Allan, 'Accountability to Law' in N Bamforth and P Leyland (eds), *Accountability in the Contemporary Constitution* (Oxford, Oxford University Press, 2013) 104.

[40] See eg J Laws, 'Law and Democracy' [1995] *PL* 72, at 84ff;

[41] See eg N Barber, R Ekins, and P Yowell (eds), *Lord Sumption and the Limits of the Law* (Oxford, Bloomsbury, 2016).

[42] N Reed Langen, 'Is the Supreme Court more interventionist?', UK Const L Blog (14 October 2020).

[43] L Marsons, M Sunkin, and T Konstadinides, 'The UK Administrative Justice Institute's submission to the Independent Review of Administrative Law', UK Const L Blog (26 October 2020).

[44] R Bellamy, *Political Constitutionalism: A Republican Defence of the Constitutionality of Democracy* (Cambridge, Cambridge University Press, 2007) 260.

[45] J Waldron, 'The Core of the Case Against Judicial Review' (2006) 115 *Yale Law Journal* 1346.

disqualifies them from taking what are essentially political decisions.[46] A transformed role is also likely to undermine their relatively independent status. A former Master of the Rolls, Lord Denning, recognised that: 'if judges were given power to overthrow sections of Acts of Parliament, they would become political, their appointments would be based on political grounds and the reputation of our Judiciary would suffer accordingly'.[47] Another of our most distinguished judges, Lord Bingham, put the objection to codification rather differently observing that:

> The British people have not repelled the extraneous power of the papacy in spiritual matters and the pretensions of royal power in temporal [matters] in order to subject themselves to the unchallenged rulings of unelected judges. A constitution should reflect the will of a clear majority of the people, and constitutional change of the kind here contemplated should be made in accordance with that will or not at all.[48]

CONCLUSION

In the final analysis, any attempt at constitutional codification is unlikely to succeed unless it becomes an absolute necessity for political reasons such as in the event of Scottish or Norther Irish secession. As explained above, this is because it presupposes a consensus can be reached between many disparate political positions, not only on institutional design, but also on all the values and rights to incorporate into a new constitution. Indeed, the controversy surrounding the proposed reforms to administrative law and judicial review in 2020 and proposals for the replacement of Human Rights Act 1998 with a British Bill of Rights[49] demonstrates the scope for disagreement over such issues. As part of a more pragmatic approach it is suggested that constitutional statutes might be specially entrenched as is also recommended in the Brown Report[50] and that constitutional conventions might be clarified in a revised Cabinet manual

---

[46] J Griffith, 'The Political Constitution' (1979) 42 *MLR* 1.
[47] 369 HL Deb, 25 March 1976, cols 797–98.
[48] T Bingham, *The Rule of Law* (London, Allen Lane, 2010) 168.
[49] C O'Cinneide, 'Human Rights and the UK Constitution' in J Jowell and C O'Cinneide (eds), *The Changing Constitution*, 9th edn (Oxford, Oxford University Press 2019) 90ff. See also Chapter 7.
[50] 'A New Britain: Renewing our Democracy and Rebuilding our Economy' (Commission on the UK's Future, Labour, 2022), Chaired by former PM Gordon Brown and referred to as the Brown Report, 139.

or newly established conventions set out in legislative form[51] to address a selection of pressing issues, such as the ones identified in the opening section of this chapter. The immediate goal would be to reach a broad (all party) consensus in order to achieve specific institutional reforms. An elected Senate of the Regions to replace the House of Lords might be one such example. The overall objective, of course, would be to reinforce public confidence in the UK's unique constitutional system.

FURTHER READING

Bamforth N and Leyland P, *Accountability in the Contemporary Constitution* (Oxford, Oxford University Press, 2013).
Bingham T, *The Rule of Law* (London, Allen Lane, 2010).
Bogdanor V, *Beyond Brexit: Towards a British Constitution* (London, Tauris, 2019).
Blick A, *Beyond Magna Carta: A Constitution for the United Kingdom* (Oxford, Hart Publishing, 2015).
Blick A and Hennessy P, *Could it Happen Here? The Day a Prime Minister Refuses to Resign* (London, Haus Publishing, 2025).
Jowell J and O'Cinneide C (eds), *The Changing Constitution*, 9th edn (Oxford, Oxford University Press, 2019).
King A, *The British Constitution* (Oxford, Oxford University Press, 2007).
Laws Sir J, *The Constitutional Balance*, (Oxford, Hart Publishing, 2021).
Loughlin M, *The British Constitution: A Very Short Introduction*, 2nd edn (Oxford, Oxford University Press, 2023).
McClean I, *What's Wrong with the British Constitution* (Oxford, Oxford University Press, 2010).
Sedley S, *The Lions under the Throne* (Cambridge, Cambridge University Press, 2015).
Tomkins A, *Our Republican Constitution* (Oxford, Hart Publishing, 2005).
Young AL, *Unchecked Power: How Recent Constitutional Reforms are Threatening UK Democracy* (Bristol, Bristol University Press, 2024).

---

[51] A King, *The British Constitution* (Oxford, Oxford University Press, 2007) 362ff.

Index

access to justice, 190, 200–2, 265
accountability:
  administrative state, 188–91
  civil service, 163–5
  European Union, 21
  executive: Scott Report, 161–2
  forms, 5
  local government, 256–7
  ministers, 157–61
  Scottish executive, 222
  to parliament, 99–100, 126–37
    E-petitions, 135–6
    departmental select committees, 127–30
    NAO, 133–4
    ombudsman, 136–7
    PAC, 104, 132–3, 134
    questions, 126–7
    Wright reforms, 130–2
administrative state
  see also judicial review
  accountability, 188–91
  deregulation, 75–6
  foundations, 80
  growth, 75, 188
  judicial review and, 184–201
  liabilities, 91–2
  red light and green light theory, 185–7
Advocate General for Scotland, 168
agencies, 75, 136, 188
algorithms, 10, 75
Allan, T, 48
amending unwritten constitution, 1–2
Anne, Queen, 87
Argentina: Falklands war, 127
armed forces: Commander-in chief, 88
Asquith, HH, 36
asylum seekers, 73–4, 192–3, 211
Attorney-General, 72, 91, 92, 168, 169

Attorney-General for Northern Ireland, 168
Australia, 18, 88, 94

Bagehot, Walter, 31–2, 70–1, 89, 90, 93, 96, 147
Baldwin, Stanley, 80
Balfour Declaration (1926), 18
Barnett formula, 237, 255
BBC, 9, 236
Beaverbrook, Lord, 86
Belgium, 20, 79
Bill of Rights (1689):
  accountability principle, 174
  army and, 88
  constitutional source, 28
  free speech in parliament, 100, 108
  history, 13–14, 16
  judicial independence, 41
  parliamentary conventions, 40
  parliamentary sovereignty, 45, 51–2, 69–70
  prerogative powers and, 83
Bingham, Thomas, 271
Birch, A, 59
bishops, 87, 97, 115, 146
Blackstone, William, 47, 82
Blair, Tony:
  Cabinet government, 39–40
  departmental organisation, 150
  Iraq war, 68, 106, 148
  local government and, 247–8
  ministers, 160
  press office, 154–5, 166
  style of government, 145
Bogdanov, V, 60
Brexit:
  delegated legislation and, 135
  devolution and, 227–8, 229, 233–4, 238–41
  effect, 22–5, 26, 30–1, 50, 262, 266–7, 268

Brexit: (*Continued*)
  Fake News inquiry (2018), 129
  history, 21–2
  human rights and, 211
  Internal Markets Act, 228, 263
  judicial independence and, 74–5
  Northern Ireland and, 24–5, 225, 239–41, 263, 266–7
  parliamentary proceedings, 97–8, 99, 156, 175
  parliamentary sovereignty and, 55, 98–9
  post-Brexit legislation, 179–80
  prerogative powers and, 146
  prorogation of Parliament and, 89
  referendum, 60–1, 99, 149
  Scotland and, 238–9
British-Irish Council, 225
Brittan, Leon, 159
Brooks, Rebekka, 132
Brown, Gordon, 85, 142, 152
Brown Report (2000), 117, 228, 271–2
by-elections, 101

Cabinet:
  collective responsibility, 40, 87–8, 147–9
  composition, 147
  confidentiality, 35
  Office *see* **Cabinet Office**
  Shadow Cabinet, 104
Cabinet Manual, 37, 145, 156, 271–2
Cabinet Office:
  e-government and, 170
  expanded role, 40
  government structure, 141
  organisation, 151–2
  parliamentary committees and, 129
  policy formation, 150–4
Cabinet Secretary, 143–4, 145, 151
Calderwood, Catherine, 156
Cambridge Analytica, 103
Cameron, David:
  Brexit and, 22, 149
  coalition government, 85–6, 142, 146, 156
  Coulson affair, 166–7
  local government and, 248
  Scottish referendum and, 235
  SPADS, 152
Campbell, Alistair, 154, 166

Canada, 18, 88, 112
Carr, Lady Chief Justice Baroness, 42
Carrington, Lord, 159
Channel Islands, 225
Channel Tunnel rail link, 124–5, 137
Charles I, 12–13, 69, 100
Charles II, 13
Charles III, 88, 92–3, 95
Chief Whip, 104
Church of England, 80, 88–9, 115
Churchill, Winston, 19, 86
Citizen's Charter, 189
Civil Courts Structural Review, 190
civil service:
  appointments, 166
  codes of conduct, 165–7
  competence, 164
  employment conditions, 162
  head, 151
  history, 163–4
  neutrality, 151, 164, 264
  non-discrimination, 163
  numbers, 163
  regulation, 40, 162, 163
  role, 163–5
  rule of law and, 73
  select committees and, 129–30
  structure, 163–4
  union membership, 83–4, 173, 196
Civil Service Commission, 166
Civil War (1642–49), 13, 69, 80, 100, 108
Clegg, Nicholas, 146
COBRA meetings, 8, 153
codes of conduct:
  civil service, 165–7
  ministers, 145–6, 149, 160–1, 164, 264–5
codified constitutions:
  debate, 267–71
  features, 1–2
  human rights, 8
  trend, 267–8
Coke, Edward, 12, 70, 177
colonialism, 18–19, 79
common law:
  constitutional source, 29–30, 177, 269
  narrow perspective, 177
  philosophy, 186
  precedents, 178

statutes and, 29–30, 47–8
statutory interpretation, 178
Commonwealth, 88
compliance issue, 4
Comptroller and Auditor General, 133
confidentiality, 35, 147, 168, 170, 229
Constitution Society, 123–4
constitutional changes: methods, 1–2
constitutional sources *see* **sources**
constitutionalism:
  boundaries, 5–6
  meaning, 4
contract state, 194
conventions
  see also specific conventions
  accountability to parliament, 174–5
  collective ministerial responsibility, 40, 87–8, 147–9
  constitutional sources, 33–43
  defining, 34–8
  enforceability, 37
  importance, 27, 33, 38–43
Cook, Robin, 148
Coulson, Andy, 166–7
council tax, 255–6
counterterrorism, 207–8, 266
county councils, 254
courts/tribunals
  see also **judicial review; judiciary; Supreme Court**
  checks and balances, 186
  devolution and, 230–4
  growth of administrative tribunals, 188–9
  justiciability, 173–5
  network, 184
  red light and green light theory, 185–91
  role, 173–215, 269–70
Covid-19, 6–10, 26, 144, 150, 155–6, 160, 189, 238, 262
Craig, Paul, 23, 32, 186
Crichel Down, 136, 158
Cromwell, Oliver, 13, 69
Crossman, Richard, 158
Crown:
  immunities, 91
  liabilities, 91–2
  meaning, 90–1
Cummings, Dominic, 129, 155–6, 166, 167

Dalyell, Tam, 241n92
damages: judicial review and, 191–2
Darnel's Case **(1627),** 13
data protection, 76, 170, 171
De Smith, S, 5
delegated legislation:
  Henry VIII clauses, 75, 135
  Joint Committee on Statutory Instruments, 134–5
  parliamentary scrutiny, 134–5
democracy:
  Covid-19 and, 6–10
  emergence of Parliament, 14–16
  European Union, 21
  history, 14–16
  House of Lords and, 113
  liberal democracy, 2–3
Denning, Lord, 271
deregulation, 75, 194
devolution
  see also individual devolved nations
  abolishing, 222
  Brexit and, 227–8, 229, 233–4, 238–41
  courts and, 230–4
  Covid-19 and, 7–8
  devolution issues, 176, 230–4
  effect, 42
  England and, 241–3
  EVEL and, 125–6
  history, 218–19
  HRA 1998 and, 213
  intergovernmental relations and, 226–30
    concordats, 229
    legislation, 226–8
    policy co-ordination, 228–30
  local government and, 248, 249–53
  parliamentary sovereignty and, 98–9
  referendums, 61–2
  statutes, 29
  West Lothian question, 241–3
Diana, Princess, 92
Dicey, AV:
  administrative state and, 185
  approach, 201
  constitutional authority, 32
  conventions, 34, 36–7
  devolution and, 222

Dicey, AV: (*Continued*)
  parliamentary sovereignty, 47, 51, 54, 57, 80, 98, 178
  political sovereignty, 59
  royal prerogative, 82
  rule of law, 46, 63, 64, 65–8, 157, 185–6, 201
dress codes, 209
Dugdale, Thomas, 158

e-government, 169–71
E-petitions, 135–6
Edward I, 14, 16
Edward VIII, 80
elections:
  1997 general elections, 101, 219
  2024 general election, 98, 102, 107, 138, 157, 238
  electoral system, 100–3
  electronic voting, 103–4
  franchise statutes, 15, 29, 32, 52
  general elections and confidence motions, 156–7
  monarch's role, 86
  social media and, 103
elective dictatorship, 59, 67, 98, 104, 184, 188, 268
electoral systems:
  devolved nations, 221–2
  general elections, 100–3
Elizabeth I, 12, 16, 99
Elizabeth II, 85–6, 87–8, 90, 92, 94, 95
English Votes for English Law (EVEL), 125–6, 242
Epstein, Jeffrey, 92
equality:
  before the law, 63–4, 66
  civil service regulation, 163
  Covid-19 and, 7
  foreign nationals, 207–8
  same-sex couples, 203
Equality Commission for Northern Ireland, 225
Erskine May, 32
ethnicity:
  judiciary, 183
  MPs and, 107
  South Africa, 2

European Charter of Fundamental Rights (ECHR), 211
European Convention on Human Rights (ECHR)
  see also specific rights
  absolute rights, 205–6
  constitutional source, 31
  devolution issues and, 231–2
  HRA (1998) and, 25, 55–6, 202
  jurisprudence, 203, 212, 213, 214
  necessary interference, 206
  withdrawing from, 212
European Exchange Mechanism, 105
European Union:
  Brexit *see* Brexit
  constitutional source, 30–1
  democracy and, 21
  effectiveness principle, 53–4
  Factortame, 53–4
  financial crisis, 20
  future, 266–7
  legal primacy, 53–5
  parliamentary sovereignty and, 29, 52–5, 179–80
  political debate, 148
  subsidiarity, 217
executive
  see also Crown; ministers; Prime Minister
  accountability, 35
    Scott Report, 161–2
    to parliament, 99, 126–37
  advice to Monarch, 87–8
  collective responsibility, 40, 87–8, 147–9
  conventions, 39
  Crown, 90–1
  departmental organisation, 149–50
  parliament as watchdog, 126–37
  powers, 141–72
  separation of powers and, 46

fair trial, 12, 31, 189, 201–2
Falklands war, 127, 159
feudalism, 11–12
Five Knights' Case (1627), 13
flexibility, 2
forced labour, 206
Forsyth, Christopher, 32
Fox, Liam, 160

Index

France:
  administrative law, 184
  constitutional history, 11
  equality before the law and, 63
  EU and, 20, 21
  financial crisis, 20
  secularism, 209
franchise *see* elections
Franco, Francisco, 95
freedom of assembly: peaceful protests, 265–6
freedom of expression:
  parliamentary privilege, 108–9, 111–12
  pre-HRA, 201
  Prolife Alliance, 208–9, 210
  protecting, 9–10
freedom of information, 42, 76, 110, 154, 167–9
Fulton Report (1968), 164
future:
  assessment, 261–72
  challenges, 262–5
  codified constitution, 267–71

gender: parliamentarians, 107, 115
George I, 80, 145
George V, 36
George VI, 80, 86
Germany, 68, 184
Ghana, 19
Gladstone, WE, 17, 132
Glorious Revolution (1688), 49, 80, 108
Goldsworthy, J, 60
good governance: ground rules, 6
Gordon, Richard, 268
Gray, Sue, 144
Greece: financial crisis, 20
Green Papers, 119
Griffith, J, 38, 58, 182, 187
ground rules, 5

hacking scandal, 132
Hailsham, Lord, 59, 67
Hale, Lady, 182
Harlow, C, 185, 191, 195
Harry, Prince, 92
Heath, Edward, 85, 151
Heathrow Airport, 106
Hennessey, Peter, 151

Henry VIII, 12, 16, 17, 99
Henry VIII clauses, 75, 135
higher order rules, 4–5
history:
  colonialism, 18–19
  defining United Kingdom, 16–18
  EU membership, 19–25
  parliamentary sovereignty, 49
  qualifying absolute monarchy, 11–14
  survey, 10–25
House of Commons
  see also elections; Members of Parliament
  1832 Reform Bill, 113
  adversarial character, 104, 106–7
  Backbench Business Committee, 131
  Brexit and, 97–8
  confidence motions, 156–7
  conventions, 40–1
  dissolution, 39, 86, 156–7
  government and opposition, 104–5
  House of Lords and, 36, 41, 56–9, 118
  legitimacy, 119
  Modernisation Committee, 111, 124, 131
  Public Accounts Committee (PAC), 104, 132–3
  public bills, 119–24
  Reform Acts, 15
  Select Committee on Standards and Privileges, 109–10
  Speaker, 41, 105, 108
  terms, 58, 86, 156
  watchdog role, 126–37
    E-petitions, 135–6
    delegated legislation, 134–5
    departmental select committees, 127–32
    ombudsman, 136–7
    PAC, 104, 132–3
    Question Time, 107, 126–7
    Wright reforms, 130–2
  whips, 98
House of Lords:
  Church of England peers, 115
  composition, 114–16, 243
    political parties, 116
  expertise, 122
  gender and, 115

House of Lords: (*Continued*)
  history, 15–16
  House of Commons and, 36, 41, 56–9, 118
  Law Lords, 71–2, 97, 115, 176
  legislative proceedings, 120, 122–3
  legitimacy, 113
  peers' independence, 122
  powers, 114
  reforms, 112
    1911, 28–9, 113–14, 116, 123
    1949, 16, 41, 56–7, 58, 113, 123
    1958 Act, 115
    1999 Act, 115
    further reforms, 116–18, 243, 272
  role, 112
  Salisbury convention, 41, 123
  system, 112–18
House of Lords Appointments Commission (HOLAC), 114, 118
Hoyle, Lindsay, 99
human rights
  see also specific rights
  constitutional protection, 201–14
  constitutional statutes, 27, 29, 42
  future, 265–6
  HRA *see* **Human Rights Act (1998)**
  ICT and, 170
  pre-HRA, 201
  protection of citizen rights, 265–6
  social rights and, 65–6
Human Rights Act (1998):
  approach, 202
  balancing exercise, 205–6, 209
  Belmarsh case, 203, 207–8
  codification of rights, 3
  constitutional source, 29
  constitutional statute, 27, 52
  critics, 211
  Denbigh High School, 209
  devolution and, 213
  disapplying, 193
  ECHR and, 55–6, 202, 213
  ECtHR jurisprudence and, 203, 212, 213, 214
  effect, 10, 64, 76
  effectiveness, 211
  incompatibility declarations, 203, 208
  Lord Chancellor and, 180–1
  parliamentary sovereignty and, 45, 55–6, 180, 202–3
  Prolife Alliance, 205, 208–9, 210
  proportionality, 205–6, 210
  replacing or reforming, 211–14, 265, 271
  scope, 268
  significant cases, 206–11
  threshold, 199
  vertical v horizontal effect, 204–5
hunting, 49, 56–9
Hutton Inquiry, 68

immigration, 42, 73–4, 134–5, 159–60, 192–3, 263, 266
Independent Adviser on Ministerial Standards (IAMS), 146, 161
Independent Parliamentary Standard Authority, 111
India: colonialism, 18
Information Commissioner, 169
information communication technology (ICT), 169–71
Intelligence and Security Committee, 153
Internet: e-government, 169–71
Iran-Iraq war, 162
Iraq war, 68, 106, 148, 169
Ireland
  see also **Northern Ireland**
  Act of Union (1800), 17, 28
  citizenship, 239–40
  financial crisis, 20
  history, 17–18, 218–19
  presidency, 94
  unification, 267
Isle of Man, 225
Israel, 266
Italy, 20, 62, 124, 150, 184

Jamaica, 19
James I/VI, 16, 69, 218
James II/VII, 13
Jenkins, Roy, 102
Jennings, Ivor, 35–6, 47, 57–8, 66, 187
John, King, 11–12
Johnson, Boris:
  2019 election, 146
  civil service and, 264
  departmental organisation, 150
  downfall, 143–4, 149

Northern Ireland and, 240
    prorogation of Parliament, 89
    scandals, 160, 161, 166, 167
Jones, G, 166
Juan Carlos, King of Spain, 95
Judicial Appointments Commission (JAC) for England and Wales, 183
judicial review
    see also judiciary
    administrative law and, 184–201
    claim procedure, 199–200
    development, 67
    devolution issues, 230–4
    exhaustion of remedies and, 200
    grounds, 195–8
    growth, 200
    impact, 199–201
    justiciability, 173–5
    merits and, 198–9
    ouster clauses, 64–5, 192–3
    public v private law, 193–4
    remedies, 191–2
    separation of powers and, 46
    standing, 194–5
    statistics, 200
    Wednesbury unreasonableness, 186, 196, 198, 205, 206
judiciary
    see also judicial review
    activism, 65, 73, 198, 199, 270
    appointments, 181–4
    deference, 207–8
    dismissal, 184
    independence, 41–2, 46, 67
        red light theory, 186
        separation of powers and, 72–5, 182
    Law Lords, 71–2, 97, 115, 176
    narrow social background, 182–3, 191
    powers, 271
    prejudices, 177
    retirement, 183
jury trials, 265

King's speech, 39, 87
Kwarteng, Kwasi, 144

Lang, Fritz, 10
Laski, H, 66, 187
Laws, John, 23

legal aid, 66, 190, 201–2, 265
legal representation, 201–2
legality principle:
    ICT and, 170
    judicial review, 196, 197
    no punishment without law, 31, 206
Leggatt Report (2001), 189
legislation:
    delegated legislation *see* delegated legislation
    devolution and, 226–8
    parliamentary proceedings, 119–26
        closure, 123
        English Votes for English Law (EVEL), 125–6
        guillotine, 123
        Private Bills, 124–5
        Private Members' Bills, 124
        public bills, 119–24
    statutes *see* statutes
legislative consent motions (LCMs), 227–8
legitimate expectations, 197
Lenin, Vladimir, 2
local government:
    accountability, 256–7
    audits, 257
    centralisation, 247
    devolution and, 248, 249–53
    finance, 255–6
    liabilities, 92
    localism, 248, 254, 257
    London, 62, 243, 249–51, 254–5
    mayors, 243, 250–2
    ombudsman, 257
    service delivery, 255–6
    statutory reforms, 247–9
    types, 253–5
Local Government Commission, 254
London School of Economics, 187
Lord Chancellor, 46, 71–2, 180–1

Mackintosh, J, 152
Macmillan, Harold, 146
Magna Carta (1215), 11–12, 51–2, 69, 80, 201
Major, John, 68, 105, 106, 145, 152, 155, 191, 219
majority rule: liberal democracy and, 3

Malaya, 18–19
mandating orders, 191
Mandelson, Peter, 160
Mary I, 99
Matrix Churchill, 68, 162, 167
May, Theresa:
   2017 election, 59–60, 97–8, 102
   Brexit and, 22, 41, 146, 156
   collective ministerial responsibility, 149
   immigration policy, 159
   ministerial dismissals, 146
   minority government, 120
   Sewel Convention and, 24
mayors, 243, 250–2, 267
media:
   hacking scandal, 132
   Prime Minister and, 154–6
   social media, 9, 103
Members of Parliament:
   Backbench Business Committee, 131
   backbenchers, 106
   expenses, 109, 110–12, 130
   gender and ethnic balance, 107
   mandate, 59, 119
   parliamentary privilege, 108–9, 111–12
   Register of Interests, 110, 120
   salaries, 110
   standards of conduct, 109–12
   status, 105–6
   unseating, 111
merchant shipping, 53–4
Metropolis (film), 10
MI6, 153
ministers
   see also executive
   appointments, 86, 146
   codes of conduct, 145–6, 149
      accountability, 164
      breaches, 160–1
      revisions, 264–5
   conduct, 144
   individual responsibility, 157–61
   public interest immunity, 162
minority rights
   see also ethnicity
   liberal democracy and, 3
Model Parliament (1295), 14
monarchy
   see also Crown; prerogative powers

   abdication crisis (1936), 80
   abolition, 94
   appointments, honours and, 87
   approval ratings, 93
   assessment, 92–4
   calling elections and, 86
   commander-in chief, 88
   constitutional monarchy, 79–96
   coronation, 93
   costs, 93
   government formation and, 85–6, 142
   Head of Church of England, 88–9
   head of Commonwealth, 88
   head of state, 88
   history, 11–14, 79–81
   immunities, 64
   King's speech, 39, 87
   ministerial advice and, 87–8
   ministerial appointments and, 86
   powers, 70, 89–90
   privilege, 94
   qualifying absolute monarchy, 11–14, 69, 80–1, 99–100, 108, 262
   role, 84–9
   royal assent, 38, 87, 97
   Scottish independence and, 235
   succession, 14, 28, 89
   weekly ministerial meetings, 90
Montesquieu, Charles de, 68
Morison, J, 170
Morris, Estelle, 159
Mount, Ferdinand, 66, 151–2, 268
Murdoch, Rupert and James, 132

National Audit Office (NAO), 133–4, 158
national security, 153, 168, 207–8
nationalism, 219
natural justice, 64, 196, 197
Netherlands, 20, 21, 79, 184
New Public Management (NPM), 164–5
New Zealand, 18, 56, 88
News of the World, 132
Next Steps initiative, 151, 164–5
Night of the Long Knives, 146
Nolan Report (1995), 109
North-South Ministerial Council, 225
Northcote-Trevelyan Report (1854), 163–4

Northern Ireland:
  Belfast Agreement, 25, 213, 224, 233, 239
  Brexit and, 24–5, 225, 239–41, 263, 266–7
  broadcasting ban, 65
  citizenship, 239–40
  devolution, 29, 52, 223–6, 241
  devolution issues, 232–3
  ECHR and, 213
  Equality Commission for Northern Ireland, 225
  history, 218–19
  Human Rights Commission, 225
  North-South Ministerial Council, 225
  power sharing, 224–5
  referendum, 61
  Supreme Court and, 177
  Windsor Framework, 25, 240

OFCOM, 9, 171, 236
official secrets, 163, 167, 201
ombudsmen, 136–7, 257
O'Neill, Michelle, 239
online dispute resolution, 189–90
opposition: parliamentary system, 104–5
Orders in Council, 166, 174
Orwell, George, 10
ouster clauses, 64–5, 192–3

Paine, Tom, 1, 5, 68
Pakistan, 18
Palestine, 266
papacy, 12
parish councils, 254
parliament:
  absolute monarchy and, 99–100
  accountability to, 99–100, 126–37
    E-petitions, 135–6
    committees, 127–32
    convention, 174–5
    NAO, 133–4
    PAC, 104, 132–3, 134
    questions, 126–7
    Wright reforms, 130–2
  conventions, 40–1
  Covid-19 and, 6–7
  debates, 178
  devolution and, 98–9
  emergence, 14–16
  Erskine May, 32
  future, 262–3
  government and opposition, 104–5
  House of Commons *see* **House of Commons**
  House of Lords *see* **House of Lords**
  immunities, 64
  Intelligence and Security Committee, 153
  law and customs, 32–3
  legislative proceedings, 118–26, 134–5
  misleading parliament, 160, 162
  privilege, 108–9, 111–12
  prorogation, 89, 173–5
  separation of powers and, 70–1
  sovereignty *see* **parliamentary sovereignty**
  standards, 109–12
  survey, 97–138
  watchdog role, 126–37
Parliamentary and Health Service Ombudsman, 136–7
Parliamentary Commissioner for Standards, 109–10
Parliamentary Committee on Standards in Public Life, 166
parliamentary sovereignty:
  binding successors, 47, 51
  common law and, 29–30
  defining, 47–50
  development, 69–70
  Dicey, 47, 51, 54, 57, 80, 98, 178
  elective dictatorship, 59, 67, 98, 104, 184, 188, 268
  EU law and, 29, 52–5, 98–9, 179–80
  express and implied repeal of statutes, 50–2
  HRA (1998) and, 45, 55–6, 180, 202–3
  Jackson case, 48, 49, 56–9
  morality and, 48–9
  origins, 28
  political sovereignty and, 59–62
  principle, 47–62, 178–9
  referendums and, 60–2
  restrictions, 29, 42, 45, 52–6
Partygate affair, 144
Passport Agency, 134
patronage, 81, 146
Petition of Right (1628), 12, 13, 28

Philby, Kim, 108
political parties: funds, 101
populism, 26, 99, 261, 268
Portugal, 20
postal voting, 92
precedents, 178
prerogative powers:
    history, 79–80
    justiciability, 173–5
    meaning, 33, 81–4
    ministerial powers, 146
    patronage, 146
    statutory powers and, 82–3
Prime Minister:
    10 Downing Street office, 150–4
    appointment, 142–3
    conventions, 39–40
    guardian of the constitution, 156, 264
    nature of office, 145–7
    origins, 145
    patronage, 81, 146
    policy formation, 150–4
    powers, 142–57
    Press Office, 154–6
    rise and fall, 143–5
    shaping government departments, 149–50
principles
    see also specific principles
    constitutional principles, 45–77
    ICT and, 170
prisoners, 206, 211
privacy, 170, 206
Private Bills, 124–5
Private Members' Bills, 124
privatisations, 75, 151, 191, 194, 258
Profumo, John, 160
prohibition orders, 191
proportionality: HRA review, 205–6
protest rights, 265–6
Public Accounts Committee (PAC), 104, 132–3, 134, 158, 190
public bodies: HRA and, 204–5
public interest immunity, 162

quashing orders, 191
Question Time, 107

Rawlings, R, 185, 191
Rayner, Angela, 160–1

referendums:
    1972 EU membership, 148–9
    2014 Scottish referendum, 234–6
    Brexit, 60–1, 99, 149
    devolution, 222
    local issues, 257
    parliamentary sovereignty and, 60–2
religious freedom, 209
Rhodesia, 19
Richard Report, 220
right to liberty, 65
right to liberty and security, 206, 207–8
right to life, 206, 210
right to silence, 65
Robson, W, 66, 187
Rothschild, Lord, 151
royal assent, 38, 87, 97
royal prerogative *see* prerogative powers
Rudd, Amber, 159–60
rule of law:
    definition, 63–5
    Dicey on, 46, 63, 65–8, 157, 185–6, 201
    due process, 66–7
    equality before the law, 63–4, 66
    history, 4
    ICT and, 170
    judicial independence and, 72–3
    ouster clauses and, 64–5
    threats to, 263
Rwanda policy, 192–3, 263, 266

Sachs, Albie, 269
safeguards: debate, 6
Salisbury convention, 41, 123
same-sex couples, 203
Scholar, Tom, 264
Scotland:
    2014 referendum, 234–6
    Act of Union (1707), 17, 28, 51–2, 218
    Brexit and, 24, 238–9
    Covid-19, 156
    devolution, 29, 50, 52, 219–23
        Mark II, 236
        powers, 241
    devolution issues, 230–2, 233–4
    electoral system, 102, 221–2
    EVEL and, 125–6
    history, 16–17, 218

HRA 1998 and, 213
law officers, 223
legislative proceedings, 120
local government, 254, 255
nationalism, 219
parliament: committees, 128
referendums, 61–2
SNP dominance, 106, 234
Supreme Court and, 177
taxation, 220, 236–8
Scott Report, 68, 129, 161–2, 167
secularism, 209
security services, 63, 84, 153
Sedley, Stephen, 67
separation of powers:
 constitutional principle, 46, 68–76
 development, 41, 68–70
 fusion of powers, 70–1
 ICT and, 170
 judicial independence and, 72–5
 Lord Chancellor and, 71–2
 redefinition of power, 75–6
 Supreme Court and, 71–2
 tribunals and, 189
Sewel Convention, 24, 37, 226–7, 228, 267
Shadow Cabinet, 104
Short, Claire, 148
Simpson, Wallis, 80
slavery, 31, 202, 206
social exclusion, 170
social media, 9, 103
social security, 113, 134, 189, 268
sources
 see also specific sources
 diversity, 11
 survey, 27–43
South Africa, 2, 18, 269
Soviet Union, 2, 68
Spain, 20, 94–5
special policy advisers (SPADS), 152, 155–6, 164, 264
Spycatcher affair, 167
Stalin, Joseph, 2, 68
standing: judicial review, 194–5
Starmer, Keir, 149, 161
statutes:
 administrative state and, 187–8
 common law and, 29–30, 47–8

constitutional statutes, 28–9, 51–2
 express and implied repeal, 50–2
 parliamentary proceedings, 119–26
statutory instruments *see* delegated legislation
statutory interpretation, 178
Steyn, Lord, 214
Stop Oil, 265–6
Sturgeon, Nicola, 238
subsidiarity, 217
Sunak, Rishi, 144, 240
Sunstein, C, 2–3
Supreme Court:
 appointments, 177
 composition, 176
 creation, 41, 72, 115, 176–7
 jurisdiction, 176
 precedents and, 178
 separation of powers, 71–2
Sussex, Duke and Duchess of, 92, 93

Takeover Panel, 194
taxation, 195, 220, 236–8, 255–6
Thatcher, Margaret:
 Cabinet government, 39–40
 centralisation, 219
 civil service and, 164, 264
 courts and, 191
 Euro-scepticism, 20
 Falklands war, 127
 local government and, 62, 256
 Policy Unit, 151
 Queen Elizabeth and, 90
 resignation, 107, 143
 style of government, 145
Tomkins, Adam, 35, 269
torts: Crown liability, 91–2
torture prohibition, 31, 202, 206
trade unions, 101
transparency:
 automation and, 10
 government, 167–9
treatises: constitutional sources, 31–2
tribunals *see* courts/tribunals
Trinidad, 19
Truss, Liz, 144, 264
Turpin, C, 35
Twitter, 9

United States:
  civil service, 164
  Congress: select committees, 127–8
  constitutional history, 11
  constitutional ideology, 2
  founding fathers, 2
  Iraq war, 148
  judicial appointments, 182
  President, 124
  Senate, 117
  separation of powers, 68–9, 182
  Supreme Court, 49, 179, 182
  Watergate Affair, 69, 128

Van Caenegem, R, 4
Victoria, Queen, 80, 90

Wade, William, 32, 48
Wales:
  Brexit and, 24
  devolution, 29, 52, 219–23, 241
  devolution issues, 231, 232
  electoral system, 103, 221–2
  EVEL and, 125–6
  history, 16, 218
  local government, 254, 255
  parliament: committees, 128

  referendum, 61
  Supreme Court and, 177
  taxation, 237
Walpole, Robert, 39, 145
Watergate Affair, 69, 128
***Wednesbury* unreasonableness,** 186, 196, 198, 205, 206
West Lothian question, 241–3
Westland affair, 159
White Papers, 119
William, Prince, 92, 95
William and Mary, 13–14, 16
Williamson, Gavin, 146
Wilson, Harold, 60, 85, 148, 149, 149–50
Windrush scandal, 159
Windsor Framework, 25, 240, 266–7
Windsor-Mountbatten, Andrew, 92–3
Woodhouse, D, 161
World War I, 18, 82
World War II, 18
Wright, Tony, 130
Wright Report, 130–2

Young, A, 99
YouTube, 9

Zimbabwe, 19